Designing and Conducting Research

Related Titles of Interest

Thinking Critically About Research Methods
John G. Benjafield
ISBN: 0-205-13917-5

Experimental Methodology, Sixth Edition
Larry B. Christensen
ISBN: 0-205-15506-5

Developing Research Skills: A Laboratory Manual, Third Edition
Helen J. Crawford and Larry B. Christensen
ISBN: 0-205-15569-3

Research Designs in Clinical Psychology, Second Edition
Alan E. Kazdin
ISBN: 0-205-14587-6

The Undergraduate Researcher's Handbook: Creative Experimentation in Social Psychology
Ralph J. McKenna
ISBN: 0-205-15537-5

Research and Evaluation in Education and the Social Sciences
Mary Lee Smith and Gene V Glass
ISBN: 0-13-774050-6

Statistical Methods in Education and Psychology, Third Edition
Gene V Glass and Kenneth D. Hopkins
ISBN: 0-205-14212-5

Second Edition

Designing and Conducting Research

Inquiry in Education and Social Science

Clifford J. Drew
Michael L. Hardman
Ann Weaver Hart

University of Utah

Allyn and Bacon
Boston • London • Toronto • Sydney • Tokyo • Singapore

First edition was published under the title
Designing and Conducting Behavioral Research,
Copyright © 1985 by Allyn & Bacon.

Library of Congress Cataloging-in-Publication Data

Drew, Clifford J. (date)
  Designing and conducting research : inquiry in education and
social science / Clifford J. Drew, Michael L. Hardman, Ann Weaver
Hart.—2nd ed.
    p.   cm.
  Rev. ed. of: Designing and conducting behavioral research. c1985.
  Includes bibliographical references and indexes.
  ISBN 0-205-16699-7.—ISBN 0-205-16698-9 (paper)
  1. Psychology—Research—Methodology.   2. Social sciences—
—Research—Methodology.   3. Education—Research—Methodology.
I. Hardman, Michael L.   II. Hart, Ann Weaver (date).   III. Drew,
Clifford J. (date).   Designing and conducting behavioral research.
IV. Title.
BF76.5.D68   1996
150´.12—dc20   95-16474
                                                                   C I P

Printed in the United States of America

10 9 8 7 6 5 4 3 2 1   99 98 97 96 95

Contents

Preface

The world of social science research has experienced a number of stimulating developments during the past twenty years, and this new edition of our book reflects many of those changes. In particular you will find examinations of qualitative research methods that have emerged as an important approach to investigations in educational and social science research. These additions have been integrated into previous material and constitute the focus of discussions in two new chapters. Another major change in the past two decades relates to the widespread use of computers in our daily activities. We have mentioned computer use at numerous points throughout this text, noting how they can be effectively employed to perform particular research tasks. We have consciously chosen not to add a separate chapter on computer use for several reasons. It is our assumption that most students have already largely integrated computers into their daily lives. Additionally, space limitations and book focus precluded creation of such a chapter.

We hope the additions and revisions in this volume will increase its usefulness. Despite all the changes, the basic purpose of this book remains consistent with that which guided the writing of the first edition: it provides an introduction to research that emphasizes the fundamentals of planning and design. The basic design of an investigation represents the foundation on which successful research is built, irrespective of methodology or approach employed.

Many college courses that carry the title "Introduction to Research" should still be more appropriately labeled "Introduction to Statistics." This has changed little during the past 30 years, although courses emphasizing design are beginning to surface more often in the curriculum. The purpose of this book is to provide a first step into the world of research. The material presented herein can serve as an initial conceptual framework for students without a background in research. From this beginning the student may then either proceed to more advanced work or terminate the study of research with a general working knowledge of what research involves.

Practice is one of the best teachers. This has certainly been our experience in teaching students how to conduct research. Yet in most courses there is neither adequate time nor resources to permit the application of the concepts and skills discussed. To at least partially meet this need, practice problems have been included to simulate as much as possible the situations faced by beginning researchers. These simulated problems provide the student with a paper-and-pencil substitute for application of the material presented. They have all been field-tested on students over several years.

In certain areas several simulations are presented on a given topic. This has been done for two reasons. First, the simulations in general progress from the elementary to the more difficult. This sequence of difficulty was determined over several years' use in introductory courses on research. Second, the multiple simulations are included in certain areas simply to provide additional practice in applying the material. Frequently such practice is important to the beginning researcher.

The simulations may be used in a variety of fashions, depending on the instructor's preference. They may be effectively used in class sessions for both individual and small-group participation. It is generally more effective to complete the relevant simulations immediately after reading a given section than to wait until the entire chapter has been read. Therefore the text is flagged with instructions directing the reader to the appropriate simulation for material just read. Each simulation is accompanied by simulation feedback. Usually it is helpful for a student to read this feedback immediately after completing a given problem. The feedback provides a check on the student's performance for that problem and is useful before proceeding to the next simulation or further reading.

We are indebted to many whose wisdom and frustrations have contributed to the conceptualization of this volume. It is always risky to name specific individuals since some will undoubtedly be overlooked. Such practices are, however, customary and appropriate despite the risk. First and foremost are our students, who have helped us learn to teach about research, served as primary impetus for the book, and also served as the experimental subjects as we tried out new material or new simulations. Sincere appreciation is also extended to our colleagues who read portions of the manuscript and made suggestions. We are particularly grateful to our reviewers, Donald Bubenzer, Kent State University, and David Mank, University of Oregon. They provided invaluable feedback and suggestions that helped guide our work.

C. J. D.
M. L. H.
A. W. H.

About the Authors

Clifford J. Drew is Coordinator of Instructional Technology in the office of the Vice President for Academic Affairs at the University of Utah. He is also a Professor in the Departments of Special Education and Educational Psychology. Dr. Drew came to the University of Utah after serving on the faculties of the University of Texas at Austin and Kent State University. His professional interests include research methods in education and psychology, mental retardation, human development and disabilities, graduate and professional training, applications of computer technology in instruction, and research methodology.

Dr. Drew has published on many topics in special education and related areas, having made over 100 contributions to the professional literature on subjects including mental retardation, research design, statistics, diagnostic assessment, cognition, evaluation related to the law, and instructional technology. His most recent books, *Mental Retardation: A Life-Cycle Approach* (Merrill, 1996) and *Human Exceptionality: Society, School, and Family* (Allyn & Bacon, 1996), are his 18th and 19th respectively. Dr. Drew has served on the board of directors of the Far West Laboratory for Research and Development in Education, has chaired the National Ethics Committee of the American Association on Mental Retardation, and is a Fellow of that organization. He is listed in numerous honorary biographical volumes, including *Who's Who in America*.

Michael L. Hardman is Associate Dean for Research in the Graduate School of Education and Professor of Special Education at the University of Utah. His newest books are *Introduction to Persons with Severe Disabilities* (with J. McDonnell, A. McDonnell, and R. Kiefer-O'Donnell; Allyn & Bacon, 1995), *Human Exceptionality: Society, School, and Family* (5th edition, with C. Drew, and M. Egan; Allyn & Bacon, 1996), and *Mental Retardation: A Life-Cycle Approach* (6th edition, with C. Drew and D. Logan; Merrill, 1996).

Dr. Hardman, who completed his doctorate in educational administration at the University of Utah, has published in numerous national journals within the field of education and has directed several national demonstration projects on inclusive education and transition from school to adult life. Dr. Hardman received a Joseph P. Kennedy, Jr. Foundation Public Policy Fellowship in 1982 and served as a staff member in the United States Senate, where he drafted legislation in the areas of vocational rehabilitation and the education of students with disabilities. He is very active in both professional and advocacy organizations, having served on national boards and committees for the Association for Persons with Severe Handicaps, Council for Exceptional Children, the ARC, and the Kennedy Foundation. He is currently the national president of the Higher Education Consortium for Special Education.

Ann Weaver Hart is Dean of the Graduate School and Professor of Educational Administration at the University of Utah. Prior to her appointment as dean, she served as Associate Dean of the Graduate School of Education and as a full-time faculty member at the University of Utah. Before joining the university's faculty, Dr. Hart was a junior high school principal in Provo, Utah. Her research focuses on educational leadership, the design of work in educational organizations, and academic freedom at all levels of education.

Recent books include *Principal Succession: Establishing Leadership in Schools,* (SUNY Press, 1993), and *The Principalship,* with Paul V. Bredeson (McGraw-Hill, 1996). She has also published research papers in numerous books and refereed journals. Some of her recent publications include "Work Feature Values of Today's and Tomorrow's Teachers: Work Redesign as an Incentive and School Improvement Policy" in *Educational Evaluation and Policy Analysis,* "Creating Teacher Leadership Roles: The Impacts of Core Group Support" in *Educational Administration Quarterly,* and "Reconceiving School Leadership: Emergent Views" in *Elementary School Journal.*

Chapter *1*

Introduction and Background

What is research? There are many different conceptions of what constitutes research. If you ask six different scientists what research is, you may receive six different answers. At least you would probably receive varying sets of words. Some may respond with very lofty and complex definitions. Others might be somewhat more casual in their responses, using terms that actually seem to be a part of the English language.

It is often difficult for students to find a clear and useful definition of research. Many research courses begin with a discussion of the content, and that content frequently focuses on a limited part of the research process, such as statistics. You might infer that the definition of research is supposed to become self-evident as the discussion progresses. Perhaps an instructor assumes that you already know what research *is* and that your purpose in taking the course or reading a research text is to become thoroughly familiar with the intricacies of the process. Yet in many cases, the course's purpose for the student is to fulfill requirements for graduation. The course is probably required, and the text is likewise required (perhaps this text, for that matter). Research design is not a topic that most students study as an elective.

Every author makes certain assumptions concerning readers and we are no different. Assumptions are necessary to function in daily life. They are based on a variety of factors such as knowledge about the world, past experience, and even faith. Assumptions become troublesome only when they are faulty for one reason or another (e.g., incorrect or partially correct knowledge, limited or irrelevant experience). Our assumptions about our readers are reasonably simple. They are based primarily on many years of experience in teaching research design as well as our earlier years as students trying to learn about it. We believe that research has been taught for decades in a limited manner that is ineffective and, therefore, has had some unfortunate side effects. We also assume that many of you are *not* reading this book because of a life-long love affair with the topic. However, we believe that research *is* something worth learning about (for reasons other than graduation requirements). These perspectives, as well as others that may not be so prominent, have significantly shaped our approach to teaching research design and the nature of this book. Given this context, let us return to our initial question: What is research?

Research is a systematic way of asking questions, a systematic method of inquiry. The purpose of research is to obtain knowledge or information that pertains to some question. The question may be very simple (such as "Which of these treatment methods is most effective?") or it may be more complex. The emphasis of this definition is on the term *systematic.* There are many ways of asking questions and obtaining information. Research is a method that attempts to undertake this task in a systematic fashion to obtain objective and unbiased information. The definition of research we have just presented above is simple. Beyond this level of abstraction, there are many descriptive characteristics involved in research that we will return to throughout this book. At the outset, however, a general definition will serve quite well.

The term *research* has traditionally generated a variety of misconceptions on the part of the uninitiated. It would seem that a shroud of secrecy has been placed over the act of research, either purposefully or by accident. (Many students would swear that professors teach as though the research process were something that *must* remain a secret—known only by the chosen few.) The net outcome of this situation is a generalized lack of information concerning what goes on in a research laboratory, the nature of the research process, and what research results mean. All of this has tended to generate both a mystique and a suspicion of the whole process by lay and student populations alike. The researcher has been caricatured as a strange sort of person with rather solitary habits and preferences, somewhat of a mechanistic egghead. These are unfortunate misconceptions and stereotypes. The process of conducting research is anything but mystical, and it certainly is not mechanistic. This will become increasingly clear as you progress further into the content of this volume. While certain individual researchers may indeed be somewhat different, strange, perhaps even weird, as a group researchers are no more like that than the general population. Overall, they exhibit no less or greater variation in personality or preferences than their neighbors.

Research has typically been an anxiety-producing topic for students. Particularly for the beginning student, research generates a certain amount of mental anguish, perhaps outright fear. In fact, the most consistent description of what research is may be found among students. To many research is basically an academic hurdle that must be conquered but that has little relevance to the real world (see Box 1.1 for an illustration of this). Additionally, for many students, research is synonymous with statistics, and that means mathematics (which *really* raises the anxiety level).

These perceptions of research are, again, unfortunate misconceptions that must be corrected to fully understand the research process. For example, it is critical to understand from the outset that research is much more than statistics. Statistical analysis represents only one step in the overall research process. The statistics used in research should more accurately be viewed as tools, much as an automobile mechanic uses screwdrivers and wrenches. The mechanic's tools are of little value if there is not a clear understanding of how an automobile operates. Likewise the researcher who does not know how to initiate the logical process of asking questions will have little meaningful use for statistical or other scholarly tools—some of which involve no statistics at all.

Why Read and Learn about Research

This discussion of research began with some brief attention to what research is and is not. We hope this offsets, to some degree, certain commonly held misconceptions of research and researchers. We also began with a general definition of research as a systematic method of inquiry. It is important at this point to examine why the study of research design is worthwhile. The purpose of this section is to address that question from two perspectives—the consumer and the professional.

Research and the Consumer

In discussing issues related to why study research, it seems appropriate to initially focus on the consumer perspective. This view is seldom examined, and yet it may provide one of the most compelling rationales

---

BOX 1.1

An experienced scholar recently shared at a national meeting the results of a survey he had conducted. This survey investigated student perceptions of research that they had conducted for their own graduate programs. After completing their studies the vast majority of students reported that they *did not change their minds* when their findings contradicted conventional wisdom. These students did not believe the results from their own research. They saw their research results largely as being separated from their own real worlds.

for becoming familiar with the research process. People are consumers of research in nearly every facet of their daily lives; research does relate to the real world despite what the students in Box 1.1 thought. Science and research produce new knowledge on a daily basis, and that new knowledge provides society with more choices. Providing more choices is certainly a strong, consumer-oriented rationale for research; but the consumer must be equipped to take advantage of new options. In addition, research consumers can be easily misled if they are uninformed or naive about the research process.

In the general lay arena, however, research often seems to be used more to control choices than to provide options. The student of research quickly becomes quite cynical concerning the manner in which research is used (mostly misused) to manipulate consumers. A few examples make this point painfully clear.

Some of the worst offenders in terms of misusing research are the people who develop and present advertising on television. At least one secret to selling a product on television is rather simple: employ an actor (preferably someone who is not well known as a film personality), put that individual in a white coat behind a desk (with rows of books on the wall), and the product to be sold suddenly appears scientifically credible. It always helps if the actor can also tell some sort of story to drive the point home. Often the line begins something like this: "At a famous research center in the East…" One example of this type of selling is the commercial in which a well-known toothpaste was claimed to be "unsurpassed in the prevention of cavities when compared to the other leading brands of toothpaste." The wording of this line was carefully drafted. The obvious implication is that this brand—Brand X—is more effective in preventing cavities; however, that is not exactly what is said. The term *unsurpassed* specifically means that the other leading brands were not any better than Brand X. Most likely there was no difference among them. If Brand X were really more effective, the advertisers could be expected to emphatically say so.

Another rich source of purported consumer-oriented research is the news media. A few years ago, for instance, a headline appeared that captured the imagination of many who were rather sleepily gulping their morning coffee. (Headlines are worded just for that purpose.) It read "A Kiss Means Success." The essence of the story was that a husband who kisses his wife good-bye in the morning lives longer and earns a great deal more money than a man who fails to perform that ritual. Although such a claim is less serious than claims about tooth decay, it exemplifies misinformation similar to that of the television advertisement. One implication of this news story is that the kiss *causes* the husband to live longer and make more money. Such an implication cannot be taken very seriously however, since it should be obvious that this type of reasoning is more romantic than logical. In fact, it would be rather humorous if it weren't such an insult to one's intelligence.

Lay consumers are inundated on a daily basis with what appears to be research information and its implications. Without some knowledge of the research process, they are at the mercy of those who present the information. Laws requiring truthful advertising will not help anyone make intelligent decisions. After all, the toothpaste advertisement was not really untruthful. It is important for you, as lay consumers, to have enough background concerning research methods to make intelligent evaluation judgments regarding marketing claims that are supposedly based on research.

Research and the Professional

A sound perspective as research consumer is also relevant to most professionals. Professionals often encounter situations similar to those confronting lay consumers. The content may be different, but professionals too have a strong need to be familiar with the research process. Once again, a few examples will illuminate this point, some also involving the news media. One serious illustration of the misuse of research information occurs regularly in schools across the United States. Headlines scream that Shady Hill Elementary School's third graders performed two points below (or ten points above) the national average on this year's standardized reading test. The story often implies—or even directly attributes—the blame or credit for these scores to the teaching staff at Shady Hill. In fact, there may be a variety of influences that are likely to be contributing to these scores. It may be that a local high-tech scientific firm moved its design plant, thereby relocating most of its scientists to another community. If the children of these scientists represent a significant group in the school's enrollment, school-wide average performance could easily decline two points.

Most professional practitioners operate as service deliverers in one form or another on a daily basis. Counselors interact with clients, educators teach students, psychologists use tests to evaluate individuals, and so on. A question arises: Why does a professional select a particular technique or strategy? Which counseling method, teaching procedure, or test should be used and why? These questions are not easily answered, particularly since professional consumers receive a variety of sales pitches that often resemble the television advertisements noted earlier. All exhort you to use their test, their material, or their techniques. Although there are some consumer safeguards (e.g., the American Psychological Association's *Standards for Educational and Psychological Tests and Manuals*), the professional consumer still has the responsibility of evaluating the basis on which a procedure or technique was developed. Clearly some methods have been developed on a very sound basis with a solid research foundation, whereas others have not. It is also clear that selection of materials and techniques by the professional consumer has not always been undertaken after careful consideration of the relevant research.

The selection of instructional material by teachers presents an interesting example of how some professional decisions are made. Some teachers decide which materials to use on the basis of second-hand information from others. Their principal or a textbook committee may suggest particular materials (or even require them). Perhaps another teacher casually indicates that a particular material is "good." Frequently the basis for the "good" rating remains unspecified. It may be that the individual making the recommendation mentions that the material is based on research, but this is not a typical basis for the suggestion. Further investigation concerning the research results and the technical soundness of such research (if it actually exists) is even less typical.

This all begins to sound very much like the sales proposition involving that infamous "research center in the East." In fact there are more similarities than many professionals would like to admit—and teachers are certainly not the only professional consumers involved. Professional practitioners (administrators, psychologists, supervisors, teachers) often find themselves inundated with salespeople and advertisements expounding the virtues of a wide variety of products. The marketing process for professional products has the same goal as that for any other arena—selling. The same tactics are often used; and despite a reluctance to admit it, a large number of professional consumers are ill-equipped to question the research claims used to sell products.

The basic purpose of this section is to discuss some of the reasons why it is important to learn about the research process from a consumer perspective. There is no intent here to suggest (as some of our students have claimed) that everyone has to become a researcher. We *do* contend, however, that some understanding of the research process is important to being an intelligent consumer. Certainly not all decisions require an awareness of the scientific method. There are many times, however, when it would be most helpful to be able to question some of the claims made by people who are selling (manipulating). The examples of professional consumerism given here are necessarily limited both in number and scope; but it is difficult to imagine how one can intelligently keep abreast of the professional literature without an understanding of the research process; and it is clear in most fields that a person cannot succeed as a professional without reading the relevant literature and making some thoughtful judgments. Most professionals have long since learned that they should not accept without question everything they read.

There is a variety of means used by most professionals to keep current regarding research and developments in their fields. Almost without fail they subscribe to authoritative publications (e.g., journals, monographs, or annually published compendiums) that present research results and developing trends in their fields. Increasingly they are also subscribing to electronic bulletin boards and other on-line electronic publications that provide the latest information and debates in the field. Personal computers have achieved such a high level of utility in the past decade that they are commonly employed in multiple fashions to access information as well as to perform a host of other personal and professional functions.

Why Conduct Research

We do not intend to transform everyone into researchers. There may, however, be some who have such a goal or who might be interested. Moreover, professionals seek information about the effects of their be-haviors and choices. Consequently we feel a need to briefly discuss the reasons why research is conducted.

The reasons for conducting research are nearly as varied as the people who are involved. Some would suggest very grand and glorious motivations such as solving the ills of society. Others might be much more personal and indicate that research is just plain fun. Neither of these extremes should be ignored; they are both genuine and powerful reasons for conducting research.

Over 30 years ago, Sidman published a most articulate discussion concerning the variety of purposes involved in undertaking research. Acknowledging the value of research based on theory, Sidman cau-tioned that the beginning student should not submit to a rigid insis-tence that all research "must derive from the testing of hypotheses" (1960, p. 4). He discussed the value of several other reasons for perform-ing experiments: (1) to try out a new method or technique, (2) to in-dulge the investigator's curiosity, (3) to establish the existence of a be-havioral phenomenon, and (4) to explore the conditions under which a phenomenon occurs. Much more recently, Bailey (1994) saw reasons for conducting social research along two dimensions: (1) studies that describe what is happening and (2) studies that explore why or how something happens.

The preceding discussion emphasizes that research is conducted to solve problems, to expand knowledge, and to increase understanding. These reasons are commonly accepted by both lay and professional groups. However, Sidman's comment concerning curiosity raises a com-pletely different justification that is not generally discussed. Some would claim that the curiosity of an investigator is not adequate rationale for conducting research; such justification sounds too frivolous and all too much like the "ivory tower." This type of argument is very much a part of a way of thinking that demands that every piece of research must directly relate to the immediate solution of a practical problem. Such thinking ignores, however, the established fact that many problems can-not be immediately and effectively solved until a foundation of basic knowledge exists. Often the development of such a body of knowledge is possible only through the accumulative investigations of many researchers who may well be studying questions that seem removed from the practical, "real" world. The demand that every piece of research be immediately and obviously relevant also ignores the history of solutions to immediate problems that have occurred because some researcher was indulging a curiosity many years before. It is not uncommon to find answers that may be theoretically interesting but that will not find their way into application until problems arise at a later time. From our point of view, indulging an investigator's curiosity is a very good reason for conducting research. The benefits from a practical perspective may not be immediate, but lack of immediacy is outweighed by more reasoned inferences at a later time that ultimately lead to more effective decisions.

The previous discussion sounds like a debate regarding basic versus applied research. This is a popular argument in some circles and one in which we do not wish to engage. *Basic research* involves investigation of questions that are interesting but may have no application at the present time. This is occasionally called *pure* research, but that term connotes a value judgment that is not particularly helpful (as compared with impure research?). *Applied research,* on the other hand, is used to designate investigations aimed at solving problems of immediate concern. Arguments concerning applied versus basic research are confusing because the issues have been presented as both method issues and value judgments. This is unfortunate because a great deal of time and energy has been spent on the debate itself. Essentially the debate can be reduced to the value-judgment issue regarding whether research should be conducted that is not immediately applicable. If conducted carefully, the methodology for basic and applied research is the same; only the content and setting differ. The task here, however, is to explore technically sound research designs, not to debate value-judgment issues. There is good reason to conduct research that is basic as well as that which may be characterized as applied. There is *no reason* for conducting research that is unsound, regardless of the topic being investigated.

We are strong advocates of Sidman's approach regarding the purposes for research. All of his reasons are powerful justifications. Most active researchers seem to be, at one time or another, motivated by all of his reasons for undertaking investigations. This places the question of Why conduct research? on a very personal level, and that seems quite appropriate. We have already noted that research is fun (not discounting the fact that it is also work). It is most certainly a pleasure to obtain an answer to a question that one has, regardless of whether curiosity, theory, or an immediate social problem motivates the research. There is tremendous personal satisfaction in gathering your own data— much more than reading someone else's report. The senior author will never forget the exhilaration when he received his first questionnaires back for a sociology study as an undergraduate.

As the years have passed, we have begun to appreciate other personal benefits of conducting research. A natural part of the process is writing. The expression of thoughts, ideas, and findings in writing is one of the most demanding tasks a person can undertake. It requires a completeness and clarity of communication that is simply not involved in routine conversation. Spoken communication, even if it is rather formal conversation, often includes considerable nonverbal gesturing to accentuate, provide emphasis, and complete thoughts that are only partially expressed by the actual words. Most people do not even notice these behaviors since they are so accustomed to both using and experiencing them. Although reliance on nonverbal aids may be acceptable in spoken communication, writing does not admit such luxuries. Consequently it is challenging for most people to write in an articulate fashion. Despite the struggle, a great deal of satisfaction accompanies completing the written report of a particular piece of research.

The entire research process, from designing a study to writing the report, can be one of the most growth-producing experiences available. Each step requires the exercise of disciplined thought balanced with an appropriate dose of creativity. The conduct of research has many similarities to the writing of poetry. You can almost feel the mental growth each time a successful study is completed. For us, this is a very compelling, personal reason for conducting research and one that is as powerful as any of the more lofty justifications that are typically offered.

The Research Process

Reference has been made to the research process although only certain portions of it have been described. As a whole, the research process can be conceptualized in a circular or closed-loop fashion in the manner illustrated in Figure 1.1. The process begins with the research question or problem. The research question may arise from theoretical dilemmas presented by other research, a practical problem needing solution, or the curiosity of the individual undertaking the study. In the case of quantitative research and all experimental designs, the research idea must be distilled into a very specific question, which may take the form of a hypothesis or several hypotheses. In the case of qualitative or naturalistic studies that involve the exploration of naturally occurring or contemporaneous processes, the research idea must be consistent with general questions about how and why things occur. Once this has been accomplished, the study must be designed in a manner that will avoid potential difficulties and permit the researcher to answer the question. The research design is critically important and essentially involves a rigorous and meticulous planning procedure. Planning should include

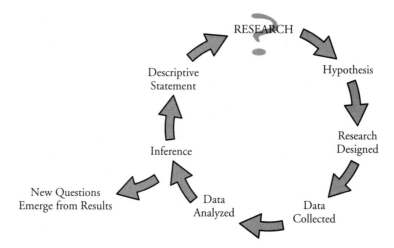

FIGURE 1.1   Closed-Loop Conceptualization of the Research Process

the operational details of actually conducting the study and recording data. You are now ready to begin executing the investigation. Data are collected and then analyzed. Once this is done, the results must be interpreted in terms of the research question that completes the loop. If executed properly, the question should be answered, the problem solved, or at least a first step taken toward achieving this end. And as indicated in Figure 1.1, the study may generate other questions — a matter that occurs quite often.

The preceding discussion presents a simplified view of the overall research process. A variety of obstacles may intervene at each step, and many details have been omitted. These will be discussed in greater depth throughout this volume. What has been examined, however, is the research process as a whole. The field has often been guilty of focusing on one portion or emphasizing one step to the exclusion of others. Such a limited perspective has frequently given laypeople and beginning students an inaccurate view of what is really involved in research. Creating such perspectives (knowingly or unknowingly) has generated many misconceptions and often contributed to unfavorable opinions about research. We hope that this volume will serve to inform, as well as correct misconceptions in cases when that is appropriate.

Foundations of Research

Several additional topics should be considered before discussing the central design aspects of conducting research. Although these topics are somewhat peripheral to the major concern of designing and executing research, they serve to round out the information required for a full understanding of the process. As noted, the purpose of research is to obtain knowledge or information. Research is a systematic method of asking questions. It involves the scientific method when variables can be manipulated, which warrants discussion. It also involves systematic inquiry that reveals the essential features of naturally occurring social events (Eisner, 1991). Both the scientific method and other systematic research traditions are to some extent different from the way in which people generally conduct their daily lives. This section is aimed at placing research in perspective with other approaches to knowledge about the world.

Four Ways of Knowing or Fixing Belief

Many years ago, Kerlinger (1973) outlined four different ways of knowing or fixing belief, which remain pertinent to research conducted today. These methods of knowing include tenacity, authority, a priori, and science. Each approach involves a different set of characteristics and sources of information. Additionally, each of these methods is used to a greater or lesser degree by different sectors of the population (Brown, 1992). The different ways of fixing belief are useful in placing research in perspective with regard to other approaches to inquiry.

The first means of fixing belief is known as the method of *tenacity*. Using the method of tenacity (derived from the idea that an individual holds tenaciously to existing beliefs), something is thought to be true because it has always been true. If something is known by the method of tenacity, essentially a closed system exists; closed in that it is not particularly amenable to the input of new information. In fact, the very nature of tenacity may prompt the individual to hold to a belief even in the face of nonsupportive evidence. Schon (1983) points out that people, even experienced professionals, often become so accustomed to common events and experiences that they selectively ignore information that contradicts previously held beliefs. He calls this "selective inattending" (perhaps the students in Box 1.1 were involved in this).

Another approach to knowing or fixing belief, *reference to authority*, involves citing some eminent person or entity as the source of knowledge; if someone who is well known (an authority) states that something is the case, then it is so. Reference to authority relieves the believer from having to consider alternative information. The method of authority is not clearly and definitively a bad method of knowing; much depends on the authoritative source, and even more depends on the way in which the believer uses the method. If it is used in a totally nonthinking, closed-system fashion, there are obvious weaknesses. Used in this manner, no consideration is given to nonsupportive or conflicting evidence. When this is the case, the progress of knowledge and ideas is painfully slow and depends completely on the progress of the authority.

A third way of knowing or fixing belief is the *a priori* method. A priori, by definition, refers to "before the fact" and is primarily based on intuitive knowledge. In subscribing to the a priori method, one knows that something is the case before the gathering of information by experience or even in the absence of experiential data. Usually the a priori approach is logical or in harmony with reason. The weakness in the method lies with the question of whose reason is used. Humans have certainly been known to commit errors of reason or logic. Unless the information system is open to data from experience (experimentation or observation), such an error of logic may initiate a line of thought that is characterized by progressive errors.

The fourth method of knowing is called the method of *science*. The method of science is characteristically different from the other three ways of fixing belief. It is based on experience external to the knower, in that the primary source of information is observation that is designed to be objective. The method of science has a *built-in self-correction factor,* which distinguishes it rather dramatically from the other ways of knowing. This self-corrective factor is operative because the system is open and public. The work of a scientist is public not only in terms of end products (results), but also in the terms of means by which those ends are obtained. A researcher must describe in considerable detail the procedures, materials, and subjects and must even show the path of logic used to reach the question or conclusion involved. This degree of openness or public exposure attempts to ensure that subsequent investigators may know as much as possible about previous work in order to be able to replicate (duplicate) an investigation. Independent replication operates the self-correction factor of science, and all knowledge must remain open to eventual falsifiability if new data come to light.

Research has its foundation in the method of science. Nevertheless, one has only to read a research article to observe great diversity within the method of science and the use of at least segments of two other methods of knowing. Certainly reference to authority is operative in research. The researcher is continually citing the work of others. This use of the method of authority, however, is considerably different from utilizing authorities solely as a closed system in which conflicting evidence is not acknowledged. Furthermore, research serves to openly challenge authority when evidence is not in agreement. Research also uses basic components of the a priori method of knowing—logic and reason. Again, the way in which logic and reason are used in research is considerably different from use of the a priori method as the sole source of knowledge. Researchers are usually required to openly show the path of reasoning by which conclusions are reached. If the logic is faulty or in conflict with experiential evidence, it is challenged by the method of science. By virtue of its public nature, science can effectively make use of portions of the other methods of knowing and avoid pitfalls inherent in them. Refereed review of scientific research by peers capitalizes on the virtues of these qualities.

Inductive and Deductive Reasoning

Reasoning and logic represent vital components of the research process—elements that, if absent, weaken and jeopardize the process so severely as to render it useless. Without the input of reasoning, knowledge would not progress at all since the relationship of one idea to another, or of data to an idea, is based on this essential element.

Two rather distinctive types of reasoning are involved in the broad spectrum of research efforts—deductive and inductive reasoning. *Deductive reasoning* uses logic that moves from the general to the specific. Deductive reasoning is characterized by statements that were initiated from a general idea, model, or theory, and from these statements something is inferred about a specific case (if the [general] theory is correct, then I should be able to observe this [specific] behavior). *Inductive reasoning,* on the other hand, reflects the reverse type of logic. Inductive reasoning uses logic that is launched from a specific case or occurrence and moves to inferences concerning the general (if this [specific] behavior occurs, then this [general] theory is supported).

Both types of reasoning are used in behavioral research. Examples of deductive reasoning may be found in introductory statements of research articles. Deductive reasoning is being used when researchers are examining a theory, model, or body of knowledge (general) and hypothesizing a specific behavior that they expect to observe. Inductive reasoning often drives exploratory qualitative inquiry, when theory is lacking or just developing, when the area of study is new, or when controlled, experimental research has suggested that behavioral patterns exist that the researcher would like to examine in natural settings. Inductive reasoning is also the primary means by which data generalization is accomplished. When a researcher is writing the discussion section of a research article, the discussion is based primarily on the data obtained. From the data (specific behavioral occurrences), inferences are drawn back to the theory or model (general) that was mentioned in the introduction. Additionally, generalizations are usually being made about the population (general) from the subjects' performance (specific).

Differences between Experimental Science and Common Sense

There are several distinctions between science and common sense that are useful in placing the scientific method in the context of daily life.

There is a general theme that threads its way through the differences: science is characterized by a more systematic approach to problems than is common sense, and it always leaves the door open for new approaches or knowledge that may dramatically change beliefs about truth or reality. The extent of a scientist's reliance on systematic inquiry is described in several of Isaac Asimov's works (e.g., Asimov, 1960): a nonscientist is certain without proof while a scientist accepts proof without certainty.

There is a distinct difference between science and common sense in the use of theoretical structures and concepts. Science systematically constructs theories and conceptual schemes, uses them, and submits them to repeated tests, as Asimov suggested when he said the scientist is never certain. A person who operates primarily on a common-sense basis generally does not use theory and concepts in the same fashion. Often theories and conceptual structures are applied loosely and not systematically. Explanations for the occurrence of events may not be supported by the logic relating those explanations to a conceptual scheme. They may not even relate to accurate data about the events.

A second difference, closely related to the first, speaks to the issue of theory development and testing. The method of science systematically generates and tests theories, hypotheses, and ideas. The term *systematic* here again becomes the key. If a given theory is presumed to be operative under conditions X, Y, and Z, science demands the systematic examination of events under conditions X, Y, and Z. A common-sense approach to testing, on the other hand, tends to be much less concerned with systematically testing an idea under all relevant conditions. Selection bias frequently enters into the choice of test situations and the viewing of test results. Often an idea such as "all Republicans are conservative" is tested unintentionally under conditions that ensure support for a preconceived notion. Information that does not support the hypothesis may be discounted or ignored and not included as a part of the test. Proverbial in-law stories exemplify this type of information bias.

A third difference between science and common sense involves the concept of *control.* This concept will become a central focus in later chapters on experimental designs. Here again, the systematic approach is relevant. All science arose from the observation of naturally occurring events. The social and behavioral sciences (such as anthropology) cannot always control natural processes in existing groups or cultures. Paleontologists cannot experiment with extinct animals. Experimental science built on these traditions and relies on the concept of control, which essentially involves eliminating possible influential variables except the one being tested. Common sense, to the contrary, may operate in such a loose fashion that several factors are allowed to vary at once. This may mean that any one of two or three influences might have generated the results observed, in addition to the one being studied (as in the case of Shady Hill Elementary). Under such circumstances scientists would probably throw up their hands and view the data as uninterpretable, certainly not attributing the results to any one influence. From the less systematic framework of common sense, the interpretation may suggest a result caused by one influence, which, since two or three are operating, may well be in error.

A fourth distinction between science and common sense involves the interest level concerning relationships among phenomena. The layperson is frequently interested in relationships between phenomena in a somewhat loose and unsystematic fashion. Interest is generated primarily when there is great personal relevance involved. To the contrary, the scientist becomes almost obsessed with the relationships between phenomena, personally relevant or not. There seems to be a continual question-asking process in operation (e.g., I wonder if this material would be more effective if ... or I wonder if that behavior is influenced by...). Such an inquiry approach seems to frequently spill over into the nonprofessional life of the scientist. It is not clear whether this curiosity is a part of the animal (i.e., whether individuals with such a bent gravitate to science) or whether the nature of the training generates such behaviors in those who choose science. Such curiosity is, however, apparent and reported frequently in the daily lives of scientists. (This is certainly not meant to imply that *all* scientists are this way or that is *always* the case even in some scientists. What is true for the population may not be true for any given individual.)

The fifth difference between science and common sense relates to explanations of phenomena. Explanations of events that flow from the method of science tend to be stated in terms of the observable, the logical, and the empirically testable. A common-sense explanation, on the other hand, frequently involves reference to metaphysical influences. Metaphysical explanations cannot be tested. Such statements as "Working hard is good for one's moral character" and "Suffering builds character" are metaphysical statements. Although powerful parental statements when you were a child, such explanations do not fit well into the observable empirically testable framework.

Science is, in one way, a systematic extension of common sense, and some claim that the two need to be connected to enhance the utility of science (Staats, 1993). There is certainly a conceivable continuum between the two, and they are probably not best thought of in an all-or-none fashion. The primary factors that seem to be involved are concepts of systematic inquiry, logic, objectivity, and observable phenomena.

Rationalism versus Empiricism

Throughout the history of human existence, various methods of inquiry have been used as the search for knowledge has proceeded. You may have noticed that methods of inquiry can be viewed in a number of different ways. One manner in which inquiry may be categorized relates to the source of knowledge—internal or external. This conceptualization is relevant from a historic viewpoint and may be distinguished as rationalism versus empiricism.

Rationalism is a method of inquiry that primarily uses an internal source of knowledge. Characteristic of inquiry in ancient Greek times, rationalism views the intellectual examination of ideas as *the* means by which knowledge progresses. Little if any emphasis is placed on that which is external and observable except as the objects are to be manipulated. Instead the emphasis is on logic, reasoning, and intuitive intelligence. Rather than observing a phenomenon to see if a given event occurs, the user of rationalism may draw conclusions as to whether it occurs by using a logical progression of ideas. Rationalism is the primary method of theoretical science.

Empiricism emphasizes knowledge that comes through factual investigation, with the facts discovered through sources external to the investigator. The primary means by which information is obtained involves direct experience and observation through the senses for a particular situation. The empirical approach is the primary method of observational and experimental science.

Different phases of history have been characterized by different modes of inquiry and knowledge seeking. In reaction to the introspective, intuitive approach of rationalism, inquiry has occasionally swung to the other extreme—strict empiricism, with the *only* acceptable source of knowledge being that which is directly observable. The rationalistic approach to inquiry, in isolation, is subject to considerable possibility of error because of the virtual absence of a monitor on the progress of ideas, using observation or experiential checkpoints; and it is possible for progressive error to operate if a series of ideas are generated from the foundation of a false or weak premise. Thus, although rationalism may permit rapid progress, the probability of error is high. Strict empiricism, on the other hand, progresses painfully slowly if it is used in isolation. Some strict empiricists are reluctant to infer or interpret to any degree and are more inclined to merely view the data as a behavioral description. Progress will be infinitesimal if behavioral descriptions must result from observations under all possible conditions without permitting the use of logic or reason to draw inferences from pieces of data. The strength of empiricism is its constant contact with the reality of experience. This substantially reduces the error potential that is so high with pure rationalism. Current research approaches tend to represent a blend of rationalism and empiricism. Reason and logic are used to draw inferences from empirically derived data. Such a blend fortunately combines the strengths of the two approaches, as each tends to offset the pitfalls of the other.

Nomothetic Net

Related to the discussion of empiricism and rationalism is a topic that is concerned with the manner in which theories are constructed. A theory or model usually involves a descriptive explanation of why some phenomenon occurs. In such an explanation, certain aspects of the theory are frequently observable or have been observed, whereas others are either not directly observable or have yet to be observed. Theoretical structures are usually formed by drawing intuitive or logical connections between observed and unobserved aspects of behavior. The points and their connective links together become the theory and form what is known as a *nomothetic net,* a nomologic network or nomologic structure (Smith & Glass, 1987). Cronbach and Meehl (1955) described the nomothetic net in the context of test validity as an "interlocking system of laws which constitute a theory" (p. 290). In the context of research, the points or behavioral events may relate within the network as "(a) observable properties or quantities to each other; or (b) theoretical constructs to observables; or (c) different theoretical constructs to one another" (p. 290). This conceptualization of theory construction has emerged in a number of diverse behavioral science areas ranging from career development (Niles & Sowa, 1992) to personality research (Eysenck, 1992; Gurtman, 1992; Paulhus & Martin, 1987).

The nomothetic net conceptualization of a theory is analogous to a fishnet. The knots or points where the strings join may be thought of as the points (either observed data on performance or hypothesized behavior expected before observation). The linking strings between knots are analogous to intuitive or logical links that suggest relationships between known behavioral data points and hypothesized behavioral performances. Figure 1.2 illustrates the nomothetic net that represents a behavior theory. Points A, B, C, K, L, and M represent results of investigations. The other points, D, E, F, G, H, I, and J, represent hypothesized or expected behaviors. The theory builder may scrutinize known points A and B, saying in essence, for instance, that if A is the case and likewise B, then perhaps a child's memory operates like D. Similarly the theoretician may inspect B and C and hypothesize a composite picture of the child that looks like E. The question might then be raised concerning the existence of both D and E, supposedly composite pictures of the child from known data. The process is not unlike photography. One might take three different photographs of an object, each from a different angle and thus each providing a different piece of information. If one looks at any two of the photographs, a somewhat different mental image of the whole may be generated.

Further inspection of Figure 1.2 indicates three intuitive points (F, G, and H) that are two steps or intuitive links removed from observed data points. These are examples of what Cronbach and Meehl (1955) described as relationships of "different theoretical constructs to one another"

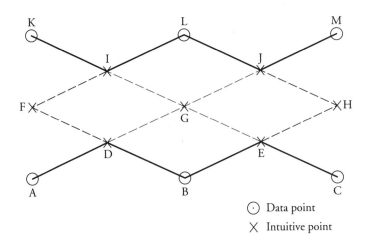

FIGURE 1.2 **Hypothetical Representation of a Behavior Theory as a Nomothetic Net**

(p. 290). Such intuitive points may represent attempts to hypothesize more completely what the phenomenon will look like from two or more previously hypothesized constructs. The logic links that proceed to these second-order constructs are represented in Figure 1.2 by broken lines. This is intended to suggest a weaker inference than those that are only one step away from observed data points. Because known information is further away from intuitive points F, G, and H, their soundness must be viewed as much more tenuous than that of points that are more closely linked to existing evidence. The further a theorist moves away from known data, the weaker the inferences must be considered. The intuitive points then may become studies to be conducted. As investigations are subsequently completed, there are more knowns and fewer intuitive points, placing the theory on an increasingly firmer evidence base. It is also expected that the nature of some of the intuitive points will be altered as data are obtained that suggest theory modification.

The nomothetic net conceptualization of theory construction illustrates nicely the manner in which empirical and logical processes work together in research. It is in this fashion that empiricism and rationalism blend in current research and theory. Actually the fishnet analogy is descriptive of the way in which theory serves to generate research and the theory is, in turn, tested by empirical investigation. If one has made accurate inferences in generating the nomothetic net, it ought to function as a sound fishnet would in scooping fish. Assuming that point G is a solid knot, it ought to "catch" or predict the behavior of a child. This would be either supported or negated by the data from an investigation of point G. If, instead, point G is not an accurate inference, the knot will be unsound and the child will slip through the hole in the theory net (i.e., the theory will miss or not predict performance). This situation would then suggest a change in the theory, assuming that the experiment was appropriately executed to test the theory in the first place.

Inquiry conducted outside arenas in which researchers can control the interaction of variables then adds to this controlled interaction between rationalism and empiricism. Picture the nomothetic net tossed into the complex sea of interactive social processes in natural settings. The truth of the net's knowledge still holds, but its operation is substantially affected by the complex forces at work in the natural setting. "Tides" may disrupt the efficiency of the net; "temperature" may weaken the strength of the knots. The researcher then exchanges the advantages of control for the complexities and advantages of generalizability (a topic to which we will continually return).

Epistemology: Social Science and the Nature of Social Reality

By now, the reader will have noticed that a wide range of methods undergird the systematic inquiry process known as research. Before closing this introductory chapter, one more dimension of the knowledge and knowing tradition in human inquiry requires attention. Just as the logic of rationalism and the logic of empiricism contribute to the accumulation of knowledge over time, no discussion of research is complete without a brief introduction to the intellectual traditions that drive our views about what knowledge is and how it is best acquired.

The entire discussion of research up to this point has been guided by the assumption that behavior and social reality are driven by discoverable, universal principles. The philosophy of science is also enriched by strong traditions about the nature of the human experience and driven by vastly differing assumptions about the universality or uniqueness of human experience. These differences are embedded in *epistemology*.

Epistemology is the theory of science that investigates the origin, nature, methods, and limits of knowledge. Social scientists who conduct research and professionals who use research to help make practical decisions rely on beliefs about how knowledge is acquired and whether social knowledge is transferrable from one situation to another. In the earlier discussion of ways of knowing and fixing belief, we addressed methods that all assume knowledge is fixed and transferrable, but the traditions of science (and the research designs and methods explored in future chapters) are a bit more complex.

Positivism

Much of modern science is based on the logic of empiricism discussed above. In the nineteenth century this empiricism led to the development of a strong belief in the philosophy of science known as *positivism*—the belief that positive data drawn from observations of objective facts and their relationship to natural law are the only truth on which to rely. The term positivism was originally used by Auguste Comte in the 1820s, although it developed from ideas of the scientific revolution. It extended beyond the natural sciences, however, applying the assumptions, methods, and prestige of the natural sciences to social sciences, law, philosophy, and many other areas of scholarship. A mathematician by profession, Comte believed that social problems could be solved by applying the methods and logic of the natural sciences directly to all of society's ills.

John Stuart Mill was a disciple of Comte's. Mill hoped for a predictive and scientific sociology that would develop out of history and make possible the use of behavioral observations to project generalized patterns of human interaction. These ideas are more prevalent in our popular culture than many imagine. Asimov, for example, uses the question of the uniqueness versus predictive generalizability of human social interaction as the foundation for his popular *Foundation* series. In this series, Asimov explores the solar system's future through the creative tension between a predictive sociology of "psychohistory" (that would absolutely predict the future) and the important effects of one person not predicted by the general theory. In this sense, he foreshadowed chaos theory's famous butterfly effect—the unpredictable and powerful influences of small changes in one factor on entire systems.

The ideas of Charles Peirce grew out of these traditions. Peirce argued that all important natural and social questions could be answered using the common observations of empiricism and the logic of rationalism. Peirce's ideas have come to be known as *logical positivism*. In contrast to Peirce, Karl Popper maintained that only the incorrectness of a theory can be inferred from empirical evidence, not its truth. Scientific knowledge must remain always and forever open to future evidence that may falsify an old theory. This openness directly conflicts with the knowledge of authority described earlier, which accepts truth on the basis of statements by the authority which are never open to challenge.

Phenomenology

The genealogy of our views about what is scientific thus leads to an important distinction about the nature, origins, and methods of knowledge. Burrell and Morgan (1979) point out that social and behavioral research is undertaken from a variety of perspectives about the nature of knowledge, ranging along a continuum from the completely phe-nomenological to the positivist. Phenomenologists argue that individual and circumstantial variables are extremely powerful in naturally occur-ring settings, such as classrooms, schools, communities, or cultures. Phenomenologists contend that this potency of individual variables will make them completely unique in critically insurmountable ways—not predictable. From this view a social scientist's main task is to reveal, describe, and interpret (through qualitative research methods such as ethnography) so accurately and richly that readers experience the set-ting as though they were insiders (Gregory, 1983). The empathic experi-ence is paramount.

The Debate

The logical positivist position was described earlier. From the positivist perspective, social knowledge is discoverable and generalizable just as natural science knowledge is. Devoted researchers need only ask the right questions and systematically build on small increments of knowl-edge in order to find this discoverable truth. Totally subjective approaches to social science stand on the phenomenological side of this debate. Totally objective approaches to social science stand on the positivist side (also termed functionalist). Morgan and Smircich (1980) examined some of the assumptions involved in the phenomenology-positivist debate. They point out that the purely subjective perspective of human reality views our experiences as projections of the human imagination and belief. As humans (and researchers) move along the continuum, they view reality as socially constructed rather than objectively experi-enced. As researchers move closer to the objectivist stance, they may view reality as a field of experiential information that exists only in context, as a concrete social-psychological structure to be discovered through a process of controlled experimentation or survey research. Figure 1.3 pictorially represents the nature of social knowledge on a continuum from the subjective to objective perspectives.

Debates among scientists and researchers along this continuum are fierce and, apparently never ending (e.g., Adler, 1990; Sahlin, 1991; Van-Lill, 1989). We do not find these debates productive for the purposes of this introduction to research design because they require that students of research accept a paradigm of social reality at the beginning of their professional or scholarly career—on the basis of insufficient experience—when rich traditions drive both extreme positions. There also is the possibility that no neutral empirical ground of shared facts can be found on which to judge between competing paradigms. In reality, no facts are theory-free and no theories are free of fact, observation, or interpretation.

In summary, traditional quantitative studies in the social and behav-ioral sciences are based on the assumption that general principles or laws govern the social world, much as they govern the physical world.

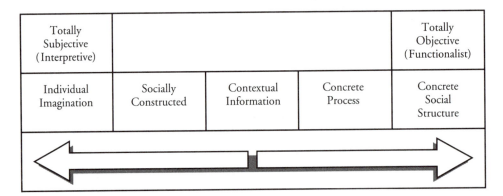

Totally Subjective (Interpretive)				Totally Objective (Functionalist)
Individual Imagination	Socially Constructed	Contextual Information	Concrete Process	Concrete Social Structure

FIGURE 1.3   Nature of Social Knowledge

These principles can be discovered if researchers work long and hard enough and will eventually provide the foundations for predicting all human behavior. The social scientist need only exert enough effort, ask the right questions, and pursue carefully controlled and generalizable research; social reality is universal and discoverable. On the other end of the continuum of beliefs, social reality is seen as unique, phenomenological. Each personal or group experience is intrinsically shaped and governed by the perceptions, interpretations, and unique interactions of the people involved. It can never be replicated, only accurately described so that the reader of research comes as close as possible to understanding, even vicariously experiencing, the social reality involved.

These differences in beliefs about the fundamental nature of social experiences may seem to split hairs, but inexperienced researchers can become trapped in critical problems surrounding rigor unless they are clear about the view of social reality that dominates their own views. As a consumer of educational and social science research, a reader must understand the assumptions about social reality dominating a researcher's design in order to adequately and accurately interpret the meaning of reported findings. Beliefs about the origin, nature, methods, and limits of knowledge thus lie at the base of all questions about the appropriate design of activities meant to acquire knowledge. The epistemological debate among researchers revolves around these issues (Howe, 1985). Qualitative and quantitative data gathering and analysis techniques are a part of this debate. We will place the particular research designs being discussed along this continuum and challenge you as readers to actively interrogate your own beliefs about knowledge and appropriate methods for its discovery as you study and practice research design through this volume.

C h a p t e r 2

Different Research Approaches

Chapter One began with a simple definition of research as a systematic method of inquiry. This is a rather broad definition that essentially identifies the purpose of research as one of obtaining information pertaining to some question or set of questions. Obviously there may be many different types of questions. As might be expected, there is a variety of approaches to obtaining answers. The approach selected depends on several factors, including the nature of the question, the setting in which the research is to be conducted, and the background and disciplinary orientation of the researcher. Although each approach is different in some rather significant ways, all involve the basic components outlined in Chapter 1: generally speaking, the research question or problem must be specifically identified and distilled into researchable form, the study must be designed in a technically sound manner, the data must be collected and analyzed, and results must be interpreted. In certain types of qualitative research there are significant variations on these themes, which we will note. The purpose of this chapter is to discuss different approaches to conducting research.

Distinctions between Research and Evaluation

Differences between evaluation and research have been subjects of discussion and debate for many years. Early considerations of this topic often seemed to be unproductive and characterized more by debate than by serious examination. However, significant progress has been made in recent years, and a brief discussion appears warranted to place both in perspective.

There are many situations in which the distinctions between evaluation and research are minimal, if they exist at all. In fact, for many researchers, evaluation is considered as simply a specific application of data collection that requires much the same rigor as research. In some cases the methods employed are indistinguishable whereas in others there are some differences.

One distinction occasionally emerging between research and evaluation involves the generic purpose for which such an effort is initiated. In certain circumstances evaluation is undertaken as a basis for making informed decisions intended to result in some rather immediate action. Such decisions might pertain to selecting the most effective procedure, material, or organizational structure. Evaluation studies may also address such questions as "Does this technique (material, treatment) work?". These purposes obviously involve questions of utility with a sense of implementation in the relative near future (as opposed to some action which may be taken years or decades in the future). Some research efforts also share this type of purpose. The purposes of applied research efforts often include similar, if not identical, goals. However, the broader concept of research includes other purposes. Basic research is primarily focused on knowledge acquisition; the immediate application of such knowledge is a secondary consideration.

Some evaluation methods have developed that highlight variations in purpose which are different from the immediacy of application. For example, many years ago Provus (1969) presented a description of evaluation that emphasized its conceptual distinctions from research and served as a forerunner of further model development in the field. Provus's concept has since developed into what is known as the Discrepancy Evaluation Model (DEM). He outlined evaluation as the process of "(a) agreeing upon program standards, (b) determining whether a discrepancy exists between some aspect of the program and the standards governing that aspect of the program, and (c) using discrepancy information to identify the weaknesses of the program" (p. 245). This notion highlights one of the distinctions that often differentiate research and evaluation. Essentially the DEM compares performance with some agreed-upon standard to identify potential discrepancies. By virtue of the fundamental purpose of research, predetermined performance standards are not involved when the goal is primarily knowledge acquisition.

In some cases evaluation appears to be a form of applied research with the generalizability of results as the primary difference. Evaluators may have a primary intent of collecting information that is relevant only to the local decision to be made. Researchers, on the other hand, would often like their results to be applicable in other settings, even when they are conducting applied research.

Evaluation may still be considered a form of applied research at the most abstract level. However, the gap between the two appears to be widening. As evaluation techniques have developed and the conceptualizations matured, evaluation has become a credible field of study with increasing attention to sophisticated methodology (Anspach, 1991; Svyantek, O'Connell, & Baumgardner, 1992). The distinctions between evaluation and research have become more evident over the past few years and may be even more notable in the future.

Differing Research Perspectives

We mentioned at the beginning of this chapter that there are different approaches to conducting research. These differing approaches are the result of a number of factors including the wide variety of questions, the settings in which research is to be conducted, and the disciplinary background of the individual undertaking the investigation. Obviously this is only a partial list of the factors that contribute to divergent research perspectives. Even such matters as the investigator's personal preferences may strongly affect the particular method selected. Such specific differences are far too numerous to completely catalog and such an inventory would serve little purpose in this text. There are, however, some generic characteristics of various approaches that are important to consider in becoming acquainted with the research process.

Disciplinary Perspectives

A great deal of discussion has occurred about the nature of a discipline, the characteristics of a discipline, and the vast differences between disciplines. Occasionally the tenor of such discussions has been reduced to consideration of whether or not a particular field warrants the status of a discipline. Although such debates may serve to inflate some professional egos at the expense of others, they are not helpful in furthering the primary purpose here—to more fully understand the research process from various disciplinary perspectives.

Obviously vast differences exist between many disciplines (e.g., medicine versus anthropology, anthropology versus psychology). What is seldom noted, however, is that there are a number of similarities as well. For example, many of the problems faced by medical research are similar to those encountered in psychology, sociology, and education. In some cases although the specific context or content may differ, viewed broadly, the problems are quite similar. For instance, all researchers are faced with complex ethical problems as they attempt to conduct research; there are ongoing and vigorous debates within several disciplines over the philosophical approach to research (Brown, 1992), preferred methodologies (Bailey, 1992), the link between science and practice (Burdine & McLeroy, 1992; Staats, 1993), and applied versus basic research. Consequently an examination of disciplinary perspectives must go beyond issues concerning what is or is not a true discipline (discipline has been defined by some simply as a field of study). If people are to profit from the advances of science in general, it is important to explore various disciplinary differences and similarities regarding the general character of research in the disciplines, methodologies used, and the fundamental views of research in the larger disciplinary mission.

It is neither feasible nor productive to discuss every possible field of study in this text. Our purpose here is to be illustrative rather than exhaustive—students can learn much about the general scientific process by reviewing the techniques, problems, and perspectives of various fields. All too often one's perception of a problem and the approach used to examine that problem are unnecessarily narrowed by a single disciplinary focus.

Certain disciplinary distinctions are more ambiguous than they might appear on the surface. For example, if someone is investigating the practice of medicine and studying the mental health of physicians in the process, is that person engaged in medical research? Perhaps, but depending on the perspective, it may be considered psychological research. It may also be that it is not important to determine exactly what *type* of research is being conducted. In the last analysis the most important consideration is whether or not the investigation is designed and executed in a sound manner.

General Disciplinary Image of Research

The general image of research in different disciplines varies nearly as much as the number of fields of study that one can imagine. In some disciplines research efforts are viewed very favorably and represent high status activities; in other fields research does not have such a favorable image. Although the general scientific image may not be a prominent concern to the individual researcher, it does impact rather substantially on the ability to conduct research in several ways: (1) it serves to promote or diminish funding available to support investigations, (2) it dramatically impacts the importance attached to findings that are reported, and (3) it influences, in a rather circular fashion, the current and future view of research held by professionals within the discipline (that is, attitudes and inclinations of both practitioners and potential scientists). It is difficult to separate these matters since they truly interact in a circular and progressive way. Attitudes within a discipline affect significantly the amount and type of research undertaken, which in turn influences the importance attached to reported findings. Additionally, all of these impact on the support and funding available to facilitate research and vice versa. It is not at all clear whether they are really a *cause* or an *effect* with regard to disciplinary image. What is clear, however, is the general impact of disciplinary image on science within a field.

The general attitude of a discipline toward any activity, in this case research, is largely formed and perpetuated by the training programs that prepare people to work in that field. This process has been characterized as *professional socialization* and basically follows the general notion of socialization but places it in the context of the professional environment (Hart, 1991). The socialization of professionals regarding research varies dramatically between disciplines and the impact is equally dramatic. This discussion will focus on medicine, psychology, and education to illustrate the issues involved.

One very important indicator of socialization is found in the attitudes and publicly expressed views of research by the practitioners in a given field. Research in the medical field is generally valued, even by most physicians who are not actively involved (Murata, Lynch, Puffer, & Green, 1992; Pincus, 1991). One very seldom hears a physician complain about those who are conducting medical research or berate their efforts as having little value. This is a very enviable situation and one that brings into bold relief some of the differences among disciplines. Such conditions do not exist in all fields as may best be illustrated by the status of research in education, in which practitioners seem continually at odds with those who are conducting research. One does not have to search very far to find educators who are complaining about "those ivory tower researchers," claiming that such efforts are worthless and a waste of money. In many cases, those who are most vocal with their complaints have no solid basis for their judgments. (Often one wonders how long it has been since they have read a professional journal.) Clearly, educators are not favorably socialized toward research (Drew, Preator, & Buchanan, 1982). Educators also may be uncomfortable with their research abilities and, furthermore, uninterested in acquiring training in research (Lee & Workman, 1992). Ausubel highlighted this difficulty over 25 years ago when he stated

> there is both little general acceptance of the need for educational research and little appreciation of the relevance of such research for the improvement of education. A tradition of research does not exist in education as it does, for example, in medicine or in engineering, where both professionals and consumers commonly agree that research and progress are almost synonymous. (1969, p.6)

Not all behavioral science views research in the negative light described above for education. Psychology, for example, is a behavioral science discipline in which research has a much more favored status. Research and scientific inquiry are more integrated into the practice of psychology (LaFromboise & Foster, 1992; Tsoi-Hoshmand, 1991). Additionally, the literature in psychology often examines the need for research training as a specific topic aimed at shaping personnel preparation programs (Ellis, 1992; Loughead, Black, & Menefee, 1991). Because research is more a way of life in psychology, students become accustomed to both reading and conducting investigations very early in their academic careers. The process and terminology of research is an integral part of their studies and therefore become favorably incorporated in their attitudes and conceptual view of the discipline. This represents a very important source of support for research in the field and one that should serve as an important lesson to those fields in which research socialization has been less effective.

Earlier we noted substantial differences among disciplines regarding the importance attached to reported research findings. These differences are particularly evident in the lay public. Once again the great diversity is probably best illustrated by medicine and education. Within the lay public, medical research seems to have a very high status and generate a great deal of interest. In some ways this aura appears warranted, whereas in others it seems a manifestation of western society's sacred view of the physician. Regardless of the causes, most people are simply much more concerned about advances in knowledge of human health than about human social, psychological, or educational progress. A new discovery in the field of medicine seems to be more newsworthy than a discovery in these other fields. The public will generally watch as a television newscaster describes a new surgical procedure, even if they do not understand the technical terms being used. On the other hand, a discussion of educational research is more likely to signal a raid on the refrigerator—despite the fact that the refrigerator bandit may have children in school and may never need surgery.

Our society has historically viewed physicians and medicine in a somewhat sacred manner. Most people have complained at one time or another about this doctor or that hospital—even belittled the entire medical field from time to time. Despite these complaints, the physician and the medical field continue to carry great prestige. A comparable type and degree of status is not likely to be achieved by social or behavioral science regardless of their usefulness. The impact of this perspective is extremely potent and has a substantial influence on funding and support for research. Members of Congress are unlikely to vote for funds to support activities that are not valued by their constituents.

The purpose of this section has been to discuss some disciplinary differences with respect to the general image of research and scientific effort. Some of this examination has drawn comparisons that illustrate strengths and weaknesses in certain disciplines. Certain fields fare better than others. This is not intended to suggest that research in fields that fare less well represents undesirable careers to pursue; to the contrary, these are rich and fertile fields that have a great need for talented and committed people. Many professionals view the future as involving more research in these areas than ever before. In particular, there is increasing interest in research that involves collaborative efforts between disciplines (Sheridan, 1992; Welch & Sheridan, 1995).

Research Methods and Settings

There may be no area in which disciplinary differences are thought to be so well known as the methods used and the settings in which research is conducted. Stereotypes place the anthropologist in the field studying uncivilized cultures, the psychologist in a laboratory studying rats, and the biologist hunched over a microscope studying "Lord knows what." Although stereotyped views are always somewhat misleading, they are often based on fact to some degree. The purpose of this section is to briefly discuss differing research methods and settings. Where appropriate, notations will be made regarding characteristic use of one method or another by specific disciplines. However, the major agenda here is not further stereotyping. All methods have applicability in appropriate situations, and many methods are beginning to cross disciplinary boundaries, bringing with them concerns about appropriate training (Searight, 1990). Selection of an appropriate method will primarily depend on the question under study and the setting in which the research is being conducted. The fully equipped researcher must have a variety of tools on hand to effectively pursue the answers to diverse questions that arise.

Distinctions: Experimental-Quantitative and Nonexperimental-Qualitative

Research methods can be categorized in a number of different ways depending mostly on the perspective being used. Scientists with a sociological background often divide them into two major groups—survey and nonsurvey methods. Those with a background in psychology tend to view methodology in terms of experimental and nonexperimental techniques, and both education and psychology speak of quantitative and qualitative methods. Such perspectives reflect disciplinary socialization rather than a statement of preference regarding one over another.

The experimental-nonexperimental and quantitative-qualitative distinctions are akin to reverse images: the prominent features of experimental research are often the opposite of nonexperimental, and the same can be said for quantitative and qualitative research. We choose to pair together experimental and quantitative methods as well as nonexperimental and qualitative strategies because these pairings often occur in practice—experimental researchers often use quantitative approaches and nonexperimental researchers often use qualitative approaches. However, it should be emphasized that these pairings also facilitate discussion in this text. It is not *always* the case that such pairings are present in actual practice. In fact, qualitative methodology often is used in combination with quantitative methodology. Mixed-method research such as this is becoming increasingly popular in order to effectively answer complex research questions arising in natural settings (e.g., Crawford & Christensen, 1995; Hart, 1994).

Experimentation is most often described as tightly controlled investigation in which the researcher manipulates the particular factor under study (e.g., treatment) to determine if such manipulation generates a change in the subjects. Nonexperimental researchers tend to observe, analyze, and describe what *exists* rather than manipulating a factor under study, and they are often concerned about *not controlling* or manipulating the environment. Experiments often occur in laboratory-like circumstances, or the investigator may impose significant controls on existing settings such as minimizing noise or stimulus factors that are unrelated to the study. Nonexperimental researchers and those employing qualitative methodology are more likely to emphasize preserving the naturalness of the setting.

Quantitative investigators and those using experimental methods have a tendency to begin their studies with clearly stated questions, fully developed hypotheses to fit these questions, and a research design manipulating contrived circumstances aimed at answering these questions. Qualitative investigators may differ from their experimental-quantitative colleagues with regard to this question–hypothesis–design phase of the study. Whereas quantitative-experimental investigators place great value on specifically defining the question, developing the hypotheses, and planning the design to fit, qualitative researchers take a different view. They are more likely to let theories, questions, and hypotheses emerge from the environment and subjects under study. In their unwillingness to intervene in naturally occurring events, qualitative researchers may begin their work by being generally interested in a group rather than a research question. Definitions may emerge as the study proceeds.

Quantitative experimental researchers may manipulate conditions as noted above and collect data that are reduced to some numerical representation of what is being measured (such as the number of attempts to solve a math problem, the number of verbal outbursts, etc.). Researchers using qualitative methods tend to collect data that are in a form other than numerical representations. They may record actual verbal utterances which occur naturally in a family setting, or they may describe the natural history of some problem as it emerges in a child. Words are not uncommon as a form of data and the analysis is performed on these words or on ideas suggested by them (whereas a quantitative researcher might count the words that represent certain types of errors). Further, the qualitative researcher is more likely to observe the child in his or her natural context, attempting to understand the child's perceptions of reality—sometimes known as phenomenological reality (Borg, Gall, & Gall, 1993). Although the data are in different forms and the types of analyses vary, both qualitative and quantitative researchers are likely to use computers to perform part or all of their analyses. It is not uncommon to find powerful laptops in field settings for both types of methodology.

Distinctions between quantitative-experimental and qualitative-nonexperimental methods vary depending on the perspective held by the person. From an elementary and uncomplicated standpoint, these approaches can be conceptualized in terms of two intersecting dimensions that represent the distinctive features of the two paradigms. On one dimension is the factor of control—one's degree of willingness to alter the natural environment or naturally occurring events and define matters on an a priori basis (that is, before the study begins). The other dimension relates to the data, with one extreme involving the reduction of all measures to numerical representation while the opposite extreme records data in words (descriptions of events, feelings, etc.). Both of these dimensions may be viewed as a continuum and many researchers today are using combinations of strategies. Figure 2.1 presents a pictorial representation of these intersecting dimensions.

Historically, the majority of research in education and psychology has employed quantitative methodology. However, during the past 10 to 15 years, qualitative research methods have gained popularity, both as

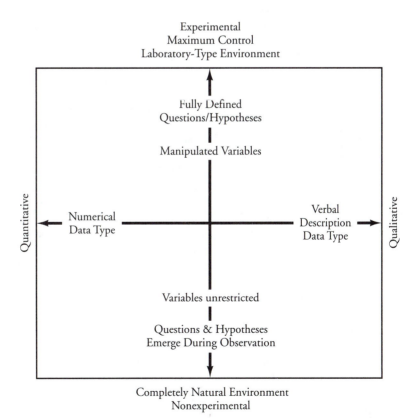

FIGURE 2.1 Intersecting Dimensions of Distinctions: Experimental-Quantitative and Nonexperimental-Qualitative

distinct research strategies and as a companion to existing quantitative techniques. Lancy (1993) indicated that "qualitative research has gone from being fringe, marginal, unscientific, to fashionable ..." (p. 24). Lancy's terminology is worthy of note, particularly the word "fashionable." There is a fluid quality to what methodology is popular, and the enthusiasm for various methods often grows and subsides without a fully developed, clear concept or language to support their statuses. Methods may not have sufficient time in the spotlight to mature as methodologies. Some believe that this is the case with the current status of quantitative-qualitative choices, although maturity seems at hand (Bogdan & Biklen, 1992; Lancy, 1993; Miles & Huberman, 1994).

Clearly, there is much that differs between the qualitative-nonexperimental and quantitative-experimental approaches; in fact, elements that are considered desirable by one strategy are often thought undesirable by the other. Qualitative research methodology has emerged because of limitations in the quantitative-experimental paradigm; researchers desire to learn more about the complexities of naturally occurring events. Heated debates have understandably been generated by the tension between these approaches (Fraenkel & Wallen, 1993; Lancy, 1993). However, it is crucial to remember that these methodology wars will subside as transitions continue. Researchers on both sides are presenting well-reasoned arguments for both paradigms and incorporating elements of both when appropriate (Hart & Bredeson, 1995). These methods each have advantages and limitations which we will discuss.

Experimental-Quantitative Approaches

Quantitative experimental approaches to conducting research have a long and rich history that has crossed many disciplinary boundaries including early work in agriculture and psychology. Sir Ronald A. Fisher is often cited as the father of quantitative experimental methodology in the social sciences for his work during the early part of the twentieth century (1925, 1926, 1935). There was, however, another author who actually predated Fisher in describing this methodology with still another field in mind—education. The work of W.A.McCall (1923), although not cited frequently, is viewed as a classic in behavioral science experimental methodology and has had a significant impact on current thinking regarding this approach to research. Although experimental approaches have been stereotypically associated with certain disciplines, McCall's methodology has been used by many researchers in medicine, biology, and numerous others. It is a powerful tool when the topic and setting are appropriate for its use. As with our earlier discussion on the emergence of qualitative methodology, some disciplines not often associated with experimentation and quantitative methods are beginning to incorporate it into their research tool kit (e.g., anthropology).

Experimental research is most commonly associated with laboratory investigations in which the experimenter tightly controls all the outside influences that might contaminate the results. If this is successfully accomplished (i.e., controlling all extraneous influences), any change observed in the subject(s) is presumed to be caused by the variable that was manipulated and is being studied. It will become evident in this volume that controlling all influences except the one under study is a major problem confronting experimental researchers and is of central importance. It will also become evident that there are many variations of the experimental approach and that the stereotype of a precise laboratory investigation does not always hold true. However, the experimental approach remains a very powerful technique.

It was noted above that the experiment involves a study in which the researcher *manipulates* the factor under study. A brief discussion of this idea is needed to further examine experimentation. The factor under study—the variable that an experimenter manipulates—is known as the *experimental variable.* It is also called the *independent variable,* but in this book the term experimental variable will be used to avoid confusion with the use of the term independent in certain other research contexts. Obviously if the researcher is going to observe change in the subjects, there must be some means of measuring that change (e.g., improved reading performance, faster time in running the mile relay, reduced number of classroom disruptions).

The measure of change is known as the *criterion measure,* that is, the process by which a researcher determines if change has occurred. In using quantitative criterion measures, the number of correct responses on a test may be recorded; a stopwatch may be used to measure time; or any number of other techniques may be included, depending on the study. The criterion measure is often called the *dependent variable,* since the change (if it occurs) is presumably dependent on the researcher's manipulation of the experimental variable. For purposes of this book, the designation of criterion measure will be used to avoid a term that often confuses the beginning researcher.

The experimental variable, in terms of the previous discussion, is the factor that a researcher manipulates. It may be a particular treatment in pharmacy research, such as drug A compared with drug B; it may involve the comparison of teaching methods, such as programmed instruction compared with reading a book. In any case, a researcher manipulates the treatment. In the literal sense, this is not always the case. Sometimes a researcher is interested in a variable that cannot be easily manipulated or that has already been "manipulated" by nature. An example of such a situation might be found if the researcher were interested in studying brain damage. In this case an investigation might be designed whereby subjects who have been brain damaged are compared on some learning task with subjects who are not brain damaged.

Obviously the researcher does not have the freedom to sample a large group of subjects and inflict brain damage on half of them. Instead it is more likely that the brain-damaged subjects will have to be sampled from a group of individuals who are already known to be so afflicted and the non-brain-damaged subjects from a group known not to be so afflicted. In this type of situation, the experimental variable is formulated on the basis of preexisting differences between the groups as distinguished from circumstances in which the researcher creates differences by actually manipulating the treatment. Such a format is known as a *quasi-experimental* design, whereas the term *true experiment* (or just experiment) is reserved for cases involving actual manipulation of the variable under study.

The discussion of experimental methodology has thus far focused on, and used examples of, studies in which groups of subjects are used. Variations on this theme will be explored in greater depth later in this volume. There is, however, another approach that must be mentioned under the general topic of experimentation—*time-series designs.* Time-series experiments have come into more frequent usage during the past 30 years and are often associated with operant conditioning or behavior modification research. In fact, time-series designs have often been labeled as single-subject designs because of their frequent use with individual subjects. Such a label is somewhat misleading since they can be and are used in situations in which more than one subject is studied. The particulars of this type of experimentation will be treated in greater depth later in this volume, although some brief discussion is warranted here. Since time-series experiments often use a single subject, this abbreviated examination will be couched in those terms.

Time-series experiments involve investigations in which the experimental variable is basically studied across different phases of treatment. Essentially these phases compare a subject's performance without treatment (termed baseline) and with treatment. The fundamental purpose is to determine whether the initiation of treatment will generate a change in the subject's performance or behavior. The simple diagram in Figure 2.2 illustrates the basic concept underlying time-series designs.

Figure 2.2 illustrates a data display that might result from a time-series format that is known as an *A-B design.* In this type of experiment, the researcher records data on the subject for a time without treatment involved (phase A, known as baseline). After the researcher has enough data to reliably indicate the subject's untreated performance level, phase B (treatment) is initiated. The experimental variable in this case is the treatment, with two specific conditions in that variable— treatment absent and treatment present. Time-series experiments represent situations in which the researcher actually *manipulates* the experimental variable. A variety of time-series design formats may be used in different situations and will be explored in greater depth in later chapters.

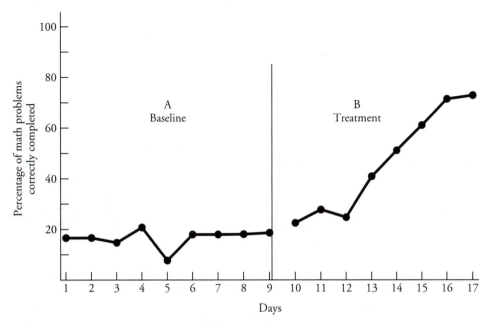

FIGURE 2.2   Example of a Time-Series Experiment Format

Advantages and Disadvantages.   There are advantages and disadvantages to all research approaches. In most cases the selection of one method over another is a matter of discretion depending on the question, setting, and a variety of other considerations. No particular approach is uniformly inferior or superior for all research questions.

Experimental approaches to research have several advantages over nonexperimental procedures. First of all, the very nature of experimentation involves a greater degree of control exercised by the researcher. The basic aim of the investigator is to control all extraneous influences and manipulate the experimental variable. Regardless of which specific design is used, the experimenter wants to arrange matters so that the factor under study varies (the experimental variable) and others do not. Thus one of the advantages of experimentation involves the amount of *control* that can be imposed.

Because of the control exercised in experimental research, this approach comes as close as any to establishing *causality*. In this case, causality refers to the notion that manipulation of the experimental variable caused any change observed in the criterion measure. If the only difference between two groups of children is the instruction they received, then differences in their scores might be attributed to their instruction. Such an idea is very appealing since it represents the firmest type of evidence that could be obtained in an investigation and therefore is a definite advantage of experimentation. However, as strong as this advantage is, it must be viewed in a relative sense and is subject to misinterpretation by those unfamiliar with the scientific process. Researchers are reluctant to assume causality with a great deal of certainty—particularly in the behavioral sciences. Notice that the word *prove* is seldom used by researchers at all (except those alleged scientists selling toothpaste on television). Despite all the care taken to control extraneous variables, there is always the possibility that somewhere there was an uncontrolled outside influence. There is even some probability that the results could be caused by chance, and statistical analyses used in research are based on assessing the likelihood that results could or could not be explained by chance. The process of experimentation is one that comes as close as possible to establishing causality, although a single study in no way accomplishes this end. Later portions of this volume will examine this process in much greater detail.

Quantitative researchers tend to use numerical representations as their data. Although they may be observing the behavior of children, they prefer to categorize these behaviors, count them (e.g., number of tantrums in a school day), and perform their analyses on the resulting numbers. This tends to be both a strength and a limitation of the methodology. There is no question what is to be done with the criterion measure—there is a counting process and after the numbers are tallied, researchers either describe what happened, look for differences (between groups or between pre- and post-treatment assessments), or look for relationships. For well-trained quantitative researchers, this is a clearly defined process and much easier for them to understand than trying to interpret data in the form of general words or feelings. However, data that are reduced to numbers may be difficult to interpret and understand. The researcher may know quite well *what* occurred, but he or she may not have much evidence regarding *why* it occurred. Quantitative data, as both a strength and a limitation, is a marvelous example of why some researchers are recommending combinations of methodology—using the best of quantitative methods to learn clearly what happened along with the best of qualitative strategies to better understand why it occurred.

Speaking specifically of experimentation, further disadvantages are closely related to the control advantages noted earlier. Because of the control involved, experimental research is often conducted in a somewhat *artificial environment*. The degree to which the environment is artificial varies greatly, depending on the manner in which the study is planned and executed. A laboratory experiment may represent an extremely artificial setting, whereas an experiment conducted in the field may be less so. Results of an investigation may be substantially different in an artificial environment from what they would be if the same topic were studied in a natural setting; and it is the researcher's task to determine the most appropriate situation. In certain instances, steps can be taken to offset this disadvantage as will be seen later.

Another limitation may be thought of as a subtopic under the broader concern of artificiality. Experimentation, by its very nature, often involves activities, people, and materials or apparatus that are unfamiliar to the subjects. Consequently these factors may be considered artificial and alter the manner in which the subjects behave. As before, such an influence may make the results different from what they would be if the subjects were performing activities and encountering people or materials with which they were familiar. This is why experimental research is often said to be "reactive" in the sense that subjects may react to these influences and not perform normally. These matters also can be overcome to a considerable degree if the researcher is thorough in planning ahead.

Disciplinary Utilization. Many different disciplines have used experimental-quantitative research as a cornerstone of scholarly inquiry in the field. Certainly the so-called hard sciences such as biology, chemistry, and physics have long found its elements to be basic in their approach to research. In social science, the field most frequently associated with quantitative experimentation is psychology, although there are vast differences between the subdiscipline areas of psychology. Researchers in the field of education have also used experimental-quantitative research heavily, although as with psychology, there is great variation between subareas of study in the general field of education.

Research using experimentation and quantitative data has begun to emerge in certain social science areas that have traditionally been associated with nonexperimental-qualitative investigation. Perhaps the most notable are sociology and anthropology, in which considerable attention is now being given to experimentation (e.g., Bailey, 1994). Experimental research is essentially a new and (to some) foreign approach in these disciplines. Such changes do not occur easily, and there are some interesting perceptions and arguments advanced both pro and con.

Anthropology serves as an excellent example. The stereotyped view of anthropological research often involves a caricature of a slightly grubby person in a pith helmet and khaki shorts busily recording field notes in an uncivilized part of the world. Although this perception is obviously a popularized one, it also has certain elements that are also shared by professionals in the field, and it captures many activities associated with traditional anthropological research. Such research has been known as *participant observation* wherein the researcher participates in the environment being observed (participant observation is generally viewed as a qualitative research method). To some degree more experimental approaches are emerging in anthropology, just as participant observation as a form of qualitative research is appearing more frequently in education. Somewhat revolutionary to some disciplinary conservatives, this development has resulted in what is termed the *emic* versus *etic* debate. The emic (from *phonemic*) perspective involves the contention that the most useful concepts for research analysis are those that the subjects themselves use and find meaningful (thus letting the research question emerge from the actions and concepts of the subjects being observed). The etic (from *phonetic*) view, on the other hand, holds that scientific data should be analyzed in terms of the concepts developed by the researcher. There are appealing points to both sides. The purpose of this section, however, is not to debate but to indicate that experimental research is now being considered as a part of the investigative framework in fields where it was previously ignored. Likewise, qualitative research methods are emerging in fields that were previously characterized by experimental methods (Eisner, 1993). Such changes do not come easily since our disciplinary narrowness often eliminates many potentially useful techniques.

Nonexperimental-Qualitative Approaches

There is a variety of nonexperimental and qualitative approaches to conducting research. Like experimentation, nonexperimental and qualitative methods have a long history of use by many disciplines and have been the basis for inquiry in many different settings. As we have said, in some ways these approaches may be thought of as the reverse image of experimental and quantitative paradigms. Researchers using such methods tend to observe, analyze, and describe what *exists* rather than manipulating a variable under study. They do not use direct control (such as in a laboratory) in the same fashion that is characteristic of experimentation. In fact, one of the prominent features of nonexperimental-qualitative research is that there is a distinct preference for preserving the natural environment. In large part, there is a distaste for altering the naturally occurring events. Qualitative researchers often go to great lengths to minimize researcher effects. At this point, there are some deviations from the closed-loop research process described in Chapter 1 (Figure 1.1). Although some qualitative investigations still follow this general model (i.e., beginning with a specific question), others follow a different course, and the questions emerge from the information collected as the study progresses (see Figure 2.1). These latter studies are more clearly on the natural end of the control continuum of Figure 2.1.

Survey research represents a type of nonexperimental investigation that may collect qualitative data, quantitative data, or a combination thereof. Survey research involves asking questions of a sample of subjects who are presumably representative of the group being studied. The questions are related either directly or indirectly to the topic under investigation, and the answers provided by the subjects represent the data. Surveys are conducted using questionnaires or interviews and may investigate a broad range of topics. Most people have been involved as subjects in surveys of one type or another. Some surveys are designed primarily to collect descriptive information such as age, annual income, and political affiliation. (Note the first two of these, age and income, are quantitative data whereas political affiliation is more likely considered qualitative.) Others are aimed at determining attitudes or opinions concerning some particular topic (e.g., type of automobile preferred, perceptions of the president's effectiveness). In many cases both descriptive and attitudinal questions are included in the same survey if the purpose of the study requires both. Examples of this latter type of survey can be found in marketing research in which the goal is to determine what products appeal to certain segments of the population.

As suggested above, survey research may be undertaken for a variety of purposes. The researcher who conducts a descriptive survey may wish only to describe what exists in a given population at a particular time. In this type of study, the descriptive information obtained represents the answer to the research question. On the other hand, a comparative survey may be conducted to see if there is a difference between two groups of subjects or between the same subjects at two points in time. This type of study may be undertaken, for example, to test some sociological theory concerning the two groups. There are many variations of survey research and a number of considerations that must be involved in planning and executing such investigations. These will be explored in greater depth in later chapters.

Observation is a second nonexperimental method. Actually, classifying observation as a separate method and purely nonexperimental is somewhat misleading. It is being described here simply because manipulation is not inherent in the process. Observation is basically a data collection technique that is used in many different types of research and is *not* the exclusive property of nonexperimental or qualitative research. Many investigations that clearly involve experimentation and collect quantitative data also use observation as a means of gathering information. Therefore, since observation cuts across different research methods, it is necessary to examine various types of observation.

One way of classifying observation techniques involves viewing the observer as either a *participant or nonparticipant.* As previously mentioned, in participant observation the individual conducting the investigation actually participates in the setting or activities being observed. As the term suggests, the nonparticipant observer plays an outsider role and does *not* actively participate in the environment. Participant observation has long been the traditional method of conducting field research in anthropology as studies have been undertaken on various cultures. (The term *ethnography* is also used in such investigations.) Research of this type is most often associated with the study of primitive cultures (perhaps the classic being Margaret Mead's *Coming of Age in Samoa*). It is also being used, however, to investigate subcultures within more contemporary societies (e.g., Spradley's *You Owe Yourself a Drunk: An Ethnography of Urban Nomads,* 1970). In participant observation, it is typical for the observer to literally become a member of the culture or group under study. Data are often qualitative, recorded in the form of field notes representing the observer's perceptions of events that occur. It is not uncommon for the participants in the study to be unaware that they are being investigated since the observer either becomes or appears to become (to the group being studied) a part of the environment. Nonparticipant observers, as just noted, do not actively become involved in the environment under investigation; in this role, the observer does not become a member of the culture or group. Data collection through nonparticipant observation may be either unknown or known to the group being studied. In some cases the observer is evident (since there is no pretense of group membership), whereas in others the observer may not be obvious (such as observations through a one-way mirror).

A second method of classifying observation involves the *amount of structure* imposed on the study. Structure can be viewed in terms of both the observer and the environment for the investigation. The observations may be arranged so that little or no structure is imposed on the manner in which the data are collected (e.g., field notes recorded without any guidelines). On the other hand, the observer may be given a great deal of structure, such as a protocol or checklist used for counting and classifying behavior frequency. The structure of the setting may be similarly viewed. The observer may record data in a completely unstructured environment—that setting in which the subjects habitually live. The opposite end of this continuum would be when subjects are observed in a totally artificial or foreign setting such as in a laboratory experiment. Observation is a very useful and powerful data collection procedure that spans many disciplines and settings. Although observation has been discussed briefly, many specific details must also be examined before an investigation of the procedure can be started.

Advantages and Disadvantages.   To some degree, the advantages and disadvantages of nonexperimental and qualitative research have already been encountered. Almost by definition, nonexperimental and qualitative investigations are described in terms of what experimentation is *not.* Consequently the advantages of quantitative experimentation partially represent the disadvantages of nonexperimental research and vice versa. However, it is important to note the word *partially;* it will become evident later in this volume that *characteristic* advantages and disadvantages are being discussed. The ingenious researcher will be able to circumvent problems to some degree by the manner in which procedures and instrumentation are planned.

One of the disadvantages noted previously under experimentation involves the artificial environment in which such studies often occur. As discussed earlier, such an artificial setting may influence the manner in which subjects behave and therefore alter results. What is a disadvantage of experimental research here becomes an advantage for certain nonexperimental investigations. Some nonexperimental research involves the primary purpose of studying subjects in their natural habitat. To the degree that this is accomplished, the subjects being investigated should behave in a natural manner and the study itself will not influence the data. Clearly, however, not all nonexperimental research is conducted in a naturalistic setting; in fact, some may be nearly as contrived and artificial as a laboratory experiment. In such circumstances, the advantages discussed here would obviously be lost.

Many advantages and disadvantages of nonexperimental research depend on the type of data collection technique being used. For example, a survey study may be quite economical if the data are collected with a mail-out questionnaire. The expense of reproducing questionnaires and postage may be relatively minimal. On the other hand, a survey conducted using interviewers might be very expensive. Personnel costs for trained interviewers can be quite high, not to mention transportation and living expenses (if the interviewer is away from home). However, there are notorious problems with mail-out questionnaires that must also be considered—such as response rates and accuracy.

There may also be difficulties with the data collected in observation studies. In some cases, inexperienced researchers have not made explicit decisions whether they are compiling quantitative or qualitative data—and may not have sufficient background to know the ramifications of such a decision. For example, it is not uncommon for beginners to elect a questionnaire strategy using open-ended questions in order to avoid the analysis of numbers because of a fear of math. Certainly there is some mathematics involved in analyzing quantitative data. However, there are also prescribed procedures for analyzing data that are in qualitative form, and these are rather involved if adequate rigor is to be present in the study. One limitation of nonexperimental-qualitative research is that it appears easier to the uninitiated and therefore invites participation by novice researchers for the wrong reasons. Qualitative methodology should be used because it fits the research setting or question, not because of an erroneous assumption that it is more simply accomplished—it is not.

It is clear, then, that there is great variation regarding advantages and disadvantages of nonexperimental and qualitative research depending on the particular method used. In many cases the particular data collection procedure must be considered in isolation to fully explore the method and its specific benefits or problems. Such a complete and detailed discussion far exceeds the scope of this section but will be addressed in considerable depth in later chapters. This brief section has served to illustrate that *no* given approach is totally free of problems. Each has certain strong points that must be weighed against its weaknesses in determining how the research question is to be studied. This also emphasizes the need for fully equipped researchers to have knowledge of a variety of investigative techniques. Otherwise the studies conducted (questions explored) will be severely limited and actually determined by the tools available. This is no more acceptable in research than it is in auto repair.

Disciplinary Utilization.   Many different disciplines have and continue to use nonexperimental and qualitative research approaches. It is obvious from the discussion above that participant observation has been a traditional means of conducting inquiry for anthropology. It is also used in sociology, psychology, and education. Survey research has often been undertaken in sociology, but it is also conducted in psychology, education, business, and political science. As these different disciplines are noted, it is important to recall the earlier point that it is not always clear exactly what type (in terms of discipline) of research is being conducted. If a researcher—a sociologist by training—is studying the subculture of a junior high school, is that individual conducting educational research, sociological research, or psychological research?

Without proceeding further it becomes abundantly clear that, in general, each discipline uses every type of research at one time or another. Despite the disciplinary stereotypes that many hold, it also becomes evident that disciplinary narrowness creates many problems for the scientist who wishes to examine a variety of research questions. The optimal situation would favor researchers who were conversant with many methodologies, perhaps sufficiently knowledgeable that they could actually implement investigations in the various modes. If this cannot be accomplished, the minimal hope would be that researchers can understand approaches to inquiry other than those typically associated with the discipline in which their preparation occurred.

Chapter *3*

Ethical Issues in Conducting Research

Researchers have always been accountable for ethical behavior while conducting their investigations, although concerns about *researcher ethics* have received increased attention in recent years (Freedland & Carney, 1992; Wheeler, 1994). As with many issues, the ethics of science receive greater attention as they become more salient and immediate in people's lives. This attention influences attitudes about science in general, as societal awareness increases and the abuses committed by a relatively few researchers receive wide-spread publicity. Recent revelations regarding radiation experiments of the last three decades in the United States have raised critical issues about ethics and consent in science for all citizens (Wheeler, 1994).

Partly as a result of increasing publicity about abuses such as these, a greatly heightened sensitivity to the rights of individuals has emerged in our society. The purpose of this chapter is to explore some of the ethical issues involved in conducting research. Thoughtful consideration of these issues is extremely important for beginning researchers, and experienced investigators, as well as the research consumer.

The importance of ethics in research is dramatically illustrated by highly public and repugnant abuses or social-value violations. The most widely known examples of such abuses occurred in the experiments conducted on Nazi concentration camp prisoners during World War II. These experiments involved grossly inhumane activities that were essentially viewed as unthinkable in civilized society. Yet recent new reports on U.S. radiation research have been openly compared to the Nazi experiments. Perhaps because of the wartime context, general sensitivity of the lay public has not been substantially heightened on a long-term basis. More recent evidence, however, clearly indicates that ethical concerns (and potentially harmful outcomes) cannot be limited to wartime mentalities and concerns about prisoners. It is also important that they not be limited to deliberate manipulations of human factors. For example, information came to light in the 1970s and 1980s about serious health problems resulting from nuclear testing in Nevada during the 1950s. Was this a violation of ethical research practices, since it did not directly involve research on human subjects? Such questions are not easily answered, but in hindsight it seems obvious that precautions should have been taken.

The topics to be discussed in this chapter are not nearly as dramatic as the examples just presented. *Most* do not involve torturing subjects by immersion in ice water, death from cancer caused by nuclear fallout, or teenagers' swallowing nuclear cocktails. (Note the emphasis on *most*; some abuses differ only by degree.) The chapter focuses primarily on issues, activities, and situations that are far from black-and-white in terms of ethics. More liberal researchers may think that some of these issues do not warrant discussion; but a balanced presentation remains our goal. There are no simple answers or solutions. Although guidelines are suggested, each researcher must assume the burden for considering ethical issues for each investigation.

Up to this point, we have referred only to ethical issues in general terms with a few examples. However, by the end of this chapter, you may begin to have a somewhat defeatist view: with all these problems, why should one even try to conduct research? This is a common response for new researchers, and is frequently voiced when difficulties are encountered while obtaining approval from agencies and institutional review boards or obtaining consent from subjects.

Nevertheless, researchers press on. As suggested by Best and Kahn (1989), a researcher's perseverance is triggered by a curiosity that leads to speculation—conjecture about ". . . the operation of the universe, the great forces beyond our control" (p. 1). Speculation then leads to inquiry and attempts to increase knowledge and dispel ignorance. The question becomes not only a matter of whether it is ethical to conduct research but whether it is *unethical not to engage in inquiry.* Are researchers guilty of unethical conduct if they do *not* engage in systematic inquiry conducted with the safety of subjects in mind and with their full informed consent?

While ethical considerations may initially be viewed as roadblocks to getting the study underway, they are an important part of research. Attention to the ethics of an investigation requires extra thought and effort, but the payoff for a study that is not only methodologically intact but ethically sound can be extremely exhilarating. This chapter cannot provide a "complete ethical checklist" that covers all questions, settings, or concerns. Such a task would be impossible and not even terribly helpful as you thoughtfully consider and decide about each research situation you might encounter. Although some guidelines are relatively firm, the best insurance against unethical research practices is the knowledgeable individual scientist who can intelligently consider the circumstances being faced. Ethical issues will be discussed in three major categories: (1) ethical issues related to subjects, (2) ethical issues related to particular research approaches, and (3) ethics and professionalism. It will become evident that certain matters (e.g., informed consent) are relevant concerns in more than one of these categories. In fact, the categories of discussion are interrelated in a variety of ways and are separated here only for instructional convenience.

Ethical Issues Related to Human Subjects

> *Except in minimal risk research, the investigator establishes a clear and fair agreement with research participants, prior to their participation, that clarifies the obligations and responsibilities of each. The investigator has the obligation to honor all promises and commitments included in that agreement.* (American Psychological Association, 1989, pp. 31-32.)

Whether researchers are psychologists, educators, or anthropologists, the primary responsibilities to their subjects are clear cut: (a) obtain consent, (b) protect from harm, and (c) ensure privacy. There is, however, one area of responsibility that is less clear for both the researcher and the subject: intentional deception. In this section, we will examine each of the more clearly defined areas of responsibility, as well as the ethical dilemmas imposed by intentional deception.

Consent

Consent, in the context of research, involves the procedure by which the subjects choose whether or not they wish to participate in a study. The researcher's task is to ensure that subjects have a complete understanding of the procedures to be used in the study, any risks involved, and the demands placed upon them as participants (Best & Kahn, 1989). They must also understand their right to withdraw from the study at any time. Consent is a dominant issue in research with human subjects.

There are two forms of consent: direct and substitute. *Direct consent* is the most preferred because agreement is obtained directly from the person to be involved in the study. *Substitute consent* or third-party consent is given by someone other than the person to be involved in the study. Substitute consent may be obtained when it is determined that persons do not have the capacity to make the decision or are dependent on others for their welfare (such as children under the age of 18 or people with cognitive and/or emotional disabilities). Both direct and substitute consent must meet the requirements for *informed consent.*

From a legal standpoint informed consent involves three elements: *capacity, information,* and *voluntariness.* All three elements must be present for consent to be effective. It is also important to understand that consent is seldom (if ever) permanent and may be withdrawn at any time. (The act of withdrawing consent must also include the elements of capacity, information, and voluntariness.)

Capacity.   Capacity is a person's ability to acquire and retain knowledge. The ability to evaluate the information received and subsequently make a choice based on this evaluation is integral to the element of capacity. Based on the ability to acquire, retain, and evaluate information, a person is deemed *competent* or *incompetent.* Competence is determined by legal qualification and ability. Legal qualification is most often viewed in terms of age; individuals under the age of majority (generally 18 years) are considered to be legally unable to make certain decisions. Children's rights are then legally protected by obtaining permission from parents or legal guardians. Children's rights are ethically protected when, no matter who is giving the consent, that person has a primary interest in the child's welfare.

The second factor in determining competence is the individual's ability to give consent: does the individual understand the nature and consequences of giving consent? This factor is again relevant to the involvement of children in research studies but is applicable to others as well (such as persons with cognitive or emotional disabilities and prisoners). First, from a legal standpoint, a person is considered competent unless they have been adjudicated through the court system as being incompetent. It cannot be assumed that because individuals of adult age have cognitive or emotional disability, they are not competent to make decisions regarding their individual welfare. Second, even if the individual is deemed legally competent, it does not relieve the researcher of the responsibility to ensure that the participant understands the information provided and can exercise free power of choice. It is clear even from this brief discussion that the capacity element is not simple. It often becomes even more complex in the context of implementation, which will be discussed in later sections.

Information.   The determination of whether information has been communicated to a participant in an effective manner is based on both *substance* and *manner.* In other words, what information was given, and how was it presented. Turnbull (1977) suggests that "the concern is with the *fullness* and *effectiveness* of the disclosure; is it designed to be fully understood, and is it fully understood? The burden of satisfying these two tests rests on the professional" (p. 8). Literally interpreted, this statement suggests the researcher's duty is to see that the information given to the potential subject is designed to be fully understood and *is* fully understood. This perspective places a great responsibility on the investigator and makes assurance that effective consent has been obtained even more complicated.

Voluntariness.   Voluntary consent is concerned with each individual's ability to exercise free power of choice without the intervention of force, fraud, deceit, duress, or other forms of constraint or coercion. This right to exercise choice must be present throughout the entire research process. The intent of this interpretation is that any such constraint or coercion must not be either *explicit or implicit* on the part of the investigator.

The collective consideration of all three elements of consent has great impact on the manner in which a study is planned and executed. Each research situation presents a different set of circumstances, and consent procedures must be adapted accordingly. For investigators in certain areas (such as child development, mental retardation, mental health), the type of subjects frequently studied require special consideration and protection (Morris, Niederbuhl, & Mahr, 1993). Such subjects will receive repeated attention in our discussion and examination of consent issues regarding *who* and *when*.

Consent: Who.   The question of who may give consent is not a difficult one for adults who have not been adjudicated as being incompetent. Adults can give consent to participate in research, and one must be an adult to do so. It is also clear that they must consent on a voluntary basis and with complete information concerning the nature and consequences of participation.

Many individuals who are not competent and in need of special consideration and protection are generally thought to be unable to give consent on their own. They may be lacking in capacity because of cognitive or emotional disabilities, or because they are legally too young. They may appear very vulnerable to either explicit or implicit coercion (thus violating the truly voluntary element of consent). They may have a combination of these and other characteristics that render them unable to exercise free will and make decisions. For individuals in such circumstances, the question becomes one of who can give consent on their behalf (and what considerations must receive attention in the process).

The answer to the question of who, is the parent, guardian, or other agent legally responsible for and authorized to act in the person's behalf. Although this may seem simple, it is not; and the prerogative of consent is not constant. It varies greatly from situation to situation and among subjects. For example, legal and ethical writing seems to suggest that parents may generally give consent that permits withholding of treatment from (and ultimate death of) infants who are born with significant genetic anomalies at birth. However, literature and the courts have also suggested that it is *not* the parents' sole prerogative to give consent for sterilization of children with mental retardation (Drew, Hardman, & Logan, 1995; McDonnell, Hardman, McDonnell, & Kiefer-O'Donnell, 1993). This seems paradoxical since in one situation the outcome may be death and in the other a person is merely rendered incapable of procreation. (The qualifying word *merely* is not meant to suggest that the latter situation is insignificant; it does, however, seem somewhat less dramatic than a decision to let someone die.)

Although the preceding examples are somewhat removed from our central concern, they serve to illustrate and openly acknowledge the complexities of consent and also to highlight the difficulty in determining who can consent on behalf of others. It is interesting to examine the differences between the consent situations in these cases. It seems that the parent, guardian, or other agent (e.g., institutional administrator) can probably give consent until it comes to someone's attention that the interests of the consenter are at odds with what may be the interests of the subject. For situations in which subjects cannot provide their own consent, the researcher should *not* assume that parental or other consent is sufficient. Although it is for the most part, one should constantly be vigilant in situations in which it may not be. The American Psychological Association (APA) (1989) suggests that obtaining legal consent from the parent or guardian does not relieve the researcher of respecting the wishes of the child. The APA suggests that if the child is ". . . capable of making some reasonable judgment concerning the nature of the research and of participation in it, permission should be obtained from the participant as well as from the responsible adult or guardian" (p. 34).

The conventional notions associated with consent may not be appropriate for children, however. Abramovitch, Freedman, Thoden, and Nikolich (1991) point out that consent is a legal term and generally is not considered appropriate to use with minors. A child's agreement or refusal to participate is more appropriately described as *assent or dissent.* In order to gain more understanding about children's capacity to assent or dissent to participation in research studies, these authors conducted a series of studies on the capacity of children between 5 and 12 years of age to make such decisions. Their findings confirmed that children do have the capacity to make meaningful decisions about their participation, but there were problems in ensuring that they can make these decisions freely. For example, many children were concerned that there could be negative consequences for them if they did not agree to participate or asked to have the study stopped while in progress. Some children also felt pressure to agree to participate and continue once they started since their parents had already agreed to their participation. The researchers strongly suggest that these influences be taken into account when designing consent instructions and interpreting children's responses. Keith-Spiegel (1976) further illustrated this point when she noted what might well be one of those old rules to live by: *"Obey thy Mother and Father—and anyone else bigger than you are"* (p. 56). Although the letter of the law may suggest that parental consent is all that is necessary, the researcher would be foolish, and likely unethical, if input from the subjects were not included. Such considerations may also be appropriate and advisable for "risk" areas other than age (such as mental retardation or mental health problems). Investigators must use their best professional judgment in determining who should be involved in the consent process.

Consent: When.   Some research circumstances clearly require consent, whereas others are more subject to debate. Risk to subjects may include a number of different situations ranging from actual physical harm in the form of pain to potential psychological harm such as emotional stress. Similarly the forfeiture of personal rights may vary greatly from a serious invasion of privacy to a situation in which the subjects are not threatened in any significant fashion.

The factors involved in when consent should be obtained are similar to those regarding who can provide effective consent. Researchers must exercise their best professional judgment. However, the general rule of thumb is *when in doubt, ask for permission* (Mauch & Birch, 1983). If it is unclear whether consent is needed, it may be prudent to err on the side of caution. Mauch and Birch listed some important areas where permission must be sought:

1. Permission to use children or persons incarcerated or under guardianship as research subjects, including permission to contact such individuals as jailors, physicians, employers of a business, teachers or principals, armed service personnel, or to systematically gather data in work, recreation, health care, or education settings for research

2. Permission to use instruments for data-gathering purposes, where such instruments were designed or developed by others, whether such instruments are copyrighted or not

3. Permission to examine, for research purposes, personnel records, student records, and other records containing personal data, where such data are not a part of the public domain and open to everyone

4. Permission to use long passages, charts, tables, and other material from the work of others, whether copyrighted or not, unless such material is in the public domain or unless blanket permission to use it, or reproduce it with credits, is printed on the material in such a way as to indicate that the authors and publishers intend the material to be freely used (1983, p. 137-138).

Consent: How. The method of obtaining consent will vary greatly depending on the situation involved and the degree of potential risk for subjects. If the study creates little or no risk or potential invasion of privacy, consent may be obtained less formally (i.e., orally). In such circumstances, subjects may be orally informed of the nature of the investigation (assuming that the capacity element is present) and give spoken consent. In situations when subjects are placed in a more risky position (e.g., potential harm, stress, substantial invasion of privacy), consent should be obtained in writing. This is typically accomplished by providing both written and oral explanations of the study, and the subject indicates consent by signing the written form. In certain cases the provision of both oral and written explanations is not possible, such as in a survey using mailed questionnaires. Usually the subject's willingness to complete a questionnaire is adequate indication of consent. A written explanation of the survey should be included with the questionnaire (often as a part of the instructions on the questionnaire) with a clear indication that responses to the questions are voluntary. In all cases, the researcher must remain cognizant of the three elements of consent and also inform the subject that consent can be withdrawn at any time. Figure 3.1 is a sample statement of consent.

Harm

The investigator protects the participant from physical and mental discomfort, harm, and danger that may arise from research procedures. If risks of such consequences exist, the investigator informs the participant of that fact. Research procedures likely to cause serious or lasting harm to a participant are not used unless the failure to use these procedures might expose the participant to risk of greater harm or unless the research has great potential benefit and fully informed and voluntary consent is obtained from each participant. (APA, 1989, p. 53).

The most basic concern in all research is that individuals *not be harmed by serving as subjects* (Lindsey, 1993). In the context of research ethics, harm must be viewed broadly. Harm may include extreme physical harm, as illustrated in the World War II Nazi experiments, but also involves such factors as psychological stress, personal embarrassment or humiliation, or any of a myriad influences that may adversely affect the subjects in a significant way.

Vulnerable Types of Research. Certain types of studies appear to present particular difficulties in terms of potential harm to subjects. Research that involves physically dangerous treatment may present very

1. Subject's name _____

2. Address _____ Tel. No. _____

3. Purpose of study. (Be sure it is clearly stated in layman's terms so that the subject will understand what you are attempting to accomplish.)

4. Experimental methods—risks involved, if any.

5. I have been informed of the nature of the research and the risks, and I voluntarily agree to be a subject. I am at least eighteen years of age, having been born on _____ . I understand also that I may withdraw from the study at any time or refuse to answer a particular question without penalty.

6. _____
   Signature of subject

7. _____
   Signature of person obtaining consent

8. Date _____

The above statement is to be signed in duplicate with one copy being kept by the researcher and the other by the subject.

NOTE: If you have any questions about the research, do not hesitate to ask the researcher, whose phone number is _____ . If you have questions about your rights as a subject, please contact the chairman of the Human Subjects Committee, Syracuse University, Professor William Johnson, 423-4288, or his secretary, Linda Smith, 423-4289.

Source: Krathwohl, D. R. (1988). *How to prepare a research proposal* (3rd edition). Syracuse, NY: Syracuse University Press, p. 105.

FIGURE 3.1 Statement of Consent

real possibilities of harm if the treatment is inflicted on the participants. Unfortunately, there are examples of such investigations in which ethical principles were violated in an extreme fashion. Some of these include such acts as the injection of live cancer cells into humans (without the consent or even knowledge of the subjects) and experimental infection of subjects with syphilis (without treatment and, in fact, resulting in death among some of the participants). One can hope that these types of studies are not being conducted in the 1990s, but they must be noted as examples to keep us mindful of the extreme acts that may occur and must be guarded against.

Other areas of research must also be viewed as high risk in terms of potential harm to subjects. For example, some studies are specifically designed to investigate the effects of psychological or emotional stress. Such research represents extremely difficult circumstances, especially when the procedures involve actual infliction of stress. From the outset there is always the possibility that a subject may have a physical crisis such as a heart attack as a result of the stress. Additionally, the distinct possibility exists that the stress itself may be harmful to subjects from a psychological standpoint. This might be a particular concern with subjects who have a high degree of vulnerability—such as either identified or unidentified mental health problems—a topic that will receive further attention.

Vulnerable Subjects. Some studies may be characterized as having a high risk for harm because of the particular subjects being studied. Individuals, by virtue of characteristics associated with age or disability, can be rendered relatively powerless in exercising free will when choosing whether to serve as research subjects. Such subjects may be less capable of understanding potential harm, or they may feel openly or implicitly coerced in some fashion. Individuals who are institutionalized or incarcerated, such as prisoners, persons with severe disabilities, or people with serious mental illness, may agree to participate in a study either because they feel they should to show evidence of good behavior or to gain approval of their institutional supervisors. Unfortunately, some of the worst examples of ethical violations have occurred with such subjects.

Highly vulnerable subjects should not be taken advantage of, and researchers investigating topics involving such people must exercise particular care in executing their studies. Very young children, elderly citizens, or individuals with disabilities may be easily convinced that most activities are important, are of little harm, and should be engaged in for the benefit of society. The scholar who is seriously concerned with research ethics must remain especially alert to ethical issues regarding harm when studying such subjects. Vulnerable subjects pose a dilemma because there is a real need to study these subjects to improve their lives and to benefit society. Consequently, these difficulties will likely be encountered by all researchers sooner or later. Thoughtful and knowledgeable consideration provides the primary source of guidance for procedures.

How Much Is Harmful? Researchers continually face questions regarding what is meant by a *high degree* of vulnerability and a *potential, substantial, or significant risk.* These are not easy questions to answer. Although the terms suggest quantification, they refer to topics that are very difficult to quantify precisely; the terminology is related to perceptions, values, or judgment. Little likelihood exists that there will be widespread agreement concerning exactly what is meant. However, the topic cannot be ignored; the broad perspectives must be examined. The question is reduced to: "How much (harm) is harmful?"

You may have already decided for yourself how much threat, stress, or pain can be considered harmful. If you have, it would not be unusual for your determination to be near one end or the other of the continuum—that is, the position that nothing should ever be done in research that would possibly pose the slightest imposition or threat of stress on a subject versus the position that the paramount interests are of science and the betterment of society and an individual subject's distress or harm should largely be discounted in favor of the potential benefit for the greater number. Although both of these viewpoints have been argued and thoughtfully considered, neither extreme can be accepted as a blanket rule. Harm is simply too complex, and the continuum must be explored more completely (and ultimately judicious caution exercised).

Some researchers have fallen back on *consent* as a means of dealing with the harm issues. They argue that potentially harmful studies can be undertaken only if the subjects have effectively consented (have the capacity to understand the potential risk, have full information concerning any harm to them that may occur, and voluntarily agree to subject themselves to such harm). Since consent is an essential prerequisite to such investigations in any case, this would seem to afford little in terms of fully attending to the problems of harm to subjects. Consent, even under the most careful precautions, does not render an investigator free to assume no further responsibility regarding potential harm.

Another approach to addressing the issue of harm to subjects is the *cost/benefit ratio.* This approach involves a comparison of the potential benefits of a given study with the potential risks to the participants (cost). The assumption is that if the benefit of the study outweighs the potential harm, the study can be considered ethical and vice versa. For example, suppose an investigation were proposed that had potential for solving the inflation problem in the United States. However, to conduct the study a sample of 1,000 participants would be required to divulge personal details concerning amount of income, sources of income, and the manner in which every dollar was spent. Certainly this represents a substantial invasion of privacy—but clearly the inflation problem badly needs a solution. Do the benefits outweigh the harm? This becomes a matter of individual judgment.

The idea of assessing costs and benefits has considerable appeal, but how is this task accomplished? It may be a rather simple matter in business, but in many cases we are confronted with factors that defy measurement. How does one evaluate and predict the harm that might be inflicted on a subject? An equally difficult question involves how one measures and predicts benefit; and further, how does the process of balancing subject harm with potential benefit proceed? These problems lack precise solutions and require careful evaluation. The evaluation process must involve a review by professionals other than the investigator proposing the study (often an institutional or agency "human subjects committee"). If assessments were solely the prerogative of the researcher, an obvious conflict of interest could influence the decision. (After all, the researcher has a vested interest in the study.)

As much as possible, research should be planned and executed in a manner that minimizes harm to subjects. A study is always more ethically justifiable when there is little likelihood of risk. If there is a possibility of harm to the participants, it should be as minor as possible. Additionally, the researcher must be concerned about how long the effects will last after the study is completed and whether they are reversible. It is desirable to deal with an effect that can be easily reversed and one that has a short post-investigation duration. A potentially harmful effect also should be detectable early so that the study can be terminated if necessary.

Privacy

The value attached to individual privacy has varied throughout history, and vast differences are still evident from one country to another. Privacy has, however, taken on the status of a right that is highly treasured in contemporary western society. As with other ethical considerations, privacy has become an increasingly valued right due both to serious abuses as well as to a generally heightened sensitivity to individual prerogatives.

Seeking privacy is an act of seeking seclusion or confidentiality—removed from public view or knowledge. Total privacy is virtually nonexistent, and people are required on occasion to yield a certain amount of privacy for one reason or another. In some cases this is done voluntarily to obtain something in return (e.g., a person divulges certain personal information to obtain a loan or credit card). Even in these circumstances there have been rather dramatic changes recently in the kinds of information that can be requested. There are, however, other situations in which it is less clear whether the information is being obtained voluntarily. This latter type of action endangers an individual's free choice of privacy.

Science is based on the collection and analysis of data or information. In particular, behavioral and social scientists collect and analyze data concerning humans both as individuals and groups. This is the point at which the goals of research and the right of privacy may be in conflict. Frequently, research of this nature is aimed at obtaining information concerning attitudes, beliefs, opinions, and behavior. Thus, the pursuit of the goals of science, even while guarding against unnecessary invasion of subjects' privacy, presents complex issues.

In considering privacy related to the conduct of research, several factors need to be addressed. First, the *sensitivity* of the data in the view of the individual or group being studied must be considered. For example, certain types of information may be viewed as sensitive under any circumstances. Data concerning sexual experiences or preferences represent information that many people would want to keep private. Other information may be less sensitive, such as one's favorite color. Additionally, many types of information would be considered situationally sensitive: information that might be divulged under certain circumstances but not others (such as age, weight, personal income). A greater probability of invading privacy occurs when the data being collected are sensitive or potentially sensitive. Under such conditions, the researcher must exercise extra precaution and always proceed with great care.

The *setting* in which research is being conducted may also be an important factor in considering potential invasion of privacy. On one end of the continuum there are those settings that are nearly always considered private, such as a person's home. The other end might be represented by a setting in which privacy is not generally assumed, such as a public park. Some settings may be only situationally private—a person's home cannot be considered private when a realtor is show-ing it to a prospective buyer. Clearly the researcher must consider the setting in which the data are collected if undue invasion of privacy is to be avoided.

A final point to be addressed regarding privacy involves *how public* the information is going to be. As a subject, you may not believe that your privacy has been seriously threatened if only one or two people know (such as the researchers collecting the data). It is a totally differ-ent story, however, if the investigators publish your name and personal opinions in the local newspaper. In so doing, they have made the infor-mation (which may be very sensitive) available to the general public. This makes it possible for those reading the newspaper to identify *you* as the individual holding those opinions. Such a breach of confidence should never occur, but this example is not without basis in reality. The researcher must remain very alert concerning the degree to which pri-vate information remains confidential, particularly when such informa-tion is of a sensitive nature.

To sum up, the researcher cannot ignore privacy in any study. If a potential problem exists, consent should always be obtained. Addition-ally the subjects should be assured that the data will be held in strict confidence to protect anonymity. Few studies require that data be main-tained (certainly not published) in a form in which subjects can be personally identified. In general, researchers should invade the privacy of subjects as minimally as possible. If a potential of privacy risk exists, the investigator should take all precautions possible. Any study that substantially invades privacy obviously may place the subjects in a risk position. Such procedures also place the conduct of science at risk, by reducing the level of public trust vital to the successful pursuit of knowledge.

Deception

Research deception involves a misrepresentation of facts related to the purpose, nature, or consequences of an investigation. In this context, deception refers to either an omission or a commission on the part of the researcher in terms of interactions with subjects. Regarding an *omission,* deception could mean that the investigator simply does not inform subjects, either completely or at all, about important aspects of the study; part or all of the information is withheld. A *commission,* on the other hand, involves a situation in which the researcher gives false information about the investigation, either partially or totally. In the first case, subjects may not even be aware that a study is in progress or they may be informed only about a portion of the investigation. In the second situation, subjects generally are aware that they are involved in some type of study or activity out of the ordinary but may be given misleading information regarding the true purpose or nature of the study or activity. In either case, the researcher is misrepresenting the study.

Regardless of the precise nature of deception, it has become a very prominent problem for investigators concerned with the ethics of conducting research. Deception of one type or another has become rather widespread in behavioral and social research (Baumrind, 1985; Lindsey, 1984). A study by Smith and Richardson (1983) found that in a survey of 468 psychology undergraduates involved in research activities, about 50 percent were involved with studies using deception. Diener and Crandall (1978) cited figures ranging from 19 to 44 percent of psychological research that involved "...direct lying to subjects" (p. 74).

Although the accuracy of such estimates can always be questioned, deception presents a major problem—not least of which is that many subjects believe they are being given false information about studies in which they participate, whether or not they are really being deceived. Research subjects have become test-wise and often believe the real purpose of a given study is hidden. This is more true for certain types of participants than others (notably college sophomores, the most studied group around, but by no means limited to them). If subjects are unduly suspicious, they may be expected to answer, perform, or generally respond in an atypical manner. Such responses, if widespread, may seriously threaten the soundness of an investigation. Subjects may also attempt to respond in a manner that they think the researcher desires, or they may try to outguess the researcher and thereby "foul up" the study.

The methodological problems with deception will be examined further throughout this book in terms of its potential to weaken sound research. Subjects are affected in any case merely by the process of being in an investigation and may therefore react differently (called the *Hawthorne effect* in terms of internal validity and *artificial research arrangements* in terms of external validity). Although some of these topics have not yet been addressed in this book, the examinations, thus far, suggest that deception is a serious problem—both ethically and methodologically. Why, then, does deception occur?

Intentional deception means:

> . . . withholding information in order to obtain participation that the participant might otherwise decline, using deceptive instructions and confederate manipulations in laboratory research, and employing concealment and staged manipulations in field settings . . . Full disclosure of everything that could possibly affect a given subject's decision to participate is not possible, and therefore cannot be ethically required. (Baumrind, 1985, p. 165)

Suppose a study were being conducted on group control of individual actions. In this type of investigation, the study might focus on the amount of influence a group had on individuals' opinions about the use of drugs. This might be a type of study that would involve intentional deception to a considerable degree. If the subjects being observed (the rest of the group might actually be confederates in the study) were suspicious about the purpose of the investigation, they might be more or less resistant to group pressure than normally would occur. The researcher would therefore need to adapt for such an influence by deceiving the subject: the individual could be directly deceived about the purpose of the study, or information could be withheld. If the subject were openly informed about the nature of the study, the outcome might be jeopardized. Yet in this case, the reason for using intentional deception might also become its greatest enemy. The researcher cannot reveal the exact nature of the investigation, but the participant may be generally suspicious and alter behavior because of those suspicions (in a manner unknown to the investigator). Intentional deception is used to control factors important to the study, but suspicion of deception creates problems for control.

The control exerted may relate to the technical soundness of the study or it may relate to the generalizability of the findings (matters that will be examined in detail in later chapters). If one group of subjects receives different treatment (deception) than another, the comparison may not *really* involve the treatment. Likewise, if deception is either real or perceived by subjects, results might not be generalizable to the outside world. Methodological reasons for using intentional deception represent a double-edged sword; they have both advantages and disadvantages. The judgment of the investigator is likely to be tested.

Some reasons for using deception are purely pragmatic. Limited finances, time, and the data sources have often led researchers to use deception. For example, if it is too expensive, time-consuming, or not feasible to observe a natural occurrence of a particular phenomenon, it might be best studied by creating a simulated incident. Such a situation may arise when the researcher is studying something that occurs only rarely or creates dangerous circumstances when it does occur (e.g., emergencies). This type of deception might involve a staged purse-snatching or mugging with observations focused on the reactions of witnesses. Such an example would necessarily involve deception (and also no prestudy consent) if the witnesses are to behave naturally.

The preceding discussions illustrate some of the reasons researchers use deception and also some of the problems involved in its use. But is deception ethical? One of the most fundamental arguments against deception is that it *is* unethical and degrading to the subjects involved. Lying is generally viewed unfavorably in our society and even deemed immoral. This value places the conduct of science in a dilemma. Science is presumably undertaken for the benefit of society, so should it be associated with acts that are generally thought to be evil? This is a question that has no direct answer since it is couched in such polar terms.

Most people would agree that research cannot be clearly declared either ethical or unethical. There are many shades of gray and myriad matters that must be considered. One of the most serious issues facing research using deception is the issue of consent. If participants are involved in activities that present potential risk to them, consent is necessary. In studies using deception, effective consent is probably absent. If a study uses deception, subjects must at least be given enough information to know the possibility of risk and then voluntarily decide whether to participate. Additionally, deception exists on a continuum from relatively minor omission of information to direct lies.

Ethics Related to Particular Research Approaches

In this section, we will examine ethical considerations that are of particular concern in the context of experimental and ethnographic approaches to research. The purpose of this discussion is to inform investigators who are anticipating using a particular approach. Although the text will be brief, we will make an attempt to sensitize and refer the reader to other sources that may address a given method in more depth.

Ethics and Experimental Research

Experimental research involves studies in which the investigator manipulates the factor under study (the experimental variable). Frequently the manipulated variable represents some sort of intervention or treatment (e.g., medical, psychological, educational) that is being studied with regard to effectiveness. This manipulation of treatment raises certain ethical questions and dilemmas.

Part of the difficulty with an experimental treatment pertains to subjects who *receive* the intervention. For example, the intervention may represent training in group communication that includes a great deal of self-disclosure. Self-disclosure is a procedure used by some counselors to encourage people to talk about their feelings, attitudes, and experiences (some of which may be quite personal). Let us suppose that you are a subject and you tend to be a very private person. The ethical question is: what right does the researcher have to impose the treatment on you? After all, the way in which you deal with such matters is really your own business and represents part of your personal value structure. This example illustrates the problem nicely but does not necessarily answer the question. Certainly the researcher should have fully informed you about the nature of the activities in the process of obtaining consent. It was also the investigator's responsibility to clearly indicate that your consent could be withdrawn and that you could elect to discontinue the activities at any time. Assuming that the investigator handles consent appropriately, both in planning and executing the experiment, the problem should be lessened, although this does not completely eliminate ethical concerns.

An additional problem for subjects receiving an experimental intervention involves potential harm, the probable duration of that harm, and its reversibility. These matters have been discussed before but must be reexamined briefly here. Research of any type should be designed and executed in a manner that reduces the risk of harm as much as possible. Furthermore, if there is a potential harm risk, it should (1) be as minor as possible, (2) be reversible, and (3) have a post-experimental duration that is as short as possible. All of these qualifications are particularly relevant to ethical questions about subjects who receive an experimental treatment. If harm *is* incurred by such an intervention, the researcher should take precautionary steps to reverse the problem and see to it that the reversal is effective as quickly as possible. Unfortunately there have been examples when such precautions were not taken.

The discussion thus far has focused on problems related to subjects who receive the experimental treatment. There are equally difficult ethical problems involving subjects who *do not* receive the treatment (e.g., placebo comparison or control groups). This begins to sound like "you're damned if you do and damned if you don't." There are, however, some distinct and interesting questions related to this part of the problem. Let's suppose, for the moment, that you have discovered a very effective treatment that may significantly reduce depression. Everything so far has suggested that it is a very promising procedure. You need to conduct further investigation and want to form two groups—one that receives the treatment and one that receives a placebo activity. The ethical question raised is: what right have you to *not treat* the placebo group (deny them treatment)? The conflict becomes evident—you need a group that does not receive treatment for comparison, but do you have the right to *not* give them what appears to be a promising treatment for depression?

The ethical perspective is that the researcher has the responsibility to provide treatment to all subjects. This argument is particularly emphasized if the treatment appears very effective as in our depression example. As you can well imagine, some researchers have a very different view. This opposing perspective is often called the *natural state argument* and contends in essence that the untreated subjects are not being denied a benefit they already have, they are merely being left in their natural state.

Clearly neither extreme position can be generally accepted for all research. In the depression example, you probably do have some responsibility to provide treatment to the placebo group, particularly if it is as effective as you think. However, there is still the need to conduct a scientifically sound test. One approach to this dilemma represents a compromise that attempts to meet the goals of research and also the ethical need for providing benefit to all subjects. It may be possible to first conduct the study as initially planned—with a treatment group and a placebo comparison group. Then, after the investigation is complete and the data collected, you could provide treatment to the subjects in the comparison group. In this way you are not withholding the treatment from anyone in the study, and the data are not contaminated. Although this is a reasonable compromise, there are some minor problems. Some would contend that the delay in treatment is still harmful to the placebo group. This may be true if the duration of the study is very extended, but if not, such an argument loses much of its potency. Another problem may be expense: if the treatment is quite expensive the researcher may have difficulty funding treatment for the second group. Although this may be a problem, it is not a very compelling argument. To remain clearly ethical the researcher should simply plan the budget to allow for treatment of the comparison subjects. None of this discussion has great significance for interventions or treatments of unknown effectiveness but it becomes more relevant as evidence of promise accumulates for any given treatment.

As before, there are no simple or clear guidelines that account for every ethical concern regarding experimentation. Some of the more prominent difficulties have been illustrated, but most specific planning must be based on the researcher's good judgment.

Ethics in Qualitative Research

Many of the ethical concerns associated with ethnographic research—consent, deception, privacy—have already been discussed. They do, however, present some unique challenges in the context of any particular research approach. Chapter 2 discussed observation as one important nonexperimental approach to research. Observation has been used widely in the social sciences as a means of collecting nonexperimental data in natural settings. In particular, participant and nonparticipant observation are basic research methods used in both anthropology and sociology. Each presents some perplexing ethical difficulties with consent, privacy, and deception. These methods exemplify well some of the unique ethical problems encountered in nonexperimental research.

Effective consent is necessary yet problematic for an ethical study using participant or nonparticipant observation. While potential harm from a treatment per se is not a threat, a substantial threat to privacy exists; revelation of observed conversations and behaviors could cause substantial harm to subjects in their families, communities, or work. Also, the actual subjects of the research who have given consent may not be the only people observed. In natural settings, people move in and out of interactions and settings for many reasons. For example, a researcher may have permission to study formal and informal counselor-student interactions in a middle school. The researcher may obtain, with careful planning, informed consent from the counselors, students, and parents of the students who are in formal counseling. But the researcher may follow the counselors while they work during the day and record informal interactions among students throughout the school and between the counselors and the students. How is consent obtained from all the students, from their parents? Is consent necessary? The generally accepted rule of thumb for such observation research is that consent is not necessary when entrée to the setting is approved by the agency or institution, subjects who are actively involved have given informed consent, and other observed behavior is considered public and observable by anyone present in the setting. In other words, if the other students in the school could overhear the conversations the researcher is recording and observing because they took place in public, they do not require additional consent.

This rule of thumb does not always guarantee that no difficulties with consent will arise, however. The definition of *public* also is open to debate. One of the authors supervised the research of a doctoral student who obtained consent from the president and members of the board to observe a YWCA Board meeting. An influential community member visiting and speaking at the meeting asked who the observer was and refused to participate in the meeting when told about the study. The entire board meeting came to a halt.

Participant observation presents another ethical challenge to the researcher. The observer often lives, eats, and sleeps on a daily basis with those being observed. In such a study, the research seeks to record a broad range of details about the subjects' cultural mores, interaction patterns, social structures, and daily behaviors. The research may probe into many facets of the lifestyle of the subjects—public, private, and often sensitive. With such a pervasive scope of observation, privacy invasion is inevitable. This invasion of privacy makes effective consent absolutely necessary.

The nature of the investigation also raises some serious difficulties with consent. As with the above example, from whom should consent be obtained? Even more specifically, participant observation often requires that only the core group of subjects know the researcher is not just another member of the group. Is it adequate to obtain consent only from the group leader (e.g., the tribal chief, the school principal, the teacher, the fraternity president)? A related problem in observation studies involves the effects of obtaining consent on the behavior of those being studied. One of the strengths of observation methods comes from the study of subjects' routine behaviors in their natural environments; by obtaining consent, a researcher may alter this natural behavior. Many researchers seek to mitigate these effects by asking an inside informer to watch for changes in the customary behavior and interactions of the group and warn the researcher about them.

Another potential difficulty with observation methods, particularly participant observation, arises as the subjects become increasingly comfortable with the researchers' presence. By virtue of the observer's role, the subjects may forget that they are being studied. Some question exists whether this may mean that they are no longer consenting because their consent is no longer effective in the pure sense. Researchers must remain vigilant to protect subjects, complete rigorous research, and be sensitive to the needs of all concerned at the same time.

We mentioned privacy earlier in the context of consent. Privacy invasion represents a substantial risk in participant observation research because of the extremely private and sensitive data often collected and analyzed. Serious examinations of any cultural or contemporary group cannot take place without these data, yet their distribution raises dilemmas. One of the traditional methods of circumventing privacy problems—anonymity—can protect individual subjects. Observation studies have usually used fictitious names to disguise the identity of individuals, groups, agencies, and locations. Although this technique may be adequate in most circumstances, it sometimes fails. One of the best known examples of this failure involved Vidich and Bensman's book *Small Town in Mass Society* (1960). Anonymity was not protected despite the pseudonyms used in the publication. Some of the published information involved behavior that could be considered embarrassing and potentially damaging to the people involved, and the townspeople knew each other well enough to establish who was being discussed. Anonymity does not solve privacy questions related to sacred data in cultural studies. The revelation of sacred ceremonies, taboos, or stories, while central to a research process, may never be appropriate. Tony Hillerman described this dilemma aptly in his novel *Talking God* when he said, "The museums of the world are filled with the gods of conquered peoples."

The aura of deception, while not yet mentioned in this section, surrounds ethical questions in observation studies. In one sense, the participant observer is an automatic deceiver, becoming part of a group yet not a true member. And even with consent, the participant observer affects the behavior of others in the study by her or his behavior. This is a serious problem that cannot be ignored by researchers using this approach. It also raises complex questions about potential harm. There have been examples of potential harm when participant observation was construed as political spying. In extreme forms of participant observation, the observer might encourage others to engage in behaviors that might be harmful, illegal, or both. (The classic drug agents' sting operation in which the undercover officer sells drugs to the unaware customer is a prevalent nonresearch example, but experiences nearly this extreme have been described.) Researchers using observational techniques must continually ask themselves (and the appropriate review committees), "What harm may be incurred by the deception involved in my study?"

This section has focused primarily on ethical concerns encountered in observation. Earlier we indicated that other types of nonexperimental and qualitative research are fraught with their accompanying ethical questions (Deyhle, Hess, & LeCompte, 1992). For example, interviews are a common method of gathering qualitative data. Researchers using this method must worry about asking leading questions, deception about the nature of the interview, unauthorized taping, and undue pressure to continue in the study, among other things. The discussion here is illustrative rather than exhaustive. A complete examination of ethical issues, with any type of research, is far beyond the scope of this text. Many of the references cited in this chapter may provide additional information for the student interested in pursuing a particular topic.

Monitoring Ethics in Research: Institutional Review Boards

While the investigator is ultimately responsible for ensuring that there are no ethical violations in a proposed study, the federal government has also established an additional assurance in the conduct of research—the institutional review board (IRB). IRBs are composed of five or more members who are representatives of an institution (such as faculty or administrators) as well as lay people who have no association with the institution. The IRB is charged with reviewing the purpose of the research and the proposed methodology as it relates to potential risk and/or benefit to the subjects involved. This review body is also directly concerned with issues of informed consent and a subject's right to privacy. As suggested by the APA (1989), the following questions are considered appropriate for review by an IRB:

Will dangerous or potentially harmful procedures be employed? If so, what precautions have been taken to protect participants from the possibly damaging effects of the procedure? Will inordinate demands be made upon the participants' time? Will the research involve deception or withholding information? If so, what plans have been developed for subsequently informing the participants? What plans have been made for providing the participants with an explanation of the study? In general, what will the participants gain? (p. 47)

Many researchers are supportive of IRBs and view them as a protection not only for human subjects but for researchers as well (Howe & Dougherty, 1993). The IRB can assist the researcher by spotting potential pitfalls that can be overlooked by an individual investigator, thus protecting reputations and avoiding litigation. Other researchers see the IRB as an unnecessary governmental intrusion into the research process. They view IRBs as overly cumbersome, unnecessary, and dictatorial. From this viewpoint, IRBs were established to deal with the very few who violate ethical standards, while punishing the many ethical researchers with unwieldy governmental requirements.

Regardless of the position one may take on the need for IRBs, they are a federal requirement. Institutions receiving federal funding must establish committees to approve *all* human and animal research. Research is defined as any "systematic investigation designed to develop or contribute to generalizable knowledge" (Guidelines, 1991, p. 1). This includes student research for theses and dissertations as well as individual faculty endeavors. Investigators must receive IRB approval on any research involving human or animal subjects whether the study is receiving federal dollars or not. An institution that fails to meet IRB requirements may put its federal funding in jeopardy.

While some scientists believe that abuses of effective informed consent are a thing of the past, others disagree. Paul Knudsen, Executive Coordinator of the Committee for the Protection of Human Subjects at the University of Texas at the Houston Health Sciences Center, suggests that paper consent forms are less important than the way in which subjects are approached. "It is all well and good to design the most wonderful informed-consent form in the world, but if a person in authority with a white coat and stethoscope walks into a room and tells a patient, `I have a great study that is just right for you,' it doesn't matter what the forms says" (cited in Wheeler, 1994, p. A9). Critics like Knudsen point out that researchers who review their colleagues' proposals are under subtle pressure to approve because their own work will come under review by the same bodies. A number of reforms consequently recommend that more citizens and nonuniversity scholars sit on review boards.

Collegial review bodies, such as IRBs, do not negate the individual researcher's responsibility for ethical decision making. The final ethical responsibility rests with the investigator. The APA (1989) indicates "The investigator should seek advice with respect to the potential costs of the research procedures to the participants, even if there is no legal requirement to do so...Collegial review can neither substitute for nor diffuse personal responsibility" (pp. 20-21).

Ethics and Professionalism

We now turn our attention to the researcher in the context of the profession. Many of the topics to be discussed in this section are not often openly addressed in print, although they are frequently the topic of debate in the hall or staff lounge. These topics also seem to be of great interest to students as they observe the professionals whom they intend to join as colleagues. Ethics and professionalism could easily consume an entire volume but will only receive abbreviated examination here. Three issues will receive special focus: (1) integrity during the execution of the study, (2) integrity related to publishing, and (3) sanctions for breaches of integrity. We hope these topics will provide a background and sensitivity that will prompt further thought and inquiry by the beginning researcher as questions arise.

Integrity During Execution of the Study

Any breach of integrity during the execution of a research study, whether it be unintentional errors or outright falsification of the data, invalidates the investigation. One of the most basic purposes of science is the acquisition of objective and accurate data about real phenomena. Reality is fluid, situational, and certainly variable depending on one's perspective. But somewhere underlying the conduct of science there is a philosophical assumption that some truths can be determined. This places a very important responsibility on science and scientists to undertake their efforts in a totally honest fashion. This is not a statement that reflects a value judgment or moralizing. It simply reemphasizes a fundamental principle on which scientific investigation is based.

This chapter has emphasized the importance of integrity in research and focused thus far on execution. The question that is naturally raised in this context relates to why breaches of integrity occur. Although a variety of influences can result in these problems, none make such acts justifiable. However, their discussion helps to more fully understand them and take preventive precautions.

Factors influencing breaches of integrity involve some rather powerful social pressures, particularly among beginning researchers. As suggested by Fox (1990), one of the most powerful factors is the "pressure to publish." Researchers are constantly pressured to "get into print." This pressure may place such a stress on investigators that they either unintentionally or purposely alter or fabricate data. To protect against such acts investigators must be overly diligent in their efforts to be objective.

In 1830 Charles Babbage (cited in Campbell, 1987) coined the term *forging* (inventing research data) to describe a basic type of fabrication. There are two variations of forging: *trimming* and *cooking.*

> Trimming occurs when the researcher smooths irregularities in the data, to achieve a better fit between actual and expected results. Cooking occurs when the researcher retains or reports only those findings that fit the hypothesis. Both variations, while more subtle than complete fabrication, still represent dishonest science. (Campbell, 1987, p. 72)

Great value is placed by many on the *elegant* investigation: the study that is designed in a clever manner to investigate a particularly difficult question. We are not discounting the value of such research; it is an admired and a sought-after goal. It does, however, seem to be overemphasized at times to the exclusion of other concerns. Additionally, ethical problems arise when strong pressure (often implicit) leads to inaccurate data collection. For example, such pressure may occur when a research assistant believes that significant results *must* be obtained and either consciously or unconsciously alters the data. Other circumstances may have the same net outcome. Often the data collection process is laborious, boring, and even extremely difficult. This has led to incidents in which research assistants actually record fictitious data rather than conscientiously observe subjects (sometimes known as *dry labbing*).

Research assistants and beginning researchers are not the only scientists vulnerable to breaches of integrity. In fact, some very prominent individuals, with widely known reputations, have been discovered in or accused of unethical research execution. One example concerns the work of Sir Cyril Burt, a noted British psychologist. Burt is a particularly difficult case since the allegations of scientific misconduct against him were made after his death, making it impossible for him to respond. The controversy is further complicated by two factors: (1) there is no question that Burt was a very well-known scientist—he was knighted in 1946 in recognition of the importance of his work—and (2) the topic of his investigations was, and remains, very controversial—the heritability of intelligence. The allegations include (1) estimating certain levels of intelligence (parents of certain twins) but later reporting such estimates as solid data, (2) listing people as co-authors on research reports who may never have existed, and (3) producing data that represented answers supporting his theoretical beliefs that are unusually precise fits to predictions (some say impossible). These points have been countered by supporters of his work, on the basis that while the inconsistencies may represent a degree of carelessness, the errors are basically trivial, do not seriously undermine the strength of the heritability-of-intelligence position, and certainly do not warrant the accusations of fraud. The arguments have been intense on both sides, often representing varying perspectives on the intelligence issue as much as the problems involved in the ethics of science. However, one cannot ignore the difficulties and suspicions generated in relation to the conduct of research. In some senses the scientific endeavor is as much on trial as the work of Burt, which illustrates very well the fundamental problems involved with breaches of integrity (confirmed or alleged). It should be noted that this is not the only example—other fields of science also have their unfortunate incidents or allegations.

All researchers must take precautions against integrity breaches related to the execution of research. However, it is impossible to have *every* data collection effort fully supervised or observed by more than one researcher. Ethical integrity in science, as in many other fields, is mainly an individual undertaking. However, we can hope that one factor that may have an important influence is the recent more open discussion of breaches of integrity and the resulting problems and potential outcomes.

Integrity Related to Publishing

Publishing is an integral part of the overall research process. Figure 1.1 characterized the research process in a closed loop fashion. An investigation is undertaken to answer a question of presumed importance; the loop is not closed until the results are interpreted in relation to the original question. The work of a scientist is public and publishing is the means by which it is made public. For the most part, a published research report describes the closed loop. The research question is presented, accompanied by the rationale concerning why the question should be studied, a description of the execution, the results, and an interpretation of those results related to the question. Considerable detail (e.g., subjects, procedures, analysis) is included in such a report, which has the effect of making the researcher's work open for public scrutiny by the scientific community. This public scrutiny helps to make science objective and is why publishing is such an important part of the research process.

Because publishing is an important part of research, it is also an important factor in the career of a scientist. Scholars use publications as one means of determining the capability and performance of a researcher. Successful publication of research in a respected journal or book provides at least some evidence that the work has withstood review by the scientific community. Such evidence clearly enhances the researcher's employability, rank, and salary. In fact, some institutions (e.g., some universities) will terminate professors if they have not published a reasonable amount during the first few years of their employment (often the first five to seven years). These realities of academic life place pressure on researchers to publish. Although the pressure is not undue (five to seven years is a substantial period), some tend to exaggerate the intensity of this pressure and ethical problems may result.

One of the ethical problems that may arise relates to our earlier discussion of integrity during execution. There may be a temptation to report the investigation somewhat differently than the data collected would indicate. In quantitative research this may be a situation in which significant differences are reported but the data did not actually show statistically significant differences. Such incidents have ranged from circumstances in which "it was close" and the data were changed slightly, all the way to dry-labbed results. In qualitative research, the scholar may fail to convey quotations or observations that contradict or raise questions about his or her conclusions. Obviously these acts represent serious breaches of professional integrity, and one would like to hope they seldom occur. Some reports, however, suggest that the frequency may be disturbingly high (Fox, 1990).

Another ethical problem related to publishing involves multiple publication of the same article. This difficulty would present itself if, for example, you conducted a survey, wrote an article reporting the study, and then published the same article in two different professional journals. In fact, the rule of thumb that is usually employed does not even permit *submitting* the same article to two different journals at the same time: you submit the article to one journal and, if it is rejected, you are free to submit it for review by another journal. Many journals include such a requirement in their editorial policies.

The multiple-publication issue noted above also is much different from an article (already published) being *reprinted* in another journal or a book of readings. In this latter situation, the journal or publisher desiring to reprint your article must first request permission from the original journal. (A credit line must also be listed in the reprinted publication clearly indicating that it is reprinted from another publication and the name of that publication.) Additionally, such a reprinted piece is *not* then claimed by the author as a separate and new publication—it is merely noted as having been reprinted.

Authorship also presents several serious ethical problems in publishing. This is an area in which graduate students and beginning researchers may be particularly vulnerable. One of the first questions relates to who should be listed as author or authors. Any individual making a major contribution to the project should be listed as an author. Obviously the phrase *major contribution* is open to different interpretations. In this context, it is being used to reflect a contribution involving the conceptualization, design, data collection and analysis, and writing of the manuscript. One can insert several combinations of *and/or* between these activities to determine whether or not authorship is warranted. Once again this is an area in which one's best ethical judgment must prevail. The problem is mentioned because it seems that integrity occasionally wears thin when it comes time to list authors. All too often graduate students have been taken advantage of by unscrupulous professors who give them only a footnoted credit line, if that. (A credit line may be appropriate for minor contributions; it is *not* appropriate for substantial efforts involving conceptual and writing efforts.)

Given that a publication may have multiple authors, this raises a question regarding the order of authorship. Who is to be senior author (listed first) and who will be junior author(s) (those listed second, third, and so on)? The order of authorship should be determined in relation to the level of contribution. The person making the greatest contribution should be senior author and the others listed in order of their relative efforts. If the contribution is relatively equal, order should be determined by mutual agreement, a flip of the coin, or some other method that is acceptable to those involved. Do not be deceived by someone's claim that order is accomplished alphabetically; typically the one making such a claim has a last name that is early in the alphabet. If order of authorship does not denote level of contribution, the authors must acknowledge this and describe how the order was determined in a footnote at the beginning of the publication. Also disregard the argument that order is a trivial matter—after all with three authors the citation is usually "Senior, et al., 1994." Do you really want to be *et* or *al* if you did most of the work? Unfortunately not everyone adheres to fair and ethical principles when determining the order of authors. The main precaution that one can take is to be aware that such breaches of integrity occur and to be firm about your own rights (and do not take advantage of someone else).

Sanctions for Breaches of Integrity

Some sanctions for unethical conduct are self-evident. Certainly a breach of ethics that is made public is personally embarrassing and causes professional disgrace. It may cause one to lose a job and be unable to obtain other employment in the research community (word travels rapidly even if the publicity is not a major exposé). Most scientists belong to professional organizations such as the American Psychological Association, the American Educational Research Association, the American Sociological Association, or some other disciplinary organization. Many of these organizations have formal codes of ethics to guide members' activities. Such organizations may expel a member for unethical conduct, which is essentially an expulsion from the profession. Sanctions can be very harsh for the person who is unethical, but such harshness is clearly warranted. Each time a breach of ethics occurs, the entire field of research is disgraced to some degree. Although inconvenience may result, it is important to remember that ethical principles are not only in harmony with science but also represent the basic fiber from which the process is made.

$Chapter$ 4

The Research
Process

Thus far the research process, various research approaches, and ethical issues involved in the conduct of research have been discussed. These topics serve as the backdrop for the remainder of this book. In some areas, we must now focus more attention on what has previously been discussed in a cursory fashion. In other areas, such as ethical issues, we will make only a quick reference or brief elaboration concerning what has already been stated. A review of the basic conceptualization of the overall research process is therefore appropriate at the start of this part of the book.

In Chapter 1 the research process was conceptualized in a closed loop or circular fashion (Figure 4.1). It is obvious from the earlier discussions that there may be vast differences in methodology from study to study and between various disciplines. It is also clear that some qualitative research methods do not follow this process exactly. In certain cases the investigator may begin data collection with a less complete statement of the question, allowing the details to emerge as the information is gathered (see Figure 2.1). We will examine these variations in the research process as appropriate. We will, however, begin our examination of the research process in the context of the closed-loop conceptualization of Figure 4.1.

From the perspective of the research process presented in Figure 4.1, investigations begin with an idea that becomes the research question. The research question may then lead to some hypotheses or guesses about the topic under study, which in turn lead to the design or plan for the investigation. Data are then collected and analyzed to answer the

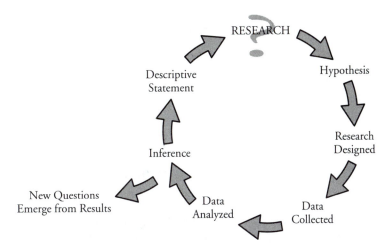

FIGURE 4.1   Closed-Loop Conceptualization of the Research Process

question, which, is the ideal outcome, and closes the loop. Along the way additional questions often emerge as fodder for future research.

This is a very simple conceptualization of the research process—one that often does not fit the stereotyped notions of science frequently held by laypeople. Many of the perceptions and misconceptions that are frequently held by beginning students and laypeople regarding research were discussed previously. These popular views of science do not help at all, and in many cases they serve to interfere with the teaching-learning process. It is important to go beyond the introductory explanations presented thus far to more fully understand research and, in turn, discard these misconceptions. One of the best places to begin is with the research idea.

The Idea for Research

Misconceptions from outside the research community do not account for all the problems facing the teaching of research. Considerable interference results from misconstrued philosophies coming from within the profession. One prime example relates to research conducted by students.

Students are often required to conduct research as a part of their academic preparation program. Such research is generally expected to result in a document or report that represents a thesis or doctoral dissertation. In most cases, well-articulated guidelines for the students are not available, which makes the task extremely difficult, contributes to the perception of mystique, and renders the experience most distasteful. The students may be given a mimeographed document that outlines format, reference forms, and other similarly critical information. It is not uncommon for such guidelines to provide guidance concerning how large the type is to be and what rag content is necessary in the paper to be used. Heaven forbid that the wrong rag content might be used, although one of the authors had a student whose thesis was returned by the library for this very reason. With these wonderful guidelines, the students begin what is perhaps their first piece of research. Completely lost at this point, they may seek assistance by turning to the college catalog to find a written description of what the thesis should be.

Although a college catalog *is* a logical place to turn, unfortunately it may serve to hinder rather than help. The descriptive statement generally says something to the effect that the thesis must be an original contribution to the field in which the student is seeking academic preparation. This is indeed a formidable task, particularly when viewed through the eyes of students with little research experience, who may interpret it literally, and who may be frightened out of their skulls. The potential anxiety generated by such a statement may be debilitating and probably inhibits the students' progress. In the first place, that the contribution must be "original" (which may imply that it must arise out of an original *idea*) is frightening enough. Placed in the context that this research must represent a "contribution to the field," the task becomes even more formidable. This situation may contribute substantially to the often-asked question "Is this (idea) enough to be a thesis?" Although such a student interpretation may be too literal, it is very real and not infrequent. The issues of educational pragmatism, realistic educational objectives, and relevance concerning how research is conducted by practicing researchers loom very prominently in this situation and should be carefully considered by professors directing student research.

We might well ask what educational objectives are involved in the production of a thesis. It makes considerable difference whether such student research is viewed as a learning experience or as an examination of competency. Unfortunately, the latter framework is implied by such statements as the catalog example and by the manner in which many faculty members approach the subject. If it is kept in mind that this is an early, if not the first, research experience for the student, the competence examination philosophy becomes ludicrous. Early student research projects should be viewed primarily as learning experiences; it often takes the practicing researcher many years to actually make a contribution that is even partially original (if one views these terms literally). From this philosophical stance, one should not be overly concerned about the source or ultimate impact of the research idea.

It is also profitable to briefly explore the world of practicing researchers. The source or originality of many research ideas studied by most professors is certainly not as it is perceived by many students beginning their thesis work. In many cases the experienced researcher obtains ideas for investigation by reading articles written by other people and noting that a gap exists in the information presented. Such an information gap might involve a variety of topics. For example, it may be that the study being reported did not focus on children of a particular age group (say 10 to 12 years of age). If the researcher reading this report thinks that the study would be improved if such children were included, this represents a perceived information gap. Often such gaps are explicitly mentioned in the discussion sections of research articles. Implications for future research are an integral part of many published articles and are nearly standard in theses and dissertations. In most cases these implications are easily identified, since the author typically uses such phrases as "future research should...," "additional study is needed...," and "further investigation might...." If these gaps and projections are of interest to the individual, they will most probably become *the idea* on which to work. What about the source? Are such ideas *original?* According to the apprehensive, literal interpretation frequently used by the student, they may not appear to be original; but, in fact, the practicing researcher working within the context of a subject area would consider them to be a *contribution.* Thus beginning researchers may give themselves a more rigorous task than practicing researchers generally require for their own investigations.

The ideas for research come from everywhere. The student who really becomes involved in a subject will find not a shortage of ideas but rather an abundance of them. Problems are generated in other people's publications, but they also appear in nearly every corner of the daily environment. Someone who is working on an idea or problem tends to assume ownership of that idea or problem (although such ownership is in no way exclusive). If an idea has been specifically mentioned by someone else as having implications for future research, the publication in which it was mentioned should be cited. Building on someone else's work, however, does not reduce the value of the current work and makes very good sense from a programmatic research standpoint.

***Turn to p. 93 and complete
Simulations 4.1, 4.2, and 4.3***

Foundations of Research: The Scientific Method

A simple definition of research was presented earlier in this book as "a systematic method of inquiry." There are many descriptive characteristics of research that are not obvious in this definition. A more complete discussion of these is important in order to gain a comprehensive perspective of the process. This section will examine some of these characteristics, which serve to conceptually undergird the research approach to inquiry.

In examining the process of research, it is useful to explore some of the assumptions underlying the scientific method. Two basic concepts that are associated with experimental-quantitative research are determinism and finite causation. *Determinism* views the events of nature as being lawful rather than chaotic, capricious, or spontaneous. From this perspective, each natural event is presumed to have a cause. Further, if those causal circumstances could be replicated exactly, the event would occur again. *Finite causation* refers to the idea that each natural event has a limited number of conditions that account for it and that these conditions are discoverable. Determinism presumes that a certain level of predictability may be achieved regarding the occurrence of natural events. Finite causation essentially presumes that everything in nature is *not* influenced by everything else. These assumptions are essential to the scientific enterprise.

These assumptions sound very similar to the earlier discussion of logical positivism in Chapter 1, and they definitely are related. To see these assumptions so blatantly stated—preserved in the form of ink and paper—is often somewhat disconcerting for researchers, even those quantitative experimentalists who depend on them. (Additionally, the issue of causality has already been noted in Chapter 2 as a vexing one for researchers.) These assumptions do not enjoy public and universal acceptance among behavioral scientists. Many researchers who would endorse these assumptions in principle would have difficulty accepting formal use of the term *cause.* In fact, a perusal of the published research in behavioral science reveals a substantial reluctance to use terms that openly suggest causation, even in the case of experiments. The discussion of results often gives the impression that researchers are masters of the elastic phrase (evidenced by such statements as "these results might suggest" and "these data would seem to indicate"). However, such seemingly indecisive language is warranted by the nature of the tools used. As noted earlier, experimental designs are often imperfect and quantitative statistical analyses are developed on the basis of probability. Consequently discussions of results are usually stated in terms that are not ironclad in their certainty. Thus a given behavior can be thought of as occurring, with a given probability, as a function of the treatment (which also means that such a result may have occurred because of chance, with a given probability). Working within these contingencies and considering the highly complex interaction of social influences, it is not surprising that many researchers are somewhat nervous about total and complete acceptance of the assumptions of determinism and finite causation. These assumptions do, however, remain as useful foundation concepts even if in behavioral reality their precise operation is difficult to observe.

It is also worth rementioning that some nonexperimental-qualitative researchers do not subscribe to assumptions that would support determinism and finite causation as described at the beginning of this section. Those who perceive social reality as unique and phenomenological see natural events as intrinsically shaped and governed by perceptions and interactions of those involved. Further, such natural events are not amenable to replication as viewed from this standpoint. Our current discussion will focus more on the positivist side of this continuum, however.

Perusal of discussions concerned with the scientific method results in a situation similar to that encountered in defining research: a variety of descriptions emerge of what is involved. We choose to employ a simple approach that is compatible with our view of research—the scientific method is a systematic manner of thinking and inquiry. From this conceptualization, a variety of dimensions within the scientific method warrant examination.

The scientific method has often been characterized as a sequence of events or activities that are initiated at a given point and that proceed through several steps in a given order. Such descriptions often give the impression that science is guided by a rigid checklist similar to that used by an airline pilot preparing for takeoff. To a certain degree, the checklist impression is useful. However, the idea of rigid adherence to a set sequence of fully articulated stages is somewhat out of phase with reality in the world of research; furthermore, deviation from some sequential checklist does not push one's work into a nonscientific category. For example, it is common for researchers to begin with a fairly specific problem or question and to subsequently think their way back through a chain of logic or rationale to a larger theoretical model. On other occasions, the actual formulation of complete and refined hypotheses may not be executed. Consequently this book will discuss scientific method in terms of three broad areas of activity rather than a sequential examination of steps. These areas of activity include (1) the problem, (2) the data, and (3) the inference. At times, however, certain sequential dimensions of the method will become evident or may be specifically mentioned as a precautionary note to the beginning researcher. Additionally, we will note areas where methodological differences occur such as those for qualitative paradigms.

The Problem

The first broad area of consideration in discussing the scientific method is the problem. Two subactivities are involved within this area: problem identification and problem distillation. Problem identification, in this context, refers to the process of finding or determining what research idea is to be studied. Problem distillation refers to the process of refining the problem or idea and making it sufficiently specific so that it is amenable to investigation. Both of these matters apply most directly to experimental-quantitative research but are also applicable in nonexperimental and qualitative studies in which the investigator more specifically describes a research question from the outset.

Problem Identification.   Considerable curiosity is evidenced by the beginning research student concerning the source of research problems and ideas. A recurring theme evident in conversation with many students suggests that, at least from their perception, they feel as if they are in an idea desert: there are no ideas around at a time when they are so badly needed. Progress beyond this point is often inhibited by an understandable reluctance of some students to admit their dilemma. (You may recognize this feeling of reluctance. After all, why emphasize to all those smart people what your weaknesses are?) It is essential, however, that the beginning student move beyond the idea-desert stage as quickly as possible. Most researchers would agree that once this movement is made, the major difficulty arises in selecting one idea from the many that pop into one's head — rather than identifying or finding them.

One perception echoed repeatedly in examinations of the scientific method is that the research problem is often generated by an obstacle to understanding. Prompted perhaps by some behavioral observation, a problem may be identified by researchers as they ask how or why a given behavior occurs. This question may then become the research problem that is to be studied. It has already been noted that problem identification frequently occurs as the researcher reads the work of others. Often authors of journal articles will facilitate the problem identification process by specifically suggesting implications for future research.

Classical experimental design has traditionally couched the conduct of research in the context of theory. From this vantage point, the statement of a problem is often viewed more comfortably if it is aimed at testing some part of a theory (e.g., some particular aspect of a learning theory or some part of a theory of forgetting). Several changes in philosophical contingencies, however, have legitimized research efforts that may not be couched in such a firm theoretical base. One example of this is represented by recent developments in applied research which, although still experimental in format, may not be based on much beyond a desire to assess treatment effectiveness. Some research of this type is based on theory but there are many investigations that are not. It is also clear that some qualitative research efforts are not launched from theory-based questions, as noted earlier.

In addition to the items just mentioned, the points made by Sidman (1960) warrant repetition because of their relevance to problem identification in its broadest sense. He contended that research should be conducted to (1) try out new methods or techniques, (2) indulge the investigator's curiosity, (3) establish the existence of behavioral phenomena, and (4) explore the conditions under which phenomena occur. Certainly these points cover a great deal of territory. The point to be made for the beginning student is that problem identification comes from several fronts. The time has passed when the only source of problems for research lay within the boundaries of major theories.

As noted, problem identification is usually the result of a gap in the information available in an area, as in the earlier example in which the researcher was interested in children 10 to 12 years of age. An information gap may exist because there is no previous investigation, or it may be the result of previous work that was poorly executed and thereby did not provide useful information. Once they begin generating research ideas, most students have little difficulty identifying a broad problem, yet from that point on they encounter great difficulty transforming it into a researchable question. This transformation process, essential to launching an investigation, usually involves a distillation or definition of the problem into a testable form.

Problem Distillation.   The point in research at which problem identification ceases and problem distillation begins is vague. Some would contend that the problem has not been truly identified until operational definitions and hypotheses have been stated. In reality, problem identification and distillation are probably a continuous process. They are distinguished here somewhat artificially for instructional convenience. For the experienced researcher, they are often indistinguishable.

As the problem becomes identified, it is often in the form of a fairly general question. For example, in reading an article you may encounter something that makes you wonder what the types of influences are that affect learning? The investigation that you have been reading may have studied the effects of response time, but something seems troublesome with that. It is at this point that you may recall (from your own experience) that response time seems to have different effects depending on how meaningful the material is. This would then represent a stage of preliminary problem identification that tends to focus and guide additional reading and search of existing studies. At this point you are beginning to distill the problem into more specific form.

Problem Specification.   One of the first tasks in problem distillation is a precise specification of the topic under study. Although this may sound rather redundant, the key term here is *precise.* As previously noted the research idea is frequently conceived in very general terms—often even vague and nebulous. To successfully design and execute an investigation, the researcher must become very clear (and specific) about what is being studied and the nature of the research question.

A point needs to be made here about the nature of the research question. It is obvious from the discussion thus far that a variety of different questions may be investigated. To list examples of each specific type would be impossible. It is possible, however, to examine the general types of questions in terms of three basic categories: descriptive, difference, and relationship. *Descriptive questions* essentially ask what is: what does this culture look like or what does this group look like? Descriptive studies are basically static, in that manipulation does not occur, and are frequently undertaken in surveys and other qualitative studies. *Difference questions* essentially make comparisons: is there a difference? Comparisons may be made either between groups or between measurements within a group. In many cases these comparisons are made between the mean scores (average) of the groups if the data are quantitative. Such a question may be phrased "Is there a difference in the average scores between these groups (or treatments)?" Difference questions tend to be most frequently used in experimental research, although nonexperimental studies may also be comparing groups or cultures. *Relationship questions* explore the degree to which two or more phenomena relate or vary together. If the researcher were curious about the relationship between quantitative measures of height and weight, the question would basically be "As height varies, what tends to happen to weight?" More specifically, if height increases, does weight tend to increase or decrease (or is there no systematic tendency)? Rather than comparing groups, the researcher records data (both height and weight measures) on a sample of subjects. With two measures on each subject, the investigator then computes a correlation coefficient, a statistical analysis that provides an estimate of the degree to which the variables relate.

One very important part of problem specification is determining exactly what type of question is being asked. Although this is a seemingly simple task, it is one that repeatedly baffles the beginning research student. Yet it is crucial for many studies; if the researcher does not know what type of question is being asked, there is a very poor likelihood that the study can be planned.

Problem specification for an experimental study involves determination of the experimental variable. The earlier discussion stated that the experimental variable refers to the phenomenon under study, that factor which the researcher manipulates to see what the effect is. For example, if you were interested in which of two treatment methods was more effective, you might design a study in which two groups were treated, one using method 1 and one using method 2. After the two groups had been treated with their respective methods for a specified time, you would then test both of them to find out which group had improved more. If other influences between the groups are equal, you are likely to suggest that the method used to treat the group that performed better is more effective. In this example the experimental variable is the method of treatment (which is what you were investigating).

One important point in defining the experimental variable is employing the *principle of generality*. The experimental variable should be expressed in terms of a statement that refers to a concept or abstraction rather than the specific treatments being studied. An illustration of this is found in the example just given in which the experimental variable was stated in terms of the abstract variable of method of treatment. This is an appropriate way to state the experimental variable as opposed to stating it in terms of the particular treatment conditions (which in this case would have been something like *method 1 versus method 2*). If the experimental variable is stated as *method of treatment,* results may then be discussed regarding the concepts involved in treating subjects. This provides more generalizable concepts and information, and generates more predictive power regarding the nature of treatments.

Problem specification for nonexperimental and qualitative research is also important unless one is using an approach where matters become defined as they emerge. Once again the same principles apply as discussed before. The topic under study must be clearly in mind before the planning can begin. For example, if you were interested in learning about dating behaviors of college sophomores, a survey might be an appropriate method for conducting the research. In such a situation, *dating behaviors* would be the problem and you would then have to specify the precise behaviors to be studied (much like specifying methods 1 and 2 before). Without this type of consideration, the survey is likely to be analogous to a fishing expedition; you may end up on the lake simply pulling in and keeping anything that bites.

The discussion in Chapter 2 clearly indicated that some nonexperimental and qualitative researchers do not agree that the problem should be specified before the study begins. This is particularly evident in anthropology, in which some argue strongly against experimental methods in favor of a more traditional view of the participant observation approach. Such a perspective is represented by the emic position discussed earlier. Those subscribing to the emic approach believe that the observer should attempt to view the problems to be investigated through the eyes of the subjects being observed. Masses of descriptive data can be obtained using this approach although it is quite limited in terms of testing theory.

Operational Definition.   Another important task involved in problem distillation relates to operational definition. Regarding this part of distillation, a researcher needs to carefully define the steps to be taken and the measurements to be recorded. This is an essential step in problem distillation and must precede implementation of the study. Suppose for the moment that a researcher is going to study the effects of material meaningfulness on learning. Full distillation of the problem will require operational definition of all terms, operations, and measures that will be involved in the study. The definitional process can be demonstrated with the term *learning.* Since learning cannot be measured directly, it must be inferred that a certain amount of it has occurred based on performance dimensions. Will the focus be on the rate of acquisition? If so, how is this to be measured? A variety of measures might be used, some preferred over others for differing circumstances. The point to be made is that learning must be rigorously defined in terms of what is observable. Similar definitional efforts would be required for the survey on dating behaviors. In all cases the definitions will have to include operational terms that are translatable into procedure. Beyond this, each aspect of the idea must also be operationally defined in the same manner to fully distill the problem. In this sense a research problem is much like liquor: it is not usable until it is fully distilled. The distillation process, as discussed above, involves two essential activities: (1) specification of the experimental variable and (2) complete operational definition of all necessary terms. Once this is accomplished, the researcher is ready to plan the steps necessary for implementing the study.

***Turn to page 97 and complete
Simulations 4.4, 4.5, and 4.6***

The Hypothesis.   Descriptions of experimental scientific methods are frequently written in a fashion that heavily emphasizes hypotheses. As a consequence, the beginning student often forms an idea of the scientific method primarily from a hypothesis formulation standpoint.

The Hypothesis as Development of Theory.   In one form, a hypothesis represents one dimension of theory development. Within this framework, the hypothesis is a theoretical conceptualization or, more informally, an idea or guess regarding how the researcher thinks the results will look. Used in this way, the hypothesis may take the form of a fairly general statement, occasionally written but often merely exchanged orally with colleagues. The statement is usually linked to the theory being tested (e.g., if the interference theory of forgetting is accurate, then the subjects should…). Used in this fashion, the hypothesis becomes a part of the logic underlying the execution of a study, thus linking data to theory.

The Hypothesis as a Testable Prediction.   Hypotheses made for a second purpose take a much different form from those of the "theory-logic" type described above. This second type represents the ultimate in problem distillation. It demands that the statement be made in specific terms and that it take the form of a statistically testable prediction. Hypotheses of this second type might appear in the following form:

1. Subjects will not differ in mean trials to criterion as a function of high versus low meaningful material.

2. Subjects will not differ in mean trials to criterion as a function of 5-second versus 20-second response time.

These hypotheses were adapted from a study that compared subject learning rate on two types of material and under two response time conditions. Indicative of the level of specificity is the fact that a testable hypothesis is generated for each experimental variable (material meaningfulness and response time). With the research problem distilled to this level of detail, conceptualization of the study is facilitated since it is broken into its most fundamental components, two experimental comparisons. (Clearly these hypotheses were used in an experiment that collected quantitative data.)

One factor that often introduces confusion involves the use of null and directional hypotheses in quantitative experimental research. *The null hypothesis predicts no difference between comparison groups.* Examples of null hypotheses are found in those just presented concerning material meaningfulness and response time. *Directional hypotheses,* on the other hand, *do predict a difference and indicate the expected direction of that difference* (i.e., which group will perform at the higher level).

From a pragmatic standpoint, hypotheses in quantitative experiments are primarily used for statistical testing and problem distillation. For the beginning researcher, the hypothesis is most valuable for clarifying the question and serves little other purpose. Under these conditions, the important concern is adequately addressed using null hypotheses, and nothing is to be gained by predicting the direction of differences. The prediction of a directional hypothesis comes into its own in the context of theory development (the first-mentioned purpose for hypotheses). In this framework, the "guess" of prediction becomes relevant from the standpoint of how well the logic of the theory functions in the clinical or applied setting with real subjects. However, for statistical testing and problem distillation purposes, the null hypothesis serves well and is probably used more frequently by practicing researchers than the directional hypothesis. For theory purposes, the directional prediction is more often used.

Unstated Hypotheses.   A student who turns to the journals for examples of the uses of hypotheses by practicing researchers may experience considerable difficulty identifying or even finding formally stated hypotheses. In most cases, the formal hypothesis—or for that matter reference to the researcher's existence—is not evident in the published research report. This does not mean that such problem distillation is not used by experimenters who publish their work; rather, in most cases the seasoned researcher has a backlog of experience that makes problem distillation nearly an automatic process. In such situations, hypotheses more often take the form of mental notes or written records that are so much second nature to performing the overall research act that they seldom appear in the published report. Formal hypotheses do, however, appear frequently in theses and dissertations. This phenomenon relates to the third purpose of the hypothesis, which somewhat overlaps the first two.

The Hypothesis as an Aid in Teaching.   The third purpose for a hypothesis tends to overlap the others because it primarily involves a *use* rather than a substantive component or addition to the research process. Hypotheses are, within this context, of considerable value in the process of teaching beginning research students how to conduct experimental research. Many beginning researchers have difficulty conceptualizing the research problem. In addition, there is frequently a strong tendency for the beginning investigator to identify a research target that is far too broad and vague to be a viable research question. In both of these general areas of difficulty, the use of hypotheses is helpful. As noted earlier, two practical purposes of hypothesis formulation include theory development and problem distillation. Both of these purposes tend to combat the beginning researcher's difficulties. Problem distillation (using a testable prediction), as exemplified by the hypotheses presented previously, serves to strongly counter the student's implicit belief that a study must be complex (synonymous with big) to qualify as research. Initially, specific testable hypotheses tend to break a given investigation into its most simple and fundamental components. This facilitates conceptualization by simplifying the concept being studied. The "theory-logic" use of hypotheses helps problem conceptualization by forcing a step-by-step articulation of the logic base for predictions.

Thus, it is not surprising to find formal hypothesis statements in student theses and dissertations. For beginning researchers, the hypothesis becomes an instructive device to guide them through the processes that have become second nature to an experienced investigator. It is desirable that the student place hypothesis formulation in proper perspective, however. It is useful for instruction, yet it is often not mentioned on paper by practicing researchers. Additionally, it is important to remember that research aimed at testing hypotheses related to theory is *not* the only legitimate type of scientific investigation.

Comments.   The first broad area within the scientific method has been identified generically as *the problem.* Referring to the research problem, the two subactivities of problem identification and problem distillation have been shown to be necessary elements in the eventual formulation of a researchable question. A variety of specific activities may be involved, serving either the identification or distillation function. Once the problem is distilled to the point that it becomes a focused, specific, researchable question, the next area to be considered is the data aspect of the scientific method.

The data phase involves a number of subparts including design and planning activities, data collection, and data analysis. It is important to remember that *issues involving the problem must be settled before entering the data phase of a scientific investigation.* Frequently a student has data in hand and "wants to do something with it" or "hates to see all these data wasted." Perhaps it is a stack of cumulative testing records from a school district or counseling center. Regardless of the individual's emotional attachment to the data (or the strength of belief that this is a quick way to complete a thesis), to launch a study in this fashion is to launch a study destined for innumerable difficulties. Often such activity is a waste of time from the standpoint of both research information obtained and knowledge gained by the student about the research act. Additionally, most IRB committees will refuse to grant retroactive approval to studies already completed because of the many problems with obtaining informed consent and other procedures designed to protect the subjects. For the most part, it is sufficient to state that the sequence of the scientific method essentially places problem issues before data issues.

The Data

Once the problem is adequately distilled, the researcher is ready to enter the next phase of activities, which coincides with the second general area of the scientific method. The second area focuses on issues related to the data to be collected. The data dimension of the scientific method most closely approximates the layperson's stereotyped conception of research generally. By now, however, you know that the data portion of research constitutes only one component in a set of related activities.

Design and Planning. As already stated, the most important decisions affecting the soundness of an experiment are made before initiating data collection. In fact, the strength of any datum is directly influenced by the preexperimental planning that determined how it was to be gathered. The more clearly the problem is articulated (distilled or defined), the more easily the data-related planning will be accomplished.

A basic concept that influences the data is that of *control.* As other aspects of the scientific method are discussed, the focus will be on interpretation of what the data or results mean. Of course it is desirable to be able to say that the data reflect the experimental variable (if we are conducting experimental research). The researcher will be able to do this only if there is confidence that the data do, in fact, reflect the variable of interest and not some other influence that has not been eliminated. This is generally known as controlled observation in experimental design. Said a slightly different way, you can infer that a change in your experimental variable caused change in the criterion measure only if all other possibilities can be discounted as causes of the change.

This principle is an essential aspect of experimental research design and an important consideration in the data area of the scientific method.

A second consideration involved in data planning relates to the *generalizability of results.* To what degree are the results generalizable beyond the specific subjects and exact setting used in the research? The essence of this issue involves the reliability of data obtained. How reliably can one obtain the same or similar results? We will consider this question at length.

A variety of influences are operative in the reliability of data. Perhaps the most evident involves the *subjects in the study.* If it is desirable that results be applicable to a given group of individuals, the subjects in the investigation must be representative of that group. (Such profoundness! Yet this is frequently a problem.) Usually this larger group is defined as the population to which generalization is desired. The researcher wants generalizability; that is, to be able to observe the same or similar performance in the general population that was evident in the sample of subjects. To obtain this data reliability between subjects and population, the experimenter must be able to assume that the subjects are representative of the larger population. In experimental-quantitative research this is primarily accomplished through the procedures used in selecting the sample of subjects (discussed in Chapter 9). Data reliability and the "goodness" of findings are also serious issues in qualitative research. Although qualitative methodology approaches data reliability in a substantially different way, the problem remains (Miles & Huberman, 1994).

A second factor to be considered in data reliability involves the *stability of measures being used in the research.* This factor is also related to generalizability, although most discussions of generalizability focus on sample considerations. In the context of data reliability, the primary concern is that the measure be sufficiently stable that a subject in the same status (e.g., physiological, motivational, or anxiety level) and performing at the same level as an individual in the broader population will obtain the same or a similar score on the measure (or provide the same or similar answers on a survey questionnaire). Thus, for the results of an investigation to be generalizable, the measures recorded must be stable enough that a given score or answer is likely to recur under the same conditions. If the measure is highly unstable, the data may indicate two different scores for the same subject status. Although behavioral science is plagued by measurement problems, it is usually possible to select or contrive measures that are adequately stable. Of course this does not mean that there is no variation in the behavior. Instead the concern is that the measure be sensitive to variations in performance and not capriciously variable when performance is not changing (that is, the variability in measure should be coincidental to performance variation).

Many investigations involve situations in which the data are collected through observation. In these types of studies, measure stability is very closely tied to the nature of the observation. Here there are typically vast differences between quantitative studies and those using qualitative methods. From the standpoint of quantitative methods, greater definition and control of the observation protocol is sought. More specific tasks requiring less judgment from the observer usually result in greater measure stability. These often translate into specific, overtly evident responses that may be counted or easily placed into discrete categories. Binary decisions are the most easily counted: the subject either does or does not respond, the response is either correct or incorrect. Such measures, when easily observed and counted, can minimize potential error in judgment and result in stable data. Qualitative researchers face different challenges in the sense that they are not counting behavioral events; instead they are concerned with recording descriptions of occurrences that allow the researcher to interpret conceptually. Qualitative researchers most often employ a set of codes, in order to record behavioral or social incidents in a manner that promotes accurate interpretation. Methodologists specializing in these approaches express concern for reliability, stability, and inter-coder agreement in much the same way that quantitative researchers do (e.g., Lancy, 1993; Miles & Huberman, 1994).

Quantitative studies may use mechanical instrumentation to achieve more measurement precision. For example, a stopwatch may be useful if one is measuring time and is not highly vulnerable to error, especially when the observer has easily identifiable cues for instrument operation. Less stability may result if it is less obvious when to initiate or terminate instrument operation.

Instrumentation may be used in another fashion to facilitate measure stability. Electronic devices are readily available that, if the research procedures permit, may be used to permanently record actual subject responses. Such approaches then allow the recorded responses to be removed to another site and analyzed later in a careful manner, without the pressure of ongoing procedures. The types of recording instruments vary, and techniques are continually being improved. Audio tapes may serve well to record verbal responses, and video tape equipment may similarly be appropriate for video records of ongoing behavior sequences. Additionally a variety of physiological instruments, such as the electroencephalogram, polygraph, and others, may be used if that type of data is desired. The advantages of such devices have already been noted. The data may be permanently recorded, and analysis or categorization may be accomplished in a relaxed and cautious fashion. Such recording of responses also permits the review of performance if any uncertainty exists concerning the nature of the response. This allows multiple checks to be made on the categorization of responses, which, in turn, serves to improve potential data stability.

The use of permanent recording devices seems to be desirable insurance for research in situations in which such procedures are possible. We have used permanent mechanical recorders as well as human observers many times. As a consequence of such experiences, a note of caution is in order. Recording devices are not a panacea; their utility is only as good as the mechanical soundness of the equipment. More than one experimenter has been dismayed when the recordings were prepared for viewing and there was no record because of mechanical failure that had been undetected. This unfortunate situation, of course, means lost subjects, lost data, lost time, and occasionally a completely aborted experiment. It is always prudent to double-check equipment before it is used in a study. Perhaps nowhere in research is Murphy's Law more applicable—"anything that can go wrong will"—than with electronic equipment. It is also important to be aware of the possible impact on subjects' behavior when a recording device is inserted into the environment. Subjects may respond quite differently when such apparatus is used since it is not part of their routine. They may become nervous, or act in a manner that they believe is socially appropriate or expected. These are issues that must be weighed carefully by the researcher since the recorder itself may alter the data.

Several examples have been given of measures or procedures that may be used to improve data stability. A variety of measurement situations also may be viewed as conditions for higher risk of instability. The probability of greater measure instability is always increased when more reliance is placed on *observer judgment* concerning the nature of a subject's response. This may occur under several conditions. Probably the greatest variation is generated when the observer is requested to categorize or code behaviors that are not well defined or easily observable. The fewer distinct cues that are available, the more difficult the task of recording data. Likewise when rating scales are used to assess constructs that are ill defined (e.g., attitudes, self-concept, anxiety), the observer is presented with a more difficult task, and often greater data instability results. Such situations may be encountered in interviews or mail-out questionnaires. Four basic approaches can help minimize such difficulties. First, the behavior or performance to be measured must be as well defined as possible. Second, the more distinctly the cues are defined for the observer, the greater the chance that accurate response records will result. Third, multiple observers can be trained to a point at which reliability is high among the group of judges as a whole. In this latter technique, the several observers serve as checks on each other, which places less reliance on a single individual's judgment. Finally, when rating scales are used (such as the Likert 1 to 5 scale), each point on the scale can be as tightly anchored as possible. A tightly anchored scale might involve very specific descriptors (e.g., 1 = 0 days per week, 5 = 7 days per week). Such arrangements can greatly increase data stability simply because the respondent's interpretation of vague descriptors (e.g., seldom, often) is less involved.

Planning or design aspects of the data component are extremely important functional dimensions of the scientific method. It is easy to see how investigations may be seriously jeopardized by errors in this area. Since the data become the central representation of subjects' behavior under the experimental conditions, their soundness must be ensured to every extent possible.

Collection.   The collection phase refers to the actual execution of the investigation and thereby involves data recording. This may include the process of administering a questionnaire, conducting an interview, or presenting an experimental task to a subject and recording responses. *This is the point at which the study is implemented.* The activities involved in implementation are most frequently described in the *procedures* section of a research article.

Perhaps the most critical aspect of data collection is performed before the actual initiation of subject testing—detailed planning of each step. Planning has been stressed throughout the discussion thus far and is being raised once again to emphasize its importance. At least two types of factors warrant attention before data collection begins. First, there are many operational details that should be planned ahead of time and that are so central to research that they are almost givens. They are present in nearly all data collection procedures. The second type of factor is much less predictable. Planning in this area is precautionary, an attempt to avoid incidents that are sporadic but may jeopardize the soundness of data collection procedures. (In research vernacular, this planning is aimed at keeping things from getting screwed up.)

In planning for both types of details, the best preparation is research experience. Frequently these items become second nature to the practicing researcher, almost to the point that it becomes difficult to recall and teach students about them. The most effective method of learning about such factors is to work with a researcher over a period of time on different investigations and to note carefully the types of details that receive attention. (This is also the most effective manner in which to learn research.) In lieu of accomplishing this at present, some areas will be suggested that may warrant preliminary planning.

Regarding the more nearly standard concerns, probably the most effective planning device is to *mentally rehearse* the entire procedure in detail. A series of questions is usually helpful:

1. *Where are you going to observe or administer the task to subjects?* This is a question that is more expansive than may be apparent at first. The actual attention to place is certainly important and a great deal depends on the requirements of the method being used (e.g., qualitative methods and observation, experimental administration of a task). If a study is being conducted in a school, do you need a separate room or will you be observing more natural settings such as classrooms? If you need a separate room, will there be one available in that school, or will you have to make other arrangements? Suppose you have a room, what is its proximity to the source of subjects? This has certain ramifications for later questions involving transporting subjects to the test area.

This question also has ramifications for the physical characteristics of the research site. What are the characteristics of the research site that are desirable for your purposes? If you are undertaking naturalistic observation, are you going to be in the room with the subjects or are you to be hidden—perhaps observing through a one-way mirror? If you need a separate research space, should it be a relatively distraction-free room? What about air circulation—might that be important? Final decisions on many of these details must await the site visitation. However, they should receive advance attention in order for you to have in mind what will or will not suffice. Frequently the advance planning involves the assessment of general tolerance levels that are acceptable regarding the characteristics (e.g., just how stimulus-free *must* it be?). Air circulation may not generally be a problem, but when the principal shows you the room (which turns out to be an unused walk-in food locker) it may suddenly present a difficulty.

2. *Where are the subjects, and how do you gain access to them?* If you are observing in a classroom, how do you gain entrance—and when? If the study requires working with children in a separate space, do you contact the teacher(s) with a prearranged list, or do they merely send children as they are free? This latter situation is desired by some teachers but could present certain sampling problems unless precautions are taken. (see Chapter 9). The distance from the subject source to the test site is usually not a big problem. One must be concerned, however, about the mental set that subjects receive during the walk to the research room. If the investigator is accompanying the subject, what transpires with respect to conversation may be rather influential.

3. *If you're in a separate room, what furniture is necessary in that space and how should it be arranged?* For example, do you want a table between you and the subject for research materials?

4. *Are your coding or data sheets in order for the subjects' appearance?* This applies in both separate research spaces as well as observations in natural settings. It is not very natural for you to be fussing around with your data sheets when students enter the classroom. Nor do you want your personal organization to be part of the experience when a subject comes into your separate research space. Both of these activities may have an influence on the subjects' behavior. For example, do the data sheets contain space for complete and convenient recording of descriptive information concerning the subject (e.g., name or code, age, sex, and data)? Are the data sheets designed for complete and convenient recording of data? Often this may have to be performed with one hand while the other hand manipulates the research materials. Can this be done efficiently and smoothly if necessary?

5. *Are your other research materials in order?* This is related to item 4 above but worthy of additional emphasis. Is instrumentation, such as a stopwatch or video recorder, in place and in good working order? How should this be accomplished to save time and not make the subjects nervous?

6. *What are your interactions going to be with subjects? If you're conducting an experiment, what instructions are you going to give them?* Give serious consideration to the nature of interactions between you and your subjects. After all, as the new element in their environment (intruder), what you say or do is likely to be noticed by them. If you're conducting an experiment or administering a test, it is a sound procedure to have instructions typed out and either memorized or read verbatim. In a slightly different context, never send a questionnaire out without a carefully constructed cover letter. The wording is crucial to the response.

7. *What is the time interval to be used for subjects to respond?* Is it five seconds in an experiment or three weeks for a mailed questionnaire? (Do not forget to allow for the mail delivery.) What do you say and/or do if this interval is exceeded?

8. *If you're working one-on-one with subjects, what is your response to the subject if an error is committed?* Likewise, what is to be said if a correct response is made? Not only is your response likely to influence any future behaviors of the subject, but you should realize that some of your verbal interchanges might become public.

9. *How do you exit or dismiss the subject when the research is completed?* Again this is most crucial when the researcher is in direct contact with the subject(s). What is to be said?

These questions are merely examples. They are relevant in a high proportion of research procedures but may not include everything that should be considered in a given investigation.

Beyond the mental rehearsal, there is one procedure that will provide further safeguards and, in fact, is so essential that it should be a standard rule (it is with our students). In preparation for data collection and wherever possible, *the researcher should actually practice the entire procedure from start to finish.* Pretest the questionnaire on a few individuals who are similar to the subjects to be used. Practice the experimental procedures or interview in a similar fashion. Practice the observation process in realistic settings, including coding the data. This rehearsal will serve two important purposes. First, it will usually highlight procedural questions that may not otherwise receive attention. Such decisions and preparations can then be accomplished before the study is to begin, which minimizes the risk of losing subjects because of procedural error. Second, it will give the researcher practice and self-confidence and polish the performance of data-collection procedures. This is essential, and it is surprising how much improvement is usually evident in the first few practice trials.

As noted previously, it is often not possible to anticipate every contingency even by following a checklist of standard procedures. Unexpected situations usually arise when the procedural rules are stretched by deviant subject performance or behavior. Tales of subject antics are exchanged in research laboratories much in the same way that the proverbial fish stories are circulated among anglers. In many cases, the researcher's judgment is tested to a considerable extent to preserve order in the investigation setting. It is also not uncommon to lose subjects because of deviant behavior, responses, or performance. This possibility can also be circumvented, to some extent, by preinvestigation planning. Such planning usually takes the form of attempts to anticipate, on an a priori basis, the possible performance or behavioral extremes. In most cases this anticipatory planning takes the form of a series of *what if* questions. Some possible decision questions are suggested.

1. What if a subject indicates openly (or subtly) that participation in the study is no longer a desirable activity? This is sometimes referred to (in cynical laboratory vernacular) as "withdrawing consent." This is a real possibility and presents a definite decision point for the researcher.

2. What if a subject asks to have the instructions repeated? What if a youngster being observed decides to engage the observer in a conversation (and you thought you were being a nonparticipant)? Are these permissible or will they contaminate the data?

3. What if a subject in an experiment makes an error and then immediately corrects it ("Oh no, the answer is…") in a fashion that gives the impression that the correct answer may have been known in the beginning?

4. How many consecutive incorrect responses are permissible before a subject is deleted from the study, and is deletion the appropriate action? Subjects with certain learning problems may persevere far beyond what is imaginable before they are deleted.

5. You're working alone with a child in a separate research space. What should be done if someone knocks on the door—or enters the room without knocking—while the study is in session? (This is guaranteed to happen at least once.)

6. Should records be kept out of the subjects' view? How should this be accomplished? Should the timing (if this is a part of the procedures) and data recording in fact be performed surreptitiously (and is this ethical)?

7. What is to be the response if a subject rises and walks around the table to see the materials?

8. What should you do if a fire drill is staged?

Turn to page 98 and complete
Simulations 4.7 and 4.8

Turn to page 98 and complete Simulations 4.7 and 4.8

It is impossible to anticipate all the contingencies that may occur during data collection. These represent only a few drawn from the authors' experiences. It is evident, however, how helpful it is to have considered even the few mentioned here. Data collection may be exhilarating and nerve-wracking, somewhat like athletic competition. It may also be repetitious and boring in certain cases. There must, however, be something addictive about data collection since researchers keep returning to it again and again.

Analysis.   Once the data are collected, the next step is analysis. This step will be treated in considerable detail later in the text and will be discussed only briefly here in the context of the scientific method.

Data analysis probably carries with it more negative connotations than any other single part of the overall research process. Most beginning research students visualize quantitative data analysis somewhat like a baptism by complete immersion in Greek symbols that make up formulas. Actually, most quantitative analyses are merely combinations of elementary arithmetic operations. In most cases, if one is reasonably prepared with the skills of addition, subtraction, multiplication, and division, the essential elements are present. The actual performance of these operations may be guided by any one of several step-by-step quantitative analysis handbooks on the market. Such handbooks (known as "cookbooks" in the profession) are based on a philosophical position that it is of little value for the researcher to memorize formulas. We subscribe to this position with considerable vigor. Consequently the discussion of analysis procedures in later chapters will include several references to computational handbooks. Selection of the appropriate analysis is often more troublesome than performing the computation.

Qualitative data are usually recorded in the form of words rather than numbers. In many cases the data reflect an attempt to capture the perceptions of the subjects from the inside. Most analysis of qualitative data is also undertaken with words as the researcher attempts to isolate themes, identify trends, interpret, explain, and even undertake some comparisons. Some consider qualitative data to be less about behavior and more about actions—and these actions carry implications about intentions, meanings, and consequences (Miles & Huberman, 1994). While some beginning students may find comfort in the absence of mathematics, they should understand from the outset that qualitative analysis is a very time-consuming and intense process.

The Inference

The data are not an end but merely a means by which behavioral and social descriptions may be made. Such a statement may appear somewhat pedantic, but it is not unusual for the impression to be given that once the data are analyzed, the study is completed. To the contrary, one of the most exciting processes has just begun, that of data interpretation and inference.

Inference is the third general area of discussion under the scientific method. In a specific sense, *inference is the intuitive process by which the researcher derives a descriptive statement from the data*; it is the *explanation* of the results. Principally based on logical conclusions from the data (related back to the theory or question that prompted the study), the outcome of the inference may be found primarily in discussion sections of research articles.

In addressing the task of making an inference, it is not appropriate to use a hit-or-miss search for explanations. In the inferential part of the research method, data are fed back into the total process in a fashion that attempts to close the information loop. At the outset, there was a research question. Some hypotheses were generated, whereupon an investigation was designed and executed to gather data relevant to that question. The process of inference essentially translates, via writing, numbers back into behavioral descriptions of what happened to propose an answer to the original research question. (See Figure 4.1 for an illustration of the closed loop conceptualization of the research process and the role of inference in that model.)

One important point needs to be considered regarding the inferences drawn from data. For the uninitiated, there is a common tendency to conceive of results as "proving" that a descriptive statement is the case. The problems of proving a theory or statement were discussed earlier. There is probably no single term that makes a researcher shudder as much as *prove*. Quantitative behavioral science has its foundation based on chance or probability theory and qualitative research emphasizes the uniqueness of interactions and events. A consequence of this is that results *tend* to confirm or support a descriptive statement, or alternatively, the results *tend* to be in disagreement with or negate a statement.

In quantitative research, results of statistical analyses are no more than probability statements. The statistical statement of "$p < .05$," frequently encountered in research reports, means that the results obtained may be expected to occur due to chance alone only 5 times out of 100. The converse of the same statement speaks to the presumed effects of the treatment. The results obtained may be expected because of influences *other* than chance (presumably the treatment) 95 times out of 100. Thus inferences in discussion sections of research articles are usually written in such terms as "These results would seem to suggest..."

rather than saying that the results prove certain statements. Quantitative researchers write in such a fashion because they are working from probability bases, not because they are that unsure of their work. Qualitative researchers are very clear about the fact that they are working with interpretations, explanations, and inferences from the observations they make. They too are working with some level of probability of correctness or some level of confidence. However, since qualitative investigators are not working with numbers, they do not assume to know what that probability is. They rely on the concept of trustworthiness to protect the research's rigor (Lancy, 1993; Miles & Huberman, 1994).

In the process of designing an investigation and interpreting the results, researchers (particularly experimental researchers) attempt to eliminate alternative explanations. If this is not accomplished and there are multiple logical explanations for a given result, the investigation has not been efficiently designed and a meaningful interpretation cannot be expected. Such an essential relationship between study design and study outcome also points up something that will be reflected throughout this text. Although the total research process is composed of several component functions, a crucial relationship ties each component together into an integrated operation. A serious weakness in any part of the research method threatens the worth of the total effort. Thus each segment must be addressed with equal seriousness and with consideration for its bearing on every other segment.

Simulations

Simulations 4.1, 4.2, and 4.3

Topic: Research ideas

Background Statement: Many research ideas come from previously published articles, dissertations, and theses. Frequently the author will either allude to or specifically note research gaps and investigations that need to be conducted in the area of interest.

Tasks to Be Performed:

1. Read the stimulus material and list any research idea or ideas that are suggested by the authors in the discussion. Write the idea statements in as complete a form as possible.
2. Copy verbatim or underline the sentence, phrase, or allusion in the passage that generated the idea.

Stimulus Material for Simulation 4.1

Simulation 4.1 was excerpted from Henderson, R. W., & Garcia, A. B. (1973). "The Effects of Parent Training Program on Question-Asking Behavior of Mexican-American Children." *American Educational Research Journal, 10,* 193–201. Copyright 1973 by the American Educational Research Association. Reprinted by permission of the publisher.

> **Discussion.** The results indicated that instruction by an experimenter using modeling procedures had a significant effect on Mexican-American six-year-olds' production of casual questions, and that this behavior generalized to new stimuli without significant loss. Although not a direct replication of Rosenthal, Zimmerman, and Durning's (1970) work, these results support their findings that modeling procedures provide an effective means of teaching children to produce generalized categories of questions, and thus the present investigation has general implications for the design of strategies for direct instruction in information-seeking skills.
>
> The most striking set of findings was that children whose mothers were trained and instructed to use social learning principles, directed toward the modification of their children's question-asking behavior, produced significantly more casual questions in each of the three trial phases (baseline, instruction, and generalization) than children whose parents were not trained and instructed to use these procedures. The implications of these findings for education may be made apparent through an analogy. Consider the baseline measurement as a reflection of a child's school entry behavior on a specific academic skill. Further consider instruction on question-asking provided by the classroom teacher. The teacher might well assume that the change in performance from baseline to instruction is attributable to her teaching.... We can note, however, that the experimental and control samples, drawn from the same population, appear to represent two different populations: high achievers and low achievers on the specific tasks investigated in this study. The differences here, however, are not attributable to differences in the abilities of the children. Rather, they are attributable to the fact that the experimental group of children received instruction and support at home and the control group did not. This situation may be parallel to the natural circumstance in which children's school performance is facilitated by the efforts of parents or siblings at home, the so-called hidden curriculum in the home.
>
> Considering the data already available which indicate that differences in home environments are highly related to differences in children's intellectual growth (Dave, 1963; Henderson, 1966, 1972; Henderson & Merritt, 1968; Wolf, 1964), the results of this study indi-

cate that parenting skills relating to the development of intellectual competence can be learned and used effectively by parents who have relatively little formal education. The effectiveness of such parental intervention is clearly evident in the results of this investigation. Anecdotally it should be noted that the mothers of the so-called "disadvantaged" children in the experimental group for this investigation were highly motivated to participate in the training program once the rationale and purposes became clear to them.

The relationship between question-asking behavior under controlled conditions such as those reported in this study and curiosity-motivated question-asking of the sort which is of principal concern to educators remains to be examined through controlled investigation. While we do not have hard data on transfer of skills studied in this investigation to more curiosity-motivated question-asking in natural environmental settings, some anecdotal information is available to suggest that generalization may occur. At the conclusion of the study, the mothers and children who participated in the experiment were taken to a facility housing wild life indigenous to Arizona and Sonora. The mothers remarked that their children were asking far more questions than usual, and many of the questions could be answered by neither the mothers nor the project staff. The mothers spontaneously began to record the children's questions. A meeting was scheduled with an employee of the museum at the end of the tour, and the questions were answered. Furthermore, at the beginning of the study very few of the participants had library cards. By the conclusion of the program every mother in the experimental group had obtained a library card for the child involved in the study and for other children in the family.

Susan Gray's (1971) report on the longitudinal results of the Early Training Project at the Demonstration Research Center for Early Education suggests that improved educational programs are necessary but not sufficient conditions for dealing with the problem of progressive retardation in the school performance of disadvantaged children. Gray indicates that "Unless the home circumstances of the child can be changed, the aversive environment which created the original problem will continue to take its toll" (p. 13). The results of the present study indicate that the efforts of parents to influence a specific set of behaviors in their children can be effective in producing in those children a significant increment of performance, over the results of instruction by outsiders.

Further research should be directed toward the problem of determining how parents may be encouraged to generalize the social learning principles, which they were trained to use for this study, to other child behaviors facilitative of intellectual development. Applied experimentation of a longitudinal nature should also be pursued to identify appropriate procedures to maintain the use of parenting skills for which training may be provided, and to determine the specific and general effects of home intervention over time.

For feedback see page 99.

Stimulus Material for Simulation 4.2
Simulation 4.2 was excerpted from Tang, F. C., & Chagnon, M. (1967). "Body Build and Intelligence in Down's Syndrome." *American Journal of Mental Deficiency, 72,* 381-383.

Conclusion and Summary. The findings partly confirm Goldstein's empirical observations: there is a tendency for shorter and fatter individuals with Down syndrome to have higher IQs than those of taller and thinner bodies, with CA [chronoloical age] controlled. However, in predicting IQ from body build in two extreme groups, forty-two percent of the total group would be incorrectly identified.

Goldstein associated other variables with the two considered in this study. Heavier subjects would suffer from thyroid deficiency and be emotionally more stable while lighter and less intelligent subjects would have pituitary disturbances and be more restless. Further research would employ more refined criteria of body build and take into account a greater number of variables as described by Goldstein.

For feedback see page 99.

Stimulus Material for Simulation 4.3
Simulation 4.3 was excerpted from Skiba, E. A., Pettigrew, L. E., & Alden, S. (1971). "A Behavioral Approach to the Control of Thumb-Sucking in the Classroom." *Journal of Applied Behavior Analysis, 4,* 121-125.

Discussion. The initial objective of the study was to attempt to control a socially undesirable response in a classroom. The results show that this attempt was somewhat successful.

An initial disadvantage that faces any experimenter attempting such a study is the physical size of the class. With class sizes ranging from 25 to 35 children, management of routine lessons can in itself be quite arduous. Attempting to control experimentally the behaviors of specific children becomes an even greater task. It is easy to see, therefore, that control of variables in such a classroom situation may be quite difficult to maintain. Some of these variables were identified during the course of the study and will presently be discussed.

The experimenter was able to observe the subject for only two 50-minute sessions per week. Effects of behavior of the subject's parents and regular teacher towards the thumb-sucking was not controllable in this study. It would be interesting to note how the thumb-sucking would be affected if the regular teacher provided reinforcement contingency every day throughout the week. Even more interesting would be the effects of combined control by both the parents in the home setting and the teacher in the school setting. Further research is needed in this area.

Another important variable of interest in furthering the control of the child's behavior is that of random reinforcement by classmates. Wahler (1967) suggested that peer reinforcement may possibly take over when social reinforcement is not provided by the teacher. Although the measurement of such reinforcement would be quite difficult to obtain the need for investigating its effects is important.

Equally important areas not covered in this study were the effects of the number of reinforcements given and the method of presentation of such reinforcements. Research has shown the importance of schedules of reinforcement in conditioning behavior. No attempt was made to schedule the frequency of reinforcements in this study.

The use of reinforcement contingency in eliminating undesirable behavior presents a wide range of research possibilities. Control of behaviors ranging from simple idiosyncratic (calling out) to more overt (aggression) can be attempted by the teacher in the classroom. The results shown in this study describe an attempt to control such a behavior (thumb-sucking) within a classroom in a public school.

For feedback see page 100.

Simulations 4.4, 4.5, and 4.6

Topic: Problem distillation

Background Statement: One of the most crucial operations in the early planning stages of research is problem distillation. This is the process of refinement that changes a general, frequently vague idea into a specific, researchable question.

Tasks to Be Performed:

1. Read the following statements, which represent research ideas stated in somewhat general terms.
2. For each simulation, restate the idea in a distilled form that makes it more specific and a researchable question. Your restatement may be rather lengthy. In the statement specify what is necessary to define the experimental variable (keeping in mind the principle of generality). Make the statement as specific as possible in terms of operational definitions.

Stimulus Material for Simulation 4.4
The idea to be distilled reads as follows: "Assess the effects of variation in teaching experience on material evaluation."

For feedback see page 100.

Stimulus Material for Simulation 4.5
The idea to be distilled reads as follows: "Compare the effectiveness of different methods of teaching reading."

For feedback see page 102.

Stimulus Material for Simulation 4.6
The idea to be distilled reads as follows: "Assess the effects of number of reinforcements given."

For feedback see page 102.

Simulations 4.7 and 4.8

Topic: Data collection

Background Statement: The text emphasized the importance of pre-implementation planning for data collection. Such precautions frequently save an investigation from being aborted (remember, Murphy's Law is the enemy of thesis completion!).

Tasks to Be Performed:

1. Read the following stimulus material, which concerns a study you are planning.
2. Make notes to yourself concerning the preimplementation planning or decisions that need attention. To the degree possible, write out those plans or answers to decision questions (realizing that the study is hypothetical). Accompany those plans or answers with a rationale as to why you elected the response given.

Stimulus Material for Simulation 4.7
You are conducting a learning experiment on third- and fourth-grade children. The subjects are to learn a set of eight words with which they are not acquainted and which are on flash cards. You are going to administer the task to each subject individually. After one exposure of each word in the list, during which you will say the word for the subject, you will require the subject to read each word to you as presented.

For feedback see page 103.

Stimulus Material for Simulation 4.8
You are conducting an investigation on the dating practices of college students. You are primarily interested in their responses to questionnaire items. These items are statements to which they will respond on a scale of 1 to 5 (highly agree to highly disagree). You want your sample to be equally distributed between men and women.

For feedback see page 104.

Simulation Feedbacks

Simulation 4.1

The most obvious research ideas in the stimulus discussion section are those preceded by the phrase *further research*. This phrase is found in the last paragraph of the discussion, and if you noted this as the area for generating research ideas, you are right on target.

The first sentence of the last paragraph reads as follows: "Future research should be directed toward the problem of determining how parents may be encouraged to generalize the social learning principles, which they were trained to use for this study, to other child behaviors facilitative of intellectual development." This is rather straightforward. The present study trained parents in the area of child question-asking. The suggestion about future research simply indicates that the authors believe that the same skills taught the parents for this purpose may well be applicable in other areas of behavior, and the question or problem being suggested is "How could parents be encouraged or taught to use the same principles with other behaviors?" How close were you with your answer?

The second sentence in the last paragraph actually suggests two research ideas. The first one involves a study to determine a way to "maintain the use of parenting skills" that were taught to the parents over a longer period. The second part of the same sentence suggests that it may be important to determine both "specific and general effects of home intervention over time." This idea implies that the authors would like to observe the effects over a longer period than was accomplished in the present study and that the time factor itself may generate some important effects.

Another idea suggested in this discussion section is somewhat less obvious, and you should not be overly distraught if you did not pick it up. It is the type of suggestion, however, that you should begin to look for in addition to the more obvious ones. This idea is found in the fourth paragraph of the discussion section. The first sentence of that paragraph indicates that the relationship between question-asking behavior under controlled conditions and curiosity-motivated question-asking "remains to be examined through controlled investigation." This, then, is open game for some researcher who is inclined to follow up. The authors also suggest that the curiosity-motivated questions may be the type that are of primary concern to educators.

Simulation 4.2

The most obvious research idea is mentioned specifically in the last paragraph of the section. Note the last sentence, which begins with the term "further research." This type of cue is a dead giveaway, and if you focused on it, that's great. The investigation that is suggested is essentially similar to the one that is reported, but the authors are suggesting two additional considerations: (1) the criteria for body build need to be refined and (2) more of the factors noted by Goldstein should be included. Particularly for the second area of expansion, the first part of the paragraph must be reviewed before you have much of an idea of what is involved. With no more information than is available here, it would seem that the factors would include some or all of the following: (1) some assessment of thyroid status, (2) some measure of emotional status, (3) assessment of intelligence, (4) a check for pituitary disturbance if you can devise such a thing, and (5) probably some observational assessment of restlessness. The authors give less guidance concerning how body build criteria might be refined, so you can do this if you are experienced in that area or have some notions other than what is provided here.

Simulation 4.3

Specific mention of research ideas in this discussion section begins in the third paragraph. The third sentence in this paragraph suggests the first idea ("It would be interesting to..."). In this sentence the authors are pondering the effect of the regular teacher implementing the management procedure each day during the week. The next sentence suggests another idea, which would combine control in the home setting by parents with the control in the school setting. If you identified these two suggestions, you are on target.

The fourth paragraph suggests another research idea. Although it is fairly specific, the authors take the entire paragraph to articulate the suggestion. The implied investigation would involve using peer management as a procedure for controlling thumb-sucking.

The fifth paragraph makes two specific suggestions, both of which deal with the area of reinforcement. In the first part of the first sentence, "the effects of the number of reinforcements given" is indicated as an area needing study. This is followed by a suggestion that "the method of presentation of such reinforcements" should be investigated. This thought is clarified in the next sentence as referring to reinforcement schedules.

Simulation 4.4

Although a variety of approaches may be taken with any given problem distillation, the most obvious in relation to the instructions would appear to be as follows:

1. The beginning point is the idea statement "Assess the effects of variation in teaching experience on material evaluation."

2. The experimental variable is *teaching experience*. This will mean that differing amounts of teaching experience will be involved in the subject characteristics. Probably one would want two or three levels of teaching experience, such as beginning teachers in their first year of teaching, teachers in their third year of experience, and teachers in their fifth year of experience. Pressing this explanation just a bit further, one may wish to constitute three groups of teachers, one each with a different amount of experience. The accompanying diagram might exemplify a pictorial illustration of this experimental variable.

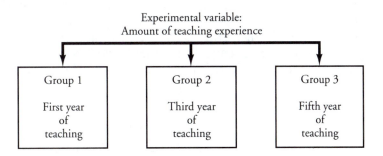

3. From the diagram it is evident that the three groups will be compared with regard to something. This leads to the principle of operational definition. Several parts of the idea require definition; one part is material evaluation, which is what will be measured. The subjects will be evaluating some material, and the researcher will be determining whether the different amounts of experience (the experimental variable) influence the way in which the material is evaluated. In other words, do teachers who are in their first year of teaching, as a group, evaluate material differently than do those in their third year of teaching and likewise those in their fifth year? It will be necessary to define in operational terms what the material is to be and the evaluation. Exactly how will the researcher record or assess the teachers' evaluation of the material? You can see that this moves into the realm of what is to be measured. Are you going to have the teachers rate the material on some scale such as the following?

Excellent		Average		Poor
1	2	3	4	5

Begin thinking in operational terms as you distill the problem.

Simulation 4.5

As before, a number of different approaches may be taken in distilling a research idea. Some may result in different studies than others. The following approach is one that you may have developed.

1. Begin with the idea statement, "Compare the effectiveness of different methods of teaching reading."

2. The experimental variable is *teaching method*. Generally the researcher will have a couple of specific methods in mind, but in keeping with the principle of generality, the experimental variable should be stated in terms of the abstract variable rather than the specific methods being compared. In the process of distilling the problem it is necessary to specify what those methods are. Suppose for these purposes that method 1 is Phonics and method 2 is Look-say. To implement the study you may wish to form two groups of children, one that is taught using phonics and a second that is taught using the look-say method. A diagram for this study might appear as shown.

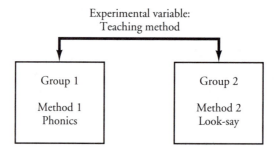

3. Now the term *effectiveness* needs to be operationally defined. The definition of this term will specify what is to be measured. One classic response to this is reading comprehension. This is all right as a start but is still too general. As you move through the text you will have to be much more specific to determine an observable criterion measure. In most cases reading comprehension is measured by counting the number of correct answers to questions on a test that covers a passage the children have read. It is frequently necessary to operationally define a number of factors in the research idea before it is distilled to the point that the study can be executed.

Simulation 4.6

If you reacted to the statement with something like "This one is really general," you were right. In its undistilled form this research idea is indeed vague. This makes your problem-distillation task even more crucial. Additionally, because of the vague nature of the problem there are even more ways that this may be designed. Following is one possible distillation:

1. Begin with the idea statement "Assess the effects of number of rein-forcements given."

2. The experimental variable in this idea is *number of reinforcements given*. This is what the researcher will manipulate. Probably there will be two or three different experimental conditions, such as one rein-forcement per minute, three reinforcements per minute, and six rein-forcements per minute. Of course these are merely examples, and those actually selected would be determined by the specific situation and the type of subjects being used. Note that these examples specified the time frame during which the respective numbers of reinforcements were to be given. This would obviously be a necessary part of setting up the experimental conditions.

3. Operational definitions are particularly important in the distillation of this idea since it is vague. The term *effects* once again is a word that must receive attention. It will have to be distilled into sufficiently spe-cific terms so that measurement is possible. In the present context, the definition of effects will also determine the setting that will be used; that is, it may determine whether the subjects will have to learn some material. If so, the amount they learn (assessed on some sort of test) is the way in which the effects of the experimental variable will be assessed.

4. Who will the subjects be? Description of the subjects may have to be accomplished rather soon to determine the reinforcement conditions as well as what is to be learned.

Simulation 4.7

Recall that a series of questions to yourself is frequently an effective means of preexperimental planning. A mental rehearsal of the entire procedure, as you visualize it, is often helpful. Such questions may in-clude the following:

1. Where will you administer the task to subjects?
2. Where are the subjects, and how do you have access to them?
3. What furniture is necessary in the experimental room, and how should it be arranged?
4. Are the record sheets in order? What will you record?
5. Are the experimental materials in order?
6. What about instructions to the subjects?
7. Is there a time limit for responses?
8. What will you say when the subject responds correctly? What will you say when the subject makes an error?
9. How will you dismiss your subject when the task is complete?
10. What about the unexpected?

Simulation 4.8

As before, a mental rehearsal is probably as an effective device as exists for preexperimental planning for the data collection. You might be alerted to the fact that questionnaire studies frequently involve more problems than one might expect. Here are some factors that will probably need attention.

1. Initially, of course, you will need to have your instrument completely designed. This will require considerable thought concerning the content (both general and specific) on which you want data. Are your instructions clear? Careful consideration must be given to the wording of your stimulus items. Are there possible misinterpretations that might result in contaminated responses? A good safeguard against this is to have two or three friends (who are uninformed about your project and similar to the subjects to be used) complete the questionnaire. This may suggest areas in which clarification is necessary.

2. How will you obtain your subjects? This is discussed in detail in Chapter 9, but be alerted that this must receive attention.

3. How will you administer the instrument? Are you going to mail it? Percentage of return is frequently poor on mail-out questionnaires. How about the campus mail service? Remember Murphy's Law! Are there administrative bodies or student populations that might be upset by the content? Plan ahead to circumvent such problems; if necessary obtain permission from the appropriate big wheels.

4. What will you do if you do not receive an equal number of returns from men and women? How equal must they be for your satisfaction?

5. Other factors?

C h a p t e r **5**

Designing Experimental Research

We ended Chapter 4 with the idea that the research process involves a number of interrelated steps. We also noted that this research process is basically the same regardless of what type of investigation is being undertaken. A wide variety of influences exists as the researcher proceeds toward the implementation of a study. Some of these forces are at odds with the basic aim of research, as suggested earlier. However, it is under just such contingencies that research must be conducted and completed in as rigorous a fashion as possible. The research design or plan has already been mentioned as being an extremely crucial aspect of the total research process. The purpose of this chapter is to present the basic foundation of research design for one major approach—quantitative experimentation.

The source of appropriate research designs is frequently a bewildering problem for beginning students. Existing designs or prepackaged plans often do not fit either the research question or the situation in which the study is being conducted. This is the case even in relatively sterile laboratory settings. Consequently, researchers frequently find that they must modify basic designs or even contrive a totally new plan using components from several basic arrangements.

This chapter presents certain foundation concepts of experimental research design and a variety of design formats that are used in experimental studies. In accomplishing this task it is necessary to present several basic design formats. Although some of these basic designs may serve well for a particular investigation, they are not presented as a comprehensive catalog of all possible arrangements. Instead they are presented as sources for useful components that may be combined in a variety of fashions to suit the needs of a particular research question.

The Concept of Control

Perhaps the most nearly central idea in experimental research, basic to all design efforts, is the concept of control. Although it was mentioned earlier, this concept is such an essential concern in design that it warrants repetition. When a study is completed, the researcher will want to attribute the results to the treatment. To accomplish this with any confidence, all other possible explanations must be eliminated, or their probability must be minimized. Thus the researcher wants to *control* or hold constant all influences except that which is under study. If, for example, the researcher is setting out to investigate the effectiveness of a particular technique for teaching reading, this will be accomplished only if the other possible influences are controlled, leaving the influence of the reading instruction technique free to generate an impact. Control is the essential element in sound experimental design. The fashion in which the concept of control is implemented varies a great deal depending on the circumstances involved in the research setting.

*Turn to page 125 and complete
Simulations 5.1 and 5.2*

Two Approaches to Experimentation

Experimental research in recent years has been characterized by two distinct approaches to designing studies: time-series experiments and traditional experimental designs. Time-series experiments have come into more frequent usage in the past 30 years, often in operant conditioning or behavior modification research. Traditional group experimental designs, on the other hand, have long been used in a variety of settings and disciplines ranging from psychology and education to medicine and pharmacology. Group experimental research was developed primarily in the context of early agricultural research whereas time-series experimentation has come into popular usage especially in the realm of behavioral science.

There are several differences with regard to both philosophy and approach between time-series designs and traditional group experimental research. Some of these differences are plainly evident (e.g., application of time-series experimentation frequently involves small numbers of subjects or even research on a single subject, whereas traditional experimental approaches are usually characterized by much larger groups of subjects). There are, however, some distinctions that hold greater importance as well as some similarities that are often overlooked. With the broad range of research problems that face the practicing researcher (or even the consumer of research), it is no longer the case that one can afford to be equipped with a narrow range of tools. The purpose of this section is, therefore, to present an overview of the basic concepts of design, both time-series and group experimental approaches.

To begin the overview, it is important to note the similarities and differences between time-series and group experimental designs. From the outset both methods have the same goal, that of producing information. Since this is the basic objective of all science, it is not at all surprising that this is a commonality. It should be mentioned, however, that because of the different manners in which questions are addressed, the type of data generated is different, as we will explain shortly. Additionally, because of the various settings involved in their typical applications, the data tend to be put to different use.

A second similarity between the two methods involves use of the *concept of control.* As was mentioned previously, this is an essential component in sound experimental design. Consequently, both time-series and group experimental designs are vitally concerned with the concept of control. The researcher must be able to attribute any effect observed to the treatment being studied. However, the ways in which the concept of control is implemented differ greatly between the two approaches.

Differences between time-series experiments and those using group experimental designs have been alluded to previously. Research using time-series designs tends to be concerned with the behavioral process as well as the product. The terms *process* and *product* should be clarified. Time-series researchers record several sets of observations over a specified period, under both baseline and postintervention conditions. As a consequence of these procedures, investigators not only have information regarding the influence or product of the treatment, but they also have considerable information concerning the behavioral characteristics of the subject as change was occurring *(process).* This concern for process as well as product is an important strength of the multiple data points gathered (often continuous measurement) in time-series designs. Group experimental designs, on the other hand, tend to focus more on the behavioral *result* or *product* of the treatment being studied. Fewer measurements are usually taken on each subject in investigations using group experimental approaches. The method, in general, involves formulation of a sample of subjects, administration of a treatment, and assessment of treatment effects. From this standpoint, a single performance measure per subject is often the source information. (If more than one measure *is* obtained, such data are certainly much less frequent than in time-series designs and are not usually in sufficient number to observe the process.)

An additional distinction between time-series and group experimental designs relates to the *generalization of results*. Group experimental research involves standard procedures that focus on generalizing descriptive statements to broader groups of individuals than those used in the actual study. This will become more evident in Chapter 9 with the discussion of sampling procedures. Time-series experiments, because of restricted numbers of subjects as well as subject selection, are less focused on generalization of results. Although time-series researchers usually do not openly deny a concern for generalization, the nature of the method used tends to seriously detract from it, because when working with a single subject or with small numbers of subjects, the probability of such subjects being unrepresentative is considerably greater than with a larger group. Additionally, the manner in which a subject is selected must be considered. Time-series investigations tend to be pragmatically responsive to needs in more naturalistic settings (such as controlling undesirable behavior in the classroom) rather than suited to gathering knowledge with samples that represent a characteristic population. This frequently results in problem behaviors and subjects being presented to the experimenter rather than the experimenter taking a given problem to a population. Consequently, generalization of results tends to be limited and is somewhat of an abstraction that might be stated as "relevant to all those like... [the subject]." This problem is not insurmountable even in the time-series method. It does, however, require numerous replications of single-subject experiments that are conducted with generalization as a focused purpose. It is also important to note that results of traditional group experiments are not automatically generalizable merely because of the approach. Generalization must be a concern of the researcher in designing the study if results are to be generalized, regardless of method. This topic is further explored in later discussions of external validity.

It was just noted above that problems are often brought *to* the experimenter in time-series research. Because of the nature of the time-series approach (suitable for use with small numbers or a single subject), the time-series designs are particularly powerful tools for use with clinical populations and/or behavioral disorders. Some of these may be low-incidence disorders for which it would be very difficult to obtain access to a large enough population to execute a group study. Thus we can use time-series designs and function as behavioral scientists (collecting scientifically sound data) and at the same time meet our responsibilities as clinicians by treating the individual subject (Gelfand, Jenson, & Drew, 1988).

Both time-series and group experimental designs have important strengths and problematic pitfalls. Neither should be systematically viewed as being preferable over the other. There are myriad problems and situations involved in the settings in which research must be conducted. Under certain conditions, time-series approaches will serve more effectively than group experimental designs, and vice versa. It is imperative that researchers be aware of the various design characteristics so that they can have more options with regard to what can be investigated.

Time-Series Experimental Designs

Time-series or *continuous measurement* research is not totally without a history of usage. It has been used for a considerable period of time in economics (Davis, 1941) and was implemented occasionally in earlier behavioral science work (Arrington, 1943; Thomas, Loomis, & Arrington, 1933). Its popularity, however, as well as its methodological sophistication has grown dramatically in recent years with an increasing interest in behavior modification. It is beyond the scope of this book to explore in depth all the dimensions and details involved in designing continuous measurement investigations. It is possible, however, to provide an overview of basic design concepts. Readers interested in further study should consult sources devoting more focused coverage to time-series experimentation (e.g., Kazdin, 1992; Kratochwill & Levin, 1992).

Several initial factors must be considered since they are essential elements in continuous measurement research. It is suggested by the term that this approach to research involves continuous or at least nearly continuous measurement. In actuality it involves a series of observations taken on the subject over a specified period. This is a distinctive feature in relation to other research approaches, in which a single (or at least far fewer) data point(s) represents the source of information. The number of measures taken varies considerably depending on the situation, which leads to a second basic consideration. Usually there are a number of phases in any experiment, each one representing a different experimental condition. The number of measurements or data points within any phase must be sufficient to determine a *stable performance estimate*. The purpose of changing from one phase to another is to demonstrate behavior change presumably caused by the new condition. This cannot be established with any degree of certainty unless the behavior rate or performance level is stable before the change.

The question of when behavior may be considered stable is one that continually plagues students of time-series experimentation. Obviously there are some behaviors that are never stable in the sense that no variation occurs, but usually it is possible to establish a reliable estimate of the behavior pattern, which serves as a comparison for the data in the next phase. For example, it may be that considerable variation occurs in the frequency of a behavior but it is cyclical and varies rather reliably around a particular level at certain times. Behavior fitting this description is illustrated by Figure 5.1 and would be considered an

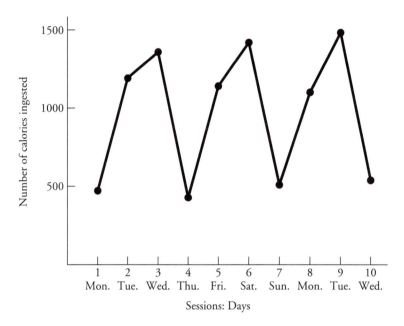

FIGURE 5.1 Hypothetical Data with Great Variability But That May Be Considered Stable Because of the Cyclical and Reliable Pattern

adequately stable basis for implementing a phase change. However, the data would not have been considered adequate for a phase change by session four since the regularity of variation was not evident at that point. Likewise, the fictitious data presented in Figure 5.2 are not sufficient to indicate a phase change. Gelfand and Hartmann (1984) provided a rule of thumb for the length of a baseline period in terms of data stability. They suggested three sessions (as a minimum) plus one additional session of data collection for each ten percent of variability (variability being determined by taking the highest rate minus lowest rate divided by the highest rate). They noted, however, that scheduling difficulties may make this rule impractical, requiring attention or intervention regarding some of the problems causing the data variability.

The different phases are important and correspond to various experimental conditions. Before demonstrating the effect of any special treatment, it is necessary to determine what the performance level is without the treatment influence. This is usually accomplished by recording performance level of the subject in a natural or nontreated state. Such a condition and the data generated are called *baseline.* When sufficient data have been recorded to establish the usual or stable baseline performance level, the researcher then begins experimental treatment. For purposes of this discussion, the initiation of treatment will be called the *intervention.* (In actual experiments, it is usually labeled by the specific treatment term such as *extinction* or *reinforcement.*)

The A-B Design

The A-B design is essentially a two-phase experiment. Although it was frequently used in early work, the A-B design involves some very serious weaknesses. Expansions that were developed to circumvent these pitfalls have essentially replaced its use entirely. It is presented here only because of conceptual simplicity, which facilitates basic understanding of time-series formats in general.

The two phases constituting the A-B design are baseline (A) and intervention (B). The baseline condition is implemented first and continued until a satisfactory estimate of pretreatment performance level is obtained. After a stable rate of baseline behavior has been established, the intervention or treatment condition is begun. Figure 5.3 illustrates a data display that might result from an A-B design experiment.

The vertical center line in Figure 5.3 represents the time of intervention or phase change. Basic to the A-B design is an assumption that performance change after intervention is a result of the treatment. The major difficulty with the A-B design lies in the absence of supporting evidence for this assumption. Suppose, for the moment, that baseline

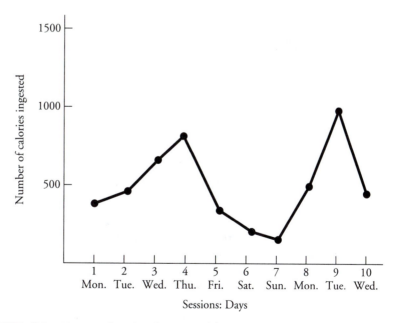

FIGURE 5.2　Hypothetical Data That Would Be Viewed as Insufficiently Stable to Warrant a Phase Change

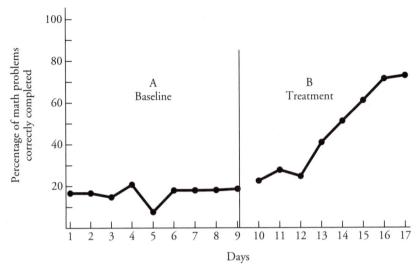

FIGURE 5.3   Example of an A-B Experiment

data are stable, and then a rather dramatic performance change is evident, which occurs at the same time as the intervention. In viewing such data, one might be compelled to attribute the performance change to the treatment. This may, in fact, be the case. There are, however, some alternative explanations. It could be that other influences occurred simultaneously with the initiation of treatment. In the example in Figure 5.3, suppose the intervention involves Johnny being fitted for glasses. The experimenter would therefore like to say that the dramatic improvement in math performance in phase B occurs because Johnny is now wearing corrective lenses. Suppose, however, that about the time Johnny was fitted for glasses, the teacher, distressed by his poor performance, also began to provide him with one-to-one tutorial assistance. Is the performance change caused by the glasses, the tutoring, or both? The experimenter really cannot say with certainty. Here is a situation in which the change in performance might be caused either in part or wholly by influences other than the experimental treatment. Without additional convincing evidence, the researcher will find it difficult to be assured that the treatment alone resulted in the behavior change. Such difficulties are discussed in greater detail in Chapter 8.

One additional note must be made. It has repeatedly been mentioned that the baseline data *must be stable before intervention.* This is an *essential* element in any time-series experiment. Otherwise, performance change evident in the data may merely represent an extension of an already existing trend and may not be the result of the intervention at all.

*Turn to page 125 and complete
Simulations 5.3 & 5.4*

The A-B-A-B Design

In an effort to circumvent some of the pitfalls of the A-B design, re-searchers extended that basic model into a four-phase format, the A-B-A-B design. Frequently called the *reversal design,* the A-B-A-B basically involves a sequential replication of baseline-intervention-second baseline-second treatment intervention. Figure 5.4 illustrates a hypothetical data display for an A-B-A-B design.

The purposes of the first two phases in the design are the same as for the A-B design. The B_1 condition is terminated at the time that the performance level or behavior rate is stable. At that time, the condition is reversed such that the pretreatment baseline contingencies are rees-tablished (A_2). The assumption underlying this procedure is that if the treatment being studied is the influential or controlling variable, that which generated behavior change in B_1, then removal of this treatment condition ought to reestablish the behavior at the baseline level. The A_2 condition is continued until the performance level returns to or nears the A_1 baseline or stabilizes. If this occurs, it is presumed that the treat-ment is the factor influencing the behavior. At this point, the experi-mental treatment contingencies are reinstituted (B_2). If behavior returns

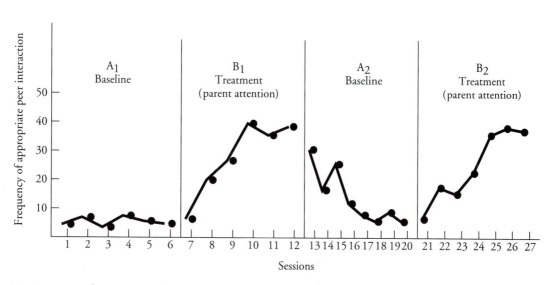

FIGURE 5.4   Example of an A-B-A-B Design

to the first intervention level, this is taken as further confirmation that the treatment is controlling the behavior.

The A-B-A-B design is not without weakness. First of all, the assumptions concerning the controlling variable are supported only if the data reverse nicely to or near the initial baseline level when A_2 is instituted. Likewise, as noted previously, if condition B_2 reestablishes the performance at or near that evident in B_1, further strength is provided for the assertion that the experimental treatment is controlling the behavior. However, such support is not available if the data do not fall nicely into this pattern. Suppose the behavior does not reverse in A_2. There may be several reasons for this. The first involves the possibility that the experimental treatment is not controlling the behavior; other influences occurring at about the same time as the intervention at point B_1 may have changed the performance level (as in the previous example). Alternatively, the treatment may be so powerful that the effects are not reversible even with treatment withdrawn. A third possible contaminant might be that some unknown influence may have intervened to maintain the B_1 performance level at the same time that the experimental treatment was withdrawn. Another possibility is that the behavior itself is not reversible. Certainly the reinforcement history of the subject has changed, and it is doubtful that the subject during A_2 is the same organism that existed before treatment was ever instituted. This is most salient in target behaviors in which obvious learning is involved as a function of B_1. Acquisition of skills is rather difficult to reverse, and the A-B-A-B design should not be used in such circumstances.

The reversal design must be used with considerable caution. As just noted, it is of doubtful utility if the target behavior involves obvious learning or skill acquisition (e.g., academic areas). It may be used effectively if behavior is being maintained by contingencies in the environment, perhaps an undesirable behavior, and if those contingencies may be altered to decrease the rate of behavior occurring. The primary strength of the design is visible when the data evidence reversal under A_2 and reestablish a changed level under B_2. Without this evidence, the researcher is left primarily to speculation concerning the treatment effectiveness.

Beyond the interpretation difficulties presented by nonreversal, other considerations must receive attention in use of the A-B-A-B design. It was mentioned earlier that time-series experiments are often conducted for pragmatic purposes rather than primarily for knowledge progress. Under these conditions, it is not unusual to encounter situations in which reversal of changed behavior is undesirable or unethical. If, for example, a child is exhibiting self-destructive behaviors, it is not likely that the experimenter will be inclined to reestablish such behaviors to strengthen confidence in what controlled the behavior. (A parent is not likely to be impressed by the contribution to science when the child has a bruised head or broken bone because of A_2.) The danger may simply be too great to permit reversal. Consequently, under such conditions the A-B-A-B design is not desirable.

Turn to page 127 and complete
Simulations 5.5, 5.6, and 5.7

The Multiple-Baseline Design

In situations for which the reversal format is either undesirable or has a low probability of effective demonstration, alternative designs must be used. One such alternative, the multiple-baseline design, has received considerable attention in recent years by researchers conducting time-series experiments. In the multiple-baseline design, data on more than one target behavior are recorded simultaneously. Termination of baseline on the different behaviors is staggered in a fashion illustrated by the hypothetical data display in Figure 5.5.

As is evident in Figure 5.5, the baseline condition on behavior two is not terminated until the experimental condition for behavior one has been established. Likewise the phase change for behavior three is con-

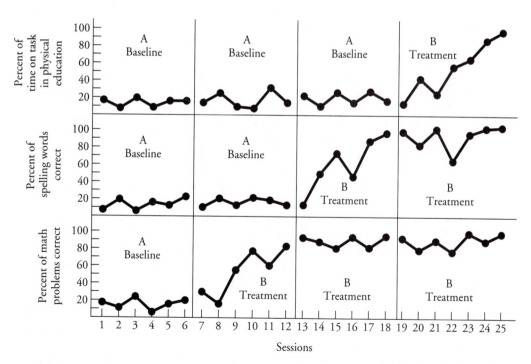

FIGURE 5.5 Hypothetical Data Display for a Multiple-Baseline Design

ducted in a similar fashion regarding the data for behavior two. The assumption undergirding multiple-baseline designs is that the second behavior serves as a control for behavior one, and the third behavior serves similarly for behavior two. Presumably the continued baseline level on behavior two (after B has been instituted on behavior one) represents what would have occurred with the treated behavior had the experimenter not intervened. Thus, if the intervention on behavior two also results in a rate change (as exemplified in Figure 5.5), this is viewed as confirmation that the treatment was the influence that generated change in behavior one. Similarly, behavior three is viewed as a checkpoint for behavior two. If the base rate remains stable and then intervention results in a rate change (again as in Figure 5.5), this is viewed as further confirmation concerning the treatment being the controlling agent. The absence of rate changes in behaviors two and three under continued baseline conditions (the staggered portion) is of vital importance to this design. Continuation of stable base rates is presumed to indicate the absence of coincidental influences other than the treatment that might have generated changes in the respective treatment conditions.

As with most designs, both in time-series and group experimental research, the multiple-baseline design is not without vulnerability to certain pitfalls. Similarly to reversal designs, the multiple-baseline approach shows strongest support for basic assumptions when the data fit nicely into the pattern exemplified in Figure 5.5. The two foundation assumptions involved in the design are that (1) the continued or staggered base rates on behaviors two and three will remain stable while other respective behaviors are under treatment and (2) the control behaviors will change rates when treatment is specifically applied to them. (The present discussion is worded in terms applicable for three or more behaviors; there are also applications in which two behaviors are used.) Several difficulties may be encountered with these assumptions. First, suppose continued base rates on the control behaviors do not remain stable (i.e., they also change when treatment is applied at intervention points on other behaviors). One explanation might involve influences other than the treatment that occur coincidentally with intervention. If this were the case, such other influences (e.g., unknown reinforcers in the environment) would probably not be applied only to the target behavior (e.g., behavior one in Figure 5.5) but more generally and thus might generate rate change in control behaviors. Under these conditions, the experimenter would have no way of knowing whether the treatment was powerful enough to generate rate change at all. Alternative explanations would leave the researcher in an equally confusing situation. Perhaps the treatment was so powerful that the observed base rate change in control behaviors was caused by generalization of influence. It may also be the case that the behaviors are too closely interrelated, such that that improvement in, say, behavior one, will result in rate changes in behaviors two or three. The behaviors must be sufficiently independent from one another to negate such an outcome. Regardless of which alternative actually occurred, change in rate when baseline condition is in effect seriously jeopardizes the strength of multiple-baseline experiments and frequently leaves the researcher with uninterpretable results.

Failure of those behaviors that were previously control behaviors to exhibit rate change on intervention also presents the researcher with problems. Suppose, for example, that the rate of behavior two did not increase when B (treatment) was applied to it. Again several possibilities might be operative. It may be that the treatment is effective only for certain behaviors (in this instance, behavior one). This could mean simply that all the behaviors under study are not controllable with the same treatment. One essential assumption of the multiple-baseline design is that the target behaviors are *all* amenable to control by the experimental treatment. A second possibility might involve the absence of control of the treatment at the beginning. If the change in behavior one was caused by some other coincidental influence and not the treatment, the treatment might also fail to change behavior two. This possibility is somewhat remote, since it is doubtful that a coincidental influence would be so specific as to affect behavior one and not two or three, which were under baseline conditions.

Despite the difficulties noted above with a multiple-baseline design, it is one of the most powerful available for time-series experiments. It is particularly useful when reversal is either undesirable or impossible because skill acquisition is involved. As with most basic designs, many variations may be generated that permit investigation in a broad spectrum of situations. Such variations involve expansions as well as combinations of other design components. The example and discussion preceding involve multiple behaviors in a single subject. However, the basic design may also be used to study the same behavior across multiple environmental conditions or may be applied using multiple subjects.

*Turn to page 128 and complete
Simulations 5.8 and 5.9*

Traditional Group Experimental Designs

Traditional group experimentation has held a position of prominence in behavioral research for a long time. As noted earlier, many of the basic design formats were developed primarily in agricultural research and were subsequently modified or applied directly to other areas of investigation. Group experimental research is used in a somewhat broader range of investigations than time-series designs, although it too may be understood in terms of a few basic design formats. Beyond this core of basic designs, nearly endless variations and expansions have been used in particular situations. This section presents an overview of group experimental designs.

Traditional group experiments are often characterized by a single assessment on a group of subjects, in contrast to the continuous measurement found in time-series studies. When multiple measures are taken on the same subjects, they are far fewer than is characteristic of time-series approaches. (More than two or three repeated measures are unusual.) As with time-series research, group designs involve several distinctive formats.

Independent Group Comparisons

One of the most commonly used designs involves independent group comparisons. The term *independent,* in this context, simply refers to different groups for each condition. For example, group A is made up of different subjects than group B. Consequently there is little reason to expect the scores in one group to be influenced by scores in the other, and they are therefore considered independent. This term is used primarily to distinguish the separate-group designs from those in which more than one measure is recorded for the same group. When repeated measures are recorded on the *same* subjects, such as in a pre-post design (explained in the section following), the scores are *not* considered independent and the comparison is called *nonindependent.*

Beyond group independence, the number of experimental variables is an essential determinant of design configuration. The experimental variable, you will recall, is that factor or question that is under study. For example, if we were attempting to determine the effects of material meaningfulness on learning rate, the experimental variable would be material meaningfulness. If an experimenter were interested in what the effects of teaching experience are on instructional effectiveness, the experimental variable would be teaching experience. Simply, it is the variable that is being investigated.

Figure 5.6 illustrates a hypothetical design for an independent group comparison with one experimental variable, often called a *single-factor design.* This example uses material meaningfulness as the experimental variable and illustrates a study in which two groups are compared: group A received highly meaningful material, and group B received material of low meaningfulness. Single-factor designs may include more than two groups; it is not uncommon for them to involve three, four, or more groups. Each of the groups or conditions within the experimental variable is called a *level* or *condition* (for example, two levels or conditions of meaningfulness, high and low, are involved in Figure 5.6).

One basic assumption is essential to the independent group design regardless of how many levels or groups are being used. *The groups*

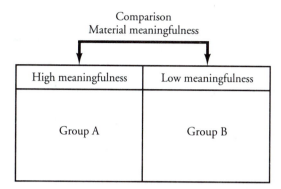

**FIGURE 5.6 Hypothetical Independent Group Comparison
with One Experimental Variable**

must be equivalent before the administration of a treatment. The usual
procedure is to constitute the groups and then to administer the experimental treatment, there being a difference in the treatments given to
groups A and B. Usually the performance score is generated either in
the process of treatment administration or on some type of test given
immediately after the treatment. If groups are not equivalent before
treatment, any differences observed in the performance measure may
be a result of group differences before the treatment rather than the
treatment itself. Therefore, if the study is to actually investigate the
effects of a treatment, the only difference between the groups *must be
the treatment.* This is the important concept of control mentioned previously. Various means of forming equivalent groups primarily involve
the way in which subjects are assigned to the respective groups. This
will be discussed in detail in Chapter 9.

Frequently a researcher is interested in investigating two experimental variables in the same study. This may be accomplished conveniently by using what is known as a *two-factor design.* (The number of
factors indicates the number of experimental variables; for example, a
single-factor design has one experimental variable, and a two-factor design
involves two experimental variables.) Figure 5.7 illustrates a hypothetical two-factor design. Note that this discussion is still focused on independent group comparisons, which means, for the design in Figure 5.7,
that the experimenter must constitute four different groups of subjects.
The experimental variables in Figure 5.7 are material meaningfulness
and amount of practice. There are two levels of each variable (high and
low meaningfulness on comparison A; ten and twenty trials on comparison B). Consequently, this design is frequently labeled a *2 by 2* or
2 x 2, which refers to the number of *levels* in each variable (each factor).

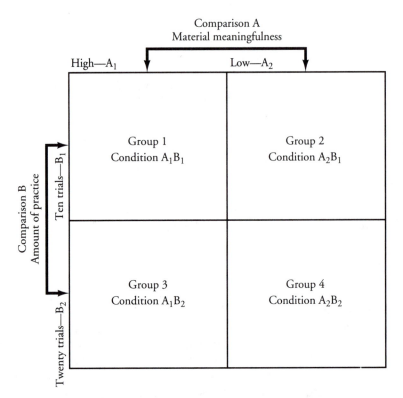

FIGURE 5.7 Hypothetical Independent Group Comparison with Two Experimental Variables

The two-factor design is flexible with regard to the number of levels in each factor. It is not necessary that the two experimental variables include the same number of levels; one may use three on A and two on B or any number of combinations (e.g., 3 x 2, 2 x 3, 3 x 4). The assumption of pretreatment group equivalence is necessary for two-factor designs regardless of number of levels, as it is for group comparisons in general.

More complex group designs may also be used if three or four experimental variables are studied simultaneously. These are merely logical extensions of what has already been discussed and likewise may involve a variety of levels within the experimental variables (e.g., for three-factor, 2 x 4 x 2 or 3 x 3 x 5). If three experimental variables are involved (A, B, and C), the pictorial representation is three dimensional, as in a representation of a cube. More complex designs, if used in a totally independent group comparison format, require a large number of subjects. They also present interpretation difficulties simply because of the complexity of results with several experimental variables. Although complex designs are useful on occasion, the simpler experiment often provides a more clear-cut demonstration of effect and is therefore preferable when possible.

Repeated-Measures Comparisons

There are situations in which the experimenter either does not desire or is not able to compare independent groups. Under such circumstances, the researcher may choose to record data on the same group under two or more different conditions. Because the same subjects serve as the data source more than once, this type of experiment is known as a *repeated-measures design.* These designs are called nonindependent, again because the scores are on the same subjects, and the performance at time 2 is certainly not independent of the performance at time 1.

Several different applications are used in the general repeated-measures design. Frequently an experimenter will administer two different testings with either a treatment or a time lapse intervening between them. This may take the form of a pretest followed by the treatment and then a posttest. Known as a *pre-post design,* this arrangement is illustrated in Figure 5.8. As indicated in the figure, the data (frequently mean scores) are compared for the pretest versus posttest performance to determine if significant change has occurred in subject performance. If there is a difference between the mean scores of the administrations, the researcher is then inclined to attribute this difference to the intervening treatment.

The basic assumption underlying pre-post designs is that the treatment is the *only* influence that intervened between measurements. If this is actually true, the researcher may accurately infer that the treatment generated the performance change. This assumption, however, is somewhat difficult to substantiate. The only data usually available are the performance scores on pretests and posttests. The researcher often

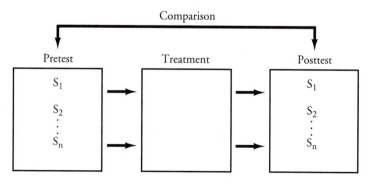

FIGURE 5.8 General Pre-Post Design Format

has little firm evidence that test scores would not have changed had *no* treatment been administered. In using the simple one-group pre–post design, there is always the possibility of unknown influence that may have occurred between tests to plague interpretation. There is also no evidence concerning how much improvement may have resulted simply from test practice. Problems that threaten the soundness of this design and suggestions for circumventing them are discussed in greater detail in Chapter 8.

We are not limited to two data points in repeated-measures designs. It may be desirable to obtain multiple assessments over a period of time to trace performance change in a more detailed fashion than is permitted by only two measures. The condition that occurs between measures may merely be time passage, or it may involve some active intervention such as the treatment suggested above. In either case, the repeated-measures design is still plagued by the same assumption weaknesses already mentioned with the pre–post format. Depending on the actual circumstances surrounding an experiment, repeated measures with more frequent assessments may be more vulnerable to test-practice effects than is the case when only two data points are used.

Despite the problems confronting repeated-measures designs, they are an essential part of a researcher's repertoire. Frequently the nature of the research question demands observation of performance change on the same subjects. Many expansions and variations are used to circumvent the problems discussed above. Usually such variations involve the addition of comparison groups, which permits measurements that will substantiate or assess the soundness of the basic assumptions.

***Turn to page 130 and complete
Simulations 5.10 and 5.11***

Mixed-Group Designs

Mixed-group designs involve two or more experimental variables, with independent groups on one or some of the variables and repeated measures on the remaining variable or variables. This type of design is called *mixed* because of the use of both independent groups and repeated measures (i.e., it "mixes" independent and nonindependent comparisons). Figure 5.9 illustrates a mixed two-factor design in which material meaningfulness is the independent comparison and recall time is the repeated comparison. As illustrated by Figure 5.9, this merely means that two groups are formed, with one being administered condition A_1 (material of high meaningfulness) and the other A_2 (material of low meaningfulness) and that both groups are tested for recall immediately (B_1) and after 24 hours (B_1 and B_2).

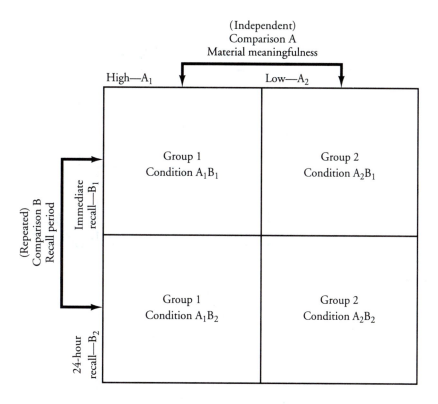

FIGURE 5.9 Hypothetical Two-Factor Mixed Design

The mixed-group format is extremely flexible. If three experimental variables are being studied, the researcher may design the investigation with one variable independent and two repeated or with two independent and one repeated. Figure 5.10 illustrates both of these options.

The same basic assumptions are operative with mixed designs as with other group comparison formats. More complex designs may be used on occasion, although interpretation of results becomes more difficult.

Design Alternatives: Comments

This chapter has outlined a wide variety of options regarding quantitative experimental designs. There is no single answer to the frequently asked question "Which is the best?" Each approach has its strengths and limitations, as we will see in even greater detail in later chapters. They serve different purposes and operate under different situations. Research-

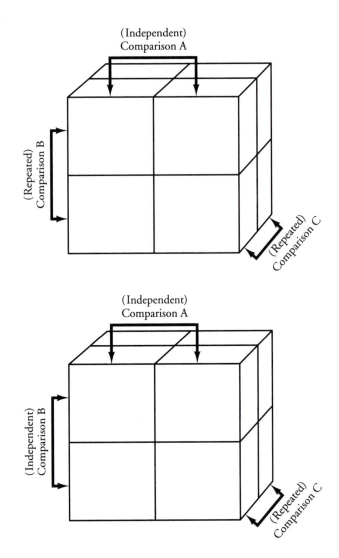

FIGURE 5.10 Option Examples for Three-Factor Mixed Designs

ers must assess the contingencies that are operating in an investigation being planned. The task then becomes selection and, usually, modification of the basic design format to be used.

Turn to page 132 and complete Simulations 5.12, 5.13, and 5.14

Simulations

Simulations 5.1 and 5.2

Topic: Concept of Control

Background Statement: The text has discussed the importance of what is known as the concept of control. This is a crucial factor in experimental research. Practice is one of the most effective means by which the concept of control becomes knowledge that is practical and functional. Try your hand at applying control in these simulations.

Tasks to Be Performed for Simulation 5.1:

1. Refer back to the diagram that was presented in the feedback for Simulation 4.4. This suggested a group study, using three groups with one experimental variable, teaching experience.
2. Apply the concept of control to attempt the formulation of groups equivalent other than in terms of the experimental variable. Make specific notes as to factors that might necessitate control attention. How would you control the factors you have noted?

For feedback see page 134.

Tasks to Be Performed for Simulation 5.2:

1. Refer back to the diagram that was presented in the feedback for Simulation 4.5. This suggested a study with two groups and one experimental variable, teaching method.
2. Apply the concept of control to attempt the formulation of equivalent groups other than in terms of the experimental variable. Make specific notes as to factors that might necessitate control attention. How would you control the factors you have noted?

For feedback see page 134.

Simulation 5.3

Topic: Basic design arrangements: time-series A–B

Background Statement: Recall that the A–B time-series is one that has two phases, baseline and postintervention. Certain evidence concerning the strength or weakness of an experiment may be available merely by visually inspecting data displays.

Tasks to Be Performed:

1. Inspect the hypothetical data display presented here.
2. Comment regarding the strength of the design, noting as specifically as possible the rationale underlying your notes of strengths or weaknesses (for example, what about the concepts of control and phase change timing?).

For feedback see page 135.

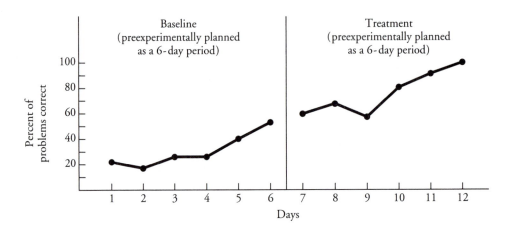

Simulation 5.4

Topic: Basic design arrangements: time-series A-B

Background Statement: Several basic design arrangements form the basis for most experimental designs (in modified form) used in behavioral science. These are rather easily portrayed by diagrams, which are helpful for the beginning researcher in terms of identifying the appropriate design format.

Tasks to Be Performed:

1. Diagram a study with the following characteristics:

    a. Difference question
    b. Time-series design
    c. A-B format.

2. Insert hypothetical data on your diagram (indicating not only your hypothetical criterion measure but also the experimental variable). Explain the important decision point or points if there are any (e.g., timing for phase change).

For feedback see page 136.

Simulations 5.5 and 5.6

Topic: Basic design arrangements: time-series A-B-A-B

Background Statement: Recall that the A-B-A-B time-series design is one that has four phases. Several aspects of this design are crucial to its soundness, and occasionally certain strengths or weaknesses are evident from visual inspection of the data.

Tasks to Be Performed for Simulation 5.5:

1. Inspect the hypothetical data display presented below.
2. Comment regarding the strength of the design and interpretation of the data, noting as specifically as possible the rationale underlying your notes of strengths or weaknesses.

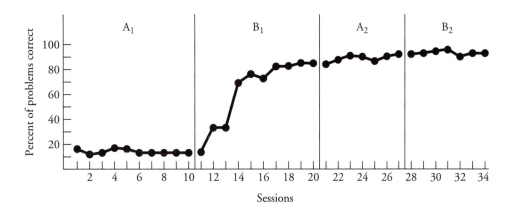

For feedback see page 136.

Tasks to Be Performed for Simulation 5.6:

1. Inspect the hypothetical data display presented below.
2. Comment regarding the strength of the design and interpretation of the data, noting as specifically as possible the rationale underlying your notes of strengths or weaknesses.

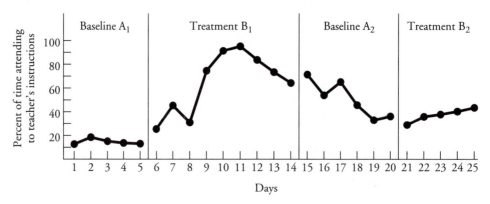

For feedback see page 136.

Simulation 5.7

Topic: Basic design arrangements: time-series A-B-A-B

Background Statement: Several basic design arrangements form the basis for most experimental designs (in modified form) used in behavioral science. These are rather easily portrayed by diagrams, which are helpful for the beginning researcher in terms of identifying the appropriate design format.

Tasks to Be Performed:

1. Diagram a study with the following characteristics:
   a. Difference question
   b. Time-series design
   c. Reversal format.

2. Insert hypothetical data on your diagram (indicating not only your hypothetical criterion measure but also the experimental variable). Explain the important decision point(s) if there are any.

For feedback see page 137.

Simulations 5.8 and 5.9

Topic: Basic design arrangements: time-series multiple-baseline

Background Statement: The multiple-baseline design is one that involves several intricacies in terms of implementation and interpretation. Visual inspection of data displays provides a number of checks regarding how the experiment was accomplished.

Tasks to Be Performed for Simulation 5.8:

1. Inspect the accompanying hypothetical data display.
2. Comment regarding the points of concern and strength.
3. Suggest possible interpretations or reasons why the data may have appeared as illustrated.

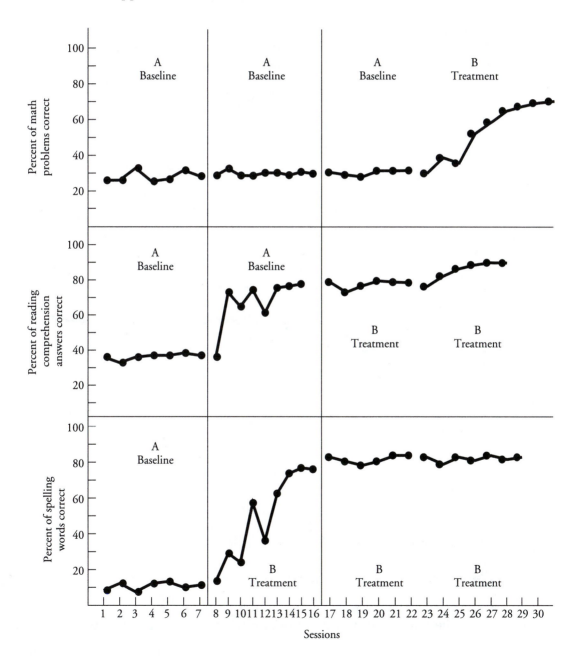

4. If weaknesses are noted, how might these be addressed? For example, how could the problem be avoided, or how could the researcher's interpretation of results be confirmed or checked?

For feedback see page 137.

Task to Be Performed for Simulation 5.9:

1. Inspect the accompanying hypothetical data display.
2. Comment regarding the points of concern and strength.
3. Suggest possible interpretations from the data.
4. If weaknesses are noted, how might these be addressed? For example, how could the problem be avoided?

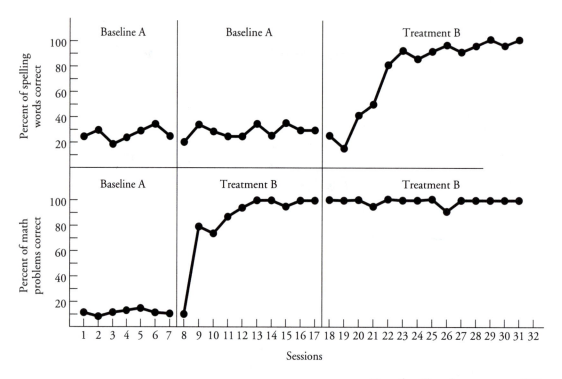

For feedback see page 138.

Simulation 5.10

Topic: Basic design arrangements: group experimental

Background Statement: Traditional group approaches to designing experimental research are considerably different from the time-series approach. Although the same type of data displays is not relevant (since continuous measurement is not involved), diagram inspection remains a useful approach to practicing knowledge application.

Tasks to Be Performed:

1. Inspect the accompanying diagram and answer the following questions:

   a. Is this a difference or a relationship question? What is the rationale for your response?
   b. What is the experimental variable? Express this, keeping in mind the principle of generality.
   c. Is this a repeated measures or an independent design? What is the rationale for your response?

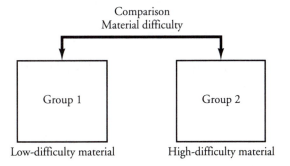

For feedback see page 139.

Simulation 5.11

Topic: Basic design arrangements: group experimental

Background Statement: Inspection of diagrams permits application of design knowledge and skill from one angle. Frequently, however, one is required to generate diagrams from a set of information. This is essentially what is required when you are designing an investigation yourself. If you can diagram an experiment accurately, then you usually have a pretty adequate functional knowledge of research design.

Tasks to Be Performed:

1. Diagram a study with the following characteristics:

   a. Difference question
   b. Group experimental design

c. One experimental variable
   • Teaching method (three different types)
   • Independent groups

2. Label carefully the experimental variable on the diagram and be certain that it is evident where the comparisons are being made.

For feedback see page 139.

Simulation 5.12

Topic: Basic design arrangements: group experimental

Background Statement: Traditional group approaches to designing experimental research are considerably different from the time-series approach. Although the same type of diagrams are not relevant, diagram inspection remains a useful approach to practicing knowledge application.

Tasks to Be Performed:

1. Inspect the accompanying diagram and answer the following questions:

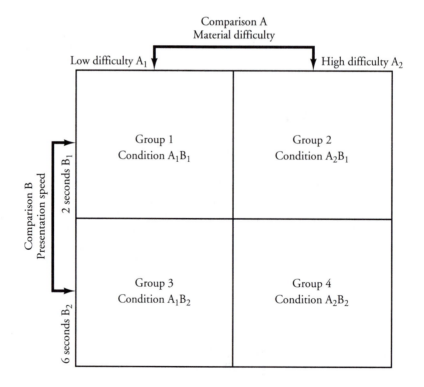

a. Is this a study that is asking a difference question or a relationship question? Why?
b. How many experimental variables are involved? What are they? Remember the principle of generality.
c. Is this an independent design, a repeated measures design, or a mixed design? Why?

For feedback see page 140.

Simulation 5.13

Topic: Basic design arrangements: group experimental

Background Statement: Inspection of diagrams permits application of design knowledge and skill from one angle. Frequently, however, one is required to design an investigation rather than describe one that is already designed. Construction of a diagram from a set of descriptive statements is essentially the task that is required when designing an investigation and therefore is presented here to simulate such a task.

Tasks to Be Performed:

1. Diagram a study with the following characteristics:

a. Difference question
b. Group experimental design
c. Two experimental variables (both independent comparisons)
   • Teaching method (three different types)
   • Amount of practice (two amounts or levels)

2. Label carefully the diagram with respect to experimental variables, and be certain that it is evident where the comparisons are being made.

For feedback see page 141.

Simulation 5.14

Topic: Basic design arrangements: group experimental

Background Statement: Occasionally difficulty is encountered in moving from a general diagram of an experiment to the specific details that are involved. This simulation begins with your diagram from Simulation 5.13 and becomes a bit more specific.

Tasks to Be Performed:

1. What were the three different methods to be compared under the first experimental variable (what did you specify as method A_1, method A_2, and method A_3)?
2. What were the two levels that you will compare under the second experimental variable (comparison B)?
3. Now, write down a description of what the subjects will be doing in group 1. In other words, what is condition A_1B_1? Your description can be fairly short and take the nature of: "Subjects in group 1 will receive condition A_1B_1, which means they will be taught with the _____ method and will receive _____ practice."
4. Now describe the conditions for the other groups in the same fashion.

For feedback see page 142.

Simulation Feedbacks

Simulation 5.1

In any group study, application of the concept of control is a clinical process. Recall that this concept essentially requires that groups be equivalent on all variables *except the one under study*. Certainly there will be some factors that one may not think about. However, it is important to attend to all that seem to require control and that can be thought of at the time the study is planned. Some might be as follows with regard to the study in the feedback for Simulation 4.4:

1. The three groups should all evaluate the same material, with the same instructions and time limits and on the same instrument under the same or similar conditions.
2. There should be no reason to suspect systematic preference of one group for one type of material over another (such as might be the case if, say, the members of group 3 had all received intensive training in Distar on the writing of behavioral objectives and the other groups had not).
3. All groups should be from similar backgrounds, teaching in similar situations with similar types of children.
4. Others?

Simulation 5.2

You will recall that the concept of control in group studies requires that the groups be equivalent on all factors except for the experimental variable. In the present example the groups are receiving two different teaching methods. Some factors that may need attention in terms of control are as follows:

1. The setting. The children from both groups should be taught in the same setting or in settings as similar as possible. This might include matters such as rooms, teacher–pupil ratios, and others.
2. The teacher. All precautions possible should be taken to prevent differences in teacher enthusiasm, experience, effectiveness, and so forth between the two conditions. This is a tough one to control. Perhaps the same teacher might be used for both. Still there is the possibility of preference differences. This problem plagues behavioral researchers endlessly.
3. The subjects. Both groups should consist of children with similar ability, from similar backgrounds, and of similar ages. This can frequently be accomplished by rigorous assignment procedures.
4. The instrument. The same test for reading comprehension should be used with both groups.
5. The time. There should not be any systematic difference in when the two groups are taught or tested. If one group is always taught or tested in the morning and the second in the afternoon, there is a problem. Also pay attention to the duration of the experiment; you do not want one group to receive more training than the other.
6. Others?

Simulation 5.3

Several problems are evident from the data display, mostly interrelated.

1. There is a preexperimentally determined period for both baseline and postintervention measurement periods. Although the importance of preexperimental planning has been emphasized, the length of time that observations continue should be determined primarily by data stability in a time-series experiment, and a strictly predetermined time period presents a problem.
2. Data stability has been emphasized as crucial in time-series designs. The data in phase A are certainly not stable at the time of intervention. Instead, an upward trend is evident in at least the last two performance observations. The performance level in phase B could well be caused merely by an extension of this trend rather than by the intervention. Likewise, data collection in phase B is terminated while the performance is still on an apparently increasing trend. Consequently you do not know how much change would ultimately result.
3. Because of the problems noted above, the concept of control is not apparently operative in these data. You would hope that change in performance level could be attributed to the intervention. Since the

data were not stabilized at the point of intervention, however, the postintervention performance level could well be caused by influences other than the treatment. This would seem to be a definite possibility in these data because of the upward trend in performance level, which began before the intervention and generally continued afterward.

Simulation 5.4

Since you were asked to draw the diagram in this simulation, considerable latitude is possible concerning exactly how your drawing might appear. In basic form it should resemble the data display diagram in Figure 5.3.

The most crucial decision point in your hypothetical study is the phase change from baseline (A) to treatment (B). It is important that the data appear stable, which would require that your graph largely follow the guidelines suggested by Gelfand and Hartmann (1984) presented in the text. Likewise the data should appear stable by the end of phase B. How did you do?

Simulation 5.5

Recall that one of the crucial factors in any reversal design is the reversal itself. The present data do not evidence that essential reversal of performance under phase A_2. There was nothing that would have predicted this as the experiment proceeded. Baseline was stable; a dramatic performance change occurred under treatment phase 1 (B_1) and then stabilized nicely. Problems became evident as the reversal was attempted (A_2) and performance level did not return to the pretreatment level.

These data are difficult to interpret. Can the change in B_1 be attributed to the treatment? Not with any degree of certainty. Why? Review the discussion in your text and note the possible alternative explanations.

What problems may have generated these results? What do you do now? Would you replicate the experiment? Would you choose another behavior? Are there other alternatives?

Simulation 5.6

This particular data display presents a somewhat confusing situation. The crucial violation of sound design practices occurred at the end of the B_1 phase when the data were not stabilized before reversal was implemented. Note the definite decelerating trend in the data during the last three observations. The apparent reversal in A_2 could therefore be caused by a continuation of this trend.

On an overall basis, the change in B_1 could be caused by influences other than the treatment. This is a possibility presented by the deceleration in B_1 and the ineffective B_2 reimplementation of treatment.

What should have been done differently? Once the data began to decelerate under B_1, this phase should have been continued until the data stabilized. This would have given more information concerning the effect of the treatment (or lack thereof).

Simulation 5.7

Since you were asked to draw the diagram in this simulation, considerable latitude is possible concerning exactly how your drawing might appear. In basic form it should resemble the data display diagram in Figure 5.4.

The phase changes are, of course, extremely important decision points. Your diagram should portray stable data for several observations before the change points.

In A_1 you should have the label *baseline,* and your hypothetical data should appear in concert with the suggested guidelines of Gelfand and Hartmann (1984) before the phase change. There will often be variation from observation to observation in terms of the subject's performance, but the guidelines just noted take this into account. Phase B_1 should be labeled *treatment,* and the treatment should be specified, such as *parental attention, reinforcement applied,* or some other indication that communicates what the treatment was. Depending on what the data are supposed to represent, this phase may show a rather dramatic change in performance level (if the treatment worked). It is also important in this phase that the data stabilize before the next phase change (to A_2).

Phase A_2 is the reversal phase or a return to baseline conditions. This should be so labeled in your diagram. Again, depending on how your hypothetical results turned out, this phase may show a dramatic change in performance level in which the data return to or near the baseline level in the first phase. This is assuming that you selected a reversible behavior. Did you do so? Check your label on the criterion measure side of the graph, which tells what performance or behavior is being assessed. Is it something that will probably revert to baseline when the treatment is withdrawn? If you have questions about this, review the text pages covering this problem. The data should again be stable in phase A_2 before the change to B_2. Phase B_2 should probably include a performance change that might resemble that which occurred in B_1 and then stabilize before observations are terminated. How did you do? Have your instructor inspect your diagram if you are unsure.

Simulation 5.8

Probably the most effective way to inspect a multiple baseline data display involves a sequential inspection from behavior 1 through behaviors 2, 3, and so on. One should also, however, attempt to view the total display to obtain an overall interpretation.

In this particular data display, the behavior 1 phase change sequence appears to be appropriate. Under Phase A, the baseline condition, the data appear to be stable in what could be called a stable low rate. There is probably no doubt that adequate data are available and that the phase change to B is appropriate. As the change occurs in behavior 1, it becomes dramatically evident that something has influenced the behavior rate in the subject. If one views only the data in behavior 1, there is little reason to believe that the treatment is not the effective agent generating change.

In this data display behavior 2 is where problems become evident. The behavior is stable under the first baseline phase, which coincides with the baseline for behavior 1. However, during the second baseline phase (which coincides with the initiation of treatment in behavior 1), there is a dramatic change in the rate of behavior 2. In fact these data appear as though the treatment has been applied to behavior 2 as well as behavior 1. Consequently it is not certain that the implementation of treatment in behavior 1 generated the change, since a similar change appears in the data for behavior 2. It could be that something other than the treatment generated the change in behavior 1 and that it also was evident in behavior 2.

Moving to behavior 3, there is evidence of stable behavior frequency under all three baseline phases with a general trend toward change under treatment, which would suggest that the treatment is effective. Overall, however, the researcher should have some concern regarding the design of the study represented by this data display. One cannot be terribly confident that the treatment is generating the change in behavior although in two cases it appears to be so. That is, data for behaviors 1 and 3 would suggest that the treatment is probably the factor generating change; but with behavior 2, a substantial change in rate occurred when that particular behavior was still under baseline and behavior 1 was under treatment. Because the data did not fall nicely into the phase change pattern (since there was a change under baseline with behavior 2), the set of evidence is not terribly strong although the data are suggestive. Probably what occurred is that behaviors 1 and 2 were not sufficiently independent, and the implementation of treatment in behavior 1 generalized to behavior 2. Of course there is no strong evidence for this—it is merely speculation—but one might suspect that this occurred with these data. This emphasizes the importance of selecting behaviors that are independent and that can be treated in sequential fashion, so that generalization does not change those behaviors not under treatment.

Simulation 5.9

The data display presented in this simulation provides what is probably a classic example of everything appearing to go right. For behavior

1 (math problems) there was a stable baseline evident at around the 10 percent correct level for seven sessions. This is certainly sufficient data to consider a phase change, which was initiated on behavior 1 at that time. Beginning with session 9 there is a rather dramatic increase in the percent of math problems correct, which moves all the way to 100 percent and, with three minor variations, remains at 100 percent for the remainder of the observation sessions.

Behavior 2 (spelling words) is somewhat less stable than behavior 1 but certainly is within a narrow enough range that an estimate of untreated performance level is evident. This is particularly the case since 17 sessions are available under baseline before treatment is begun. Behavior 2 also responds rather dramatically to the treatment with the level of spelling words correct approaching 100 percent and varying around that level until session 32, when it was determined that the behavior was probably as stable as it was going to be and observation was terminated.

Simulation 5.10

This is a difference question. The difference question asks, "Is there a difference between..." and compares two or more groups or measures. The arrow in this diagram indicates that the performance of group 1 will be compared with the performance of group 2.

The experimental variable is material difficulty. Without knowing any more about the specifics of the study, the question can be stated as "Comparing subject performance as a function of material difficulty." Another way of looking at the same descriptive statement might be "The effects of material difficulty on subject performance." The principle of generality requires that the experimental variable be expressed in terms of the abstract construct (material difficulty) rather than the particular levels or conditions within that variable (which would be like the material A versus material B approach, noted earlier as inappropriate).

This is an independent design, since different groups of subjects are compared (one group receives the low-difficulty material, and a second group receives the high-difficulty material). The repeated-measures design would require that the same subjects be tested under both conditions, which is not indicated by the diagram.

Simulation 5.11

Since you were asked to draw the diagram in this simulation, considerable latitude is possible concerning exactly how your drawing might appear. It should resemble the diagram shown here and should be labeled in the same fashion.

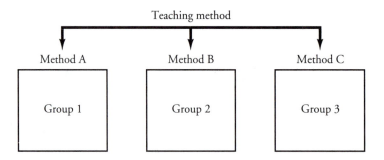

Simulation 5.12

This simulation presented a series of questions related to the diagram that was included. Responses to those questions will be outlined in the same sequence as they were presented. As you read the simulation feedback responses, refer back to the diagram and keep in mind your own responses to the questions.

1. This study is asking a difference question. As before, difference questions suggest comparisons between groups or groups of measures.
2. There are two experimental variables involved. Comparison A is designated as material difficulty, whereas comparison B is presentation speed. This would generally be called a two-factor design because there are two experimental variables. Each experimental variable has two levels or conditions within that variable. For comparison A, material difficulty, there is low difficulty and high difficulty material (also designated A_1 and A_2 respectively) and for comparison B, presentation speed, B_1 is a two-second presentation, whereas the B_2 condition involves a six-second condition.
3. This is an independent design, that is, for both experimental variables there are independent comparisons with a different group for each condition. This is evident from the indication that there are four different groups involved, groups 1, 2, 3, and 4. Each group functions under only one condition and is not measured under more than one condition, thus there is a totally independent design on both experimental variables. Group 1 receives condition A_1B_1, which is the intersection of low difficulty material and two-second presentation speed. Group 2, on the other hand, is operating under condition A_2B_1, in which high difficulty material is presented at the two-second presentation speed. Group 3, condition A_1B_2, receives the low difficulty material at the six-second presentation speed, whereas group 4 receives high difficulty material at the six-second presentation speed (condition A_2B_2). These types of notations are frequently helpful as you proceed through an

experiment to prompt yourself and keep in mind exactly under what conditions each group is being tested (or which treatment is actually being administered).

Simulation 5.13

Although a variety of details may differ in the way your diagram is arranged, the following general format will hold. If you have drawn the basic configuration shown, you are on target. Here is a brief review of certain information about this design.

Task 1 (part c) required that the design be totally independent, that is, that both experimental variables should be set up as independent comparisons. What does that mean in terms of this experiment? Simply stated, it means a different group for each condition, which in this case resulted in six different groups of subjects (group 1 received condition A_1B_1, group 2 received A_2B_1, and so on). The two experimental variables are teaching method and amount of practice. Three methods of teaching are involved in the first experimental variable and two levels of practice are involved in the second. Because this is an experiment involving two experimental variables, it is generically called a two-factor design. Specifically you will see such a configuration called a three by two or 3 x 2, which refers to the different numbers of levels under each variable.

Proceed to the next simulation and become a bit more specific in terms of the details of your diagram.

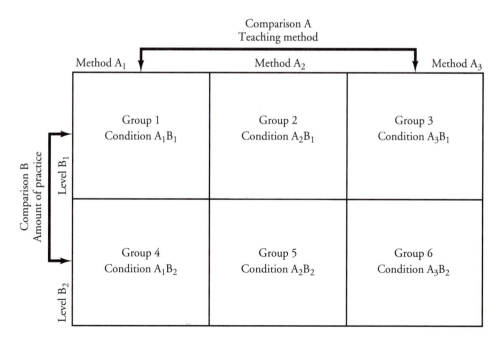

Simulation 5.14

Because of the variety of possibilities in responses that you might have, this simulation should be checked with your instructor. This will be the quickest way of obtaining specific feedback.

In general you should have six different sets of conditions, one for each group. The conditions are dictated by the specifics that you attached to each level of the two experimental variables. If you called method A_1 the authoritarian method and level B_1 six practice trials, A_1B_1 will receive the authoritarian teaching method and six practice trials. Your description should continue in this fashion for each group.

Chapter 6

Designing Nonexperimental Research

Throughout this text we have stressed the point that the dimensions of research are somewhat fluid. Ethical considerations vary greatly depending on the individual perspective, the field of study, the situation involved, and the methodology used. The content and procedures for the study differ along the same lines. Likewise, the language used to describe the theoretical and methodological concepts is also quite variable. This chapter focuses on the design of nonexperimental research as contrasted with experimental research. We are not, at this point, focusing on qualitative methods, although some of these procedures may be employed to collect qualitative data. The primary discussion of qualitative research methodology is found in Chapter 7.

However, the distinction between the categories of experimental and nonexperimental research may be somewhat arbitrary, again depending upon the personal perspective and the professional field of study. For example, instead of using the terms *experimental* and *nonexperimental* to distinguish between specific categories of research, an investigator may employ such terms as *nonsurvey* and *survey* research. Our use of experimental and nonexperimental classification schemes is for communication and instructional convenience, but it is important to remember that they are somewhat artificial and that the language is fluid, particularly as one crosses the boundaries of various professions involved in research.

The term *design* (used as a noun) has typically been associated with experimental research. The researcher uses a specific design to investigate a given topic. In nonexperimental research, *design* begins to have less meaning. Nonexperimental research focuses more on methods of investigation (e.g., survey, observation) rather than the design of the study. There are a number of parallels, however, and the notion of designing a nonexperimental study is still very relevant. Despite terminology differences, the general research components for nonexperimental and experimental investigations remain basically the same. Certain procedural matters will change; some dimensions will be emphasized more, while others will be emphasized less. However, beyond these differences, the fundamental process with which this book began will remain relevant (see again Figure 1.1). Initially there is a research question, the question is distilled into operational form, the study is planned, the data are collected and analyzed, and the results are interpreted in terms of the original question. Because some different emphases, topics, settings, and methods are now involved, a brief examination of these processes is warranted in the nonexperimental context.

The initial idea for an investigation is often rather general and lacks specificity. To actually implement a study, it is very important to eliminate vague areas through problem distillation. The first area needing attention in the distillation process *is very precise specification of the problem or question* to be studied. A researcher must be very clear and specific regarding the research question that is being addressed.

Precise specification of the research question is particularly crucial to nonexperimental studies because there are a broader range of questions typically addressed. Three basic categories of questions have been discussed: descriptive, difference, and relationship. Nonexperimental researchers may work in all three categories. Researchers using experimental designs tend to focus primarily on difference questions.

There are several general distinctions between different types of research questions. The descriptive question basically asks *what is.* Descriptive research attempts to describe the existing behaviors, opinions, attitudes, or other characteristics of the group or culture under study. Difference questions ask *is there a difference?* Investigations addressing difference questions may be comparing the opinions, behaviors, or characteristics of two or more groups or cultures. Relationship questions investigate the degree to which two or more phenomena *relate or vary together.* A researcher undertaking a study such as this may, for example, be interested in the relationship between marriage and annual net income. The question might read as follows: "As the length of marriage varies, what tends to happen to annual net income?" (That is, as the length of marriage increases does annual net income tend to increase or decrease?) Rather than comparing groups (as in the difference question), the researcher records quantitative data on a sample of subjects (both the length of marriage and annual net income). With two measures on each subject, the investigator then computes a correlation coefficient, which provides an estimate of the degree to which the variables relate.

Any given study may involve more than one type of question. For example, a researcher may be investigating the relationship between marriage and family income but also be interested in possible differences between geographic regions of the country. In this type of study, both a difference question and a relationship question are part of the same investigation. In order to avoid confusion in the conceptualization, execution, and interpretation of the above study, it must be clear that there are two distinct research questions being addressed.

The second vital step in problem distillation is *operational definition.* A clear operational definition of terms, activities, measures, and other important factors must be completed prior to beginning the study in order to avoid the need to make immediate (and potentially incorrect) decisions in the field. All terms, activities, and so forth, must be specifically defined in a fashion that will permit someone to know exactly what is to be done or what is considered a complete response. For example, what is meant by annual net income? Does this mean merely "after-taxes income," or does it also take into account necessary business expenses such as union dues or membership dues to professional organizations? Unless these matters are clarified, the investigation is likely to involve considerable error in the implementation process and the results will be less precise. If you can answer the question "What exactly do you mean by..." (e.g., net income), you probably have the term operationally defined. If you cannot answer such questions, do not begin the study.

The remainder of the research process involves the data stage (planning for collection and analysis) and the inference or interpretation of results. These steps are vital components in nonexperimental research. For example, it would be devastating to your entire project to send out all your questionnaires and then find out that your instructions or questions were unclear. If your instructions are vague in an experiment, by contrast, you may lose data only on the first subject or two. The designing of nonexperimental investigations must be undertaken with great care; your priority decisions and questions must be made and answered early. Reviewing Chapter 4 will facilitate this process and is helpful for both the experienced and beginning researcher.

The labels that are attached to nonexperimental studies tend to reflect the methodology used for data collection (e.g., survey studies, observation studies). Consequently, the planning of nonexperimental research will be discussed in this same fashion.

Survey Research

Survey research involves asking questions of a sample of individuals who are representative of the group or groups being studied. Survey studies may have a variety of purposes (e.g., describing, comparing, correlating). As is true in all research studies, problem distillation is the first step in the process. Assuming that this has been completed, the next step in designing a survey involves planning the procedures to be used in collecting data. This will include developing the instrument and determining the sample to be drawn. A variety of sampling techniques can be used, and each involves very specific procedures that must be carefully planned and executed. These will be examined in detail in Chapter 9.

Surveys typically use two general procedures for data collection: questionnaires and interviews. Questionnaires may be distributed by hand (such as in a group meeting or class session), or they may be mailed to the respondents. Similarly, interviews may be undertaken on a face-to-face basis or by using the telephone. Each specific procedure has certain strengths and weaknesses that must be considered by the researcher in the process of selecting an appropriate technique.

The essential task of any survey is to obtain information from a sample of respondents that relates to the question(s) being studied. Although this sounds simple enough, it can often be a formidable undertaking. Great care must be exercised in planning a survey investigation to facilitate successful execution of the study. The factors to be addressed differ somewhat between questionnaire and interview research and will therefore be discussed separately.

Questionnaire Investigations

If a questionnaire study is being designed, there is an obvious need to construct the instrument itself. This seemingly simple task has many pitfalls that may seriously threaten an investigation if they do not receive attention during the preexecution planning. For example, the questionnaire must be constructed in such a manner that it will extract accurate information from the subjects. The questions must be written clearly and in a fashion that minimizes the possibility of misinterpretation by respondents. There are also certain factors to be considered in construction of a questionnaire that can either encourage or discourage responses by the subjects. This section will focus primarily on design issues rather than the development of the questionnaire (although questionnaire format creeps in). Questionnaire construction will be discussed in more detail in Chapter 10, which examines measures, instruments, and tasks.

The two methods of questionnaire distribution (by hand or by mail) have different strengths and limitations that must be considered. Mailed questionnaires may represent a substantial savings of time and money and may also permit greater accessibility to geographically dispersed respondents, which is less feasible with questionnaires distributed by hand. The financial investment for a mailed questionnaire might be limited to the postage expense, the paper needed for instrument reproduction, and the personnel costs involved in instrument development, reproduction, and mailing. No one would dispute that each of these is becoming increasingly expensive, but postage is still less costly than paying someone to personally distribute the questionnaire. The accessibility of subjects may also be a major consideration. Clearly, if respondents are geographically scattered, the mailed questionnaire may be the only option.

Problems with mailed questionnaires must also be carefully considered. Mailed questionnaire studies are often plagued by a small percentage of respondents completing and returning the questionnaire (low response rate). In fact, this is an often used argument against mailed questionnaires. Related to this difficulty is the problem of slow response. Subjects may take their time in returning the questionnaire, and the researcher has little means of controlling their behavior. Additional difficulties include a lack of control regarding the nature of subjects' responses and the potential of receiving information from a biased or atypical sample. It is difficult to argue against the idea that there is likely a difference between those subjects who respond and those who do not (and, therefore, between the respondents and the intended sample in general). Most of the factors involved in careful design of mailed questionnaires focus on circumventing such problems. Some of the factors involved in the planning of mailed questionnaires may vary depending on the type of question being asked. Others are more specifically related to the procedures used in questionnaire investigations. A synthesis of the areas that are particularly problematic with this type of study can be reduced to two major categories: (1) the low response rate and (2) the accuracy of the subjects' responses. Clearly, a researcher has limited means of controlling the respondent once the study is under way. Consequently, all precautions possible must be taken before the study is initiated to circumvent both accuracy and response rate difficulties.

One question that often plagues beginning researchers concerning the issue of low response rate is just how low must it be before there is trouble? Of course, answers to this question are diverse, but the investigators must begin with the basic assumption that what they really want is that all respondents return a complete questionnaire. Whereas this would be the best of all possible circumstances, it seldom occurs. Some studies using mailed questionnaires have response rates as low as 10 percent, which is generally considered inadequate. Some authors suggest that a 70 percent response rate can be considered adequate, and less than that warrants little confidence in the results (Borg, Gall, & Gall, 1993). It should be noted, however, that such guidelines represent judgment statements. There is no wide consensus among researchers regarding these figures as being set in concrete. For example, Bailey (1994) suggests that researchers should not be satisfied with low response rates and that the serious researcher should undertake several steps to substantially increase the return. According to Bailey, a properly constructed questionnaire and appropriate follow-up by the researcher should result in a 75 percent response rate. Additionally, response rates of 90 percent and above are quite possible.

There are certain factors related to response rate that warrant further examination. One of these is the *length* of the questionnaire. Respondents are more likely to complete a one- or two-page questionnaire than they are one that is four or five pages in length. There are no rules regarding optimum length for a questionnaire, but it seems clear that the shorter it is, the more likely you are to obtain a satisfactory response rate.

Another response rate factor regards the *ease* with which a respondent can complete the questionnaire. Obviously, this includes the length of the questionnaire, but other factors also influence the effort required to complete the form. If there is little time and effort required, there will probably be a higher return rate (and perhaps more accurate and honest responses) than if the process is time-consuming and difficult. Part of this will be determined by the clarity of instructions provided for the respondent. Unclear instructions are likely to cause confusion regarding what is to be done and may even cause many subjects to "deep-six" the questionnaire. Open-ended questions may have the same effect. Such questions take more time and effort because they require the respondent to write out the answers.

One of the best procedures for circumventing the difficulties mentioned above is to conduct a *pilot test* of the instrument. A pilot test simply involves asking a few individuals to complete the questionnaire before the actual study is begun. The pilot test provides information regarding whether the instructions and questions are clear and whether the time and effort required on the part of the respondents is reasonable. It is very important that the pilot test be conducted with individuals who are similar to the respondents in the sample; otherwise, the pilot will tell little or nothing concerning how the actual respondents will react.

A variety of other steps can be taken to improve the response rate in mailed questionnaire studies. It is a commonly accepted practice to include a *self-addressed, stamped envelope* for subjects to use in returning the questionnaire. This obviously reduces the imposition on respondents and substantially influences the return rates. The nature of the *cover letter* may also be important. It is somewhat unclear whether or not a personal letter (Dear Mrs. Smith) is more effective than one that is rather impersonal (Dear Occupant). What is clear, however, is that the body of the letter is important. A shorter letter results in a higher response than one that includes long and involved statements. Additionally, a letter that has a coercive tone is less effective than one that involves a somewhat more permissive appeal to respondents.

Respondents are more inclined to complete and return a questionnaire if they are convinced that the study is legitimate and of value. One factor that may influence this perception relates to *organizational sponsorship* of the investigation. A study being sponsored by a credible government agency (if you can find one), a university, or some other well-known and respected organization is likely to be viewed as more legitimate than one that is not. Subjects are generally more responsive to an investigation with such sponsorship than to a study with no apparent organizational affiliation. It is important to note, however, that not all organizational sponsorships may be viewed favorably. Certain sponsors may be viewed with suspicion by respondents, such as those that may have a commercial motive (e.g., the salesperson appears at your door two weeks later). Although sponsorship of a questionnaire investigation is important in terms of response rate, an investigator must carefully consider the impact of the particular affiliation on the subjects being sampled.

Respondents are most likely to complete and return a questionnaire if they attend to it as soon as they receive it. Obviously, a researcher cannot stand over the shoulder of each subject, but there are certain precautions that can be taken in terms of *mailing.* The response rate is substantially lowered if the questionnaire arrives just prior to a major holiday or vacation time. Researchers should attempt to avoid these times or any other periods that may have a similar effect. Subjects may be inclined to delay response until after the holiday has passed, and if it is an extended holiday, they may decide afterward that it is too late to respond. Precise control is usually not possible because of many unknown influences (e.g., mail service). An investigator must also know a fair amount about the population being sampled to avoid potential problems. If school personnel are involved, for example, it is better to sample in September than in May.

Follow-up is also a step that may improve the return rate in questionnaire studies. Bailey (1994) cited evidence suggesting that response rates may be increased as much as 20 to 30 percent when follow-up is involved. In general, three follow-up contacts is the optimum. Any more contact is often viewed by the respondent as harassment. The initial follow-up may be a reminder letter. The second contact should be a second reminder letter with another questionnaire attached. Finally, the third follow-up should be a telephone call. A number of specific issues require attention in deciding the nature of follow-up procedures (e.g., timing, protection of anonymity, content of the follow-up, etc.). The beginning researcher who anticipates undertaking a questionnaire survey should consult a volume specifically devoted to this research method (e.g., Berdie, Anderson, & Niebuhr, 1986).

Turn to page 157 and complete
Simulation 6.1

Interview Investigations

Interview investigations have the same basic purpose(s) as questionnaire studies but simply use different data collection procedures. Interview investigations use personal contact and interaction to gather data necessary to address the question or questions being studied. Such contact may be made on a face-to-face basis or by telephone. Each procedure has its strengths and weaknesses that must be considered as the researcher decides which approach to use.

One difficulty related to interview studies is the high costs involved. If the interview is conducted on a face-to-face basis, costs can be extremely high. An interviewer's salary is often considerable and may include travel and lodging expenses. This is one area in which the *telephone interview* offers a significant advantage over face-to-face procedures. Telephone interviews can be undertaken without travel expense and can be completed very quickly (when compared with face-to-face interviews). The telephone interview greatly reduces expenses, but there are problems involved that may be so significant as to seriously limit its use.

Perhaps the most difficult problem involved in telephone interviews is sampling bias. Obviously, the only respondents who can be contacted using this procedure are those who have telephones with listed numbers. Immediately this makes the telephone survey less appealing for studies that need to sample a broad cross section of the population: certain segments may not be accessible. This problem must be carefully considered as one examines the telephone survey as a potential means of data collection. Telephone interviews may also be plagued by the perception of the respondent regarding the motives and/or credentials of the interviewer. Everyone receives a share of telephone calls that could be suspect for one reason or another. The telephone has even become a major instrument of burglars who want to determine whether a person is home; they may even obtain information regarding personal possessions through a fake interview. There are many reasons to be somewhat suspicious of telephone calls from unknown persons. These same factors greatly influence the type of data that can be obtained using a telephone interview. Although the telephone interview has certain advantages, these are often judged to be less compelling when balanced against the problems involved. Telephone surveys tend to result in about a 5 percent lower response rate than face-to-face interviews (Fraenkel & Wallen, 1993).

The *face-to-face interview* also has certain strengths and limitations. Generally speaking, the interview is a social interaction between people and is subject to all of the influences that affect such interchanges; and these influences are probably greatest in the face-to-face interaction. Certainly, a face-to-face interview is vulnerable to all of the potential biases that may be represented in the person of the interviewer. Data recording might be substantially altered to the degree that an interviewer has a personal investment of opinion regarding the outcome of the study. It may also be influenced by the perceptions of the interviewer in terms of the subject being interviewed. Suppose that the interviewer holds some bias regarding a particular religious group. If a respondent is encountered who belongs to that particular group, it is not unreasonable to suspect that the interaction with that individual will be different from interactions with individuals who are not so affiliated. Data may even be consciously altered in such circumstances. Clearly, the interaction involves at least two individuals: the respondent and the interviewer. Consequently, the respondent must also be considered as possibly contributing to the bias problem. Even if respondents do not know you (the interviewer), they may have certain reactions to the way you appear. In response to such perceptions they may or may not be cooperative, honest, and open. Thus, the personal interaction may be a significant factor in interview studies, in terms of both the interviewer and the respondent. These problems cannot be ignored as one plans an interview study or selects a procedure to be used.

The researcher must pay attention to certain considerations to maximize the effectiveness of this interaction and facilitate an accurate survey. One factor involves the *characteristics of the interviewer.* It is a commonly accepted fact that interactions between individuals of the same race or ethnic background are different from those that occur between persons of different races. This also seems to be the case regarding interview studies. If a study involves a particular racial or ethnic group, the researcher should be careful to use interviewers who represent the same population. Accurate and honest responses are more likely to occur between individuals who share personal characteristics. This is also true for social status: respondents are more inclined to provide accurate and honest information to interviewers who are, or appear to be, from the same social class. This factor extends as well to matters of clothing and grooming. Interviewers should dress and groom in a manner that will be similar to the sample of respondents; but the interviewers should maintain a balance between this perspective and one that legitimizes their role as professional interviewers. If interviewers are going to work in a low-income area, they should not be dressed in an elegant fashion; but at the same time, they should be attired so as to provide credibility to their role. (Unless, of course, they are being deceptive in their activities as an interviewer, an issue that was discussed at considerable length in Chapter 3.)

Personal characteristics of age and sex may also be important. In some cases, it seems that same-sex interviewers should be used, whereas in others the evidence is less conclusive and even confusing. A researcher must carefully consider the topic under study and the nature of the questions being asked when making this determination (e.g., are sensitive questions being asked that would probably result in a same-sex combination being more effective, or does it seem inconsequential). Concerning the age of the interviewer, it appears that in some situations the most effective interview can be conducted with the interviewer and the respondent being about the same age. At other times, it appears that the interviewer should be older than the sample group to provide the credibility and maintain the legitimate role perception necessary for an accurate survey. If there is a question in the investigator's mind, the topic should be examined at length, either by reviewing the literature or by undertaking a pilot study to provide empirical evidence related to this methodological concern.

Interviewer behavior is another influential factor in the success or failure of the data collection process. One of the first tasks that must be accomplished is the creation of a favorable impression on the respondent. Such initial perceptions may set the stage for a successful interview or lead to a complete refusal to participate. A respondent must be immediately convinced that the interviewer is legitimate and the study is of sufficient value to become involved. However, this task may be somewhat more difficult than in a questionnaire investigation, because an interviewer is physically present and can represent more of a perceived threat than the arrival of a questionnaire in the mail. The interviewer should always present credentials and identification papers and provide an explanation of the purpose and nature of the investigation. Although the respondent should not feel coerced, the interviewer will probably be more successful if the tone of the conversation assumes participation on the part of the person being approached. An extremely important factor in the success of the interview is to clearly establish rapport.

An interview may involve the use of a questionnaire or standardized protocol. The instruments should undergo pilot testing prior to being used in the actual investigation. Interviewers using such procedures should be careful to follow instructions in a consistent fashion to ensure standardization of the data collection process. There may be occasions when an interview study is conducted without a structured interview protocol. Such procedures, although useful in certain circumstances, do not provide the same caliber of objective and consistent data as those involving a standardized protocol.

Turn to page 158 and complete Simulation 6.2

Observation Studies

Observation may be used in a variety of investigations, including experimental and nonexperimental research as well as qualitative studies.

The observation method is being discussed in this chapter because it is often employed to collect quantitative data. Observation of a qualitative nature will be examined in the following chapter.

Two factors become immediately important in planning the observation process: (1) the setting and (2) the structure imposed on the observations by the investigation itself. Both of these factors can be viewed in terms of a single concept: a continuum of structure. The setting may be very structured, such as a laboratory study, or it may be a totally unstructured setting in which the observer records information in a presumably natural setting. The investigation may also involve a continuum of structure that is imposed by the investigation itself. In a fashion similar to the interview discussion, observations may be recorded using very structured categorizations or the counting of behaviors (e.g., a behavior checklist, rating scales), or they may be recorded as field notes without a specific guide for the observer. Specific operational procedures for conducting observations will vary considerably depending on the structure of the setting as well as the structure imposed by an investigation. In fact, each individual investigation may have certain features that make it unique as compared to other studies. An examination of all such possible variations is beyond the scope of this text. Consequently, this discussion will be limited to certain generic considerations involved in developing a system of observation.

The first factor that must be addressed in planning an observation study is to identify *who* is to be observed. For some investigations, this may involve identifying the general group to be studied. In others, it may mean a definition of the types of individuals to be observed (e.g., 12-year-old males with IQs between 70 and 85). Regardless of the type of study, the basic aim is to precisely describe the subjects who are going to be included for observation. The study cannot even be planned without such a definition.

Another factor that must be accomplished very early in the planning process is a determination of *what behaviors* are to be observed. This task will require an operational definition of the actual focus of the observations (assuming that all of the possible behaviors that might occur are not of interest). For example, a researcher may be studying the aggressive behaviors between 12-year-old males. In this context, aggressive behavior must be defined—is it physical, verbal, or both? In another study, an investigator may wish to observe the verbal communication between 19-year-old female students. A number of factors must be defined and/or described, especially if the observation is to be somewhat structured. The definition of behavior must be sufficiently precise so that an observer can reliably determine when it occurs. This means that the researcher must also attend to some other issues related to the behavior, such as defining any and all conditions under which the observations will be made. In what setting is the verbal communication between 19-year-old females to be observed? We know they are to be students, but more details are needed to implement the observation. Are they to be in small groups or large groups? Will the observation be in a natural setting such as the student union, or will it be a contrived setting such as a class discussion (real or otherwise)?

This raises still another factor that must be determined and described in detail: What will be going on in the *setting?* In examining the communication between 19-year-old female students, the researcher will be primarily interested in studying communication (patterns, frequency, duration) under certain conditions that would include a particular type of setting and a particular type of activity. Other studies might be specifically designed to observe communication regardless of what was happening. If this is a part of the study, controlling the activities would not be a part of the procedure. This should, however, be determined from the outset (and the question should always be addressed during planning).

Time must also be a consideration in defining the conditions under which an observation study will be conducted. In this case, time should be thought of in at least two ways. The researcher may want to define the time (when—day, month, year—the data are collected. For example, the researcher may want to study communication patterns in 19-year-old females as they first rise in the morning. Such a study might place a restriction on the time of day or define time in terms of the first hour after rising. The second view of time may involve a time interval for observation and data recording. In this type of situation, the researcher may be interested in observing the frequency (number of occurrences) per hour of a given behavior. Time must be specified so that there is a constant frame of reference. If this is not done, the data may not be accurate and consistent. For example, two groups may interact the same number of times; but one may generate 47 interactions in 30 minutes, whereas another may generate 47 interactions in an hour.

Behavior observations have been discussed thus far without reference to methods of recording. In fact, the discussion above may even suggest the writing down of each behavior—separately, completely, and in words. Although such procedures may be used in qualitative research, it is more likely that other means will be preferred for quantitative studies. Usually, certain types of behavior (e.g., the aggressive behavior in the earlier sample) or the different kinds of behavior exhibited by a particular type of subject will be of interest. Consequently, one task that usually must be undertaken is the development of a system for *categorizing and coding behavioral occurrences.* Behavior might be roughly categorized into "aggressive" and "nonaggressive," with each being operationally defined. Specific behaviors should then be observed in each category and coded to facilitate recording by the observer. The subcategories might include both physical and verbal behaviors as well as those behaviors directed toward peers and adults—aggressive-physical-peer-directed, aggressive-verbal-peer directed and so on. Obviously, there are a great many possibilities, which would vary depending on the focus of the investigation. The coding of behaviors becomes very important if there are many subcategories to be observed; otherwise, the actual recording procedure may become extremely cumbersome. For example, in the rough outline above, symbols such as A-P-P, A-V-P, and so on, may be used to represent each possible behavior. In most cases, a carefully designed data sheet will be used so that the observer is required only to make a quick mark on the form if a particular behavior occurs. There are several possible approaches to coding behaviors, and the researcher must decide which best suits the study being planned. In some cases, an existing system will function very nicely. For others, the best approach may involve adaptation or development of a system that is specifically suited for that particular study.

A variety of recording methods may be considered, depending on the nature of the investigation. One of the simplest procedures is known as the *tally method,* which is used to record the number of times that a particular behavior occurs. Once the behavior is clearly defined and coded, the observer tallies on paper (or with a hand counter) each time there is an occurrence. The observations must be recorded in relation to a time frame such as a session or a prescribed interval (e.g., five minutes). This permits the determination of rate: the frequency per session. Another recording procedure that may be used is known as the *duration method.* The duration method is useful to determine how much time a subject spends engaged in a behavior. In this case, the observer would probably observe an individual subject for a time, starting and stopping a stopwatch as the behavior began and ceased. Observations may also be recorded using the *interval method.* This procedure might be used if you were interested in whether or not a particular behavior occurred during a given interval. Using such a method, the observer would simply mark the interval on the recording sheet if the behavior occurs during that period. The behavior might be continuous throughout the interval, or it may carry over from a previous period and cease halfway through the interval. In each of these conditions, the interval would be scored as an occurrence. The interval recording method may be useful when it is difficult to count the individual occurrences of a behavior. A subcategory of interval recording is known as *time sampling.* Time sampling is useful when an observer cannot watch the subject continuously and, instead, samples the observations by looking at the subject on a systematic basis (e.g., at the end of a time interval). Sampling may permit observations on a group of subjects simultaneously. If the target behavior is evident at the time the observer samples, it is recorded as an occurrence.

There are many variations in the way observation data can be recorded. Each procedure has different characteristics and the data may differ substantially depending on the method chosen. Different research questions, subjects, and settings all influence the decision regarding which method will function most effectively. The primary purpose of this discussion has been to sample some of these considerations and emphasize the importance of specifying which recording method will be used prior to beginning observations.

Another factor that must receive attention in observation studies is the reliability of the data recording. Every collection procedure will include a certain amount of error, whether the recording is accomplished by a machine or a human. A machine recorder may be calibrated incorrectly and thus not accurately represent what actually occurred. Clearly, a human recorder may also be subject to error: a behavior might be overlooked or recorded inaccurately. Consequently, observation studies must include certain precautions that attempt to determine observer reliability. This is typically accomplished by using two or more observers (either continuously or on a periodic, spot-check basis) and calculating the degree to which they agree. Such procedures are known as *determining interobserver reliability.*

There is a variety of methods for calculating interobserver reliability, and the circumstances related to the investigation will dictate which should be used. A procedure that is commonly used involves determining *percentage agreements* (including simple percentage agreement, effective percentage agreement, as well as other variations). Percentage-agreement methods are conceptually simple and easily computed, which has certain appeal in terms of convenience and interpretation. This procedure is the measure of reliability most commonly used in behavior-modification programs (Gelfand & Hartmann, 1984). It asks the question "How much (what percentage) of the time did the two observers agree regarding the data recorded?" Despite the advantage of simplicity, percentage-agreement methods have certain limitations. One serious limitation pertains to the number of observations recorded. In particular, if there are very few observations (opportunities for agreement), percentage-agreement methods may provide a very imprecise picture of interobserver reliability. For example, if there was only one opportunity or observation and both observers agreed, the reliability would be represented by a 100 percent estimate. On the other hand, if there was one agreement out of two opportunities the estimate of reliability would be 50 percent. Consequently, there is a great deal of variation with small numbers of observations, and the reliability estimates might be very misleading as compared with estimates for the same behaviors observed many more times.

Correlational methods may be used as well to estimate interobserver reliability. The use of correlation techniques for this purpose is conceptually similar to asking any relationship question. The purpose is to determine the degree to which factors relate or vary together. Thus, if we have a positive correlation between two observers' recorded data, they tend to vary in the same direction. As observer A records an increased frequency, observer B also tends to record an increased frequency, which is some indication of the degree to which they agree or are reliable. The degree to which they agree is represented by the correlation coefficient. Correlation methods of assessing interobserver reliability have certain strengths not evident in percentage-agreement procedures. Correlation measures are not influenced by chance agreement in the same fashion as percentage-agreement methods. Additionally, correlation coefficients have a definite mathematical interpretation regarding variation between observers. Correlations may also be used for further statistical analysis if this is desired in the particular investigation being planned. Correlation estimates are not, however, without problems. First, they are more difficult to interpret from a statistical point of view. Second, there are problems with correlation procedures when occurrences are infrequent (opportunity for agreement or disagreement). Third, if there is little variation in the data recorded, the correlation coefficient obtained becomes less precise. In summary, the correlation method overcomes certain problems but is limited in other respects. A researcher must determine the type of interobserver reliability method that will be used based on the specific characteristics of the study. It is important, however, that some reliability assessment be made to provide greater credibility to the results obtained.

Simulations

Simulation 6.1

Topic: Questionnaire studies

Background Statement: Low response rate is a common problem that plagues survey researchers, particularly when questionnaires are mailed to respondents. This simulation focuses on this difficulty and presents you with the delicate task of advising your new employer.

Stimulus Information: You have recently been employed by Monolith Oil Corporation as a research associate. Due to the energy crisis, Monolith executives have decided that they should become aware of the opinions of consumers. (This is definitely something new—since when do the opinions of consumers play an important role, particularly with oil companies?) As you arrive on the job, you are summoned to the president's office regarding a questionnaire study that has been conducted on consumer views of the energy problem. By way of background, you are told that the problem is one of what appears to be a very negative response. (The consumers did not think that there was an energy crisis but did believe that the oil companies were reaping unjustifiable profits from the public.) Obviously, this is not what the president wants to hear, and so you are being asked to show how the study was conducted incorrectly. Disregard your personal opinions for the moment and consider the facts surrounding the study. The questionnaire was six pages long, it was mailed to respondents with no follow-up, and there was a 10 percent response.

Tasks to Be Performed: Tactfully, give the president advice. What information would you give the president? Was the study conducted correctly? If not, what would you suggest?

For feedback see page 158.

Simulation 6.2

Topic: Interviews

Background Statement: As you know from the material presented in this chapter, many influences may affect the success of an interview study.

Stimulus Information: You have been asked to serve as a consultant with the department of sociology of Northern Delta University, which is undertaking an interview study in a predominantly black neighborhood in Detroit. The researchers are relatively inexperienced in terms of interview studies and have asked your advice regarding the procedures that should be used.

Tasks to Be Performed: Because you have just completed "Research 32," you have considerable information concerning interview studies. What will you suggest?

For feedback see page 159.

Simulation Feedbacks

Simulation 6.1

First, assume that you have enough reserve (no pun intended) of tact that you do not lose your job. They really screwed up in a number of fashions, but you're not going to say that directly. The questionnaire was probably too long; they did not need that much information, and it probably contributed to the low response rate. The other major problem was the lack of follow-up. As you recall, the text suggested that the use of appropriate follow-up procedures might increase response rate as much as 20 to 30 percent. However, this would only raise the response rate to a maximum of 40 percent. Is that enough? Probably not. There is another, even more delicate issue that relates to sponsorship. How might Monolith Oil Corporation letterhead influence response rate? It might be better if the study were conducted by an independent research organization that did not suggest conflict of interest. This might be a very difficult point to make with the president. Good luck!

Simulation 6.2

The most obvious suggestion involves the population that is to be involved in the survey. If the interviews are to be conducted in an area that has a predominantly black population, the interviewers should most likely be black. This would hold for any particular ethnic or other subgroup. You may have to provide advice regarding the general factors influencing success or failure of interview studies: for example, grooming and dress for the interviewers, the appropriate presentation of credentials, and the manner in which sensitive questions should be presented. Although you might expect the researchers to know about these influences, you must remember that Northern Delta University is not exactly in the academic mainstream. How did you do? Would you have at least considered the general areas that should receive attention?

Chapter 7

Designing Qualitative Research

In Chapter 2, we presented an overall scheme for viewing qualitative, quantitative, experimental, and nonexperimental research designs and methods. This scheme introduced the use of qualitative data to study human behavior. The chapter included some central concepts of social science research that uses descriptions of naturally occurring social events as the data from which general patterns and concepts about human behavior can be drawn.

When we discussed the growing popularity of qualitative methods in behavioral research, including education, we pointed out that while the quantitative/qualitative distinction is convenient, qualitative research designs vary considerably along many of the same principles that distinguish among other kinds of research—control versus realism, internal versus external validity, phenomenological versus positivist. (Remember the epistemological debate about knowledge and how to acquire it, introduced in Chapter 1?) Qualitative researchers also differ in their beliefs about the unique nature of social experiences, debating whether any social situation and event involving a unique person or group of people can ever be replicated (Benjafield, 1994). They often deliberately and systematically fail to "honor one or all elements of the blessed trinity" of experimental research: (1) theory driven, (2) hypothesis testing, and (3) generalizable (Peshkin, 1993). Repeatedly, we have emphasized that beginning researchers should be familiar with all the major traditions of research, so that they will be able to assess the appropriate methods for each research question and develop a better understanding of their own views of knowledge. We agree with the opinion expressed by Warwick (1973) when he said that "every method of data collection is only an approximation to knowledge. Each provides a different and usually valid glimpse of reality, and all are limited when used alone" (p. 190).

In this chapter, qualitative research approaches commonly used in educational and social science research are introduced that represent a variety of perspectives. Details about the scholarly traditions of qualitative inquiry, the planning and execution of qualitative studies, methods for data collection and analysis, and the applications of qualitative research to understanding research problems are discussed.

When to Use Qualitative Methods

You recall the caution that beginning researchers sometimes turn to qualitative methods out of a fear of mathematics and a belief that, since words and language are familiar, qualitative research will be easier than quantitative research. As you will see in this introduction to qualitative research design, qualitative methods are time-consuming, labor-intensive, and expensive. Developing scholars need a commitment to rigorous inquiry on which consumers of the research can rely when making general statements and drawing conclusions from the research process. These rigorous methods can be found in both quantitative and qualitative traditions.

The methods of qualitative research have their roots in anthropology, a social science primarily devoted to the study of unique human cultures. As we noted earlier, the stereotypical anthropologist in pith helmet and khaki shorts trudging through the jungle eating grubs and other native foods encompasses only a small fraction of the scholarly tradition that is anthropology. Rich descriptions that render for the reader a clear and accurate picture of the nature of each culture form the basis of anthropological studies. No assumption that these descriptions, and analyses of more specific relationships within the culture, are generalizable or even transferrable to other cultures—is part of this scholarly tradition.

However, accumulating, rigorous qualitative studies contribute to the development of general concepts or theories about human culture. Cultural or sociological concepts that appear across cultures, even as the details of the cultures differ dramatically, provide the foundation for social science theories. The main features of qualitative research therefore make it generalizable to theory rather than generalizable to different research populations. Yin (1991) argued that expanded theory is the major goal of qualitative inquiry.

While the experimental, quasi-experimental, and nonexperimental designs discussed in earlier chapters provided social scientists with foundational knowledge about their disciplines, educators and other social scientists have found that important aspects of their fields are best studied in environments that place serious limitations on the researcher—natural settings where richness and complexity are accompanied by messiness and lack of control. Researchers who design studies requiring natural settings are constrained in their ability to apply the standards of rigor appropriate to experimental and quasi-experimental methods we have discussed. Jerome Kagan, a renowned experimental child psychologist, pointed out, for example, that much of what we know about the behavior of small children has been learned in artificially controlled experimental settings in which they are separated from their customary sources of security and social support (1978). While such knowledge is critically important, it is safe to assume that advances in knowledge about the natural psychology of the child require an understanding of the children's behavior in their customary surroundings. Kagan called for a program of research on children in their natural settings, surrounded by their caregivers, parents, siblings, or playmates, to expand knowledge about their normal behavior.

The critical variable in this call, for a variety of research approaches and designs, is the researcher's ability to study events as they naturally occur. As we have repeatedly reminded, this quality also limits the control and manipulation of variables. Consequently, qualitative methods are uniquely suited to studies imbedded deeply within a setting of naturally occurring interactions among people. Qualitative research methods are most appropriate in very specific situations when the research problem or question does not allow for high control and the manipulation of variables. More specifically, qualitative methods are suited to designs that seek to answer questions:

1. requiring natural surroundings;
2. examining unfolding and uncontrolled events;
3. requiring the exploration of *reasons* for behavior and the ways in which behavior unfolds;
4. needing exploration, explanation, description, and illustration; and when
5. small sample sizes and few global settings exist.

First, qualitative methods provide an answer to Kagan's challenge to learn more about how people behave in their customary surroundings. Educational settings, like other social situations, are very complex. Children react to each other, respond to their friends sitting next to them, complete (or fail to complete) problems and assignments for many reasons that spring from their personal lives, environments, and interactions with peers. For example, recent research on underachieving talented African American children has revealed that the pressure not to achieve in school, not to "act white," is sometimes intense for inner city black children. These pressures extend to all racial and ethnic groups who seek aggressively to establish an identity and sometimes find the line between identity and exclusion difficult to distinguish (*Frontline*, 1994). To study these children's achievement and failure patterns, scholars must study them where the pressure occurs and record their perceptions and interpretations in their own words. Qualitative methods are appropriate, therefore, for researchers who seek to understand how people make sense of their surroundings and the people and circumstances that shape their lives (Bogdan & Biklen, 1992; Miles & Huberman, 1994).

Second, many critically important behavioral processes can best be understood as they naturally unfold. Rigorous and high-quality experimental research cannot be used to study these social processes, because events must be examined as they occur without manipulation or control. The critical variables affecting unfolding events are not known in advance but must be discovered and observed. Much as detectives carefully expose the critical facts and events as they investigate events in the past, qualitative researchers observe and describe events as they occur. When contemporaneous social processes are the focus of study, qualitative methods offer a natural alternative to other designs (Schatzman & Strauss, 1973).

A third situation for which qualitative methods are well suited occurs when the researcher seeks to understand the reasons behaviors occur as they do and how these behaviors occur. A long tradition of research affirms that human beings' behaviors often are shaped by their interpretations and beliefs as strongly and as surely as by objective events around them. Even the source of information, the social status of the person who conveys information, and the acceptance and beliefs of others in the group have been shown to shape people's choices (Markus & Zajonc, 1985). An aspiring gang member may, consequently, choose to believe what the home-boys say about the intentions and motives of a teacher who tries to befriend him rather than believe the teacher. Whether the teacher is truly supportive or not, the students' beliefs about that support will often determine how they choose to act (Likert, 1967). Contemporary, real life phenomena and the whys and hows that shape them are best studied using qualitative methods (Schatzman & Strauss, 1973).

The need to explore, explain, describe, and illustrate behavior and interactions to better understand them and uncover poorly understood variables provides a fourth situation in which qualitative methods are very appropriate (Yin, 1991). For example, a researcher may seek to explore the cognitive processes that fourth graders typically employ when solving story problems in mathematics. The question is not which logarithms or methods work best when children use them but how do nine-year-old children typically think about mathematical problems? A design that allows the children to talk about what they are thinking and doing as they work on a math problem gives a researcher a view about what the children are doing, choices they make as they seek to solve a problem, and their rationales for making these choices. Later on in a research agenda, after the researchers know more about the cognition of fourth graders, specific teaching methods based on age-appropriate mathematical reasoning that thereby teaches mathematics more effectively can be developed and tested using experimental designs.

Finally, researchers often need to conduct inquiry when small sample sizes and few global settings exist. In-depth study that yields important concepts about social behavior over time is very intensive; the trade-off is large sample sizes with less depth of inquiry. Qualitative methods allow the researcher to approach the subject, probe the setting, and describe reality in a more natural fashion and in great depth (Lancy, 1993; Lincoln & Guba, 1990). Widely read examples of this kind of inquiry in education include Cusick's (1973) study of social relationships among student body officers and athletes within a comprehensive high school, *Inside High School,* and Wolcott's (1973), *The Man in the Principal's Office.* This tradition is well established (beginning in the 1930s with Willard Waller's classic work) and growing. The most widely read study of the culture of teaching produced in recent decades, Lortie's (1975) *Schoolteacher: A Sociological Study,* is still considered among the most revealing descriptions of the teaching profession.

These examples of general situations in which qualitative methods are uniquely appropriate are by no means exhaustive, but they provide a guideline for researchers who wonder whether qualitative methods are appropriate to answer their particular research questions. Yin (1991) provided three standards that researchers can use to help them determine whether qualitative methods fit their particular research problem. Yin suggests that these methods should be used when:

1. the phenomenon under investigation is contemporary,
2. the boundaries and context of the study are not distinct, and
3. the researcher has little control over the phenomenon being studied.

Violence and gang problems in public schools provide examples of a major educational and social problem that meets these criteria. Gang membership changes with time, and gangs develop, split, and change their norms, sometimes as frequently as their leaders change. This places contemporaneous, immediate time requirements on a scholar interested in studying them. When gang interactions spill from the streets into the schools, the boundaries of context change constantly and fit the indistinct nature of Yin's second criterion. Finally, no researcher could ever maintain the illusion of having any control over the phenomenon of gangs in schools. While many variables affect the situation, each school and gang mix is unique, and no opportunity to manipulate or control these variables exists. Peshkin (1991) has conveyed these factors vividly and insightfully in his book *The Color of Strangers, the Color of Friends: The Place of Ethnicity in School and Community*.

Any scholar seeking an appropriate research design must pay attention to the research context, because one faces the temptation to let a preference for methods rather than the nature of the study shape their choices. The design must be the logic that links the data to be collected and the conclusions drawn to the initial questions of the study. Research questions inform the sampling frame, instruct where the researcher goes to get answers, suggest with whom one talks and what one observes, and set the conceptual framework into action (Miles & Huberman, 1994). Thus, careful identification of the questions is critical, and the choice of research design (including qualitative methods if appropriate) then can flow from the nature of the research questions.

Educational researchers using qualitative methodologies also differ along the phenomenological/positivist continuum discussed in Chapter 2. Consequently readers and research consumers should take care not to assume that all scholars who use qualitative methods share the same assumptions about the nature of knowledge and ways of knowing. But scholars designing qualitative research must be very clear about where they stand in order to assure the accuracy and trustworthiness of results and the integrity of communication of findings to readers. This stand is, in the last analysis, a value and belief judgment, and researchers who avoid clarity of perspective risk the danger of bias by cloaking value judgments with names such as objectivity, truth, and science.

Some Comparisons of Qualitative and Quantitative Designs

In addition to the situations for which qualitative methods are uniquely suited, researchers can investigate different aspects of the same problem using both qualitative and quantitative methods in mixed-methods designs (Crawford & Christensen, 1995). A few examples of research settings will illustrate how researchers use qualitative and quantitative data to learn different things about some social and educational problems.

Researchers interested in the psycho-social development of children, the responses of children with and without intellectual disabilities when disabled children are mainstreamed into regular schools and classrooms, or any number of other aspects of children's social development and learning in school settings might need to observe their behavior. Using a quasi-experimental design, the children could be carefully selected on the basis of the characteristics of interest, placed in a controlled setting, and their actions observed through a one-way mirror. Using this scenario, researchers often build on their hypotheses and supporting theory to design a structured observation instrument. Raters or observers are trained to recognize the behaviors of interest and research variables are explicitly chosen in advance and listed on the recording summary sheet. At regular and predetermined intervals, raters judge and categorize observed behaviors and make a record of their observation. Frequencies, intervals, and kinds of behaviors can be systematically compared in this way using *quantitative* data. (This approach was discussed in greater detail in Chapter 5.)

A playground, learning center, or classroom setting is more natural, however, and provides a natural context. Theory may be poorly developed, or experimental or quasi-experimental data may have provided clues that existing theory is failing to explain. In these circumstances the more natural setting provides additional information while lacking control. The researcher does not want predetermined categories or theories to direct his or her attention or shape the observation by masking new or poorly understood dynamics, so the structured observation instrument and trained behavior raters are useless in the search for this new aspect of children's interactions. The researcher instead needs to be a keen observer who can vividly and accurately record what is seen—*qualitative* data—for later analysis and interpretation in descriptive prose. Days or even weeks might be spent observing and recording the interaction of children with and without disabilities as they interact in school. The sample of children is the same; the knowledge acquired by the two methods is quite different; but each method contributes a different part of the whole picture.

In both these situations, the inquirer (researcher) is the instrument gathering information. The interaction of the inquirer with the events or with the subjects (perhaps the teacher and students being observed) is a reality of qualitative and quantitative methods. In the qualitative example, the reactivity of the investigator with the subjects might affect both the investigator's observations and the subjects' actions. In the quantitative example, the researcher would not be observed by the subjects, but the training of the raters and reliability of judgments about predetermined categories affect the data. The quality of behavioral data recorded in quantitative form depends on the observational abilities of the persons doing the counting and on the level of agreement between different observers. This factor is called inter-rater reliability. Just as a thermometer measures temperature and a clock time and these instruments can be calibrated to make them more reliable, so can training and experience improve the reliability of observers or raters.

The above examples exaggerate the clarity of distinctions between qualitative and quantitative methods. Earlier, we pointed out that social scientists vary in the level of their commitment to a belief in the uniqueness or regularity of social phenomena. The examples from anthropology we have used draw on the uniqueness of each culture studied. Researchers also use qualitative data to look for regularity. The text of an interview or the script of an observation can be coded for regularly appearing patterns and the codes counted, for example. These data can be displayed in matrices, summary sheets, and graphs to help the researcher understand qualitative data. (We return to analytical techniques briefly in this chapter and expand on them in Chapter 15.) Another example of the lack of clear distinctions between so-called objective, positivist research and subjective, phenomenological research can be found in survey methods (See Chapter 6). A respondent may be asked to record a subjective feeling or judgment and quantify it on a Likert-type scale representing level of agreement or disagreement with a given statement or intensity of feeling. A scale from one to five or from one to seven is commonly used in this type of research, but the data rely entirely on respondents' feelings and understandings, even though the quantitative nature of the data once recorded makes them seem more objective than a textual description.

As you can see from these few examples, qualitative and quantitative distinctions lie most firmly in the final form of the data—whether they are recorded as numbers or words—yet the research methods using these kinds of data share many similar features. Each is concerned that the study accurately and reliably represent the people, behaviors, or activities under study and that it reveal concepts that are theoretically or empirically generalizable (either to the human experience or in specifically rational and replicable ways). While many researchers use very technical terms to convey these values and standards of rigor, qualitative researchers are more likely to use practical, common terms to describe them. Table 7.1 provides some examples of basic research questions and concepts and the qualitative and quantitative terms that label them. These are not complex concepts, but the beginning researcher sometimes feels overwhelmed by the many design issues he or she must address in order to protect the quality of the study. Checklists, guidelines, and principles are the best guide; no one need memorize long and complex design alternatives. We continually return to themes of rigor, however, because our experience with beginning students tells us that poor design (not poor research execution or inexperience with statistics or field notes) poses the greatest threats to research quality.

Standards of Rigor

As with other kinds of research designs, qualitative researchers must ask specific questions regarding conceptualization and research process in order to assure the trustworthiness of a study. Table 7.1 provides an introductory framework for this question-asking. Certain steps in the design, data gathering, and data analysis process can help researchers avoid pitfalls and maintain trustworthiness (Crawford & Christensen, 1995; Guba & Lincoln, 1989). In this chapter, we focus on research design and data gathering for qualitative methods. Qualitative data analysis

TABLE 7.1   Criteria for Assessing Qualitative Research

Question	Qualitative Term	Experimental Term
Is it the right thing to do; is it needed?	Appropriateness	Problem significance
Can we trust the researchers?	Unbiased	Objective
Do the results stand up; same results with repetition?	Dependable	Reliable
Can it be used in various settings; is it situation free?	Generalizable	Externally valid
Are the results subject to contamination?	Credible/Authentic	Internally valid

techniques are discussed in Chapter 15. Just as with the designs and methods discussed earlier regarding experimental methods, the two main issues qualitative researchers must face to preserve rigor are reliability and validity. After a brief review and examples, different terms applied by qualitative/naturalistic researchers to their standards of rigor will be discussed. In Chapter 8, we return to the concepts of internal and external validity in qualitative and quantitative research in greater detail.

Reliability in qualitative designs has much the same general meaning as it does in quantitative designs: under similar circumstances, can the study be replicated with similar results? Are the results an accurate reflection or rendition of what actually occurred, of relationships, of observed interactions (Bogdan & Biklen, 1992; Miles & Huberman, 1994)?

Internal reliability means that objectivity is maintained and the findings will be similar within the site (Lecompte & Goetz, 1982; Lecompte & Preissle, with Tesch, 1993). For example, in a given group of youths, a researcher describing social patterns can expect (if the findings are internally reliable) that expectations, beliefs about what is right and wrong, and pressures for conformity will be similar among those who belong to the group, and the researcher will describe and elucidate them in a way that resonates with the youth being studied. Further, another researcher might use different language but would discover the same general expectations, beliefs about right and wrong, and conformity pressures using a quality research design. Five steps can help the qualitative researcher protect internal reliability:

1. Use low inference descriptors.
2. Use multiple researchers whenever possible.
3. Create a careful audit trail (record of data that can be followed by another scholar back from conclusions to the raw data).
4. Use mechanical recording devices where possible (and with permission).
5. Use participant researchers or informants to check the accuracy or congruence of perceptions.

For qualitative researchers, *external reliability* suggests a replicability of concepts across and between sites. We emphasize that phenomenological designs reject this standard out of hand, because they rely on the assumption that all social experience is essentially unique. Yin (1991) argues, however, that designs across sites such as comparative case studies make it possible for researchers to describe patterns existing in broader social environments and describe more abstract or general concepts related to specific research findings. This is the feature we referred to earlier as theoretical generalizability. Procedures that help protect external reliability include:

1. Clearly specify the researchers' status or position so that readers know exactly what point of view drove the data collection.
2. Clearly state who informants are (or what role they play in the natural context) and how and why they were selected or chosen (while maintaining confidentiality).
3. Carefully delineate the context or setting boundaries and characteristics so that a reader can make judgments about similar circumstances or settings.
4. Define the analytic constructs that guided the study (describe specific conceptual frameworks used in design and deductive analysis).
5. Specify the data collection and analysis procedures meticulously.

As in quantitative designs, *validity* in qualitative research captures the accuracy or truthfulness of the findings. Lecompte and Goetz (1982) find validity to be a strength of qualitative research, because it sets findings within natural settings, free from the contaminating effects of control or variable manipulation. Other researchers refer to this feature as "trustworthiness," "credibility," and "authenticity" (Miles & Huberman, 1994). As with the other important standards of rigor, specific features of a research design can help protect the validity of a qualitative study.

First, duration and intensity of data gathering assure that a plethora of important events and details is recorded over time, involving all the important participants in the group and in many different situations and combinations. This prevents unique or unrepresentative events from receiving unwarranted attention and importance in the analysis. In quantitative designs, these unrepresentative events would be represented as *outlier data,* perhaps as a lone point separated from other observation points on a scattergram. Probability alphas (as will be discussed later) protect statistical analyses of quantitative data; time in the field and multiple, in-depth records of events protect qualitative analyses of data.

Second, rich and supportive data from a variety of sources improve the likelihood that a researcher will be able to create a valid description and complete a valid analysis. Consequently, qualitative researchers often practice *rich description,* the detailed, accurate, and vivid description of settings, people, and interactions similar to the skilled work of an essayist, nineteenth-century naturalist, or art or theater critic. Rich description challenges a scholar's writing skills, demanding accurate and vivid—not florid and hyperbolic—prose. Beginning researchers sometimes have difficulty keeping the purple prose out of their vivid descriptions; but, as with all writing, care, practice, and numerous revisions can hone the qualitative researcher's writing skills.

A rigorous qualitative research design must include safeguards against common threats to validity. Validity is most often threatened by:

1. history and maturation,
2. setting, participant, or context mortality,
3. observer or researcher effects on events and behavior, and
4. spurious conclusions.

The best safeguards against history and maturation spring from detailed, meticulous, and accurate records in which any history effects will appear. Mortality is a threat to all studies whether quantitative or qualitative. Carefully secured effective informed consent and positive relationships between researchers and subjects can help protect against mortality. (Researchers should also meticulously respect the important protections required by Institutional Review Boards for Research with Human Subjects described in Chapter 3, when designing qualitative research.)

Researcher effects may be very subtle, but any new member of a group will change in some way the mix of behaviors, actions, and unfolding events. Researcher effects can be minimized by a number of interventions. First, researcher effects often decrease significantly as the researcher spends an extended length of time in the setting and participants become accustomed to this presence. Recall that we discussed this natural outcome as an ethical dilemma for the ethnographer in Chapter 3. The observer becomes commonplace; people become accustomed to being observed and monitor and adjust their behavior less and less.

A second way in which researcher effects can be mitigated is to check with members of the social setting under study. The researcher should check discretely with insider informants for their observations of differences in behavior between times when the researcher is present and when the researcher is not. Often, a single informant can be asked to pay attention over time to these changes (researcher effects), and the researcher can take steps to acquire data about times when he or she is not present, seek other sources of data, and openly describe and acknowledge behavior changes in the report of findings.

Disengagement from the field provides another way to mitigate researcher effects on a study. Bias, beliefs, and perceptions of the researcher while deep within the group can color analysis, so it is best to leave the setting for the analysis phase of research. It is also prudent to interview participants who remain about any differences that emerge as time passes.

A final major threat to validity arises when researchers sometimes reach inaccurate or spurious conclusions from the data gathered. In the search for ways to mitigate against their own biases and beliefs, researchers must acknowledge that they have preferences for certain ways of knowing and kinds of knowledge, professional beliefs and knowledge about the phenomenon under study, and personal preferences. Even with quantitative data, researchers may misinterpret the meaning of their findings following the analysis of data, drawing false analogies or conclusions (see discussion in Chapter 4). In qualitative designs, a researcher can guard against spurious conclusions by:

1. asking for participants' feedback and reaction to emerging themes or conclusions (checking with participants),
2. maintaining contact with all participants in the setting and avoiding isolation,
3. maintaining contact neutrality and objectivity by avoiding forming close or personal relationships with a few participants,
4. disengaging from or leaving the site during final analysis,
5. seeking independent corroboration of data and analysis from multiple informants,
6. using multiple sources of data (documents, observations, interviews— see following sections),
7. deliberately seeking disconfirming evidence of negative cases as conclusions begin to coalesce,
8. asking colleagues and peers to examine and review data and to audit emerging findings and conclusions to see if they follow logically backward to the data, and
9. keeping a research journal that describes the research process in detail and the researcher's feelings and affective responses.

In summary, standards of rigor in qualitative research rely on processes that protect the reliability and validity of the study as surely as they do for other research methods. The principles of confirmability, dependability, and credibility are firmly grounded in rigorous qualitative research. Transferability also is a principle of qualitative research that accepts certain premises of positivism, based on assumptions about the replication of patterns in social science and theory development.

Earlier in this chapter, we pointed out that qualitative or "naturalistic" researchers often use different terms to describe principles of rigor than do social scientists using quantitative methods. Guba and Lincoln (1989) offered a comparison between terms based on quantitative and qualitative traditions that is useful in helping the new researcher draw comparisons. They argue that a rigorous design attends to the study's truth value, applicability, consistency, and neutrality. Truth value or internal validity leads to credibility. External validity or generalizability leads to applicability. Consistency or reliability leads to auditability (a traceable chain of logic). Neutrality or objectivity provides confirmability. Table 7.2 summarizes some helpful analogies between terminologies.

What beginning researcher would not want his or her study to be credible, applicable, consistent, and neutral? Issues of rigor must be resolved *in advance and during the design phase* in qualitative research, just as they must be addressed during the design phase in quantitative designs. Rigor cannot be rescued in the throes of the study when the researcher is enthusiastically embroiled in a setting with interesting and valued people engaged in socially valuable and admirable activities. Rigor also cannot be recovered during analysis if the data are fundamentally flawed by poor design and execution.

Data Collection

Because the data used in qualitative research come in the form of words—researchers' and participants'—some important principles affect the technical soundness of a research design using qualitative methods. These soundness principles relate directly to the preceding discussion of the general validity or trustworthiness of qualitative research. First, researchers should seek data from a variety of sources and of different types. This process of checking data sources and types is often called *triangulation* (see also Chapter 8). A researcher can triangulate data by drawing

TABLE 7.2 Standards of Rigor for Qualitative Research

Truth value or internal validity → Credibility
Generalizability or external validity → Applicability
Consistency or reliability → Auditability
Neutrality or objectivity → Confirmability

Source: Guba E. G., & Lincoln, Y. S. (1989). *Fourth generation evaluation.* Newbury Park, CA: Sage.

upon different kinds and sources of data (usually three or more, hence the term) or by utilizing a design involving multiple researchers (Lancy, 1993). A design may triangulate by employing interviews of people with very different points of view (teachers, students, parents, administrators), by gathering existing documents that provide multiple perspectives (school board minutes, faculty meeting minutes, school records), and by spending extended time in the field observing and recording behavior as it occurs.

The researcher also must practice questioning, listening, observing, and recording data. You will recall from our earlier discussion of the research process that we require all our students to practice the procedures and processes they will use to carry out their research before conducting the actual research activities. This can mean testing a survey on a group of people similar to the subjects, rehearsing an interview protocol, practicing with recording devices in settings similar to the research setting, or carrying out any other activity on which the research depends. In several contexts, we have referred to the qualitative researcher as the research instrument. This comparison is apt, because the quality of data analyzed is absolutely dependent on the quality of data recorded, and it takes practice and care to acquire these skills. Consequently, we ask our students to practice taking field notes and developing expanded field notes from audio and video tape, to write "thick description," and to prepare practice cases. Practice makes perfect is trite but true.

These practice techniques help prepare the qualitative researcher to collect research data. Three different types of data can be collected in qualitative research. The most common sources of data used in this tradition are *interview, observation,* and *existing documents* or *archival research.* Wolcott (1992) referred to these activities in everyday terms as *asking, watching,* and *reviewing.*

Interview/Asking

The interview is one of the most commonly used methods for gathering qualitative data (we also discussed interviews briefly in Chapter 6). In Wolcott's terms, the researcher asks those in the know. Interviews can be highly structured or completely open-ended, depending on the purpose of the interview, the researcher's familiarity with and knowledge about the setting, and the exploratory or confirmatory nature of the study. When designing an interview study, it is important to keep in mind important issues about the relationships between the research, the interview guide or protocol, and the respondent.

Asking requires questions and answers. Consequently, the interview process is highly interactive, and good interviewing techniques take considerable practice. The new researcher should not be discouraged, however, because a relaxed manner, asking questions well, note-taking, appropriate use of follow-up probes, establishing trust, and keeping track of responses come with time. The important thing for new researchers to remember is that research interviewing is a way of gathering data and differs substantially from the less formal interviewing they may have done in the past—interviewing a job applicant, for example. Detailed records, careful attention to the substance and affect of responses, and unfailing politeness will go a long way in improving the quality of the interview process and of the data gathered.

Advantages and Disadvantages of the Interview. As a data-gathering technique, interviewing is flexible, personal, subtle, and can provide information in great depth. It also is expensive, time-consuming, and vulnerable to manipulation by the subject and lack of thoroughness on the part of the interviewer.

Interviewing has a number of advantages as a data-gathering technique. First, while the actual format can be more or less detailed, a semistructured or open-ended interview is a more flexible way to gather data than the survey or other tightly constrained or preestablished methods. The respondent has the most detailed information and can enlighten the researcher about unfamiliar aspects of the setting or situation. The respondent, then, can add great insight, perspective, or even new issues that the researcher may not have predicted or anticipated in advance. Consequently, interviews provide a method for discovery research. Naturalistic interview techniques depend on as open a process as possible. With a willing and talkative subject, the entire interview may consist of only one major question, "Tell me about ...," followed by clarifying probes.

Second, interviews provide a method through which the meaning of behaviors and events for the people involved can be conveyed. Following observations, for example, the researcher may wish to interview participants and ask them why they said or did something or how they were feeling when something happened. The data are very personal, and personal perceptions and meanings thus have an opportunity to emerge during the interview process.

Third, since interviews are personal and provide personal perspectives, the researcher can gather information and perspectives that are unique to the individual being interviewed. While there are some circumstances in which group interviews can be useful—time is limited or the group's discussion and members playing off of each other provide important information—individual interviews offer the opportunity to gather data unaffected by other members of a group.

Finally, dialogue between interviewer and respondent is possible to clarify questions and responses, ask for more information, or follow up with probes that elicit additional information. When a response is not as detailed as the researcher would like or when a respondent's answer is ambiguous or unclear, the interviewer can rectify lack of clarity in the data on the spot. The interviewer also can request permission to call back or ask additional questions if they arise during data analysis and can establish a rapport or personal relationship that makes respondents more likely to agree to a follow-up. Follow-up questions are often the most important part of the interview process. They encourage more information but can also provide information to the respondent about the inquirer's attitudes and expectations, so care must be taken not to bias the respondent.

Interviewing also has disadvantages as a data-gathering technique. Many new researchers seriously underestimate the effort and skill required, and the quality of the data is totally dependent on the quality of the interview process.

The first major disadvantage of interviews is that they are time-consuming. They require that the researcher and respondent spend time one-on-one and often require travel and preparation time for the researcher. Each respondent must commit much more time to the research process than might be required for a written survey or more structured response format or for observation. Time also is consumed after the interview is over, transcribing audio tapes or preparing systematic field notes.

Second, interviews are labor-intensive. The researcher must be prepared to devote considerable effort and commitment to the research process. Often, an interview study requires that several research assistants be trained and employed to help gather data, and this can be very expensive. Not only is considerable effort required to collect the data, but, as we just pointed out, the preparation of systematic field notes or the transcription of interview tapes takes a great deal of labor and time. Substantial labor and time also are associated with data analysis. A rule of thumb used by many qualitative researchers is that *time in the field equals time in analysis.* In other words, if you take six months to interview, observe, and gather archival data, you should plan on at least six months of laborious data analysis. You soon may envy your friends who are "stat jocks" and run their analyses on computers overnight.

A third disadvantage of interviews as a data-gathering technique is the practice and skill required. Many educators or other social service professionals who have interviewed others for jobs or spent time talking with parents, students, or clients are surprised at the level of effort and skill required to elicit detailed, honest, and open responses during a research interview. The interview process takes intense concentration, the ability to listen, write, and anticipate a future question all at the same time, and strong human relations skills.

Informal interviews that occur naturally within a research setting also often require considerable memory and concentration. In some research settings (informal conversations, meetings, social interactions), note-taking is intrusive and inappropriate. While the researcher may have permission to conduct a study, the particular situation in which data are gathered make note-taking, taping, or other methods for re-cording responses impossible. The inquirer then must withdraw as soon as possible and depend on an accurate memory to record data. This post hoc note-taking requires meticulous attention to detail and sensi-tivity on the part of the researcher. Care should be taken to allow as little time as possible to pass before post hoc notes are recorded.

Fourth, interviews often sacrifice breadth for depth. They may pro-vide in-depth data while neglecting breadth of data because of the limitations of time and effort, the inability to interview everyone who has something to offer in a setting or situation, and the time-consuming nature of the process. Consequently, interviewing often is used in con-junction with other forms of data gathering to fill the need for in-depth data while not constituting the sole method employed.

Fifth, as previously noted, the reliability and validity of the data can be threatened by biases of the interviewer. If an interviewer is too encouraging or reveals a positive or negative attitude about the responses being given, there is serious danger of leading the witness, so to speak; yet it is important to be warm, courteous, and open. Respondents no-tice when their statements are being greeted with approval, and the simple process of head nodding can affect the nature of the data given. Interviewers may selectively record some data in greater detail because of researcher biases and leave out other data for the same reason. The interviewer is the instrument (see discussion of instrumentation as a threat to experimentation in Chapter 8), and biases affect the calibra-tion of the instrument and threaten the data as surely as a poorly ad-justed mechanical instrument. This is a major component of the re-searcher effects we referred to earlier.

Finally, interviews are a very inefficient way to gather some kinds of information. They are not appropriate for basic statistics, a broad range or survey of opinion, or for sampling general attitudes. Research-ers should carefully choose methods that sample broadly for these kinds of data and rely on interviews for more focused, in-depth data needs.

Interview Techniques. When designing research that involves in-terviews, researchers can ask themselves some simple questions that will help protect the quality of the process. These questions help the researcher prepare, ask good questions, record the data appropriately, and attend to the social context of the interview to assure the highest quality of data possible.

When getting ready to conduct an interview, one should ask: Who will conduct the interview? Should the principal investigator or some-one else interview respondents? Is there a same-sex or different-sex interviewer issue that needs to be addressed because of the social set-ting, beliefs of the respondents, or topic of the study? Are trust or pre-established relationships important? What reasons might there be for seeking an outside interviewer, such as preserving anonymity for the respondents? The subjects may be acquainted with the principal investigator, or there may be a power differential that threatens the quality of the responses. Besides the researcher, others who may become involved include: (1) someone to interview, (2) someone to record, (3) interviewers representing constituent groups (e.g., teachers, administrators, parents, students), and (4) friends and confidants of the respondent.

Another important question in the preparation process is: Who should be interviewed? This is not an idle question. The researcher may need to seek the answer in the original research questions or in the setting itself. One might ask an insider informant with whom the researchers should talk. Constituent groups should be represented, as should a broad range of opinions. If insufficient variance in responses seems to occur, the researcher should ask participants if there is anyone they should interview who does not agree with the majority in order to check the representativeness of responses. But the researcher should also constantly use the resources and knowledge of people within the research setting to make sure people possessing important information or representing important points of view are included. One also should seek a variety of perspectives (where one sits determines where one stands), deliberately search for outsiders/outliers who represent an important point of view or power source, and seek multiple sources for the same information to check for its confirmability. One can systematically sample people's views on various organizational levels and with various responsibilities relevant to the research question. To protect the reliability of the data, an interviewer must be especially careful to ask respondents only for data about which they have firsthand knowledge and that they can provide freely and candidly. Unlike experimental designs, qualitative research designs using interview techniques often allow the sample of people to be interviewed to evolve naturally as more is learned, the researcher follows hunches, and hypotheses and patterns suggest new directions for discovery.

After selecting the interview sample, the researcher should decide explicitly how the interview will be conducted. As we discussed earlier, individual interviews yield the most personal and possibly the most unique data, but they are costly in time and effort. Some alternatives can include interviewing members of groups in pairs or in groups. These decisions should take a number of important issues into account: (1) reliability, (2) candidness, (3) the protection of respondents' confidentiality and protection of the respondent from possible negative effects for participating, (4) the threat of "group think" in a group interview (Janis, 1982), (5) stimulation of ideas by others—spontaneity and liveliness, and (6) time constraints. The researcher should select a time and place for interviews and make appointments with respondents that can be meticulously kept. Respondents are doing the researcher a favor and giving of their time and information, and should be treated with the utmost consideration and respect. Interviewers can count on some subjects missing or forgetting appointments; this is simply part of the reality of field research.

Careful preparation in other areas is also important. A researcher should gather background data on the setting, selected respondents, and topics of interest and use existing documents and records, written accounts by others, or other interviews already conducted to prepare for each interview. This preparation can take a number of forms. First, as just noted, the researcher should make substantive preparation that will make it possible to avoid asking people what can be found out more efficiently in other ways. This is a waste of people's time and makes the interviewer appear too lazy to do important background work. Second, careful preparation provides stimulus for questions and the opportunity to be sincere and informed. Third, the interviewer should practice each specific interview protocol and develop interviewing skills to avoid wasting the respondent's time, repeating questions or appearing (and being) unorganized, and failing to get and record good information. An interviewer who knows the subject and the interview protocol will be relaxed, friendly, and expeditious in the interview process instead of fumbling for notes and checking for the next question while half-listening to an answer.

This planning process also includes the questions to be asked. Researchers should plan so that they ask good questions and do not "shoot from the hip." Most Institutional Review Boards for Research with Human Subjects ask a researcher to provide either preplanned interview guides, sample questions, or (at the very least) the topics, tactics, and directions all interviews will take. If open-ended or naturalistic interviews are planned, these must be accurately described so that the logic of discovery is justified. In most cases, a specific interview guide should be prepared in advance. This careful planning is important for several reasons: the interview will fit the person and the situation; important questions will not be forgotten or overlooked; the time the interview will take can be planned and respondents informed in advance how long the interview should last.

Several simple procedures can help make this advanced planning pay off with a successful interview. First, most researchers leave space directly on the interview guide for note-taking and plan explicit probes (follow-up questions) if the responses are stilted or not forthcoming or questions need clarification. If an interviewer asks follow-up questions not included in the guide, the questions should be written down in order to have a record of exactly what was asked that elicited a specific response. Audio tape recordings (and sometimes video tapes) provide verbatim records, but they are not always possible, and researchers sometimes do not have sufficient resources to transcribe all tapes.

Second, good interviews often begin with a broad, open-ended question that allows the respondents to answer however they choose. This provides the opportunity for respondents to talk openly and at length, puts them at ease, and provides high quality information without the interviewer prompting or unduly influencing the form and substance of the data. This tactic requires careful listening skills and familiarity with the interview guide in order to avoid asking questions later in the interview that the respondent already has answered.

Third, make certain interview questions use everyday language that is completely familiar to the person being interviewed. Research jargon is deadly in an interview.

Fourth, ask unambiguous questions that have been tested on people like those in the research population. Any time spent explaining questions is time wasted. It irritates the respondent and degrades the relaxed and trustworthy atmosphere of the interview.

Fifth, ask only one question at a time. Like survey research, interviews must give the respondent the opportunity to answer a given question, leaving no doubt about the connections between question and response. Additionally, when two or more questions are asked at the same time, respondents may be distracted or ramble, trying to think of what they are going to say next. Sometimes they may even be unsure whether they have answered the question or may leave out a part of their response so that the question must be asked again or rephrased.

Sixth, ask no leading questions. Researchers already know what they believe. The interviewer's task is to find out what the respondent believes or knows.

Seven, anticipate needs respondents might have for help thinking through an answer, and plan probes or follow-up questions in advance to prevent fumbling and uncertainty. Probes can provide clarification, elaboration, and encouragement. However, researchers should also learn to use silence—about three seconds or more—to encourage lengthier and more complete responses and to avoid prematurely cutting off a respondent who is thinking through a response. When an interviewer jumps in prematurely with the next question, the response is incomplete.

Eighth, interviewers must think fast on their feet and construct follow-up questions in the interview as they go. As a series of interviews is conducted, the researcher also will see patterns in the guide that require specific follow-up questions to improve the interviewing process. The researcher should always ask respondents at the end of the interview if it would be all right to get back to them if further questions arise or if clarification is needed later. This is, of course, possible only if the subjects have given their consent for their identity to be recorded in association with the data. If the interviewer has promised total anonymity (as distinguished from confidentiality), then no record identifying respondents may be kept. Anonymity is sometimes necessary in settings for which the safety or well-being of the respondents is unacceptably threatened by any existing record.

Ninth, questions should be posed in a context or setting that reminds, draws out, and increases the memory of the respondent. This also provides recognition and recall and improves the detail of the response. This is why the interviewer should travel to the respondents' environment if at all possible rather than asking respondents to come to an office or classroom.

Tenth, save the most difficult questions for the middle of the interview, and end on a less stringent note. Record the affect or tone of the interview and note any hostility, friendliness, reluctance or reticence, or general discomfort on the part of the respondent. The trustworthiness of the data depends on the interviewer's ability to assess the quality of the data provided. Table 7.3 summarizes the various steps important in conducting a qualitative research interview.

TABLE 7.3   Conducting a Qualitative Interview

Getting Ready

- What do you need to know?
- Is this the best way to learn what you need to know?
- Who will be interviewed?
- Who will do the interview?
- Where will the interview take place?
- How will the interview be conducted?
- Has enough time been planned to cover the questions; is the interview a reasonable length?

Asking Good Questions

- What adjustments in questions might be necessary to this particular situation?
- How should the questions be ordered; why is a particular order best in this situation?
- Are the questions unambiguous and do they contain only one question each?
- What follow-up questions or probes might be needed to get the most complete information?
- Do the questions suggest an answer the interviewer would prefer; do they put words in the respondent's mouth?

Keeping Track of Responses

- How will responses be recorded?
- What impact might the recording method have on the people being interviewed?
- Is the recording method acceptable and ethical in the situation?
- How does the recording method serve the best interests of the inquiry while protecting the respondent?
- What are the trade-offs between different recording methods in this particular situation?
- Does the interview guide apply to all the people you wish to interview; what adjustments might need to be made for people in particular roles or with different responsibilities?
- Does the interview guide provide sufficient flexibility?

(Continued)

TABLE 7.3 *(Continued)*

Understanding Your Effect/Affect?

- Does my relationship with this person inhibit their ability to be candid?
- Am I open and relaxed?
- Is a relationship of trust and rapport in place?
- Is the purpose of the interview clear to the respondent?
- What signals do I send the person being interviewed through eye contact, nonverbal cues, verbal reinforcement?
- Does the person being interviewed believe that the information will be kept confidential; will it?
- Can I expect to finish the interview without distractions; how will I prevent interruptions if possible?
- Can I compensate for the effect of distractions?
- Can I listen to what is said and keep the respondent's statements free of distortions?

Turn to Page 187 and complete Simulation 7.1

Recording the Data.   As we noted previously, interview data can be recorded in a number of ways. Some important guidelines help assure the accuracy and usefulness of recorded data.

First and foremost, researchers should take copious notes. This requires the ability to listen, think, and write at the same time. Although this process often is very accurate, it does leave room for disputation or controversy if only one person is in the room; but note-taking is often less obtrusive than tape recording. Many interviewers are beginning to use quiet laptop computers to record responses. People are becoming increasingly comfortable with their presence, many prefer them to tape recorders, and respondents can see immediately what the researcher has written if they would like to review an exact sentence or phrase. It also can be advantageous to use one interviewer and one note-taker; but trust, confidentiality, and spontaneity are more difficult under these circumstances.

Audio tapes are a common method for recording interviews. They are accurate and indisputable, but they can be very intimidating to some respondents. Tapes sometimes dampen candor, require greater trust, and often require assurances that the tape will be destroyed after the inquiry is completed, because voices can be recognized. Experienced researchers often recount experiences in which respondents have asked them to turn off the tape recorder before they will answer a particularly sensitive question or open up at the end of the formal interview when the tape recorder has been turned off. The transcription of tapes is very expensive, so researchers often request permission to tape an interview and then take copious notes that later can be expanded or developed into systematic field notes by checking sections of a tape.

Interviews are human interactions, and the interviewer affects the quality and quantity of data gathered directly. This point was also noted in Chapter 6. It requires practice to set an open and relaxed atmosphere during interviews. This atmosphere may depend on where the researcher and respondent sit, privacy, body language, or small talk.

The trust and rapport necessary for a successful interview often are a function of current or past interactions, but they can be notably affected by careful planning on the part of the researcher. For example, social workers and sociologists find that parents in economically disadvantaged neighborhoods who are themselves poorly educated often find the school an intimidating, even a hostile, place and are reluctant to go there. The school would be an inappropriate place to interview such parents.

A researcher also should be careful to make the purpose of an interview or conversation clear to the respondent. If possible and depending on the purpose of the interview, respondents should have the assurance of confidentiality. They also should have confidence that the inquirer will use discretion and that their responses will be free from distortion. If confidentiality is not possible, the respondent should know this at the outset before giving permission to be interviewed. Respondents have every right to immediately halt any interview that extends beyond the topic or scope to which they have agreed and to refuse to answer any or all questions (see effective informed consent discussion in Chapter 3). The researcher communicates the importance of the person being interviewed by assuring privacy, freedom from distractions, and respect. When respondents feel confident that their rights are being respected, they will be more likely to give useful and trustworthy responses.

Finally, as we pointed out earlier, you must not lead the witness. The interviewer must be careful about communicating attitudes to the respondent through eye contact, nonverbal encouragement and responses, or verbal reinforcement to responses. This leading process can be completely nonverbal and does not require that you say something as obvious as "Don't you think mainstreaming is a superior way to educate children with moderate intellectual disabilities?" Interviewing is a very personal process and can be successful or not depending on its nonverbal, interpersonal aspects. If researchers signal by their behavior that they are in a hurry, that interruptions are more important than the person being interviewed, that they value the response they are getting, and so on, they will influence the nature of the information.

Studies relying primarily on interview data can take the form of journalistic reporting (Guba, 1981), oral histories (Altenbaugh, 1991), anthropological life histories (Watson & Watson-Franke, 1985), or folklore and storytelling (Jackson, 1987; Miles & Huberman, 1994). This discussion is a very brief introduction to a highly developed data-gathering technique. We suggest that you see Spradley's *The ethnographic interview* (1979) for a more complete discussion of interviewing techniques and their application to qualitative methods.

Observation/Watching

Interviews provide a method for collecting data imbedded in the interpretations, perceptions, and experiences of respondents as just described. However, observation provides a direct method for the qualitative researcher to record human behavior and events as they occur—by watching. In Chapter 2, we introduced the concepts of participant and nonparticipant observation. The lines between these two kinds of observation are not as clear as this dichotomy suggests. An anthropologist might join in daily life, participate in ceremonies, and live side-by-side with the subjects as a form of participant observation. More purely, a sociologist might live as a tramp or homeless person on the street in complete anonymity and without the knowledge or consent of the subjects.

Other disciplines also experience the fuzzy line between participation and nonparticipation. Wolcott cautions that "most so-called participant observer studies in education warrant that label only in the sense that the researcher was physically present" because "researchers seldom become involved as genuine participants" (1992, p. 20). However, the level of detachment and involvement shapes much of the data, so researchers should be acutely aware of the differences and variations on these two techniques.

Nonparticipant Observation.   Nonparticipant observation strategies include nonreactive, unobtrusive research and the subjective approaches of criticism or connoisseurship (discussed in Chapter 15). The researcher, as Wolcott pointed out, is not directly engaged in central behaviors and activities within the situation under study. The observer is acknowledged by participants but is not involved. Research reports include studies of behavior in natural settings such as classroom interaction (Bossert, 1979), descriptions of social behavior based on patterns established in animal studies (Ambrose, 1978), connoisseurship/criticism studies that link the "art of appreciation" and the "art of disclosure" as a form of educational evaluation (Eisner, 1985, 1991), and vignettes or portraiture drawn from naturalistic field study (Lightfoot, 1983).

Participant Observation.   In Chapter 2, we pointed out that participant observation is a commonly used technique in anthropology. It is less common in other social and behavioral sciences. Participant observation, for example, "is particularly difficult for most adults in classrooms, playgroups, and other characteristic settings in the ethnography of schooling" (Spindler & Spindler, 1992, p. 64). The adult insiders in schools have a very difficult time performing or fulfilling their professional responsibilities while engaging in the intense activities associated with participant observation. Participants also face a major emotional and psychological challenge. Wolcott argued that "teacher researchers, the classroom's natural participant observers, encounter great difficulty disengaging sufficiently from personal experience to be convincing as 'detached' observers" (1992, p. 20).

Depending on the purpose and context of a study and the researcher's level of access to the setting, participant observation provides an in-depth opportunity for cultural analysis often necessary to produce a high-quality ethnography. While field study in general draws on the same data-gathering techniques as participant observation resulting in ethnography, the two are not synonymous. The participant observer spends extensive time in the setting waiting for particular core events to reoccur. Erickson compared this activity to a learning experiment in which the researcher is given "multiple trials at a similar task" (1992, p. 208). The research can "alter slightly the focus of analytic attention, each time attending to some features of what is occurring" and then focus on rereading and analyzing field notes and iterative experiences with observation and reflection to "develop an interpretive model" for the study. The participant observer, through active participation, can then test emerging models by trying them out.

Recording the Data. Data collection during observation can take many forms, including structured observation protocols and the use of mechanical devices such as videotapes and audio recordings. However, the most common method remains in-depth, comprehensive field notes prepared by the observer. The structure of field notes depends on personal preferences of the researcher, but generally includes the same three categories as field notes taken during an in-depth interview: (1) an objective, detailed description of the setting, events, statements, and actions observed, (2) a record of affective aspects of the observation, including observer responses and attitudes, and (3) reflections and preliminary sense making.

Like the interview, detailed observation takes practice. Many new researchers find it demanding to record the plethora of events and stimuli surrounding them in a research setting and report that it is surprisingly difficult to decide what to record. Careful sampling of people, events, and locations within the study's parameters helps alleviate the novice's tendency to be overwhelmed by the press of too much information and data during observation research, while protecting the reliability of data gathered. If you decide to undertake an observation study, be sure to spend time practicing data-recording and ask an experienced researcher to read and critique your field notes. The quality of data collected once the actual study begins will be well worth the time spent in preparation.

Advantages and Disadvantages of Participant and Nonparticipant Observation. We have referred in several places in this text to the various disadvantages and advantages of participant observation in relation to subjects' privacy and protection, research ethics, objectivity, and depth of inquiry. A discussion of the advantages and disadvantages of participant observation in many ways captures the emic/etic controversy we introduced in Chapter 4—insider insight versus outsider objectivity and analysis. The greatest strengths of participant observation are the depth of understanding and immersion available to the researcher; participation in the activities under study as a member of the group, allowing for personal experimentation with behaviors, attitudes, and experiences; time to distinguish the commonplace from the unusual in a setting; and access to cultural patterns that explain how the participants make sense of their own behavior and culture.

The disadvantages of participant observation include the tendency to focus on frequently occurring events, sampling bias, loss of objectivity through emotional attachment, and settling too early on a particular theory about the setting. The participant observer may be tempted to accept too quickly other participants' explanations for events and miss subtle features of the culture that are so familiar and taken for granted by insiders that they do not see them. Participant observation studies involving deception also face ethical problems with effective informed consent and the protection of subjects. Even when subjects know the participant is conducting a study, many may let down their guard more than they intended over time and forget about the implications and effects of the slice of life they are sharing.

The advantages and disadvantages of nonparticipant observation, like those of other methods we have discussed, tend to mirror those of participant observation. The nonparticipant observer has the advantage of objectivity and finds it easier to maintain emotional detachment. The etic perspective can be more probing, more analytical, and can uncover tacit, underlying subtleties in the research setting. Data can be recorded immediately as events occur, and the observer can interview participants to seek explanations and information. The method may require less time in the setting, and the nonparticipant observer can openly obtain effective informed consent and is free from some of the ethical dilemmas associated with participant observation. However, nonparticipant observers also sacrifice the in-depth time-in-field, insider insights and the affective association that is a major strength of elegantly prepared ethnographies.

***Turn to page 187-188 and
complete Simulations 7.2 and 7.3***

Existing Documents, Videotapes, and Film/Reviewing

In all literate societies, written (and sometimes audio and visual) records exist in archival form. By reviewing these records, the qualitative researcher can tap the history of the social group, culture, organization, or events central to the research. These records include such things as minutes of faculty meetings, newspaper and magazine articles, diaries, videotapes of teaching events, audio tapes of counseling sessions, memoranda, and correspondence. Archival records add data that are independent of the researcher's presence, interpretation, or preexisting theories. These sources provide different perspectives and cross-checks on forms of data gathered more directly. Materials prepared by and for others serve as an important resource for field research that complement data obtained directly.

Ethical Issues in Qualitative Research

Ethics play such a critical part in qualitative research approaches that they deserve revisiting. In addition to those issues raised in Chapter 3, we emphasize that the depth of qualitative researchers' knowledge and engagement in a research setting places particular stress on the need for confidentiality and discretion. Deyhle, Hess, & LeCompte (1992) present a description of covenantal ethics to frame the central demands of ethical conduct during qualitative research. This discussion provides a beginning for qualitative field researchers by emphasizing obligations among host societies and others involved. The researcher's primary responsibility is to the subjects/participants and emerges from the personal interactions involved in field work. However, conflicting commitments do arise, and researchers must constantly be on guard to question their own actions. They must attempt to "intrude as little as possible into the culture of the subject group in the process of gathering information," develop an understanding of the world they study, affect the setting as little as possible, and attempt a neutral role as much as possible (Deyhle, Hess, & LeCompte, 1992, p. 615). While unique relationships and trust must be formed to acquire high-quality, truthful data, the balance between friend and stranger roles must be maintained.

The way in which information is obtained and how it is disclosed also present challenges. We encourage you to reread frequently the chapter on ethical issues in research as a reminder of the need to continually question procedures and their effects on those being studied.

Comments

We have tried to emphasize throughout this chapter that qualitative methods are as varied as quantitative methods and rely on widely divergent assumptions about the nature of social reality. Only three main kinds of data are collected for qualitative research—observation, interview, and archival data—even though the research reports themselves may emphasize very different aspects of the situation under study. Beginning researchers should plan to study and practice the techniques of qualitative research as systematically and carefully as they might prepare for any other form of rigorous research in order to make the endeavor worth doing and the results worth reading.

Simulations

Simulation 7.1

Topic: Preparing an Interview Guide

Background Statement: The quality of data acquired through the interview process in large part depends on the congruence between the interview's purpose and design and on the quality of the researcher's preparation. An interview guide or protocol, carefully constructed to elicit the maximum amount of data with the minimum amount of participation by the interviewer, is part of this important preparation.

Tasks to Be Performed: As an experienced researcher, you have been called by the chair of the resource education team at a large middle school in your community for help with a puzzle. The standardized tests used to diagnose student problems have failed to provide adequate information about students' educational needs. Several students the team thought would do very well are failing miserably and others in the program whose disabilities seemed more serious are thriving. The resource team suspects that differences in the students' homes may hold clues to the surprising performance of some students. Parents have agreed to talk about their parenting skills, and the team has asked you for advice about the design and conduct of the interviews. What would you advise the team as they design their parent interview study?

For feedback see page 189.

Simulation 7.2

Topic: Participant and Nonparticipant Observation

Background Statement: Participant and nonparticipant observation techniques have very different advantages and disadvantages. The gains in insight obtained through participation may be offset by ethical dilemmas and entanglements. Each field researcher must carefully balance these advantages and disadvantages when deciding how immersed in the research setting to become.

Tasks to Be Performed: Collaboration among educators and social service agencies within schools has been touted as an important innovation for the service of children's needs. You have been asked by the director of human services at your state social service agency to study the working relationships, strengths, and weaknesses emerging in an elementary school where social workers, community recreation counselors, and teachers are experimenting with a combined service program. Student learning is a major concern, as is family functioning, social well-being, and student self-concept. You are designing your study and are struggling with the decision whether to observe as a participant or nonparticipant. Prior to pursuing a research career, you worked for several years as a social worker and hold a Master of Social Work degree. What are the advantages and disadvantages of participant observation (including deceit) or nonparticipant observation. Which will you finally recommend? Why?

For feedback see page 190.

Simulation 7.3

Topic: Designing Qualitative Research

Background Statement: The methodology chosen for a study in behavioral research should be directly tied to the nature of the research question. While scholars often develop preferences for some methodologies, in part because of their view of social reality and the best way to study social questions, research designs should emanate from the question rather than the researcher's pet method.

Tasks to Be Performed: The time has come to prepare the proposal for your master's thesis and defend it to your advisor and supervisory committee. You have focused your studies on the relationships among adolescents in peer-counseling groups, and you would like to conduct your research on peer counseling. You are considering qualitative methods but are not sure whether they are appropriate. What design questions should you ask yourself before choosing a method? Under what conditions will your interest in peer counseling lend itself to qualitative methods and what data-gathering methods would you recommend? Why?

For feedback see page 190.

Simulation Feedbacks

Simulation 7.1

The advantages of the interview are: (1) it is flexible and can uncover information about the setting that the interviewer did not know, (2) it can convey the meaning of events for those participating, (3) it provides a way to gather detailed information about the situation from the participant's point of view, revealing personal perspectives that are unique to the individual, and (4) it can clarify the responses to questions emerging from other data, provide information not available elsewhere, and offer the opportunity for elaboration and explanation.

The interviewers should design their questions so that the parents can provide information about the students that the educators cannot get anywhere else. Questions should ask about the importance of school in the family and the students' feelings about school. They should elicit what a test means to the child, if the child has talked about tests, homework, assignments, or other activities with the parent(s), and how the child has described these experiences. Questions should query the parents about reading, conversation, sleep, eating, and other family patterns that are known to affect student performance and should ask for the parents' feelings about these family patterns in relation to the child's school work. Finally, the interview questions should provide a way to ask parents specific questions related to their children and their own work. Examples of school work accompanied by questions about what the parents think a child might have meant in a response, portrayed in an artwork, or assumed from a question in the schoolwork will give the researchers a personalized view of the world from the child's family's perspective.

The researchers also should carefully question who will conduct the interview for each family. If racial, religious, or social class tensions exist in the neighborhood, or if gender bias might cause parents to respond in a particular way, interviewers should be matched to the families to secure the most trustworthy responses. Parents should be treated with all the respect of any research respondent, including requests for permission to tape, assurances of confidentiality, and reminders that they are not required to answer every question and may halt the interview at any time if they wish.

Before each interview, the researchers should gather all data available about the child at the school and read and review the data. Questions should be carefully personalized to child and parents whenever possible. Reviewers must take care not to ask the parents for information about the child that the school has or should have.

Finally, the procedures for each interview should be carefully laid out—who will interview, how will the interview be recorded, etc.

Simulation 7.2

This situation is fraught with problems for you, a committed social service professional in a previous career stage, and for the professionals working in the setting you plan to study. Social service professionals have a culture of giving and helping that may fundamentally block your ability to conduct the study without intervening as a professional to rectify problems you see.

You should ask yourself some very hard questions about the purposes of the study, your own temperament, the protection of your subjects and their right to fully informed consent, and the data trade-offs that would come with either a participant or nonparticipant design for the study.

Simulation 7.3

Qualitative methods are suited to research questions that: (1) require natural surroundings, (2) examine unfolding and uncontrolled events, (3) require the exploration of reasons for behavior and the ways in which behavior unfolds, (4) need exploration, explanation, description, and illustration, and (5) involve small sample sizes or when few global settings exist. What features of peer counseling match these advantages of qualitative methods? Be specific. What questions are you asking about peer counseling, and do they lend themselves to a deductive approach with clearly definable hypotheses and tests or are they indistinct and unclearly delineated? Are you able to control the variables and phenomena of interest in your study or are they naturally occurring and outside your control within a reasonable context? All these questions need to be answered before you can answer the question: Should I use a qualitative design for my study and if so, what kind of qualitative design?

Chapter 8

Potential Design Pitfalls

In the last few chapters we have examined some key elements of designing experimental, nonexperimental, and qualitative research. These discussions included some basic design formats and considerations for the initial conceptualization of an investigation. However, the designing of a study is far from complete with only the initial conceptualization considered.

It was mentioned earlier that the planning and execution of a study seldom, if ever, fit a particular textbook example. Often the specific study being planned will require slight (or even major) variations on the basic designs discussed thus far. Each situation (i.e., setting, materials, subjects) presents a unique set of problems to be solved in order to execute a sound investigation. Some of these problems have been mentioned or alluded to in previous chapters. In most cases, steps may be taken *before* the study is actually begun to substantially reduce the effects of such problems on the investigation. It is important to note the emphasis on *before* in this statement. Thorough planning is perhaps the most essential component in sound research. Although this has been emphasized earlier, it is so crucial that it remains as a major theme throughout the text. Without a great deal of thoughtful planning before the investigation is begun, there is a considerable chance that the study will fail or, at a minimum, have serious weaknesses. This chapter focuses on some of the potential problems that may be encountered in conducting research—qualitative as well as experimental-quantitative. Although these are also textbook examples, they represent crucial *types* of pitfalls that should receive consideration in planning and designing studies.

Design Validity

Understanding design validity is vital to a conceptual grasp of all research design. Use of the term *validity* in this context is somewhat different from its use in test and measurement areas. In the arena of research design, validity might be viewed as referring to the technical soundness of a study. As a researcher designs an investigation, attention must be given to various types of validity to safeguard against problems that may prevent meaningful implications from being drawn from the results. As we discuss this topic it is important to note that investigation validity is always *approximate.* Science is a process that attempts to provide the best possible information regarding the truth (or lack thereof) of some statement, hypothesis, or explanation of a phenomenon. Investigators are continually attempting to provide the most trustworthy information possible.

Two types of research validity are of primary concern to beginning researchers planning an experiment—internal and external validity. Internal and external validity were described over 30 years ago by Campbell & Stanley (1963). Although these concepts have been refined and expanded somewhat (e.g., Cook & Campbell, 1979; Cook & Campbell, 1990), their basic form has served many working in experimental research design.

Internal validity has been equated in Chapter 7 with credibility. An experiment that is internally valid is characterized by having successfully controlled (or accounted for) all *systematic* influences between the groups being compared *except* the one under study. This, of course, is the core of the *concept of control* discussed earlier. If, for example, one were comparing two groups of children and the experimental variable was treatment method, it would be desirable to have the only systematic difference between the groups be treatment method. Figure 8.1 illustrates the type of design that might be involved.

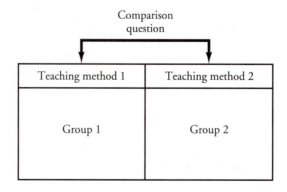

FIGURE 8.1 Design Comparing Two Methods of Teaching

As indicated by the double arrow in Figure 8.1, the research question involves the effectiveness of treatment method 1 as compared with the effectiveness of treatment method 2. The differences between method 1 and method 2 are systematic differences in the sense that one group is systematically treated with method 1 whereas the second group is systematically treated with method 2. Any other systematic differences between groups 1 and 2 may result in performance differences that would appear to be the result of the treatment method but really would not be. Consequently, to design an internally valid experiment, the researcher must eliminate all systematic differences between groups 1 and 2 except treatment method.

This same basic principle for internal validity applies to quantitative nonexperimental research when comparisons are involved. An example of such a situation may be found in a survey study in which the researcher wants to determine whether or not there is a difference between Democrats and Republicans in terms of annual income. In this case the researcher would try to make the study internally valid by ensuring that the *only* difference between the groups was their political affiliation. More detailed discussion of such cases will be presented as they are encountered in the text.

External validity refers to the question of *generalizability*. Here we are primarily concerned with what circumstances the results can be generalized to beyond those in which the study was executed. External validity speaks to the issue of how much the research setting (subjects, environment, measures, manipulated variables) is like the world about which the investigator wishes to say something. Is the sample sufficiently representative that the researcher can accurately say something about the population being studied? Figure 8.2 illustrates the nature of external validity or generalizability questions.

As before, the arrows in Figure 8.2 represent the questions being asked. How well do the results of a given investigation represent or apply, in terms of the population presumably being studied and the environment in which this population resides? Additionally, are the measures recorded representative of performance criteria that may apply in the outside world? If treatment variables are involved in the study, do they represent something that may serve as a treatment in the world outside the research setting? If a survey is involved, does the survey ask questions that are relevant to the world outside the interview or questionnaire setting? Are the questions asked in a manner that respondents can answer similarly to an "everyday" answer?

To summarize, internal validity refers to the technical soundness of an investigation. A study is internally valid to the degree that influences, beyond that variable under investigation, have been removed or minimized as systematic effects. External validity, on the other hand, speaks to the issue of generalizability. An investigation is externally

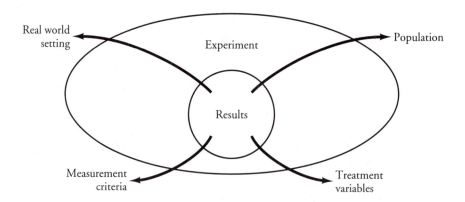

FIGURE 8.2 External Validity Questions Generalizability of Results to the World Outside the Investigation

valid to the degree that the arrangements, procedures, and subjects are representative of the outside setting, thus making results generalizable.

External and internal validity are sometimes at odds with each other. The logistics involved in designing an internally valid experiment occasionally mitigate against the achievement of as much generalizability as is perhaps desirable. This idea has already been encountered in the discussion of different research approaches. Approaches that exercise a great deal of environmental control (such as some laboratory experiments) may have great internal validity but may be less externally valid because of the artificial setting. Other experiments may have greater external validity if the environment remains more natural (e.g., an intact classroom), but internal validity may be reduced to some degree. Thus beginning researchers should realize that a given study may sacrifice some degree of either internal or external validity to achieve a greater degree of validity from the other perspective.

Maximally meaningful research must thus be thought of in terms of *programs* of research that often involve a series of different but programmatically related studies. Experiments conducted in the initial phases of a research program may sacrifice some degree of external validity to more precisely study the variables involved. Alternatively, later phases of a research program may sacrifice some degree of internal validity to achieve a better perspective of how the phenomena under study operate in the world outside the laboratory. Only the cumulative synthesis of evidence obtained in such a program of research will result in meaningful and precise changes in practice.

Design validity for qualitative investigation takes a very different form from that described above for quantitative experimentation. In qualitative research the concern still involves providing the best, most trustworthy information possible. Here, however, the issues are (1) minimizing influences of the researcher on results (researcher effects) and (2) the basic trustworthiness of the interpretation or explanation.

Minimizing researcher effects involves two broad sources of error that need attention—bias and alterations in subjects' behavior because of the observer's presence. It is important to minimize or eliminate the effects of a researcher's biases (e.g., the three P's—partiality, prejudices, and preconceptions) in both data collection and the analysis/interpretation phase. Without concern for bias, the information may be read as being an accurate representation when in fact it may be seriously slanted by preconceptions or partiality. Researcher effects also come into play by virtue of the observer's presence in the research setting. Subjects may act differently than they would otherwise, thereby giving an inaccurate picture of the circumstances. Researcher effects are serious threats to qualitative investigation, particularly because a major goal of qualitative studies is to portray a natural-state situation.

The trustworthiness of the interpretation or explanation is also a serious issue in qualitative research. This involves a number of factors, but an illustration will serve well at this point. Qualitative researchers often obtain information or data from several informers in the environment being studied. As the investigators collect such information, they begin to formulate explanations regarding matters such as what happened or why some event occurred. These become the data and clearly have a substantial impact on interpretations or explanations that emerge from the study. What steps can be taken to circumvent erroneous information coming from the informants? Such misinformation might surface because an informant saw events from a prejudiced, incomplete, or inaccurate viewpoint. It might also be the case that they lied. At any rate, it is very risky to make an interpretation or explain events based on one informant. Qualitative researchers use what is known as *triangulation* to build validity into their database. Triangulation refers to the use of multiple sources of information to obtain data (Lancy, 1993). These sources might include multiple informants, written documents or records, and any other information source that can be used to construct an accurate account of what happened. If the researcher receives the same basic story from triangulated sources, the data can be considered more trustworthy than if only one informant provides it. This enhances the validity of the research.

The design validity is crucial to the value of information obtained from an investigation whether that study uses quantitative experimentation or qualitative methods. In all cases one is *not* faced with a study that either is or is not valid—it is not a binary situation. There are degrees of technical soundness in all investigations irrespective of methodology employed. As we examine various threats to design validity you will see that there is no perfect investigation. We just keep chipping away in attempts to maximize strengths and minimize limitations.

Threats to Experimental Design Validity

Internal Validity

As we examine experimentation we find several types of influences that threaten internal validity. Each type may be operative in a variety of designs. In the following discussion, the respective threats will be examined in the context of several vulnerable designs. As the reader continues through this chapter, two points should be kept in mind. First, it is important to avoid as many threats as possible to conduct the most rigorous study feasible under the circumstances. Second, it is difficult, if not impossible, to totally eliminate all problems; nearly every study conducted has some area in which it could be strengthened. After all threats that can be circumvented have been taken care of, those remaining are something that must be lived with, so to speak, and interpretation of results must account for them.

History.   The term *history,* for experimental design purposes, refers to *specific incidents in addition to the treatment that intervene between measurement points.* The definition is critical since this is a different meaning than that commonly used for the term. As suggested by this definition, history is a threat to internal validity when the researcher is obtaining repeated measures or more than one observation on the same subjects. History represents a threat to internal validity that is difficult to circumvent. One major cause of this difficulty is that the experimenter may be unaware of historical events, and there is little that can be done in advance to prevent their occurrence. Several designs are vulnerable to this type of problem.

History may obviously affect the pre-post design in traditional group experiments. It may also influence time-series experiments if the historical event occurs at about the same time as the intervention. Additionally, history may be a potential contaminator in quantitative nonexperimental studies. For example, it may cause a problem when an incident occurs between two interviews with the same subjects. Perhaps the factor under study was merely the passage of time between the two interviews—but something traumatic also occurred during that time. To more fully discuss the history threat, some examples will be examined in greater detail.

It was just noted that history may threaten pre-post designs in group experimental studies. Suppose an investigator is conducting an experiment concerned with the effects of certain exercises on overall physical fatigue. The study is being undertaken with sixth graders and involves the administration of a pretreatment measure followed by the exercises, which, in turn, are followed by the posttreatment measure. Figure 8.3A represents a visual diagram of the experimental design. This investigation is asking a difference question. As represented by the double arrow in Figure 8.3A, the researcher will be comparing the pretest scores with the posttest scores to determine if there is a difference.

Ostensibly the only major event between these two measures is the treatment, which in this case involves certain physical exercises. Assuming that the study is internally valid, any differences between pretest and posttest performance should primarily be a result of the treatment. This may or may not be the case. History might serve to threaten the internal validity of the study. Suppose the time required for this hypothetical experiment is about two hours. The experiment is initiated at 9:00 A.M. and proceeds through the pretest and the treatment by 10:30. At this time, recess is scheduled and the children go to the playground, where a serious fight erupts. The fight involves several children from the experiment and continues for nearly 10 minutes before it is broken up. At the end of recess, the children in the experiment re-

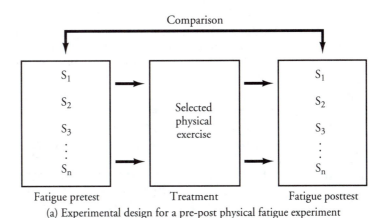

(a) Experimental design for a pre-post physical fatigue experiment

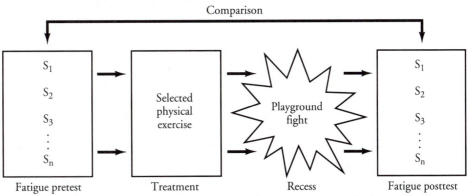

(b) Experimental design for a pre-post physical fatigue experiment with a history threat

FIGURE 8.3

turn and take the posttreatment fatigue test. In analyzing the data, the researcher finds that the measures on the posttest show significantly greater fatigue than the pretest scores. If the experimenter is unaware of the specific event (playground fight), it might be logical to conclude that the physical exercises involved in the treatment seem to produce a significant general fatigue effect in sixth-grade children. Naive concerning the history contaminator, the experimenter assumes that the design in Figure 8.3A is operating when, in fact, the data are most probably generated in the design represented in Figure 8.3B. There are two major experiences that the children encountered between the pretest and posttest. The resulting difference in scores could have been caused by either the treatment, the fight, or a cumulative effect of both. Inferences that the selected exercises generated the observed general fatigue may be in error.

How does one circumvent specific history events that may be operative in addition to the treatment? As noted previously, this is difficult because history is often out of the control of the researcher. If the researcher *is* aware of these events, a judgment must be made whether or not the events have a high probability of influencing results. This type of judgment is subjective, but if the history incident is related to either the treatment or the measure, it probably has seriously weakened internal validity. The example given represents a situation in which the measures and treatment are most likely related to the specific event. In such a case the study is probably destined for a new start. If, on the other hand, the experimenter judges little or no effect as a function of history, the incident should be mentioned in the report and a rationale should be presented concerning why it was judged to have no substantial influence. (There is no way that the experimenter could legitimately conclude that the fight did not affect fatigue at all.)

There are some preventative measures that a researcher may take to lower the probability of history looming as a threat to internal validity. Naturally, when experimental logistics permit, a shorter period between pretest and posttest is desirable. This collapsing of the time span simply does not allow as much time for history to intervene. The study, however, may not permit such a short time frame. An experimenter can also attempt to avoid times when there is a high probability of history intervening, such as recess or the lunch period.

History may also threaten the internal validity of a time-series experiment such as is often used in behavior modification studies. As noted in Chapter 5, this type of investigation is characterized by various data-collection phases. Data are collected before the treatment or intervention to establish the baseline rate of the behavior being studied. After the experimenter is satisfied with the reliability of observation and stability of behavior frequency, treatment will be initiated in phase B. Figure 8.4 illustrates a hypothetical experiment using the A-B design described in Chapter 5.

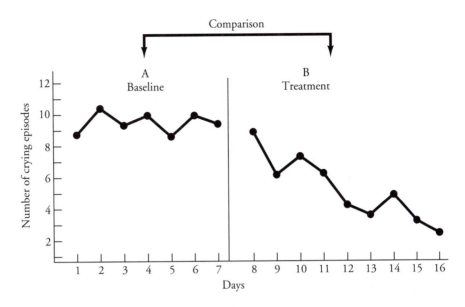

FIGURE 8.4 Example of a Data Display from a Hypothetical Experiment Using an A-B Design

This type of study is asking a difference question as suggested by the double arrow indicating comparison. Did the treatment make a difference? Is there a difference between baseline behavior frequency and that which was recorded after the intervention was initiated? The intervention or *experimental variable* may have been some aversive stimulus or reinforcement condition. The researcher, who is interested in the effect of the experimental variable (treatment), is assuming that the treatment under study was the cause of the change in behavior frequency. If some specific event *other than the treatment* occurs simultaneously with the intervention, history may be serving to threaten internal validity in the study. The change in behavior frequency evident in Figure 8.4 may be a result of the intervention, the specific history event, or a combination of the two. If the experimenter were to draw a conclusion that suggested the intervention as the cause of behavior changes, it might be in error.

Again, circumventing history as a threat may present serious problems. The researcher may do several things to guard against this threat in this type of experiment, however. First and most important, this type of experiment is often replicated numerous times before a researcher begins to draw implications from results. The chances that any particular event might systematically occur in close proximity to the intervention over a series of studies is low. Thus the data will begin to center around the effects generated by the treatment over a series of replications. Often the researcher will reverse experimental conditions (using an A-B-A-B design) after behavior has stabilized. Here again, the chances of the specific event either reversing or in some other way operating simultaneously with both intervention and reversal are low. Additionally, the use of multiple-baseline procedures has resulted in lowering the threat of history. The multiple-baseline design allows us to study treatment effect on a given subject using several target behaviors (it also has other variations as noted in Chapter 5). The probability of accidental historical incidents occurring at staggered intervals that coincide with all phase changes in a multiple-baseline design is very low. However, once again the researcher should avoid (if possible) scheduling interventions close to high-risk times when history influences are probable.

History may also represent a contaminating influence in research in which repeated measures are taken on the same subjects with only the passage of time between data recording sessions. In such a study, a researcher may be conducting an interview survey such as the brief example mentioned earlier. For example, say the investigator was interested in respondents' attitudes regarding sex as a function of phases of the moon. This might mean that an interview would be conducted during the full moon and a second interview with the same subjects during the new moon period. It would be the aim of the researcher to attribute any attitudinal differences between the two times to the different phases of the moon (a *simple* comparison survey). This would be contaminated by a history threat if, for example, a nationally televised traumatic incident related to sex intervened between the two interviews. Differences in attitudes might be caused by the moon phases, the traumatic event, or both, making results uninterpretable. Such a history threat may seriously influence results and make attribution of results to the experimental variable most difficult.

History, in the form of specific intervening events aside from the treatment or variable under study, represents a grave threat to internal validity. As is evident from the preceding discussion, the potential for weakening an investigation is present in several research approaches. In all cases, the basic idea of research design is violated. To be internally valid, a study must permit attention to the question being asked (the effects of the experimental variable) without influences from factors that are not a part of that question (influences other than the experimental variable). Once again, the concept of control is centrally involved.

Maturation. Maturation represents a second threat to the internal validity of an investigation that serves to plague behavioral scientists. Distinctive from history problems, maturation refers to factors that influence subjects' performance because of time passing rather than specific incidents. Maturation influences include such examples as growing older, hunger, and fatigue. These processes become threats to internal validity in cases in which they operate *in addition* to the variable(s) being studied. This category of threat is of concern in longitudinal research such as that conducted in human development, in which the actual growth process is involved. From the definition it also seems that maturation, in terms of hunger, fatigue, and similar such factors, may threaten a myriad of other types of research. It may be useful to explore some of the designs that are particularly vulnerable to maturation as a threat to internal validity.

Behavioral researchers often wish to observe the effects of a treatment that requires a long time, long enough to be considered a *longitudinal study*. Longitudinal designs are one of the two major approaches to research used by human development investigators, the other being termed *cross-sectional*. In longitudinal studies a single sample of subjects is repeatedly observed or tested over an extended period of time—perhaps years. Cross-sectional studies attempt to gather developmental data but not by following the same subjects over time. Cross-sectional investigators sample different groups of subjects representing several age levels (e.g., 3 to 5, 6 to 8, 9 to 11, 12 to 15). They then test or observe subjects in each group and compare across groups. Both approaches are basically attempting to draw conclusions regarding the passage of time (e.g., aging). If the *variable of time passage* represents a primary interest, then there is not an internal validity problem. However, there are situations in which an investigation may be addressing a treatment other than time but still involve a lengthy study period which may present maturation internal-validity difficulties. This is common, for example, in situations in which a school district is experimenting with a new type of program. Usually such a program assessment is approached in a general fashion that includes a pretest, the program as a treatment, and a posttest with the time involved representing a full academic year. Such investigations are replete with internal validity problems; for the purposes of this discussion, however, maturation will remain the primary focus.

The school district example above is essentially a pre–post design similar to the one diagrammed in Figure 8.3A, with a long treatment period. If the researcher proceeds with a single group, administering pretest, treatment, and posttest, a difference question is presumably being asked. This might be phrased: Was there sufficient difference between pretest and posttest performance to be significant? The inference basically involves the amount of change between the two measures. Because the assumption is that the study is being conducted with a purpose in mind (although the frustrated teacher may wonder what the purpose is, since "nothing ever changes"), the effectiveness of the treatment would seem to be directly involved in that purpose. In short, the researcher is probably attempting to attribute any difference between

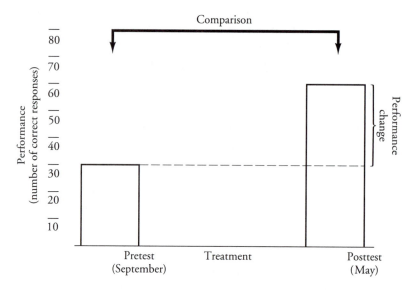

FIGURE 8.5 Hypothetical Data from a Weak Program Evaluation

the two performance measures to the treatment. The following is a brief explanation of why the investigator probably cannot attribute pretreatment versus posttreatment differences to the treatment.

Suppose, for the moment, that Figure 8.5 represents a graph of the data obtained in this study. Assuming the difference in mean scores is statistically significant, the researcher then must say something about the performance change. If an inference is drawn that the performance change is attributable to the treatment (experimental program) with no more information than the researcher has, that interpretation may well be in error. How does the investigator know that the performance change was caused by the treatment and not by the subjects' maturation? A full academic year is involved and it would be expected that as the children grow older, they will probably perform better on most academic tasks as a function of maturation. This would be particularly true with younger children. Thus the performance change might be caused by the treatment, the subjects' maturation, or both.

The question then arises regarding how the researcher might avoid or circumvent the maturation factor, which threatens internal validity in the manner suggested. With only one group, this is very difficult. To be able to say much about the amount of change that is a function of the program, the investigator needs an estimate of how much change is expected as a result of maturation. If evidence exists regarding the amount of change *on the criterion measure* that can be expected if the children do nothing but grow, change in excess of this amount ought to be due to the treatment. For example, say the children can be expected to improve by 20 correct responses on some imaginary test merely as a function of maturation. If this is true, improvement beyond that amount might be thought to be caused by the treatment. In the example in Figure 8.5, there was an average of 30 more correct responses on the posttest than the pretest. If an average gain of 15 responses is expected as a function of maturation, an improvement of about 15 responses may be thought to be a result of the treatment.

In reality, the approach to avoiding a maturation threat just mentioned above is generally not possible. First of all, the necessary solid evidence regarding untreated growth is seldom available. Even if it is available, what reason is there to think that the subjects in the study are like those from which the evidence was obtained? There are more technically sound approaches to minimizing the maturation threat to interpretation for this type of study.

In most cases, the nature of the research question suggests using multiple experimental groups. The study just discussed would probably compare the new school program with the program that had been serving the purpose previously. Certainly the selection of the new program over what was previously used must be justified (just try to get the Board of Education to hand over the money without justification). Figure 8.6 provides a visual representation of this design. In this type of design, difference questions are still being asked, but some additional elements have been included.

The design represented in Figure 8.6 has changed the question to a degree. It now appears that the effects of two instructional programs are being compared. As indicated by the double arrows, pretest versus posttest performance differences are still of interest. If subjects are randomly assigned to groups 1 and 2, the two groups should not be different on the pretest. This should be confirmed as a precaution after the pretest has been administered, but before beginning the treatment. If the groups are different, they should be placed back into the larger pool and the random assignment repeated. If the groups are not different on the pretest, the researcher is able to say much more about any differences that might exist on the posttest performance.

In a sense, the design portrayed in Figure 8.6 is still vulnerable to maturation. If there is substantial change between the pretest and posttest scores (comparison *A*), it is still not known how much was caused by treatment. There is a more solid basis, however, for saying something about the relative strength of the programs being studied. Since both groups are involved in the treatment for the same length of time, both groups of children are assumed to have the same opportunity to mature. Therefore, if one group makes greater pre-post gains than the second group, other things being equal, that greater gain might well be

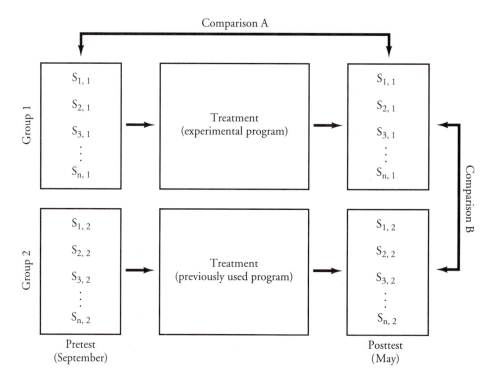

FIGURE 8.6 Hypothetical Design for a One-Year Program Comparison

attributed to a more effective program. To effectively assess the maturation gain a third comparison group is probably necessary. This third group, as suggested by Figure 8.7 would also be randomly generated but would not actually receive a treatment per se other than a placebo. *Placebo,* in this context, has the usual meaning, the sugar pill that makes patients think they are being treated when they are not.

The design represented in Figure 8.7 is an efficient design because it compares the new experimental program with the previously used program and simultaneously permits an estimate of how much change is caused by maturation. This is accomplished by using two types of difference comparisons: comparison *A* looking for pre–post differences within groups and comparison *B* looking for differences between groups on the posttest. For example, on comparison *A* for group 1, the differences between pretest and posttest performance may be caused by maturation, treatment, or both. If, however, the comparison *A* changes for group 1 are viewed in light of comparison *A* changes for group 3, more meaningful statements can be made. Group 3 receives a placebo as a treatment. The nature of this placebo activity is critical in that it must be *similar but unrelated* to the treatment. It is not desirable for the placebo to instruct in the sense that the programs under study do, since an assessment of maturation is desired. For the moment, assume that there is an appropriate placebo. Comparison *A* differences that occur in group 3 can be assumed to be caused by maturation. Any comparison *A* differences that occur in excess of the group 3 changes might then be attributed to a treatment for either group 1 or group 2. Thus it is possible to begin to say how much change is caused by maturation and how much is caused by instruction (ignoring test practice for the moment).

The *B* comparisons then permit attention to another dimension. Comparison *B* between groups 1 and 2 provides some evidence regard-

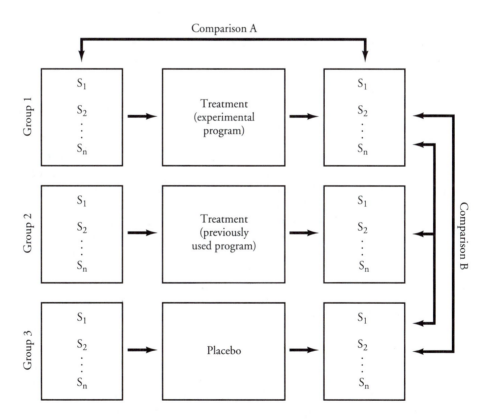

FIGURE 8.7   Hypothetical Comparison Design That Also Assesses Maturation

ing the relative effectiveness of the two instructional programs. *B* comparisons between either group 1 or 2 and group 3 permit an assessment of how effective the respective instructional program is relative to the situation that would exist if no instruction per se were provided (group 3).

It is necessary to address the pragmatic considerations of conducting such a study in the field. The value of randomly assigning subjects to the groups is obvious because with this done, a researcher has a powerful technique for equalizing groups before the experiment begins. In a school setting this may not be possible. If not, the design is seriously weakened. A second problem might be generated if the three treatment conditions (experimental, previously used, and placebo) have to be implemented by three different teachers. In such a situation, the teacher differences are systematic, one in each group, and performance differences between groups might be a result of teacher effectiveness as much as of the variables under investigation. (Imagine the difficulty in saying anything about treatment effectiveness if the teacher for group 1 is a "star," the teacher for group 2 is average at best, and the one for group 3 is terrible.) It might be more advantageous to have all three groups taught by one person for the portion of each day involving the treatment. Even this approach would necessitate careful training to minimize differences between the teacher's preference for one treatment over the others. It becomes evident that this type of investigation is vulnerable to design problems on several fronts and requires careful attention and planning.

The study just discussed above vividly represents the maturation difficulties encountered in a longitudinal investigation. Pre-post designs that involve even a period as short as a day also are subject to maturation problems such as hunger and fatigue. Their contaminating effects can be viewed from the same perspective used in the example for maturation in terms of growth. Control or comparison groups, which were suggested to estimate the effects of maturation for the longitudinal study, function in much the same fashion with a study of shorter duration.

Maturation also presents a threat to internal validity in studies in which a pre-post design is not used. In a group experimental design with only one performance measure, a serious difficulty might be presented when two or more groups are being compared. The question being asked concerns: Is there a difference between these groups? For whatever reason, an experimenter may find it most convenient to test one group of subjects completely and then move to the next group for testing. By conducting the study in this manner an investigator may be systematically introducing a difference between the groups *in addition* to the experimental treatment. If, for example, group 1 is tested in the morning and group 2 is tested in the afternoon, maturation may be operative as a threat to internal validity. The members of group 2 may be systematically different from group 1 because they may be more tired since the testing is done in the afternoon. Regardless of whether it is fatigue (tired), or different in the sense of anticipating school dismissal, it is not unreasonable to assume that their psychological state may be systematically different from that of group 1. The point of this example is that maturation, with respect to fatigue, hunger, or a number of other variables, may be different between groups in addition to the experimentally imposed differences under study. As such, results from comparisons of the two groups may be interpreted as being caused by an influence (or absence of an influence) of the experimental treatment, when actually results are caused by maturation.

This type of problem is not limited to experimental research. Clearly a survey might be vulnerable in exactly the same fashion as the example just presented. For example, consider the case in which a researcher wishes to conduct a survey on high school students' views regarding leisure time activities. In this instance, sophomores and seniors are being compared. It is most convenient to use a questionnaire that can be distributed personally, completed, and returned immediately (such as in a study hall period). It is also convenient to collect data from the seniors during the Wednesday morning study hall and the sophomores during the Friday afternoon study hall. It is hoped that no one would execute a study in this fashion—the maturation threat to internal validity is so obvious. Differences between the groups could be due to the intended comparison (seniors versus sophomores), the differences in views of leisure activities between Wednesday morning and Friday afternoon, or both.

Control for maturation threats in this type of study is relatively simple to implement. One probably cannot avoid the fact that subjects will perform differently under the influence of fatigue, hunger, or other matters. What is important is eliminating the *systematic* way in which these variables influence one group differently than they do another. In many situations, this may be accomplished easily in the field setting (such as a clinic, school, institution, or hospital).

To focus on the systematic dimension of influence, it is necessary to spread any effect of fatigue or hunger as equally as possible among all groups. To do this, a researcher will want to gather data on an approximately equal number of subjects from each group in the morning and in the afternoon, or in the previous example Wednesday morning and Friday afternoon. Thus the impact of the differing times is presumably spread evenly between the groups. Procedures for accomplishing this are simple. In the survey study, the researcher would simply have to sacrifice convenience and eliminate the practice of administering the questionnaire systematically to sophomores on Friday afternoon and seniors on Wednesday morning.

Eliminating the maturation threat in the experimental example is equally simple. One technique that is both effective and convenient involves premarking all the data record sheets before beginning an experiment. Thus the data record sheet is already labeled as being for group 1 or 2 without the exact subject's name whose performance will be recorded on that sheet. The sheets are then placed side by side and shuffled together *thoroughly*. The order of testing as well as which group "Sally" goes in is predetermined by the data sheet that is on the top of the stack. In this fashion it is also possible to go to the teacher or unit supervisor and merely ask for any subject (rather than specifically for Sally). The ongoing activities are disrupted much less than if one were to pull a subject, by name, out of therapy, reading, math, or some other activity. Since the order of testing subjects (and who will be in group 1 as opposed to group 2) is determined by shuffling, fatigue, hunger, or other maturation effects should influence both groups about equally. We have used these procedures for many years and found them to be most satisfactory both in terms of assigning subjects to groups and controlling for maturation.

Studies using time-series designs may also be subject to maturation as an internal validity threat. As mentioned before, such investigations are generally asking a difference question such as "Is there a difference between baseline and postintervention performance?" or "Does the intervening reinforcement program make a difference?" Maturation in a physiological growth sense may threaten the design if the duration of the experiment is sufficient that such growth might be expected. This is not often the case in time-series studies involving behavior modification (although it should not be discounted completely). When it is the case, however, maturation threatens in much the same fashion as has been previously discussed. If the duration of an experiment is sufficient to permit physiological growth (resulting in behavioral change), the researcher may incorrectly interpret this change as being a result of the intervention.

Many time-series studies are of such short duration that physiological maturation is not a problem. These studies are, however, subject to threats from maturation in the form of fatigue or hunger. If, for example, an experiment has a duration of a day with baseline being established in the first part of the morning, intervention and continued measurement might proceed throughout the remainder of the day but without sufficient time for contingency reversal. Fatigue, hunger, or some other influence, occurring merely as a function of time passing, may well affect performance in addition to the treatment. Thus an observed decrease in behavior frequency might represent either fatigue or the intervening change in reinforcement conditions, and interpretation becomes difficult. Some strength would be added by reversing the treatment to baseline conditions. Recall that this reversal is aimed at showing that the intervention was the influence that generated performance change. If the reversal is timed such that fatigue may be occurring, a performance drop may be caused by fatigue as well as removal of the treatment. This type of situation highlights the necessity of performance stabilization before reversal. Even with stable data, however, maturation may threaten reversal designs.

The strongest safeguard against maturation in the situation just mentioned would be replication. Additionally, replications should vary the time frame such that it would not be expected that the same maturation influences (probably unknown) would be operative. The data would then be interpreted after a series of experiments in which maturation effects, if operative, would exert their influence at a different point during the experiment, providing a clearer picture of the actual effects of the treatment.

Longitudinal and cross-sectional designs for studying human development were mentioned briefly before. We will return to these designs here since their basic purpose is to study certain effects across time, and the contamination (confounding) of interpretation may be substantial.

Longitudinal investigations assess the same subjects repeatedly over a long period of time as noted earlier. If the aim of the study is to examine time passage as an experimental variable, then maturation, in that sense, is the topic under study and is not a threat to internal validity. However, there are other difficulties that may threaten internal validity. Assume that aging is the topic of study. The typical longitudinal study involves repeated (often many) administrations of a measure during that period. It is possible that test practice will influence changes in performance (Stevenson, 1993). This would alter the average scores between comparison points *(in addition to the experimental variable)*. Also, many developmental studies are conducted over a period of years. This means that a substantial number of subjects may be lost over the period of the study. Consequently, comparisons between beginning performances (of groups) and ending performance may be altered because the groups represent different subjects. The data collected at the end of the study may differ from that at the beginning because of the lost subjects. Cross-sectional investigations circumvent the difficulty of subject attrition since they assess a number of different groups at the same time.

Most researchers have a tendency to interpret cross-sectional differences as representing developmental changes or trends similar to those in longitudinal studies of development. Such interpretations must be made with great care since there may be other factors affecting performance differences between groups. It may be that development (e.g., aging) is not the primary contributor to differences. Social changes and influences between the groups may have a significant impact. For example, there may be half a decade or more between the youngest and oldest group, meaning that these individuals may have grown up in very different environments (e.g., social mores, approaches to schooling, etc.). Differences between the groups may be due to developmental factors, differing environments, or both. Thus in developmental research we are faced with several dilemmas. Maturation is a central part of the focus, and depending on how you view it, a threat to internal validity or the experimental variable. Such changing of concepts is not at all uncommon—what is a threat in some circumstances is the topic of study in another. Research is definitely a clinical process and you must often rely on your best judgment in designing, planning, and executing an investigation.

Testing or Test Practice.   Testing or test practice threatens the internal validity of an investigation in the sense that the effects of being tested once are represented in the scores of a second test administration. The threat of test practice is most obvious in studies in which a researcher administers a pretest, a treatment, and then a posttest on the same subjects (or interviews, questionnaires, etc.). Presumably the researcher is assessing the difference between pretest and posttest performance with an intent of being able to interpret differences as due to the treatment. However, a portion of the change from pretest to posttest performance levels may be caused by test practice. This is particularly true if the measurement represents a new and unique experience for the subjects so that they may have a great deal to learn just about *how to perform.* For example, if the subjects have never encountered an achievement test before, their pretreatment performance might reflect to a great degree their lack of experience at taking such tests (as well as their knowledge of content). Just taking the pretest may teach them a great deal, which would be reflected on their posttreatment scores. It is easy to see how this influence would serve to separate their pretest and posttest scores (generate greater differences), more than might be the case if only the treatment were operative. If the researcher viewing these results infers such differences to be caused by the treatment alone, a serious interpretation error may have been committed. The differences may be a function of testing, treatment, or both.

Although the preceding example involves experimental research, the basic problem of test practice may threaten internal validity in nonexperimental research. Again, the threat of test practice is simply the effect of a first measure *on* the second. An interview (or questionnaire) may easily create the same type of situation. To the degree that respondents are sensitized, gain knowledge, or are changed in some other fashion by the first interview, data from a second interview may be altered.

To circumvent a test practice threat, a researcher may generally take one of two approaches. If subjects clearly have a background including experience on the measurement instrument, an investigator might assume that test practice will generate less performance change and therefore be less of a threat. Another alternative for the researcher would be to induce experience with a preexperimental (or pretest) warm-up. Using this approach, the researcher provides practice on the task before the first measure, which engenders at least some pretest-posttest similarity in terms of the subjects' experience. Such procedures are still somewhat weak because they do not control or assess the amount of improvement due to additional test practice. Although subjects have experience, they still may improve with more practice. A sounder procedure would involve a comparison group that does not receive the test practice, only the treatment.

To implement such a multigroup study, a researcher would initially draw a sample of subjects at random. If the plan involved having 20 subjects in each group, the sample would include 40 subjects who would then be randomly assigned to the two groups (20 to group 1 and 20 to group 2). Group 1 would then receive the pretest, but group 2 would not. Since group 2 subjects were randomly assigned from the same sample as group 1, there is little reason to believe that they are different (see Figure 8.8). Presumably the scores that group 2 would have obtained on the pretest, if one had been administered, would not differ from those obtained by group 1. From that point on both groups receive the same treatment and posttest. Any differences between the groups on the posttest should be a result of test practice, since the opportunity to learn from the pretest is the only difference between the two groups. Reference to Figure 8.8 suggests that two questions may be addressed. Comparison *A* indicates performance change from the pretest to the posttest, whereas comparison *B* estimates the amount of test practice operative. The difference between the pre-post mean scores for group 1, minus the difference between groups 1 and 2 on the posttest, presumably provides an estimate of the effect due to treatment.

Testing is also a threat to repeated-measures research, which is not strictly defined as a pre-post design. Repeated-measures research includes

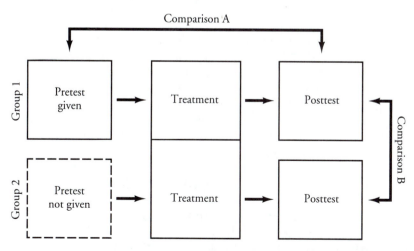

FIGURE 8.8   Pre-Post Design Controlling for Test Practice

studies in which three, four, or more assessment sessions are conducted with the same subjects. An example of such a situation might involve an investigation in which a pretest, two midtreatment tests, and a posttest are administered. There is considerable possibility for the subjects to learn from the test sessions themselves and thereby improve scores as a result of test practice rather than the treatment alone.

Classic examples of this type of threat have long plagued researchers who are studying memory or, more specifically, forgetting. Occasionally, in such studies a researcher may be interested in determining the amount of material that is forgotten over a period subsequent to the learning of a task. Often passage of time is the variable of interest such that the researcher may want to determine how much material is remembered, say, immediately, 24 hours, and seven days after the termination of learning. If subjects are tested for immediate recall and then after 24 hours and seven days, the researcher may encounter difficulty assessing the amount of material forgotten. The problem arises because the 24-hour performance does indeed represent the influence of time passage since learning was terminated. However, it also includes the testing for immediate memory performance. The testing process per se may well have provided subjects with additional opportunity to learn. Similarly, seven-day performance represents time passage (presumably promoting forgetting), but it also includes two additional opportunities for learning from the testing for immediate and 24-hour memory.

To circumvent the difficulty just described, the simplest procedure is to use multiple groups in a fashion somewhat like that suggested for the design in Figure 8.8. For example, a sample of 60 subjects may proceed through the learning task, whereupon they would be randomly divided into three groups for testing memory. There is little reason to expect that the three groups are different since they have been randomly assigned from the larger subject pool who experienced the same learning task. Group 1 might then receive an immediate memory test, whereas groups 2 and 3 would not. Group 2 would then receive a 24-hour test that group 3 would not and, finally, group 3 would receive the seven-day test. It can be assumed that the immediate memory performance for groups 2 and 3 (not tested) would be like that of group 1, and so on. Other things being equal, the seven-day performance of group 3 has only the passage of time, since additional opportunity to learn from immediate and 24-hour testing has been eliminated. By using staggered group measurement in this fashion, the researcher may attribute 24-hour and seven-day performance levels to forgetting rather than forgetting plus the possibility of additional learning.

Instrumentation. Instrumentation has also troubled researchers as a threat to internal validity. In this context, *instrumentation* represents influences on scores because of calibration changes in any measuring instrument used or changes in the observer. From the definition of the term *calibration,* one of the first examples that comes to mind is the use of mechanical devices for data collection. Suppose that a researcher was using an audiometer to gather data. If something occurred midway through the experiment that changed the calibration of that instrument (such as adjustment by a well-meaning service representative), all the data collected from that point on would be systematically different than those data gathered before the change.

As noted in the definition, however, instrumentation problems are not confined to mechanical devices. In behavioral and social science much of the data are collected with human instrumentation such as observers and scorers. The same basic problem discussed with the audiometer example is present with human instrumentation. If something occurs during the study that alters the way responses are scored or recorded, data obtained subsequent to that point are systematically different (for reasons other than the variable under study).

From a generic standpoint, the earlier discussions of history, maturation, and testing become relevant if they are viewed as applied to the observer rather than the subjects. History, the specific event (somewhat like an audiometer adjustment), might occur at a given point and systematically alter the way in which the observer records data. Factors such as experimenter fatigue and hunger exert influence more slowly but may be equally systematic in the manner in which observations are changed by the human instrument. Testing, in the sense that the researcher becomes more adept at (or bored with) testing as the investigation proceeds, may also change the human instrumentation. These are merely examples of how the influence of instrumentation changes might occur. The way in which they serve to threaten internal validity depends entirely on the design being used in a given study. A variety of designs are vulnerable, including group comparisons, repeated measures on the same subjects, time-series experiments, and field studies using participant observation.

Instrumentation as a threat to internal validity can be explored by again examining an A–B design in which baseline data are gathered for a period followed by an intervention and subsequent recording of observation data. The comparison of interest is, again, the difference in behavior frequency between baseline and the period after the intervention was introduced. It is desirable to be able to attribute any changes in behavior frequency to the intervention per se. If the researcher is inhibited in such inferences by systematic differences that occur *in* addition to the intervention, little can be said about the experimental variable.

The most serious problem is presented if the change in addition to the intervention occurs close to the timing of the instrumentation change. Under these conditions the influence of the contaminating factor may appear to be a part of the experimental effect. In terms of instrumentation problems, the most obvious difficulty is presented by changes in the observer who is recording behavioral data. For example, perhaps the experimenter, either knowingly or unknowingly, alters his or her mental set for data recording because change is expected as a function of the intervention. What occurs on the data sheet, then, is some change in behavior frequency as a result of the intervention per se, some change as a result of the observer's altered manner of recording data, and perhaps some change as a result of an interaction of the two. Since all that has been recorded is behavioral frequency, no one knows how much of the difference may be attributed to the intervention, how much to instrumentation changes in the observer, or how much to the combined influence of both.

Several approaches may be used to circumvent the potential problem noted above. Replication of experiments may help, although if the same observer is used, there is little reason to expect much assurance of control from this approach. Additionally, if other observers are used, they may also be subject to bias similar to that influencing the first observer. One approach, which may be more cumbersome but may provide more assurance of stable instrumentation, is a technique borrowed from medical research. This approach is sometimes termed a double-blind technique. In a time-series design a double-blind procedure might be one in which the person recording the data is not aware of the time that the intervention is introduced. Thus the contingency manipulation is performed by a person *other than the observer*. This would mean that the observer would not know precisely when intervention occurred except through actual changes in behavioral frequency. One difficulty with this procedure is, of course, that a research team is necessary instead of one person. Also, there may be situations presented in which it is not possible to double-blind the observer. Reversal and multiple-baseline designs provide some strength over an A-B arrangement. It is doubtful that specific observer changes will occur systematically at the same time as the various phase changes. Instrumentation changes caused by conscious or unconscious bias, however, may still be operative in these designs. Observer training, multiple observer reliability checks, and the double-blind approach probably offer the most confidence concerning avoidance of instrumentation threats to time-series designs.

Experiments in which groups are compared may also be vulnerable to instrumentation threats. The difficulty in this type of experiment is primarily a logistics consideration (that is, the manner in which the experiment is executed) rather than an integral part of the study design. Since the objective is to compare, say, group 1 with group 2, the concern must focus on minimizing systematic differences between groups that occur in addition to the experimental variable under study. Instrumentation presents the greatest potential threat of generating such differences when all the subjects in one group are tested and the experimenter then moves to the next group. Because of a variety of possible influences on the experimenter (e.g., fatigue, practice, or unconscious mental set), one group may be systematically treated differently than another. Thus the calibration of the instrument (the experimenter or observer) may change and cause systematic differences between groups in addition to the variable under study.

To control for this type of problem, an experimenter must focus on making such influences spread as evenly as possible among groups and thus remove the *systematic* dimension that may make groups different. Since there is little doubt that the experimenter will experience some fatigue or boredom regardless of what is done, a priori precautions must be taken to distribute such influence throughout the groups evenly. This may be done by randomly testing subjects from all groups such that the subjects in different groups alternate or counterbalance the order of testing. The result will be that about the same number of subjects from each group will be tested under all conditions of instrument calibration. The fashion in which this may be accomplished in the field is logistically simple and can involve shuffling premarked data sheets as described earlier.

Instrumentation also serves to threaten the internal validity of pre-post and other repeated-measures designs. Changes in the calibration of either human or mechanical instrumentation that occur between measures generate differences between the data points being compared. Since this source of difference is in addition to the variable under study, interpretation may be clouded.

Researchers are not faced with a serious instrumentation difficulty if data collection procedures involve techniques with little likelihood of calibration changes. This might be the case with a printed paper-and-pencil instrument (e.g., tests and questionnaires) used in pre-post or other repeated-measures studies. However, when human observers are used in data recording, much less assurance is possible that instrumentation is stable. One procedure that may be used (which exemplifies the difficulty in controlling this type of situation) concerns mechanical behavioral observation such as photography or videotaping. If the study involved a treatment, the pretreatment and posttreatment records could then be randomized with respect to order and rated by a panel of judges. In this fashion the data records obtained from taped behavioral observations are not identified as pretreatment or posttreatment measures. Since they need not be in order, they are less vulnerable to systematic calibration influences on the observer-raters.

Often such elaborate controls as the example just given are not feasible. When they are not, researchers may have to be satisfied with careful scrutiny of the process so they may be aware if instrumentation problems seem operative. This would represent a situation when the best the researcher can do is account for internal validity threats in the written report rather than actually control them.

Statistical Regression. An internal validity threat of statistical regression occurs if subjects have been assigned to a particular group on the basis of atypical scores. Under such circumstances a subject's placement in, say, group 1 may be in error, since the score is atypical. That individual's more normal performance may be like that of the subjects in group 2. If the misclassified subjects then regress—up or down—toward their usual performance during the experiment, internal validity may be threatened seriously (groups thought to be equivalent turn out not to be, or those thought to be different are actually not).

From the nature of this discussion it can be seen that statistical regression may create a problem when group comparisons are being made. This should not be taken to suggest that all group comparisons are equally vulnerable. If a researcher forms two groups on the basis of random assignment, for example, to compare the effects of two treatment conditions, little threat is presented by statistical regression. Because subjects are randomly assigned to groups there is little reason to expect more atypical scores in one group than the other. If, on the other hand, groups are being formed that represent preexisting subject classification differences, statistical regression may well present a serious problem. For example, if a researcher wishes to compare performance by subjects representing two levels of intelligence, a regression problem may be encountered. For reasons unknown, there may be a portion of one group whose IQ scores are atypical. Results of the comparison thought to be attributable to level of intelligence, may in fact be a function of some other factor. The researcher thinks two specified levels of intelligence are operating. In fact, because the scores on which groups were formed are partially atypical for one group, the investigator may not actually have the types of groups expected. Consequently the performance or scores may appear more like that of the actual intellectual level at which the subjects usually operate rather than the atypical score. In this sense the performance may regress toward the average level of functioning.

Control for a problem such as the situation just described is difficult, particularly in the case of comparisons that may be made between preexisting subject classifications (e.g., comparing levels of intelligence or emotionally disturbed compared with nondisturbed). (You will recall that these types of comparisons are what have been called *quasi-experiments.*) Logistically, it is always risky to form such groups with only a single score or measure as a guide. It is helpful if the subject has several scores to give at least some general credibility to the most recent one, which is often used for group assignment.

The notion of statistical regression from an atypical score is also relevant as a threat to time-series designs. A fairly common procedure called a *probe* is often used to establish the level of baseline skill or entry behaviors. This technique is usually characterized by presenting the subject with a task to be performed (or a part of the task) and assessing the ability to perform it. Based on the results of such a probe, the modification of behavior is planned and implemented. Essentially, a probe may be viewed similarly to the earlier discussed test scores used for group assignment. If, for some reason, a subject's response to a given probe is atypical (in terms of a usual or normal response), then the statistical regression problem presents itself. In somewhat the same fashion as a group design, a series of probes will provide some insurance against the atypical response being viewed as average. Time-series experiments are generally less vulnerable because of the greater number of data points usually recorded before an intervention or other phase change.

Statistical regression has been discussed as primarily a threat to internal validity in experimental investigations. For the most part, it has been most obviously a problem with this type of research. However, nonexperimental studies are by no means completely free of such difficulties. Certainly statistical regression could occur if one were conducting a survey in which groups were studied based on specific identifying data and the data were incorrect or atypical.

Hawthorne Effect.   One rather widely discussed threat to internal validity is the Hawthorne effect. The Hawthorne effect refers to a change in sensitivity, performance, or both by the subjects that may occur merely as a function of being in an investigation. Because of the experimental surroundings (e.g., laboratory), the change in routine caused by the study, or any other fashion by which subjects are made to feel special, their performance may be different than it would be if they were not subjects. Such an influence becomes a threat to internal validity with group comparisons, for example, when it is operative on one group and not the other. Under such circumstances, the members of group 1 might perform better because they feel "special," whereas the members of group 2 might not have the "special" feeling and might not perform as well because of this. This places a systematic difference between the groups *in addition* to the experimental variables. This is a serious problem since the researcher wishes to attribute differences between the groups to the treatment.

For a student beginning in research, the Hawthorne effect may become a problem because of a misconception concerning experimental and control groups. Perhaps because of the connotations of the terms *experimental* and *control* or perhaps because of a superficial understanding of these as functional concepts, the uninitiated may be led to the conclusion that an experimental group receives a treatment, whereas a control group receives nothing. If such an approach is used during the design of a study, the Hawthorne effect is likely to threaten internal validity. Assuming that the treatment somehow alters the subjects' routine (besides the process under investigation), such alteration may increase, decrease, or in some other fashion modify subjects' sensitivity to the experimental task. If "nothing" is done to the control group, differences in performance between the groups might be attributed to the factor being studied, or to the fact that one group felt special but the other did not, or to a combination. At any rate, the researcher is in a difficult position to say much about why differences did or did not occur, since the Hawthorne effect may be occurring in addition to the variable being studied.

Control for the Hawthorne effect essentially means that the systematic difference between the groups (in addition to what is being studied) needs to be removed or minimized. It is difficult to imagine an experimental treatment that is not known in some way to the subject or that does not alter sensitivity in some fashion. Many years of studying methods involved in research design have led most researchers to agree that it is difficult, if not impossible, to control the Hawthorne effect by removing it from the experimental group. Since the essence of the concept of control is to remove systematic differences (except the one under investigation) by making the groups as equal as possible, another solution to the Hawthorne effect is necessary. If the Hawthorne effect cannot reliably be removed from the experimental group, the most effective control method would seem to be to "Hawthorne" both groups equally. This might be interpreted to mean that the members of the control group are treated in a fashion that will make them feel equally special, but they are not actually given the experimental treatment per se. Since the question focuses on the effects of the treatment, or differences between a group that receives the treatment and one that does not, Hawthorning both groups does not interfere with this comparison. The absolute level of performance by groups is not as important as the relative performance compared between groups. This type of control for the Hawthorne effect has perhaps contributed to an apparent decline in the use of terms such as *experimental groups* and *control groups.* Many researchers have come to prefer the generic term *comparison groups* to avoid the misconceptions concerning what a control group adds to an experiment and how it ought to be treated.

The Hawthorne effect is definitely a concern when conducting an experimental study in which groups are compared. However, other types of research designs are also vulnerable to the Hawthorne effect, such as time-series experiments. As an illustration, refer to the simple A-B paradigm exemplified by Figure 8.9. As the intervention occurs, it is almost certain that the subject will be aware that the routine has changed. An observed change in postintervention performance may, therefore, be a result of the altered contingencies under investigation (e.g., reinforcement schedule), or the subject may have changed performance level because of the change in routine (Hawthorne), or, most probably, the performance change may be a result of a combination of the changed contingencies *and* the Hawthorne effect.

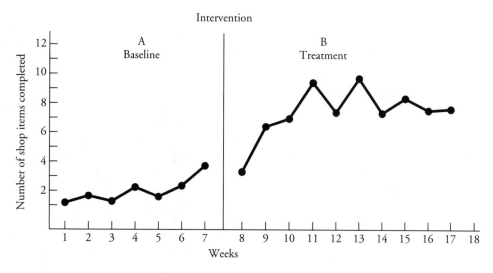

FIGURE 8.9 Example of an A-B Time-Series Data Display

How does one circumvent possible influences of the Hawthorne effect in the type of investigation portrayed in Figure 8.9? Some single-subject researchers may respond by saying "Why bother?" This type of research has been characterized by a pragmatic philosophy. From that standpoint, one might simply contend that it is of no consequence whether the Hawthorne effect was occurring in addition to the intervention. If the behavior can be modified, from an instructional point of view, that is important and that should be the primary focus. Many researchers from a single-subject background as well as from more traditional group design backgrounds would take a somewhat different stance on this issue. They would prefer a more analytical approach that at least attempts to separate the influences of the Hawthorne effect from those of the intervention. Although it is difficult to be precise, a number of possible steps or strategies may be helpful.

One difficulty involves the collection of baseline data. As noted previously, the question being addressed is essentially a difference question, comparing baseline performance with postintervention performance. If baseline data are gathered in a setting that primarily represents routine for the subjects (e.g., a classroom) and the intervention involves a nonroutine setting (e.g., another classroom or individualized instruction), the potential influence of the Hawthorne effect is immediately evident. The problem, of course, is focused on the difference created because baseline data are collected in a different setting than the intervention data. In some cases, the nature of intervention necessitates a nonroutine environment (such as a small room with reduced stimuli).

When this is the case, it is wise to also gather baseline data in the intervention environment. Additionally, since such a procedure would then influence baseline performance, baseline data collection should continue long enough to permit the subject to become acclimated to the changed environment. Most researchers require a stable behavior rate over a period before they will assume subject acclimation.

The Hawthorne effect still has a good probability of being operative when the intervention is implemented even if baseline and experimental settings are the same. There is little that can be done to eliminate the Hawthorne influence under these conditions, primarily because the same subject is experiencing preintervention and postintervention conditions (e.g., change in reinforcement contingencies). Most researchers will not, however, assess the influence of their intervention until the behavior rate has stabilized. Reference to Figure 8.9 reveals that the performance is much more erratic immediately after intervention than it is later. The Hawthorne effect is likely to be operative in its most potent form immediately after routine is disturbed. The influence of the Hawthorne effect may be expected to decline as the subject becomes acclimated (i.e., as a new environment becomes routine). Thus the stable rate of performance is assumed to be reflective of the intervention to a greater degree than rates observed immediately subsequent to intervention. However, Figure 8.9 indicates that even the later portions of postintervention data contain slight variations. The guideline for stable data presented earlier by Gelfand & Hartman (1984) is useful in such circumstances to determine how much further data should be collected.

Turn to page 236 and complete Simulation 8.1

Most of this discussion has been couched in terms of experimental research. Hawthorne-like effects can also threaten the validity of nonexperimental and qualitative investigations. We will discuss these influences under the label of *researcher effects* as we examine threats to qualitative research later in this chapter.

Bias in Group Composition.   Bias in group composition or in method of subject assignment to groups is the quintessential threat to internal validity. Use of the term *bias* in relation to groups connotes systematic differences between comparison groups *in addition* to the factor or treatment under study. The broader term *composition* is used because this threat is relevant to *quasi-experimental* designs as well as *true experimental* designs.

Recall that a true experimental design is one in which, initially, a single population of subjects is identified and sampled. Groups are then formed in some specified fashion that promotes group equality before the initiation of treatment (e.g., random assignment). Thus in an experimental design, the groups do not become different until treatment begins. A quasi-experimental design differs in that the groups are not necessarily formed from the same single subject pool. In fact, the group composition, which reflects the research question, may be based on a preexisting condition such as levels of intelligence. Such an investigation might be portrayed by the diagram shown in Figure 8.10. Quasi-experimental designs are particularly vulnerable to internal validity threats from bias in group composition. Consequently the example in Figure 8.10 will be used to examine this problem. It should be noted from the outset, however, that quasi-experimental designs have been used and continue to be used in many areas of behavioral science. They have considerable value, providing essential information to areas such as comparative and abnormal psychology, special education, and others. In considering certain questions, a quasi-experimental design is the most obvious option, but researchers must be aware of its relative strengths and limitations.

The basic problem involved in quasi-experimental designs centers around controlling systematic differences between groups *with the exception of the one under study.* In Figure 8.10 the experimental variable is intelligence, and to maximize internal validity it is desirable to eliminate other systematic differences between the groups or at least hold them to a minimum. Since this experiment is studying a preexisting phenomenon, it is necessary to be cautious and avoid other differences that may be concomitant with the different levels of measured intelligence. For example, because of the nature of intelligence tests, there is a substantial probability that the lower intelligence group (A) may have more minority children than the higher intelligence group (B). IQ tests are primarily verbal and are designed from the vantage point of white

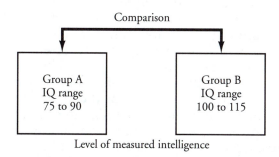

FIGURE 8.10   Example of a Quasi-Experimental Design

middle-class North America. This would handicap children with different verbal patterns as compared to those children whose total language experience has been in the same framework as the test. If, because of this test bias, group A has more minority or linguistically different children than group B, performance on an experimental task may be more reflective of this difference than of levels of intelligence. Similarly, subjects from lower socioeconomic levels may appear in greater numbers in group A than in group B. This may occur because of test bias or because of experiential background. Regardless of the reason, differences may reflect these other factors as well as intelligence. The researcher, to be precise in conducting the investigation, must decide whether intelligence is the focus of the study, or racial differences, or socioeconomic status, or all of these in combination. To study all in combination would be a poor option if the researcher desires to do much specific interpretation of results.

The quasi-experimental design raises an immediate red flag of caution because differences other than the one under study have a much greater probability of being built in. The presence of possible bias in group composition seriously inhibits the meaningful interpretation of results. There are certain precautions that may be taken, however, to minimize the probability of group composition bias in quasi-experimental designs. Initially the research question must be clearly and specifically articulated. If the experimental variable is intelligence, then, by exclusion, factors such as socioeconomic status, race, sex, or age must be controlled or held constant between groups. If the question compares subjects with and without mental retardation on some learning task, the basis for such classification of subjects must be specified. It may be that such groups are based on measured intelligence, which again activates the exclusion process of factors such as those noted above.

Working with a quasi-experimental design presents considerable challenge regarding controlling potential bias between groups. Since a researcher cannot make use of the power of random assignment, other alternatives must be used. In the absence of random assignment, the investigator is faced with the unenviable task of determining which factors are important to control—unenviable because of the potential for error involved. Not only might a researcher inadvertently omit control for some factor that is known to be influential, but risk of threat also exists from the many variables that have not yet been identified as important to control. Thus, at the outset, the challenge presented in controlling potentially contaminating variables requires considerable experience of both a research and clinical nature. A checklist of what the researcher always wanted to avoid is usually not available.

One obvious question that might be asked by the beginning researcher is: How do you decide which factors need to be controlled? These decisions are generally made based on both previous research and logic. In the case of previous research, one would probably choose to control any variable that had been shown to influence performance on the task to be used. For example, if the task involved had been previously used and results indicated that performance was influenced by different stages of child development, the investigator would be remiss if chronological age were not held constant between groups. Similarly, if gender, socioeconomic status, or other factors had been shown to influence task performance, they ought to be considered for control. For example, in the study portrayed in Figure 8.10, intelligence was the variable under investigation. If the variables just mentioned above were known to influence performance on whatever task was being used, groups A and B should not be different in mean chronological age or socioeconomic status and should have about equal numbers of both sexes or only one sex in the total study.

It was also noted that a judicious use of logic was helpful in determining what potentially contaminating variables ought to be controlled. Often previous research will not provide information directly related to the investigation being planned. In such cases the researcher must make control decisions based on information that is only tangentially relevant, laced together with logic and reason. In many instances, the researcher should just ask: What is it that might influence performance on my task besides my experimental variable? The investigator might decide that reading ability ought to be controlled and also visual impairment, since the hypothetical task requires visual input. At this point there are two general approaches to control. With the objective of making both groups equal, a given variable might be removed from the total subject pool, or it might somehow be made equal between groups but left in the subject population. In the example just noted, it would probably be wise to define the subject population at the outset as having no identifiable visual impairments and to delete children with such conditions from consideration as subjects. Similarly with regard to reading level, all children who deviated, for example, by more than a year from their age-appropriate reading level might be deleted from the potential subject pool. Even with this precaution the groups would have to be scrutinized before initiation of the experiment to ensure that they were not different in average reading level.

Operationalizing control in a quasi-experimental study is challenging. To facilitate this process, it is often useful to turn to the sampling procedure, since assignment is already somewhat predefined. Recalling the example in Figure 8.10, the research question involved comparing the performance of two groups who had different levels of intelligence. Suppose for the moment that it has been determined that chronological age and socioeconomic status as well as visual, central nervous system, and health impairments have been identified as being important for control. The question then becomes one of how to best accomplish such control.

With a quasi-experimental design, the researcher is essentially work-ing with two subject populations distinguishable on the basis of the experimental variable. In this example there will be one subject popula-tion defined by an intelligence range of 75 to 90 and a second popula-tion defined by an intelligence range of 100 to 115. One effective method of controlling the other identified factors is to define both populations as having the same characteristics on those given factors. Thus, although the subject population for group A is defined in different IQ ranges than group B, groups A and B should have a common age range and socioeconomic status. Additionally, neither subject population would include any children with identifiable visual, central nervous system, or health impairments. Given these defined characteristics, the investiga-tor can then randomly sample group A from subject pool A and group B from subject pool B. This is the essence of the process known as *stratified random sampling*, so-called because the experimenter is ran-domly sampling from different strata or defined populations (see Chap-ter 9). Experience has shown that such procedures generally result in groups that are not different on the control characteristics defined in common terms between subject populations. Precautions should be taken, however, by comparing group means or in some other fashion assess-ing the group composition on these dimensions before initiating the experiment. If they are not equal, the groups should be resampled (re-composed) until pretreatment groups are not different on the variables being controlled.

As previously mentioned, the true experimental design involves a single subject pool from which groups are formed, ostensibly with no differences before the initiation of treatment. Bias in group composi-tion does not present such a potential threat as in the quasi-experimen-tal design because of the single subject pool and thus absence of preex-isting systematic differences. Some of the initial considerations men-tioned before are also relevant for a true experimental design. As a precautionary measure during sampling, it is often wise to eliminate potential subjects who may encounter difficulties in performing the task (assuming such difficulty is not part of the normal deviation in performance). Of primary concern are substantial disabilities that are *unrelated* to the research question such as visual or central nervous system impairments.

With the advantages offered by a single subject pool, group compo-sition becomes predominately a logistic consideration. The primary concern is to form groups that are virtually equal on a pretreatment basis. One of the most powerful procedures (also easily performed) involves randomly assigning subjects to experimental conditions or groups. Earlier methodological approaches often emphasized experi-mental matching as a means of equating groups. In addition to various problems that are inherent in experimental matching, the procedure does not take advantage of the fact that, with group comparisons, group performances such as means are compared rather than individual scores. Utilizing random assignment does acknowledge the fact that group performance is the focus and aims at making pretreatment *groups* equal rather than individual subject *pairs*. Using chance in this manner results in subjects' varying at random on any antecedent factor (e.g., age or mental ability), theoretically resulting in random differences between groups that will approximate zero. Experience has substantiated the faith and theoretical base for random assignment in equalizing groups, especially if a reasonably large number of subjects is used (e.g., 40 or more per group) (Kazdin, 1992). Often there is actually zero or nearly zero difference between groups on antecedent factors. Such faith should not, however, go unchecked in any given study. Groups should be compared on antecedent factors before initiating treatment merely to check the researcher's assumption of equality. Chance variation will, in a certain number of instances, result in significantly unequal groups before treatment. When this occurs, the groups should be placed back in the subject pool and reconstituted.

*Turn to page 238 and complete
Simulations 8.2 and 8.3*

Experimental Mortality.   Experimental mortality is a threat to internal validity that has relevance to both experimental and nonexperimental research despite the term *experimental* in its label. Experimental mortality becomes a threat to internal validity when there is a differential loss of subjects between comparison groups. It is not uncommon for a researcher to lose a certain number of subjects for a variety of reasons. Perhaps the subjects are absent from school on the test day, and timing is important, so they cannot be tested at a later time. On other occasions an error in research procedures might invalidate the data from a given subject, requiring deletion from the study. In general such experimental mortality presents no serious difficulty regarding internal validity as long as the loss is approximately equal between groups. The usual procedure employed (as long as the group loss is approximately equal) involves randomly selecting replacement subjects from the same subject pool that was initially used to compose the groups. Experienced researchers will usually form their original subject pool so that a certain number of potential subjects remain as a replacement pool after groups are formed. In this fashion the composition of the replacement pool is presumed to not be different from that of the groups, thereby permitting replacement of lost or deleted subjects.

The threat to internal validity arises when groups lose subjects in different proportions. A researcher is often unaware of the exact characteristics of the subjects who are lost, in particular those characteristics that either related to or precipitated the loss. Consequently, whatever those characteristics are, they have been deleted to a greater degree from some groups than others. If replacement is then initiated by randomly selecting from the replacement pool, the researcher may be building in systematic differences between the reconstituted groups. To elaborate further, an example may be useful.

Using a hypothetical situation from the psychology learning laboratory, suppose that an experiment involves white rats as subjects. Because of qualities in the subjects (unknown to the researcher), a substantially greater proportion of one group dies than in a second group. Although the exact reasons for death may be unknown, it is possible that the subjects who were physiologically weak were more vulnerable to death. If replacement is accomplished by randomly selecting from the replacement pool, chances are that about as many strong rats will be chosen for replacement as weak rats. Thus the replacement subjects may include more strong rats than were in the group for which they are substituting. Since differential group loss requires more replacements in one group than the other, the addition of more potentially strong rats to that group might well result in built-in differences between the groups. In such a situation, an investigator faces serious problems. Excellent procedures for equalizing groups may have been implemented initially, but the mortality threat presents itself after the experiment is underway.

Circumventing experimental mortality as a threat to internal validity is extremely difficult. Depending on certain decisions by the researcher, there are pragmatic questions and issues that may be considered. One involves just how different do the mortality rates have to be before the researcher ought to be concerned? This varies from one type of research to another, and decisions are usually based on the experience and clinical judgment of the investigator. This is the type of decision that is best made before beginning an experiment. For example, based on what has been written in earlier research, an investigator may decide that any differential of more than 10 percent is going to be considered a threat to internal validity. Thus if group A lost 10 percent of the initial subjects, whereas group B lost 20 percent or 25 percent, the researcher would have the a priori caution point exceeded (that is, the differential would be 10 to 15 percent). The question then becomes one of what can be done about the threat. This may be one situation in which, after carefully examining the information available, the researcher decides to proceed but to mention the loss as a potential weakness in the findings. The investigator may account for the potential threat by indicating that it existed, what effect it is believed to have had, but that, for whatever the reason, it is thought that no substantial influence on the interpretations possible was generated. If this choice is selected, the rationale sustaining the researcher's interpretations must have considerable strength.

However, an alternative decision might be in order rather than that mentioned above. The investigator may decide that an internal validity threat is so imminent and potentially devastating to interpretation that the study should be discontinued with this sample of subjects. The researcher may choose to begin anew with a totally new sample of subjects.

Neither of the options just given is satisfactory. The first leaves the outcome in some question while the second is discouraging and expensive. The fact remains, however, that even if packaged approaches to circumventing experimental mortality do not seem attractive, an investigator must monitor each experiment to guard against it as a threat. The rigor of results is too valuable to sacrifice, regardless of cost in dollars or frustration.

Experimental mortality presents difficulties in designs other than group comparisons. An extremely vulnerable design involves the investigation in which repeated measures are administered to the same group of subjects over a long period of time. This, of course, refers to pre–post or longitudinal repeated measures designs. The repeated measures design is more vulnerable under some conditions than others. Experimental mortality is not extremely problematic in situations in which the duration of an investigation is fairly short and the researcher actively implements both pretreatment and posttreatment measures. Such control is not always possible; for example, nonexperimental investigations called *follow-up studies* are often quite vulnerable to experimental mortality.

Follow-up studies are frequently used to evaluate the ultimate effectiveness of some treatment program. These include clinical programs such as mental health treatment, vocational rehabilitation, and certain educational treatment programs. In these areas the acid test of program effectiveness is how well the clients (subjects) perform in a given environment after they leave the treatment program. Under such conditions the evaluation is often an afterthought, with a subject's status assessment on program entrance having been recorded by an admitting clinician. Regardless of how well this assessment has been accomplished, it may not have been completed with research or program evaluation as an objective. Records may be somewhat fragmentary with respect to the criteria ultimately chosen for follow-up assessment.

Yet a follow-up investigation is often designed with the program entrance records serving as the first or pretreatment data point. Because of these circumstances, such studies are occasionally called *posthoc* in the sense that existing data are used; a researcher may or may not actually see the clients during their treatment and thus may have only the pretreatment records for identification of subjects. Experimental mortality becomes a serious issue when the investigator attempts to locate subjects for follow-up assessment. Experience has shown that this is perhaps the most difficult type of study to conduct, and experimental mortality is the primary source of difficulty.

Although researchers have pretreatment descriptions (plus the occasional assessment at the point of treatment termination), they may be able to locate only a small percentage of subjects for follow-up assessment. The difficulty involves descriptions for subjects who cannot be located. Was the treatment program so effective for those subjects that they have blended into the environment to an extent that they can no longer be identified? An alternative might be that the program was not effective for them, and they became so transient that location is impossible. Neither of these explanations is supportable by existing data; in fact, they become speculations based on the absence of data.

The follow-up study is basically a nonexperimental difference question comparing pretreatment and posttreatment measures. Experimental mortality threatens internal validity because a different group composition is available at one data point than is available at the second. A researcher has little chance of knowing what the subjects look like who cannot be located. There is a substantial probability that those who cannot be located are different from those who can. Thus, if all the data are used from the pretreatment measures, the two data points are probably not comparable, since group composition may have changed. Any differences in, for example, group average scores may reflect the different composition as much as the program impact.

One solution is to use only pretreatment data from those subjects who can be located for follow-up. Although this circumvents mortality as a threat to internal validity, other problems are involved. From a pragmatic standpoint, using only this portion of data may not be an accurate assessment of program effectiveness. The questions posed previously concerning the unlocated subjects and why they cannot be located must be addressed again. There is good reason to suspect that the locatable subjects do not provide a representative sample of the clients going through the program. To use only a partial sample may therefore not be addressing the research question adequately if the question involves the effectiveness of treatment on clients entering the program.

Circumventing the difficulties of follow-up studies discussed above seems to be primarily a logistics consideration. Ideally one would wish to sample all clients entering the program and assess their change after they are out in their normal environments. To accomplish this the program evaluation must be planned in advance and a monitor system must be devised that will permit subject location.

Comments.   After being exposed to the various possibilities of threats to internal validity, the beginning researcher may be wondering if any investigation can be designed that controls or circumvents all possible weaknesses. The answer in the strictest sense is probably no. Most studies can be improved in some fashion, which is representative of the behavioral science effort to constantly refine its scientific methodology.

It should be kept in mind, however, that design changes often involve compromises or alternatives that trade improvements in one area at the sacrifice of another. Researchers must use their best clinical judgment when deciding exactly where it is most critical to implement the tightest control and where they can best afford to live with less rigorous control. Decisions of this nature are often dependent on experience as a practicing researcher.

It is also important to restate the necessity to control certain factors and account for others in the report. This is further evidence of the sacrifice in some areas to achieve tighter control in others. The process of accounting for some threats involves discussing their probable contaminating influence in the research report. Such discussion must be well grounded in logic. It is no longer acceptable to ignore the threat or even state that no effect occurred without specifying on what basis the statement is made.

*Turn to page 239 and complete
Simulation 8.4*

External Validity

As noted early in this chapter, external validity addresses the issue of generalizability of results. As indicated by Figure 8.2, external validity involves how well the results of a particular study represent or apply to the population, treatment variables, and measurement criteria presumably being studied in the world outside the investigation.

Although internal and external validity are not in direct conflict, there is a tendency for each to operate to the disadvantage of the other. This is another area in which a researcher must often decide to concentrate attention on one and perhaps sacrifice rigor with respect to the other. Such a situation does not necessarily demean the overall character of behavioral research, however. The value of research should not be assessed on the basis of a given study, but rather in terms of programs of research with a cumulative purpose. Early studies in a program of research may represent very beginning efforts at knowledge acquisition in an area. In these studies an investigator may be primarily concerned with determining how a given psychological variable operates. Since the focus is necessarily the microcosm of that factor, it probably will be desirable to make that focus as pure as possible, thereby emphasizing internal validity control. As information accumulates establishing how the factor under study operates, the researcher may then become more concerned with its influence in the real world environment. This change in focus will require increasing attention to external validity, perhaps at the expense of internal validity controls. Ultimately as a scientist approaches the real environment, data have accumulated not only on how the factor operates in a laboratory setting but also on its influence as it interacts with environmental contingencies. When generalizability becomes a concern of focus, the researcher will have a variety of threats to external validity to circumvent.

Population-Sample Differences. An entire population is rarely available to a researcher for study purposes. Even if a population were theoretically available, expense and time involved in recording data on an entire group are usually so great that it is unfeasible to do so. Consequently researchers ordinarily work with a sample of individuals selected from the population.

One obvious dimension of external validity concerns the degree to which those subjects in the study are representative of the population to which generalization is desired. If there are significant differences between subjects and the larger population, it is likely that the subjects will respond differently (on the questionnaire, interview, or experimental task) than the larger group would. If the researchers are unaware of such differences, they may interpret the results as being applicable to the population when in fact they are not.

Population-sample representativeness relates directly to the way in which subjects are selected. Chapter 9 presents a detailed discussion of sampling techniques aimed at obtaining a representative group of subjects. However, since this is such a central issue in external validity, we will undertake a brief examination at this point.

One important issue in sampling relates to the researchers' knowledge regarding the characteristics of the population and the subject pool. From this standpoint researchers may find themselves in a somewhat difficult situation. As they proceed to define the population, it is probable that a thorough knowledge of all the characteristics of the population is not available. To the degree that there is confidence concerning the importance of those known characteristics (and the relative unimportance of those about which knowledge is not available), researchers can control external validity. This speaks specifically to the approach the researchers take with regard to defining the population. Some maintain that it is better to define the population in a restricted fashion but to have more confidence in the knowledge concerning a restricted set of characteristics. The alternative position requires a much less rigorous definition of characteristics. Generalization under these conditions is viewed as an inference from the subject(s) in the experiment to a population similar to those observed. This perspective is favored by some time-series researchers.

Although we are inclined to favor the more rigorous population definition, the crucial factor is that the type of inference being made be kept clearly in mind. It is essential that researchers be aware of whether the population knowledge is reliable and that they be aware of the resulting level of confidence concerning generalization.

Artificial Research Arrangements. A second threat to external validity involves the actual research arrangements chosen for the investigation. In one sense this phenomenon is the Hawthorne effect operating as a threat to external validity. To the degree that a research setting deviates from the routine the subject is accustomed to, it may be expected that the subject's responsivity is changed. If a group of children have their daily classroom routine altered by being tested in a small distraction-free room, their performance may be either heightened or depressed as a result of the nonroutine setting. The subjects' performance on the research task may thus be different from what it would be if they were to perform the task in a nonexperimental or routine setting.

The influence of research arrangements threatens external validity to the degree that the subjects' responsivity is altered. If subjects are responding differently because of the setting, their performance is not representative of the original subject pool from which they were drawn. A researcher may have initially gone to great lengths to sample subjects that are representative of a given population to which generalization is desired. Although the subjects may have been representative at that time, they become a select, nonrepresentative group as soon as the investigation is initiated if the arrangements are substantially artificial. Earlier discussions in Chapter 2 indicated that this type of problem was particularly evident in experimental research, especially in a highly artificial setting such as a laboratory. It should be emphasized, however, that nonexperimental research may be equally vulnerable to the degree that subjects are placed in a nonroutine situation. An interview may create a great degree of artificiality depending on how and where it is conducted. In all cases an investigator must judge the degree to which external validity is threatened by artificial research arrangements.

It was previously noted that certain phases of a research program may necessitate a sacrifice with respect to external validity. When subjects are individually treated, such as is often the case in many interviews and psychological experiments, it is difficult to imagine that the research arrangements are routine. The degree to which external validity is threatened depends on the situation *to which generalization is desired.* If, for example, a researcher is studying a new method of individualized instruction, considerable generalizability might be possible. True, the results may not generalize to the classroom from which the child came, but it should be remembered that the researcher is exploring individualized instruction.

Judgments concerning external validity must include consideration of the potential application to which the study is addressed rather than automatically making reference to existing settings. From the researcher's standpoint, if external validity is a serious objective, care must be taken to arrange the research setting as much like the target setting for generalization as possible. Such arrangements may include a variety of contingencies such as the physical setting, the interpersonal arrangements, the materials being used, and perhaps many others. Here again the researcher's experience and clinical judgment must be used in deciding priority contingencies necessitating attention.

Pretest Influence. It is not uncommon to read reports of experiments in which the researcher used a pretest or warm-up task before initiating actual experimental procedures. This is done for a variety of reasons, but in general the purpose is to ensure that when subjects begin the experiment per se, the performance is reflective of the subject-task interaction and not the subjects' "learning to respond" behavior. Although it is a useful procedure for purifying the scrutiny of the subject-task interaction, such a pretest or warm-up may serve to threaten external validity. It is seldom that instructional and psychological procedures used in the field are preceded by warm-up procedures. Consequently the learning to respond behaviors are usually a part of the subject's performance in a real world setting. In some situations this difference between the research and field settings may be substantial, thereby diminishing the accuracy of generalization.

As noted earlier, a research program that is still identifying fundamental process operation may not be primarily concerned with generalization. However, if external validity *is* a central focus, the researcher must attend to pretest or warm-up as a threat. Assuming the research program has proceeded beyond the study of fundamental process, elimination of preresearch procedures may be in order to facilitate generalization. Since the initial learning to respond behaviors may be a part of performance in the field, inclusion of these influences in research concerned with generalization seems relevant. The actual impact of such pretest influence is often not known to the researcher. It may be expected, however, that the more unusual the overall task is for the subject, the more influence will result from warm-up or pretest.

Multiple Treatment Interference. The influence of multiple treatment interference as a threat to external validity is conceptually similar to that of pretest just discussed. It becomes operative when more than a single treatment is administered to the same subjects. Multiple treatment investigations present obvious analytical internal validity problems since, beyond the first treatment, a subject's performance is difficult to attribute to any given treatment (e.g., treatment 2 or 3) because of the cumulative effect. Additionally, however, the generalizability of results from treatments subsequent to the first is also questionable. Because the effects of prior treatments are often not dissipated by the time later treatments are administered, subjects may well have a depressed or increased sensitivity to a second or third research task. To the degree that such subjects' responsivity is altered for, say, treatments 2 or 3, the generalizability of results from these treatments is reduced. This, of course, assumes that a sequence of multiple treatments is not the usual setting in the population sampled.

Circumventing external validity difficulties in a multiple treatment experiment is problematic to say the least. Since subjects approach the first treatment experimentally naive (presumed free from systematic influences), results from that treatment are assumed to be externally valid if the setting is similar to that of the intended generalization. Because the subjects usually approach the second task not experimentally naive (under the systematic influence of treatment 1), they are not representative of the initial subject pool. The approach to circumventing this threat generally would require making reasonably certain that the subjects began treatment 2 also experimentally naive. In some situations researchers may depend on the passage of time to accomplish this. Such an approach is of uncertain effectiveness, and the researcher may be depending on a fallacious assumption. Alternatively, if sufficient time passes between treatments for the first to dissipate, often the research appears more like two studies than two treatments within one.

Occasionally, a researcher may be able to determine that the effect of treatment 1 is negligible on the performance in treatment 2. To be certain of this, however, a study directly concerned with such influence may be required to provide empirical evidence. In lieu of expending the effort and expense necessary to provide such evidence for methodological purposes only, a researcher may decide to avoid a multiple treatment design completely. This, of course, would be one fashion in which the researcher could be assured of avoiding the difficulties discussed above. The alternative might involve using a different randomly assigned group of subjects for each treatment.

***Turn to page 241 and complete
Simulations 8.5 and 8.6***

Comments

Thus far this chapter has discussed problems and threats involved in the basic plan and execution of experimental studies. The approach has been to focus on problems that may be encountered regarding both internal and external validity. The plan or conceptual design of an experiment is a core consideration in beginning a research effort. The same is true for qualitative research, for which threats to validity may be equally detrimental. Some of the concepts discussed thus far have relevance to qualitative studies. However, specific examination is needed because of the paradigm differences.

Threats to Validity in Qualitative Research

Some qualitative researchers use terms like internal and external validity, notions that you are accustomed to from our earlier discussions in this chapter. However, there are some substantial translations of these concepts which make them more amenable to the qualitative approach to research. Miles & Huberman (1994) use such terms as *credibility* and *authenticity* in the context of internal validity, basically referring to the question of how much truth value there is in a set of qualitative research findings. They view this dimension of validity as asking "Do we have an authentic portrait of what we were looking at?" (p. 278). External validity is expressed in terms of transferability and fittingness in the qualitative framework. Both of these perspectives are not too far afield from the manner in which we have examined validity for experimental investigations. Researchers using both qualitative and quantitative models are therefore concerned with the credibility of their findings and the degree to which they can generalize their results. With these matters in common, we will examine threats to validity that are most closely related to qualitative research circumstances—researcher effects and threats to trustworthiness.

Researcher Effects

We mentioned earlier that researcher effects may occur because of biases that an investigator may have and also because of the influence of inserting the researcher, as a new person, into an existing social situation. Bias (partiality, prejudice, or perception) may influence the manner in which a researcher collects data. It may subtly alter what is recorded and also impact the interpretation or meaning assigned to events. Because researchers are humans, they necessarily carry with them all of the preferences and dislikes that normally accompany a lifetime of experience. However, as researchers, they need to guard against these inclinations' exerting such an influence that the data become inaccurate.

There are some steps that can be employed to safeguard against bias' unduly impacting qualitative results. One helpful procedure involves the manner in which field notes are recorded. It is important to record information with a heavy emphasis on what occurred rather than including interpretation at this stage. There is ample time to interpret and explain during the analysis phase. Field notes that include a significant portion of pure description are less vulnerable to validity questions than those that become more interpretative. Additionally, it is important to provide a complete description of how the data were collected. This is a limitation found in some qualitative studies and a more detailed account of the methodology provides strength to an investigation (Miles & Huberman, 1994).

The presence of a researcher may influence the interactions and behavior of subjects being observed. Subjects are likely to act differently than they would if this stranger were not in their midst. Fortunately there are some interventions that can minimize this threat to validity. Qualitative investigators typically insert themselves into the research setting for an extended period of time—often long enough that they truly become insiders. The observer thereby becomes a routine part of the environment and subjects become more like what they were before. Although this is crucial to reducing researcher effects, at least two additional steps should be taken. The researcher should check discretely with insider informants to determine what behavioral changes they see when the investigator is present. Additionally the researcher can disengage or leave the setting. By following up and interviewing participants who remain, an additional assessment of change that might be due to researcher presence can be obtained. These further steps will help to verify the authenticity of interactions observed while actually in the field.

Threats to Trustworthiness

Qualitative investigators, like others, may reach inaccurate conclusions from the data gathered. As they collect and analyze their information they may misinterpret the meaning of their findings. Many factors may lead to such interpretations, some that are more likely to surface in qualitative studies than others. For example, it is not uncommon for qualitative research to be conducted in different cultures, where language differences exist and subtle nuances may be overlooked or misinterpreted. One example in which this may have occurred is the research of Margaret Mead on Samoa (Mead, 1928).

One area of great interest in Mead's work related to her reporting of Samoan sexual behavior. Mead's interpretation of her data indicated that extremely smooth sexual adjustments were made by Samoans with young females postponing marriage "...through as many years of casual love-making as possible" (Freeman, 1983, p. 226). This interpretation was based on her conversations with young Samoan women, and Mead concluded that premarital sex was not only customary, it was a casual pastime. This conclusion was of great interest and had a significant impact on the prevalent view of the Samoan culture. However, questions began to emerge regarding the authenticity of Mead's interpretation. Later evidence suggested that recreational sex was not as prevalent in Samoa as much as "recreational lying," particularly related to sex (Freeman, 1989). Further investigation indicated that Mead might have been in error to accept her informants' statements about sexual behavior at face value. In fact, their responses to her questions may have been prompted by embarrassment and been given in a joking manner. However, Mead took the responses seriously and did not corroborate through other sources.

This example provides an excellent illustration of a threat to trustworthy interpretation. It also emphasizes the importance of triangulation in qualitative research methodology. In order to maximize the trustworthiness of qualitative findings, it is essential that the investigator cross-check information with multiple sources. These multiple sources might include other informants or they might involve official documents and other written records. At any rate, qualitative data obtained from one source is of questionable validity.

***Turn to page 242 and complete
Simulations 8.7 and 8.8***

Comments

We have examined a broad array of threats to validity in this chapter. And we have explored these threats in many contexts, including experimental, nonexperimental, quantitative and qualitative methods. It probably doesn't comfort you to know that we have not been exhaustive in this discussion. Our purpose has been to illustrate some of the pitfalls one can encounter in designing or planning research. There is no checklist, primarily because research is a way of thinking. As you become more experienced with scientific approaches to gathering information, you begin to anticipate limitations and threats to data accuracy. Do not try to memorize; there is simply too much—and a mechanically programmed memory is no substitute for thoughtful consideration.

Simulations

Simulation 8.1

Topic: Internal Validity

Background Statement: The ability to identify and circumvent internal validity problems is essential for both the consumer of research and the person designing an investigation. Eliminating problems or potential problems is the crucial issue when one is planning a study. Identifying weaknesses permits research consumers to make their own decisions concerning how useful the results might be. As with so many other skills, practice and related experience seem to greatly enhance the ability to use knowledge about threats to research design.

Tasks to Be Performed:

1. Read the following material.
2. Note any internal validity weakness(es) that is (are) evident from this report of the experiment. Suggest how data may have been contaminated if such contamination may have occurred. Suggest a way to circumvent any difficulty you note.

Stimulus Material: Smith and Smith (1983) studied movement in an investigation that involved two experimental variables. On one variable the experimenters were investigating subject naivete about the fact that an investigation was underway. The second experimental variable involved room color. The accompanying diagram illustrates the fashion in which the study was designed.

These investigators varied the color of a contrived art gallery and found that naive subjects in a dark brown room took more footsteps at a faster pace than subjects who were placed in a light beige room. The subject groups in the brown gallery also covered nearly twice as much area, in a less dense movement pattern, and spent less time in the room

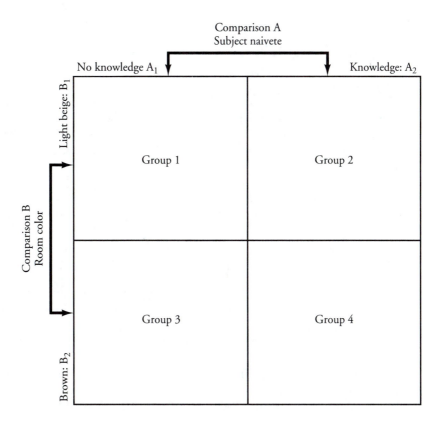

than those in the beige gallery. Under the second conditions the subjects were aware that they were in an experiment, although the true nature of the investigation was camouflaged with information that another factor was under study. In this condition, subjects were run individually through the same rooms that subjects had encoutered as groups in the condition of no knowledge. Under this condition no difference in the movement was evident between the brown and beige conditions.

For feedback see page 246.

Simulations 8.2 and 8.3

Topic: Internal Validity

Background Statement: The ability to identify and circumvent internal validity problems is essential for the consumer of research as well as for the person designing an investigation. Eliminating problems or potential problems is the crucial behavior when one is planning a study. Identifying weaknesses permits research consumers to make their own decisions concerning how useful the results might be. As with so many other skills, practice and related experience seem to greatly enhance the ability to use knowledge about threats to research design.

Tasks to Be Performed for Simulation 8.2:

1. Read the following material.
2. Note any internal validity weakness(es) that is (are) evident from this report of an experiment. Suggest how data may have been contaminated if such contamination occurred. Also be alert for other weaknesses, if any, such as logic weaknesses or inferences that may not be supportable from this study.

Stimulus Material for Simulation 8.2: Simulation 8.2 is excerpted from Drew, C. J. (1971). "Research on the Psychological-Behavioral Effects of the Physical Environment." *Review of Educational Research, 41*, 447-465. Copyright 1971 by the American Educational Research Association. Reprinted by permission of the publisher.

Rohlcs (1967) reported a series of experiments conducted on the effects of manipulating the thermal environment. Results indicated that a temperature of 98° F with a relative humidity of 70 percent did not produce thermal stress, whereas 105° F with 70 percent relative humidity did. Following the line of reasoning that anxiety might be related to this finding, the author identified high-anxiety and low-anxiety individuals and asked them to participate as subjects. None of the highly anxious subjects would volunteer.

Rohles (1967) also described an investigation of crowding and thermal stress. One group of subjects was composed primarily of juvenile delinquents, parolees, high school dropouts, and those await- ing the draft. A second group was composed of graduate students of a similar age. In crowded conditions with high temperatures, the first group exhibited a great deal of aggressive behavior. This be- havior diminished, however, in smaller groups or lower tempera- tures. The subjects who were students did not exhibit aggressive behaviors even under the highest temperatures and most crowded conditions. It was hypothesized on the basis of these findings that "if individuals who are prone to exhibit aggressive behavior are exposed to high temperatures under crowded conditions, the thresh- old for exhibiting this behavior will be lowered."

For feedback see page 247.

Tasks to Be Performed for Simulation 8.3:

1. Read the following material, which is a contrived *subjects* section in the method part of a research article. Note that the study involves a two-group comparison, which is the context within which you must look for internal validity problems.
2. Note any internal validity problem(s) that is (are) evident from this description of group composition. Suggest how data may have been contaminated if you think that such contamination occurred. Sug- gest a way to design the study that might circumvent the problems you have identified.

Stimulus Material for Simulation 8.3:   Thirty subjects with mental retardation were selected randomly from an institutional population with IQs ranging from 55 to 75 and chronological ages (CAs) of 20 to 26 years. A nonretarded sample was selected in a similar fashion from a college-student population with CAs 20 to 26 years. Subjects evidencing a speech, hearing, chronic health, or behavior problem that might inter- fere with experimental performance were eliminated from the popula- tion before sampling procedures were initiated.

For feedback see page 247.

Simulation 8.4

Topic: Internal Validity

Background Statement: As noted in the text, internal validity is as much a concern with time-series designs as it is with traditional experimental studies. This simulation presents a time-series situation and asks that you criticize and circumvent any difficulties noted.

Tasks to Be Performed:

1. Read the following material. Note difficulties as well as the experimenter's explanation.
2. Determine the soundness of the experimenter's inference. Do you agree with the explanation or not? Why?
3. What would you suggest as a means of circumventing any internal validity problems noted?

Stimulus Material: A time-series experiment was conducted on a young boy who was identified as being hyperactive. The investigator believed that the hyperactive behavior could be brought under control by positively reinforcing the child for remaining in his seat and "on-task" while ignoring (thereby not reinforcing) any out-of-seat occurrences or "off-task" behavior. Since the researcher suspected that the hyperactive behavior was being reinforced and maintained in the classroom, it was decided that an A-B-A reversal design would be used. The data collected appeared as in the accompanying illustration.

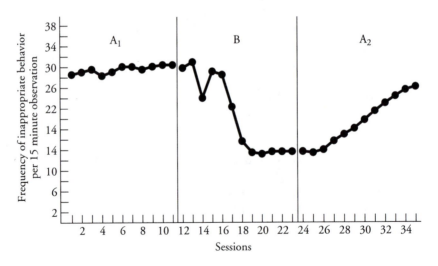

In viewing the data display, the experimenter became excited, since it appeared that the treatment (reinforcement contingencies) were effective in reducing inappropriate behavior. Baseline appeared to be stable (stable high rate) and evidenced a change under phase B. The rate stabilized nicely and showed a somewhat gentle but convincing reversal under phase A_2. Thus the experimenter was prone to suggest that the treatment effected change in inappropriate behavior.

Then some new information came to the researcher's attention. The mother had long been frustrated by the child's behavior and had consulted the local Dr. Spock (more appropriately, the family physician), who prescribed medication to control the hyperactivity. This medication was begun on the day that phase B was initiated. The medication rather than the reinforcement contingencies could have generated the behavior change in B. The researcher, however, maintained that the treatment was effective as evidenced by the reversal when reinforcement contingencies were changed back to baseline conditions.

Do you agree or disagree with the interpretation? If so, would you use it for the same or different reasons? If not, why not? How would you change the design or in some other way test the interpretation?

For feedback see page 249.

Simulation 8.5

Topic: Internal Validity

Background Statement: The ability to identify and circumvent internal validity problems is essential for the consumer of research as well as for the person designing an investigation. Eliminating problems or potential problems is a crucial behavior when one is planning an investigation. Identifying weaknesses permits research consumers to make their own decisions concerning how useful the results might be. As with so many other skills, practice and related experience seem to greatly enhance the ability to use knowledge about threats to research design.

Tasks to Be Performed:

1. Read the following stimulus material, which is a sketch of an investigation that was concerned with the treatment of acne.
2. Note any potential internal validity weakness(es) and suggest how they could be circumvented. What about external validity?

Stimulus Material: An investigation was conducted "at a famous research center in the East" on the treatment of acne in teenage boys and girls. A sample was drawn randomly from volunteers who, by self-admission, had moderate to severe acne problems. Two comparison groups were formed by random assignment with careful precautions taken to ensure equal distribution of sexes between groups. One group received the new acne treatment, while the second group received an identically packaged placebo of innocuous material. Exactly the same instructions were given to both groups by the same experimenter. Diet was controlled between the two groups.

After a four-week treatment period, the same experimenter individually interviewed each subject in both groups and assessed the severity of the acne after treatment. Data were collected by the clinical judgment of the experimenter using a standard checklist carefully designed to maintain objectivity.

For feedback see page 249.

Simulation 8.6

Topic: Study Design

Tasks to Be Performed:

1. Read the following stimulus material.
2. What type of research question is asked?
3. What is the experimental variable?
4. What type of general design approach seems appropriate?
5. Diagram the study as you see it.
6. What variables need to be controlled?
7. Now design the study in detail.
8. In relation to item 7, note categories of details that require your attention.

Stimulus Material: You have been asked to compare the effectiveness of two types of visual instruction. Both methods use filmed presentations. One presents the information in animated form (cartoon-like characters such as those used in *Sesame Street*). The other approach presents the same information in the same sequence with actual people performing the same operations that the animated characters do. The manufacturers of the films are concerned that the animation, although of high interest, may be sufficiently removed from reality that instructional effectiveness is reduced.

For feedback see page 250.

Simulation 8.7

Topic: Researcher Effects

Background Statement: Qualitative researchers can affect the content of their data and the nature of conclusions in a number of ways in the data-gathering and the analysis and writing stages of research. Qualitative researchers must be continually alert to possible effects they may have on the research setting and search for ways to mitigate these effects. The researchers' deeply held beliefs and perceptions can color what they observe or hear. Additionally, if people being studied change their behavior while the researcher is observing them in a qualitative field study, the data and any conclusions drawn from the data are threatened. In a sense, they create an artificial social situation that may differ in very important ways from the natural setting.

Tasks to Be Performed:

1. Read the stimulus material that follows.
2. Describe potential threats from researcher effects and procedures you would recommend to mitigate against researcher effects in this particular study. Write your recommendations as though they were actual research procedures to be followed in the field during the execution of the study. What additional threat(s) might you be aware of that may need to be acknowledged in the research report but are difficult to adjust for?

Stimulus Material: A school district located near a major research university is designing and planning to implement a "shared governance" program that gives teachers increased decision-making power at the school level. Researchers at the nearby university are interested in teacher decision making, participation, and collaboration in "learning communities."

Several doctoral students on sabbatical leaves from the school district to complete their dissertations are eager to study the new site-based decision-making structure's implementation in light of their interests. They are committed to increasing democratic governance structures in schools and teachers' voice on professional issues.

One student decides to make this new program the subject of her dissertation and makes arrangements with the district and the staff of a school near the school from which she is on leave to study teachers, administrators, parents, and students as they develop their school's plan. The principal volunteered the school for the new program, and the faculty agreed to participate. The researcher will spend the year observing faculty meetings, teacher decision-making committees, classroom teaching, and other activities. She also will interview some teachers and parents, the principal, the district superintendent, and members of the school board. She tells her dissertation advisor that she is thrilled about this opportunity to show how collaboration, community, and power-sharing among teachers can improve education.

for feedback, see page 250.

Simulation 8.8

Topic: Strengths and limitations: Qualitative study

Tasks to Be Performed:

1. Read the following stimulus material that was adapted from A. W. Hart (1990). Impacts of the school social unit on teacher authority during work redesign. *American Educational Research Journal, 27*(3), 503-532. Copyright 1990 by the American Educational Research Association. Adapted by permission of the publisher.
2. List the strengths and limitations you see in the study.

Stimulus Material:

A comparative case study of two schools (South and West) implementing the same work redesign structure was chosen as a means for exploring social unit factors in work redesign.... As soon as permission to conduct the study in a district implementing work redesign was obtained from the institutional review board (IRB) for research with human subjects, the superintendent, the school board, and principals were approached for access to schools. The principals of two junior high schools agreed to participate, and, after the study was explained at a regular faculty meeting, the sites were selected. Teachers were given the option as individuals not to join the project, even if their school participated. Three teachers opted out of the study.

To assure multiple perspectives with one researcher, data from a variety of sources were collected and conclusions were checked with participants with varying opinions and vested interests. Two types of data were gathered directly by the researcher: (a) systematic field notes, collected by nonparticipant observation for two days a month at each school, September through May; and (b) structured and unstructured interviews. Structured interviews with teachers, principals, and assistant principals were conducted in three cycles—September/October, January/February, and April/May. Participants initially were asked questions designed to elicit their own stories about the career ladder with as little researcher influence as possible: "Tell me about the career ladder at West." Probes focused on categories developed from the literature on school reform and work design (e.g., individual work preferences, what teachers were talking about and with whom, tasks being undertaken as part of the career ladder). These interviews (164 structured ones lasting 30-60 minutes) were recorded on audiotape and transcribed. Informal, unstructured interviews with teachers, students, and administrators occurred throughout the year. Informal interviews began as spontaneous conversations, usually in the halls, faculty room, or lunchroom or on the school grounds after school. These interviews were recorded in field notes the same day.

Like the informal interviews, observed conversations were recorded as unobtrusively as possible. To do this, the researcher would periodically leave the school and sit in her car to take notes. Other notes were taken more openly. Whenever career ladder teacher meetings, faculty meetings, or conferences were scheduled for an observation day and the teachers and administrators involved consented, the researcher observed and recorded these events simultaneously.

Systematic field notes were prepared by the researcher from the notes taken at the schools within 36 hours following observations or interviews. Notes from observations, conversations, conversations which grew into informal interviews, and the proceedings of meetings were divided into three sections: (a) an objective narrative in which the researcher attempted to provide a verbatim record of statements or an account of events which was as complete as possible, (b) researcher comments on the emotional tone of the event or interview (e.g., rushed or relaxed atmosphere, cooperative or reticent attitudes, aggressiveness, defensiveness, or resentment), and (c) reflections and emerging patterns. A scholar specializing in qualitative field research read field notes in the autumn to audit for comprehensiveness, objectivity, and follow up. Interviews were transcribed directly from audiotape.

Participants provided the researcher with existing documents, audiotapes of meetings the researcher did not attend (transcribed later), and teacher journals. Documents prepared for the study were: (a) journals of the 6 teacher leaders, 23 probationary teachers, and 3 of the teacher specialists; (b) a mid-year survey of teacher leaders and novice teachers assessing the frequency, content and process of supervision under the new structure (return rate of 95%); and (c) notes from 41 classroom observations by teacher leaders and 20 observations by principals. Participants were asked to record impressions, conversations, and events in the school (once or twice a week) that they felt were related to the career ladder. However, they failed to keep their journals consistently, tending instead to record thoughts and incidents sporadically, so journals were dominated by crises and emotionally charged experiences (both negative and positive). Participants recorded things like overt praise from colleagues, arguments in faculty meetings, complaints by a teacher to a friend about the quality of observation and feedback he or she was receiving, and rumors about the abuse of career ladder time. The journals reflected teacher rather than researcher questions and highlighted issues dominating teachers' thoughts but were episodic and unrepresentative of daily experiences.

Documents relating to the career ladder but not generated for the study included: (a) the plan, (b) job descriptions, (c) newsletters and in-service materials prepared for or by career ladder teachers, (d) official minutes and teachers' notes of task force and faculty meetings, and (e) public documents such as newspaper articles, related to career ladder events. Other data came from audiotapes and transcripts of two planning meetings of the teachers at South and 17 postobservation conferences between teacher leaders and novice teachers. . . .

Several procedures were used to mitigate researcher effects. First, a teacher at each school was asked, at the beginning of the study, to watch for any changes in behavior occurring with site visits. . . . Second, one teacher at each school who was experienced, respected by other teachers, an opponent of the new structure, and not a participant in the career ladder was identified by teachers and administrators. Interviewed formally before December and informally throughout the year, they provided a useful foil for others' ideas. Several unsuccessful applicants for career ladder positions and members of the selection committees also were interviewed. Finally, the researcher returned to the schools the following autumn to test the strength and explanatory value of conclusions by sharing them with teachers and administrators in small groups and private meetings. Several changes in the interpretation of the data were made as a result of these visits. (pp. 510-513)

for feedback, see page 252.

Simulation Feedbacks

Simulation 8.1

The most obvious internal validity threat is to comparison A. Recall that there was no difference between the movement of subjects in brown versus beige rooms under A_2, in which subjects were aware that they were in an experiment. There was, however, a difference between the movement under brown and beige conditions when subjects had no knowledge of the experiment (A_1). So it appears that knowledge of the existence of an experiment had some influence. There is a problem with such an interpretation, however. If you inspect the report concerning the way in which subjects encountered the rooms, you will find a difference between A_1 and A_2 *in addition to the knowledge variable.* Subjects in the A_2 condition were administered the experimental task individually, whereas those in A_1 were in groups. This raises a red flag immediately. Even more of a threat is evident when one considers the criterion measure of movement speed and pattern. One would expect a difference on both of these measures depending on whether a person was in an art gallery alone or with someone. Thus the differential effects of A_1 and A_2 could have been a result of the knowledge variable, the way in which subjects were administered the task, or a combination of both.

To circumvent this threat one would merely hold the way in which the task was administered constant between A_1 and A_2 conditions. Either group or individual administration might be appropriate, but it should be the same for A_1 and A_2.

Simulation 8.2

Methodological issues involved in this study were discussed later in the review by Drew. Viewing the initial paragraph first, there is a subtle inference that may be inappropriate. The critique of this inference read as follows:

> Rohles (1967) did not make specific inferences from his finding that high anxiety individuals would not volunteer for his thermal stress experiment. The reader, however, may be inclined to draw unfounded conclusions relating anxiety level and thermal environment. Such an implication, although possibly forthcoming in future research, is not given sufficient support as yet to warrant such a conclusion. It is likely that highly anxious individuals would be reluctant to participate in any experiment they are aware of.

The most serious internal validity difficulties were then discussed in the following statement. If it is helpful, diagram the basic two-group comparison and then consider how the concept of control is violated and thus internal validity weakened.

> Further reservation is in order concerning Rohles' (1967) report of the behavioral tendencies of 'aggressive-prone' subjects as compared to graduate students in high temperature and crowded conditions. At least two systematic differences between these groups could be contaminating his between-group comparisons. One might suspect that a difference in intelligence existed between the two groups. Although this may have produced behavioral differences, the second problem would seem even more compelling to prompt further study. Graduate students are, by the fact of their status, substantially adapted to the environment of the university and its scholarly research orientation. In fact, it is possible that such students are experienced as subjects. It is doubtful that the same can be said for high-school dropouts, juvenile delinquents, parolees, and those awaiting the draft. In light of this possibility, it is not surprising that behavioral differences of the nature described were noted between these groups.

Simulation 8.3

Although a variety of potential problems are evident in this statement, the most serious involves the major comparison between retarded and nonretarded subjects. Without any additional information about the study, it is evident that there is at least a two-group comparison such as that illustrated below.

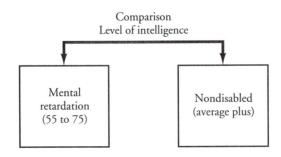

First of all, recall from your reading of the text that this would be known as a quasi-experimental design, since the different levels of the experimental variable existed in the subjects before the experiment, rather than a true experimental design, in which the subjects would be equivalent initially and the treatment would be the sole difference. The major problem with this particular study is that the level of intelligence is far from being the only dimension on which the groups are different (which is necessary if the concept of control is to be operative, creating an internally valid investigation). Initially, consider the fact that the members of the nonretarded group were college students, whereas the retarded group was selected from an institutionalized population. Despite the fact that some would contend that both sources of subjects are institutions, this is indeed problematic. People with mental retardation are institutionalized for reasons beyond their intelligence level (as are college students). For example, social and behavioral problems are frequently compelling issues in the institutionalization of retarded individuals. This would raise the possibility that there are substantial differences in the frequency of behavioral problems between the groups in addition to the intelligence variable. Also, what about cultural, ethnic, and socioeconomic status? It is not only possible but probable that a higher proportion of ethnic minorities, lower socioeconomic status (SES), and cultural subgroups are found among institutionalized retarded persons than among the nonretarded college students. Of course if the researcher is studying level of intelligence, these other systematic differences between the groups represent threats to internal validity. How might you attempt to control these variables?

Beyond the more obvious difficulties noted above, other concerns should be addressed if the study is to be redesigned. The IQ level for the retarded group is defined and involves a 20-point range. However, since the members of the nonretarded group are in college, they are apparently assumed to be average or above average in intelligence. This is a rather sloppy manner to conduct a study, and it also offers the probability of much more than a 20-point range for the nonretarded group. The two groups should at least be defined in terms of a similar range spread so that one group does not automatically have a greater variability in terms of the descriptive characteristics.

Simulation 8.4

The researcher's observations about the reversal in A_2 are based on the basic assumption of the design (that if withdrawal of the treatment results in reversal, the treatment may be viewed as generating the effect). These arguments are not, however, entirely convincing. For the moment, suppose that the medication generated the behavior change in B. It is possible that physiological adaptation occurred after a period of time and the medication was no longer as effective as it was intitially. If this adaptation began to occur at about the time that A_2 was instituted, the gradual change under the reversal condition may be a result of a lessening effectiveness of medication (rather than a withdrawal of the reinforcement contingencies). Thus the data in phase A_2 could support a medication influence as well as reinforcement contingencies.

Circumventing the problem would best be accomplished by a replication of the entire experiment and by studying the effects of the reinforcement without medication being involved. If the researcher had known of the problem before terminating the experiment, some strength could have been gained by adding a B_2 condition (making it an A-B-A-B design). This would have only been suggestive, however, and a clean replication without medication is the soundest alternative.

Simulation 8.5

It is unfortunate that so many precautions were taken to attain an internally valid investigation only to have it plagued by one threat that has been a constant problem for many drug studies. The same experimenter who administered treatment also recorded the data after treatment. Since it is not mentioned otherwise, it can be assumed that the experimenter was aware of which subjects were in the treatment group and which were in the placebo group. Particularly since the data were recorded using a checklist based on clinical judgment, there is the possibility that there was an unconscious biasing of the data, perhaps favoring the actual treatment over the placebo. This is a classic example of a situation in which a double-blind study should have been used, which would have "blinded" the data recorder from information concerning which group any individual subject was in. How about other problems?

External validity is certainly questionable from the standpoint that the intitial source of subjects for the sampling were volunteers with an admitted acne problem. Regardless of what influences may be operative to prompt the admission of such a problem (that might make them different from those individuals who did not or would not), it is doubtful that they are "like" the general population. Results are probably generalizable to other teen-age boys and girls who would admit such a problem, but it is doubtful that beyond those like the volunteers, the data are accurate with regard to external validity.

Simulation 8.6

A considerable amount of latitude was available to you in your work on this simulation. It would be impossible to anticipate all the possible details in responses that might occur. Consequently you should check with your instructor concerning aspects of your work that are not addressed below.

1. The research question being asked is a difference question, since you are comparing the effectiveness of two types of visual instruction.
2. The experimental variable is method of presentation. Depending on how you viewed the paragraph, you may have stated the variable as "degree of reality." This would certainly be appropriate, since this is the essential characteristic distinguishing the two methods.
3. This material is probably best suited for a traditional experimental approach comparing two groups.
4. Your diagram should generally look like the one in Figure 5.6 on p. 119. You would, of course, have different labels for the conditions and the experimental variable.
5. This is a particularly challenging study in which to attempt to control the necessary factors to achieve internal validity. This is an area in which you will want to exchange ideas with your colleagues and check with your instructor. You may want to be alert to such areas as content of the material, time or duration of the film, subject factors such as age and intelligence, and many others.
6. With regard to your response to this simulation, remember Murphy's Law. Review the pages in the text that discuss these types of details.

Simulation 8.7

Educators often want to study problems they and their colleagues face in their everyday work, and nothing could be more appropriate for a professional. You should have noted immediately that this very quality constitutes a threat of researcher effects, however. Because educators as researchers hold strong professional beliefs and want reforms and new programs to succeed, they suffer a built-in bias toward success. You probably noted that the researcher saw her research as an opportunity to show that collaboration and participation are good and will improve education. She immediately must be on guard because she will start looking for evidence that the new program is improving teacher morale, instruction, and learning. Conversely, she will tend to ignore data suggesting problems or potential failures and discounting impacts on learning outcomes. A well-designed experimental research study, even when the researcher holds the same beliefs, guards against these beliefs creeping into the attention-giving process during data gathering in the field.

Several procedures should be designed to mitigate against these potential effects. First, the researcher should design her observation schedule (where and when) so that she sits in on meetings which opponents of the plan and skeptics are likely to attend and voice their opinions and so that she observes interactions over time. She must remain in the field long enough to become a regular fixture in the school, so that teachers, parents, administrators, and students tend to forget she is present.

Second, soon after entering the school, the researcher should quietly ask around for the names of teachers or others who are skeptical of the reform or who oppose it. At least one or two of these people should be included among her regular informants and placed on the interview schedule.

Third, a teacher in the school who attends many of the activities associated with the new program should be asked to observe team meetings, planning and development activities, faculty meetings, etc., for differences in people's demeanor, statements, and attitudes when the researcher is not present. These should be carefully noted in field notes, and the researcher should watch for a decrease in these effects over time. If they do not decrease, sources of data about activities when the researcher is not present should be found.

Fourth, the interview sample should be chosen randomly, or a stratified random sample should be selected so that representatives of all major subgroups in the school are included (i.e., special educators, administrators, upper and lower grades, subject or content areas, staff, counselors, and psychologists). Informants with a view divergent from the majority should be added to the sample, and additional people should be added as informants mention people in-the-know that the researcher should talk to.

Fifth, as data gathering and analysis progress, the researcher should check emerging themes and patterns she is observing with the participants to see if they match the participants' experience and understanding of events. She should be tolerant of diverse beliefs and opinions among participants and should not discount variant information.

Sixth, she should seek documentary data collected and compiled by others in addition to interviews and observations. Documents could include such things as minutes of meetings, memoranda, letters, formal policies, and plans.

Finally, the researcher should subject her data and analysis to an audit by another researcher with no stake in the school, the district, or shared governance but with skill in qualitative research methods. The auditor can trace a backward map of themes and conclusions to data to check for a chain of logic and trustworthiness of conclusions. The major portion of analysis and writing, as well as the audit, should take place after the researcher leaves the school and removes herself from the setting.

Because the researcher is an employee of the school district, she will be unable to change this relationship. She suffers from a subtle pressure to conclude that the district's plan is a good one. This will be even more the case if any grant money from the state or other sources is associated with the project. She should acknowledge these ties, make arrangements with her superiors to provide a report on her research that protects participants, and inform readers of her background. During analysis, she should vigilantly look for disconfirming cases or examples of positive effects of the reform on the school or student learning and carefully avoid making unwarranted causal attributions about student outcomes.

A written record of all these procedures should be carefully kept. The researcher and her readers can then trace the procedures taken to mitigate researcher effects.

Simulation 8.8

Many of the points noted in the feedback for Simulation 8.7 were incorporated into this investigation. Data were collected from a variety of sources in order to guard against researcher bias. This was further safeguarded by checking with participants holding varying opinions and vested interests. Data were also collected at three points during the school year, allowing for additional information to be included beyond the participants' perceptions at any one point. All of these are strengths in the study. Additional strength is found in the collection of two types of data, one from field notes and the second from interviews.

One matter that is often difficult in field studies also plagued this investigation. It is always desirable to collect data from a random sample of participants in order to appropriately represent all major subgroups. Although many different subgroups did participate (e.g., teachers, principals, assistant principals), information is not available suggesting that a random sample of these subgroups was selected (and three people chose not to participate). This limitation was offset to some degree by the investigator's purposefully seeking out representation. For the most part the investigator in this study covered most of the bases for solid qualitative research. Review relevant portions of the chapter if you need additional information on any of these points.

Chapter 9

Subject Selection and Assignment

This chapter examines topics that are primarily used in experimental and quantitative research. There are circumstances in qualitative investigations in which the sampling of subjects occurs prior to initiating the data collection, and sampling is a topic of interest in qualitative research (e.g., Henwood & Pidgeon, 1992). However, as we proceed with the material on subject selection and assignment, it is evident that experimental-quantitative studies are the primary users of these tools.

Sampling and assignment are part of the many activities that are involved in the implementation of a research study. Researchers must not take the attitude that these activities represent mere logistics and are of secondary importance. Although we have emphasized the crucial nature of pre-investigation planning, it is vital that the researcher remain alert during the execution of the study. Errors during this phase plague investigators in many disciplines and can easily destroy the worth of the most carefully laid plans (Evans, Dingus, & Haselkorn, 1993; Hser, 1993; Walker & Lewine, 1993). Additionally, a complete articulation of each step in implementation, prior to actually beginning a study, is of vital importance. Pitfalls will be avoided only if the researcher attends to details in planning before they threaten the soundness of an investigation.

Subject Selection

There are several questions that must be addressed in the selection of subjects for an investigation: (1) Are the subjects appropriate for the research question? (2) Are the subjects representative? and (3) How many subjects should be used? To assure that a study is conceptually sound, a researcher must select subjects who are appropriate to the topic under study. Child development (in the usual sense) is hardly being investigated if the subjects are college sophomores. Likewise, if the intellectual status of adults who have schizophrenia is the topic, the subject's diagnosis certainly ought to fit the definition of schizophrenia. Consideration of subject variables is a part of defining the population operationally and includes a multitude of factors to which the researcher must attend.

An integral part of the subject selection issue is the representative nature of the sample. Assuming that the researcher wants to know something about how a given population responds, subjects in a study should resemble that population. Because it is doubtful that the entire population can be tested, a sample must be used that presumably will provide results similar to those that would have been obtained if the entire population had been studied. The degree to which results are generalizable, or are externally valid, is critically influenced by subject selection.

The issue of how many subjects should be involved in the study is related to concerns about the generalizability of results. This difficult question is repeatedly asked by beginning research students. Sample size is problematic because no set answer or rule may be given. Several contingencies impinge on decisions regarding what is an adequate sample.

Defining the Population

Operationally defining the population under investigation is essential both with respect to identifying subjects appropriate for the research question and obtaining a representative sample. A population refers to all constituents of any clearly described group of people, events, or objects who, for research purposes, are designated as being the focus of an investigation. Populations may be quite large (theoretically infinite) or they may be substantially limited. For example, a population might be defined as "all third-year nursing students in the United States who are enrolled in degree programs." This population would include a rather large number of individuals who are potential subjects. However, one additional restriction in the definition would dramatically reduce the size of this population. If the population were to be defined as "all third-year male nursing students in the United States who are enrolled in degree programs," the number of potential subjects would be much smaller. The essential factor in population definition involves the units or restrictions that are used to describe the set. In the first example, four restrictions were used in the definition: (1) nursing students, (2) third year of study, (3) in the United States, and (4) enrolled in degree programs. Unless the population is clearly defined, the researcher does not know what units or restrictions to use when selecting the sample of subjects (Fraenkel & Wallen, 1993). In addition, without a clearly defined set of characteristics it is unclear to whom the results are generalizable.

The descriptive characteristics used in defining a given research population must relate to the topic under study. If one is investigating some aspect of measured intelligence, then it is logical that the population definition include some unit(s) that reflect(s) intelligence specifications. Restrictions in the definition are intended to exclude subjects with unwanted characteristics. This is an important factor in conducting a precise study and should have a priori consideration rather than hasty field decisions. In the example of nursing students, the population was defined as being enrolled in degree programs. By this definition the researcher is not interested in students who are enrolled in diploma programs (degree versus diploma is a distinction made in the professional training of nurses), and such students are not eligible as potential subjects. Often, additional restrictions are added to population statements, such as "Individuals with marked visual, hearing, or emotional problems that could potentially interfere with task performance will be eliminated before sampling." Such restrictions involve subject properties that are not a part of the investigation and would contribute only error variance to the results.

Following definition of the population, the researcher must obtain or construct a complete list of all individuals in the population. This list is known as a *frame.* The construction of a frame can be an extremely difficult and laborious task unless such a listing is already available. Occasionally it is impossible to construct a complete frame as defined by the population (e.g., listing all the fish in a given lake).

If it becomes logistically impossible (or economically unfeasible) to construct a precise population frame, the researcher may find it necessary to work with a more restricted list. For example, resources may not permit the construction of a population frame for "all fourth-grade students in the state of Oregon." The experimenter may then decide to form what is known as a *subject pool* by selecting a number of districts throughout the state that are representative of the larger population. From this subject pool, a sample of subjects can be drawn to actually participate in the study. Figure 9.1 represents a pictorial example of such a procedure.

The procedure noted above certainly weakens the confidence with which sample results can be directly generalized to the initially defined population. It can be argued that if the frame is compiled from the subject pool, then this is, in fact, a redefined population that is presumably representative of a theoretically larger but not actually formed population. From a practical standpoint, it is of little consequence what term is applied. This is a field procedure that is not uncommon, and if it is implemented with care, it can provide acceptable results.

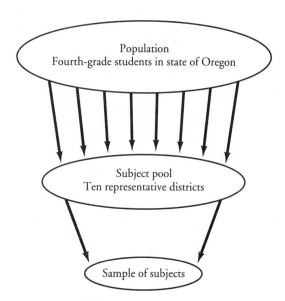

FIGURE 9.1 Subject Selection Using a Subject Pool

The subject pool arrangement portrayed in Figure 9.1 has certain advantages beyond economics. An investigation is seldom conducted without at least some subject mortality. When subjects are lost from the sample, the subject pool can then be used as a replacement pool for selecting alternative subjects. Since the original sample was drawn from this same source, there is little reason to believe that replacement subjects will not approximate those who were selected initially. Thus a researcher will occasionally form a subject pool even when a complete population frame is available. The purpose of this procedure is to allow a researcher the opportunity to replace subjects who are lost or deleted from a study due to procedural errors. This arrangement will facilitate the field operation because return to the large population frame is unnecessary.

*Turn to page 280 and complete
Simulation 9.1*

Selecting a Representative Sample

Once the researcher has a frame from which to sample, the next task is to select subjects that will participate in the study. The sample to be studied must accurately represent the larger population. If the sample is not accurate, interpretations of the results may not be accurate for individuals other than those actually used as subjects. If a researcher is unaware that the sample is unrepresentative, incorrect inferences may be drawn concerning the population.

A representative sample is crucial at two points during the process of selecting subjects. Initially, construction of the subject pool must receive careful attention to ensure a representative group. The previous example concerning fourth-grade students will illustrate this point. If the 10 districts selected for the subject pool are not representative of the state population, there is little reason to believe that a sample drawn from that pool can produce results that are generalizable to the larger population. The second point at which the researcher must be cautious is when the sample is selected from the subject pool. Identical issues are involved here; simply stated, the sample must be representative of the pool if results are to generalize to that pool, and if the subject pool is representative of the population, then results should be somewhat generalizable to the population at large.

Various Sampling Approaches

Several different sampling procedures are used in the behavioral sciences. The conditions of the study determine which procedures are to be used. The crucial nature of subject selection demands that researchers use the most appropriate and rigorous technique possible.

Simple Random Sampling.   Random sampling is probably the best known method of selecting subjects in attempting to form a sample representative of the population. Simple random sampling (occasionally called unrestricted random sampling) is a selection process whereby each individual in the frame has an equal chance of being chosen. Because each person has an equal chance of being selected, it is presumed that the population characteristics will largely be represented similarly to the degree that they exist in the population. A random sample does not totally ensure that all the population characteristics will, in fact, be represented in the sample. However, because chance is used to construct the sample, random sampling substantially reduces the possibility that a biased or unrepresentative group will be selected. More confidence may be placed in the representativeness of the sample when the population is homogeneous with regard to its characteristics. This simply makes for less diversity to be represented. Likewise, the more heterogeneous the population, the greater the chance that all aspects of characteristic diversity will not be represented.

Procedures used to select a random sample are simple and easily implemented. Any technique that ensures that all units in the frame are equally vulnerable to selection will suffice. For example, drawing names from a fishbowl will approximate a random selection process. It is necessary to have the names on individual slips of paper and to mix them well. Similarly, the names might all be placed on cards that are shuffled, after which the desired number of subject cards is selected from the deck. The shuffling procedure must be conducted carefully, however, if a random sample is to be truly approximated. Studies have indicated that casual shuffling does not approximate a chance mixing of cards. (Remember this point the next time a poker game does not seem to be giving you a fair share.)

Probably the most effective procedure for random sampling is also one of the simplest, using a table of random numbers. (There are also computer programs to perform random samples, but you need to have the knowledge in this chapter to understand and use them.) This technique requires the researcher to assign consecutive numbers to each individual listed in the frame. Once this is accomplished, a table of random numbers is used to select those who will serve as subjects. (Tables of random numbers or random units are found in appendices of many statistics books, or one might use specially prepared books of tables such as *Standard Mathematical Tables,* Beyer, 1995). To use a random number table, the researcher merely begins at any point in the table and reads systematically in any direction (vertically or horizontally). When a number is encountered that matches one of the assigned numbers in the frame, that individual becomes a subject. Numbers that are not a part of the frame list are ignored (e.g., if the number 386 appears in the table when the frame includes only 300 individuals, it is ignored). Similarly, numbers already selected are ignored once they become part of the sample (such as the second or third time that 46 appears in the table). This procedure continues until the desired number of subjects is obtained. A random number table, with specific instructions for use, may be found in Simulation 9.2 at the end of this chapter.

***Turn to page 282 and complete
Simulation 9.2***

Stratified Random Sampling. Stratified random sampling is a useful procedure when the investigation being conducted does not permit subject selections from only one population. Such circumstances may exist if the researcher wishes to study two or more groups of individuals who are distinctly different on the basis of some variable important to the research (the quasi-experimental design discussed earlier in this text). An example of such a situation is a developmental study in which three different age-level groups are being compared on a given learning task. Because developmental level is a part of the investigation, formulation of the three groups at different age levels must be forced. Certainly, one cannot expect to obtain three distinct age level groupings by random sampling from a single population.

The different developmental levels in this example actually form three different subpopulations known as *strata*. Each subpopulation or stratum constitutes a group to which the researcher may wish to generalize results. For sampling purposes, each stratum must have subjects selected from it as if one were conducting three miniature experiments. The subject group for each age level will have to be sampled in a fashion that makes that group representative of the age-level subpopulations being studied. An effective way to accomplish this is to use stratified random sampling from each of the respective subpopulations.

Stratified random sampling is accomplished in much the same way as simple random sampling. Once each of the strata is clearly defined, a subpopulation listing or frame is constructed of the individuals who are potential subjects. In the example of a developmental study, three frames would be necessary, one for each age range (e.g., group A, 3-5 years; group B, 6-8 years; group C, 9-11 years). The researcher then randomly samples from strata A, B, and C until the desired number of subjects is obtained for each.

This procedure provides a convenient method of attending to the issue of representative samples from the subpopulations. Additionally, other variables may be held constant in an attempt to equalize groups on variables other than the one under study. Using the developmental investigation as an example, it is usually desirable to have the different age groups be similar on factors such as measured intelligence. To accomplish this, the variable of measured intelligence is defined in common across groups. One would then randomly sample from all the individuals who were 3-5 years of age who had a measured intelligence between 90 and 110. Likewise, one would sample from those 6-8 years of age who had a measured intelligence between 90 and 110, and so on. There is little reason to expect intelligence differences between groups using this procedure. It is prudent, however, to check on this assumption before initiating the experiment. Such a precaution would simply be accomplished by computing group IQ means and statistically testing for differences. If groups are different, the sample should be redrawn from each subpopulation until the IQ variable is equivalent between groups. Often, the control variable means are so similar that equality is obvious even before statistical testing.

Stratified random sampling is also useful in other situations. Occasionally, the logistics of a large investigation may make simple random sampling from the total population difficult. For example, a national survey is being conducted with field offices located throughout the nation. Administrative convenience may suggest that the regional responsibility of a given field office should be defined as a stratum and a sample drawn randomly from that subpopulation. If the sample is drawn with care, there is little reason to expect that it will not represent the stratum. In fact, the composite sample of all strata should represent the larger population.

Proportional Sampling. Situations exist that may generate unrepresentative samples if either simple or stratified random sampling is used. For example, such a condition might be found if a particular subgroup of the defined population were a 10 percent proportion of the total population. In the previous discussion of stratified sampling, we implied that the subpopulation samples would be the same size. This approach would overrepresent the 10 percent group because subgroups would carry equal weight. To avoid such an error in representation (particularly when the groups are to form a single composite sample), it is often useful to sample from subgroups in the same proportion that they exist in the larger total population. This procedure is known as proportional sampling.

Proportional sampling is accomplished in somewhat the same fashion as the stratified approach. Subpopulation frames are constituted, after which a sample is drawn from each. The difference is that each subgroup sample is drawn only in the proportion that it exists in the larger population. For example, if two subgroups exist in the population, one constituting 90 percent of the population (e.g., female nurses) and the second only 10 percent of the population (male nurses), then the composite sample from both subpopulations would represent a 90 percent/10 percent split in proportional representation. This would be achieved by randomly selecting subjects from one frame (female nurses) until 90 percent of the total sample had been obtained and then selecting for the second group (male nurses), which constitutes the remaining 10 percent.

Proportional sampling is used in investigations that have a purpose different from those using equally represented strata. For investigations such as the developmental study discussed earlier in this section, equalized stratified samples are most appropriate. The developmental example is the type of study in which the subsamples are to be maintained separately and, perhaps, compared. This type of investigation is very different from the national survey example in which the strata samples are ultimately to be combined in a composite sample to be totally representative of the national population. In the latter case, the purpose of the study does not include a comparison of the subsamples. Because the inference is aimed more at describing the total national population, representative proportions are more important and probably would warrant proportional sampling. This would prevent male nurses from being overrepresented in describing the population.

Systematic Sampling. Systematic sampling is a logistically convenient procedure that may be expected to result in a representative sample *only* if the frame is arranged appropriately. Imagine that a sample of 100 subjects is to be drawn from a population frame of 1,000. The first task to be performed is the establishment of what is known as the *sample interval*. This may be done by dividing the population frame by the size of sample to be drawn. In this example, 1,000 would be divided by 100, resulting in a sample interval of 10. Now the researcher must determine at which point in the frame to begin drawing subjects. This is accomplished by randomly selecting any number from the first interval. After this has been done, subjects are selected by choosing every *k*th individual from the frame until the desired sample size is obtained. Suppose the randomly identified beginning number in the example was 7. The first subject would be the individual numbered 7 in the frame; then, using the sample interval of 10, numbers 17, 27, 37, 47, and so on, would be drawn until there were 100 subjects.

Systematic sampling is easily executed in field operations. The precision with which a systematic sample represents the population may be expected to at least equal random sampling *if* the population frame list is arranged in an unbiased fashion. A variety of precautionary checks are necessary to avoid sample problems. The major point of difficulty involves possible trends that may exist in the frame list that would result in systematic bias. If the frame is constructed in a fashion whereby individuals are listed in an order of increasing age, considerable bias may result. Because of the systematic progression through the list, two separate samples may be very different depending on the beginning number. The earlier example that began at 7 would be substantially older than a sample that begins at 2 or 3. In either case, the sample mean age may be considerably different from the population mean age, raising questions relating to sample representation. Similarly, an alphabetically constructed frame may result in a biased sample if influential variables related to surname are operative in the population. Examples of this type of problem may include concentrated pockets of minority groups that have characteristic surnames. Consequently, the precision of systematic sampling is essentially determined by the degree to which the population frame is arranged free of influential trends. As with many decision points in research, identification of a problem area is usually based on logic and experience. There is no checklist of "problems to avoid" that is functionally relevant in all situations.

Sampling often requires an investigator to combine component techniques to achieve a desired outcome. At times it may be effective to combine the concepts of stratified and systematic sampling, sometimes called *stratified systematic sampling.* As the label suggests, this approach would be used when different population frames are available and no trends toward bias are evident. Systematic sampling procedures, as described above, may then be implemented within these frames.

Cluster Sampling. Occasionally, a researcher will not find it feasible to list individuals who are potential subjects when formulating a frame.

It may be that the individuals are already grouped in some fashion into clusters (e.g., a school or geographical region would constitute a cluster of students, people, or elements). Cluster sampling is a procedure whereby the researcher lists all the clusters and takes samples from this list. Thus, instead of sampling individual members of the population, a sample cluster is initially selected from which the subjects are then obtained (Yelibi, Valenti, Volpe, & Caprara, 1993). Suppose the researcher were conducting a study involving junior high school students in a large metropolitan area. Rather than formulating the population frame by listing all the junior high students in the area, the investigator lists all the junior high schools (clusters). From this list, a random sample of schools may be drawn from which the actual subjects will be selected. The researcher may elect to use all the students available in the selected clusters or only a sample from those clusters.

Cluster sampling is similar to the subject-pool arrangement discussed earlier in this section. As with subject pools, a critical concern is that the cluster initially selected must be representative of the total population. If the clusters are drawn in a manner that promotes confidence in generalizability, similar confidence should be warranted regarding the performance of subjects sampled from those clusters.

Double Sampling. Double sampling (or two-phase sampling) is a procedure that is often useful for survey research. The term is descriptive of the process: an investigator accesses the subject twice for data. Basically, two situations warrant the use of double sampling. The first involves an intense follow-up with part of a larger primary sample. Such an investigation may be initiated with a rather large sample, using an inexpensive survey instrument. With the results of the first instrument in hand, the researcher may then elect to sample a smaller group from the first round of subjects for purposes of obtaining more in-depth data. This smaller group of subjects is usually sampled in a fashion that will ensure a representative sample of the original larger sample and, in turn, the population. It is not unusual for this smaller group sampling to be accomplished using random procedures.

The second use of double sampling is an attempt to gather missing data. This procedure, which is used most often in survey research, is used to gather the information that is absent because subjects failed to return questionnaires during the first phase. The missing data may alter the results of the investigation if those who fail to complete the questionnaire are, in some fashion, different from subjects who do return the instrument. By virtue of their failure to respond, it is probably true that these subjects are somehow different (e.g., attitude or motivation). To preserve the integrity of the first sample, the researcher may implement the next phase by drawing a second sample from nonrespondents. Usually the second phase involves procedures that are somehow more persuasive in eliciting responses, such as interviews or threats. Caution must be exercised in assuming that the second-phase data are the same as that obtained in the first phase. Certainly, the subjects are from the same first sample, but the research conditions have, by definition, changed. Double sampling may, however, preserve the sample integrity to a greater degree than selecting new subjects from the replacement pool.

Sample Size

A question that is frequently asked by beginning students in research is: How many subjects do I need? This question is often difficult to answer because there is no set sample size required under all conditions. Given different circumstances, larger or smaller samples may serve adequately. If you are interested in more depth regarding appropriate samples, we suggest you review texts that examine this topic in detail and present formulas for estimating size (e.g., Howell, 1995).

One area of concern with regard to sample size is that an adequate sample of behavior must be obtained. Certain characteristics of the population will dictate how large the sample must be to accurately predict population factors. If there is little variation in the population (i.e., if the population is homogeneous), then a much smaller sample will suffice than if more variation is present. High variability within the population indicates that the sample must be larger to permit more of that variation to be represented in the subjects selected. Behavioral science is plagued by considerably more variance than, for example, agriculture or biology. Consequently, samples in behavioral science usually require a larger proportion of the population for accurate generalization.

How does one determine population variability? The answer to such a question is often unsatisfying. Only an estimate of population characteristics can be obtained. If the researcher is conducting an investigation on a given population, there will be some unknowns regarding that population. However, clues about the population's variance may be available in previously published research. Some populations have been shown to be more variable than others over the years. Greater variability is evident, for example, in populations that are deviant on some psychological dimension. People with mental retardation are, for example, more variable than individuals without mental retardation (Drew, Hardman, & Logan, 1996). The researcher can then expect more error variance in any group of people with mental retardation, making an adequate sample necessarily larger. Information concerning such variability can often be gleaned from the published literature and samples drawn accordingly. In the absence of specific published information (such as in the case of a pioneering effort in that area), it is usually prudent to proceed cautiously. A pilot study may be useful for obtaining guidelines, or the first phase of a double-sampling design may similarly provide initial information concerning subject characteristics. Often, the early stages of a program of research are conducted with a conservative attitude that leads the researcher to take larger samples to ensure adequate power (Clark & Ryan, 1993; Dignan, 1993; Wampold & Drew, 1990).

Experimental studies asking difference questions are often designed so that the total sample of subjects is divided into two or more important groups. When treatments are applied to these smaller groups, they essentially become subsamples of the larger group. Therefore, a researcher must consider the number of treatment groups involved rather than the total number of subjects in the experiment. For example, an investigator may select 60 subjects for an experiment in verbal learning. Suppose the study is designed so that six experimental conditions are required. If these are independent conditions, such an experiment would require that the total sample (N) be assigned in some fashion to six different groups, resulting in a cell size (n) of 10. A cell n of 10 subjects is a rather small sample of behavior that may prove to be inadequate. With only 10 subjects per cell, the treatment mean is much more vulnerable to change by an atypical performance than if the group were larger. If researchers do not consider cell size from the outset, they may be dissatisfied with such small subgroups. The most prudent approach to circumventing this difficulty is to determine the desired cell n ahead of time and let the total N be determined by the accumulating ns. Our own general rule of thumb is that cell ns should not be less than 12 to 14 (although at times other logistic concerns force deviation from this personal rule). More confidence may be placed in cell sizes of 20 to 25, which results in rather large sample Ns in more complex experiments. Clearly, nonexperimental investigations also ask questions regarding subgroups that may be formed for comparisons. Bailey (1994) discussed this issue in relation to survey research. The subgroups in any study must be of adequate size to provide a credible sample of behavior, opinions, or other such data.

It should now be clear that there is no agreement concerning the "magic" minimal number of subjects necessary for a study to be sound. The number of subjects is a serious concern with respect to many aspects of design strength and research outcomes in a variety of fields (Kosciulek & Szymanski, 1993; Miller & Oshima, 1992; Stevenson, 1993). There is even great variability within particular methods. For example, Sudman (1976) reviewed several hundred survey studies and found considerable variation between surveys that sampled nationally and those that were regionally oriented. In general, he found that national surveys used samples of 1,000 or more, whereas regional studies varied considerably (50-1,000+) but tended to use smaller samples. As we noted earlier, experimental studies tend to use much smaller samples than the numbers used for survey research. The best guidance can be found by reviewing recent literature in the area being studied. Current research will provide the clearest indication of present professional practice for those substantive areas.

The researcher must also be cognizant of certain statistical considerations when determining sample size. Frequently, limited subject availability will necessitate samples that are somewhat smaller than is desirable. Under such conditions, it may be necessary to alter the statistical analyses that are to be used. A more complete discussion of this aspect of research design is found in Part III of this book.

Subject Selection for Different Purposes

Our discussion regarding subject selection has been quite general up to this point. In this section, we will discuss issues that specifically relate to the type of question being asked.

Comparative or Difference Questions. Two basic concerns of comparative investigations are internal and external validity. To recount briefly, internal validity refers to the technical soundness of a study, whereas external validity has to do with generalizability of results. The researcher who is selecting subjects for a comparative investigation must remain cognizant of both internal and external validity. There may be times during an investigation when concerns about internal validity tend to diminish the generalizability of results. In Chapter 8 this dissonance was mentioned in relation to experimental procedures, but similar conditions exist regarding subject selection. The subjects selected for a study must be appropriate for the construct under investigation. If the research question involves the study of developmental trends in learning math facts, then several age-level groups must be compared. To accomplish this, stratified age groups are formed with an explicit gap between groups. By forcing the composition of such groupings, the generalizability of results may be somewhat restricted.

The preceding statement concerning restrictions on generalizability does not mean that results do not generalize at all. Indeed, if adequate stratified sampling procedures have been employed, there is reason to believe that the *within-group* results will generalize. The point being made is that children progress somewhat continuously through a sequence of ages; it is doubtful that the results of such a stratified experiment will generalize well to children who fall between the experimentally contrived strata. Thus, results are somewhat restricted with regard to external validity by the nature of experimental arrangements that are necessary for constructing an internally valid study.

A researcher may wish to sacrifice some rigor in either internal or external validity to emphasize the other dimension. Depending on the stage of a program of research, it may be expedient to concentrate on one dimension at the expense of the second. Early in a program of research, the investigator may be more concerned with internal validity to ensure a more pure examination of fundamental constructs. As the research program progresses and data begin to accumulate concerning these variables, more attention may be addressed to the broader generalizability of results. Such alterations in emphasis regarding internal and external validity will most likely be reflected in subject-selection procedures. As the program of research progresses, it is more likely that the researcher will attend more closely to the broadest possible generalizability—thus, to the representativeness of the sample. This is somewhat different from sampling concerns that may be operative early in a research program. At these initial stages, the researcher is more likely to be most concerned that the subjects be appropriate to the construct under study. Generalizability is then limited in terms of the broader population of possible individuals to whom results might apply in the future.

Relationship or Correlational Questions.   Subject selection for investigations of relationship questions is somewhat different from selection for comparative questions. The purpose of correlational questions is to demonstrate the degree to which phenomena relate. The reasons for investigating such relationships usually involve the prediction of one variable or set of variables on the basis of measurements taken on the other variable. An example of a correlational study is the use of entrance exam scores to predict college achievement (grades). This prediction is based on correlations between entrance exam scores and college grades that were obtained on previous students. If the relationship that is observed in an investigation does not generalize to the group for which prediction is desirable, the study has lost much of its value. Thus, in subject selection, the researcher must be sure that the sample is representative of the population for which prediction is desired.

There are some characteristics of correlational methods that tend to relate results directly to sample selection. One specific factor is the variation that is present in the sample. With a more heterogeneous group of individuals, the correlation coefficient will be higher than with a more homogeneous group. If the sample is more heterogeneous (more variable) than the population, the predictive power demonstrated in the investigation will not be valid for the larger population. Likewise, if the sample is more homogeneous than the population, the demonstrated relationship (predictive power) may be lower than is actually possible in the population at large. This highlights the importance of drawing representative samples in all phases of research programs concerned with relationship questions.

Descriptive Questions.   The researcher investigating a descriptive question intends to provide a description of the characteristics, opinions, or behaviors of a given group, culture, or setting. Subject selection for a descriptive study must emphasize one concern in a preeminent fashion: accuracy of the description (external validity). A descriptive investigation that does not accurately characterize the group being studied is worthless and misleading. Therefore, a representative sample is of crucial importance in the planning of a descriptive study.

Other Questions. Our discussion thus far has focused on sampling procedures within the context of research. A variety of sampling approaches may be effectively used for questions that are not primarily of a research nature. For example, prediction is also undertaken in nonresearch settings such as forecasting election outcomes on election day. Within the last few years election prediction has become very sophisticated. Many people are amazed when winners are selected accurately with only 1 percent (often less) of the returns counted. Certainly, such a small sample would make researchers very nervous, particularly if it were not a random sample. However, the procedures used in election prediction are extremely accurate and you cannot argue with success. One reason for such accuracy is that the election sample is not randomly undertaken. A procedure known as *purposive sampling* is used, whereby data are obtained from a particular district that has consistently voted for winners. Because of this consistency, that district serves as a better prediction than a random sample of several districts.

A complete examination of sampling is far beyond the scope of an introductory design text. There are complete volumes that focus solely on sampling (e.g., Maestas & Goldfield, 1989; Thompson, 1992) for both research and nonresearch questions. The reader interested in a more comprehensive discussion of sampling theory and procedures should consult one or more of these references.

Subject Assignment

The process of assigning subjects to groups is also a procedure most commonly associated with experimental research, particularly traditional experimental studies. Consequently, this discussion will be primarily couched in terms of experimentation. Researchers involved in nonexperimental comparisons should attend to those issues in this section that may be generalized to such an approach. The main focus of subject assignment is the concept of control that has relevance to all comparison—experimental or nonexperimental.

Experiments address different questions that involve comparisons between two or more performances. These performances may be the result of a variety of designs such as: (1) baseline versus postintervention comparisons in time-series research, (2) pretreatment versus posttreatment comparisons with a single group of subjects, or (3) comparisons of two or more groups on a single performance test. The primary concern of this section is this latter example in which multiple-group comparisons are conducted that involve different groups of subjects for the conditions and also require subjects' being assigned to those groups.

Subject assignment in multigroup experiments is an important component of an internally valid study. The problem is how to divide those individuals who are a part of the sample into groups that will receive the different treatments. In Chapter 8 several examples were given in which the researcher was comparing the effectiveness of teaching methods (e.g., method A, B, or C). The teaching methods in these examples represent conditions of the type that are often compared with different groups for each condition.

The concept of control refers to the notion that these groups are assumed to be essentially equal in all respects with the exception of the variable under investigation. Thus, if teaching method A were being compared with method B, the difference in teaching methods should be the only way in which the two groups are not equivalent. The notion of control is the central issue with regard to internal validity. Subject assignment to groups is the primary technique a researcher has for ensuring control.

Assignment by Chance

Assignment of subjects to different treatment conditions is often accomplished using chance procedure. Although this procedure seems to imply that subject assignment is "left to chance," it in no way means that the procedure is unplanned or haphazard. In fact, chance assignment refers to a carefully planned and executed technique in which the researcher uses random selection to form the groups for the study.

Prior to our discussion of assignment approaches, a clear distinction needs to be made between *random assignment* and *random sampling.* Random sampling is, indeed, a separate and different procedure from random assignment and has a different purpose. The purpose of random sampling is to obtain a representative sample from the population. This is important for purposes of generalizing results to the population (external validity). Random assignment of subjects to different conditions is a technique used by researchers in an attempt to form equivalent groups. The purpose of random assignment is group equivalency, since individual variation or individual differences within groups will remain. Another concern is to ensure that subject properties (e.g., motivation or intellect) existing during the pretreatment phase are equivalent. The hope is that this will permit any posttreatment differences that may appear to be attributed to the treatment, which cannot be accomplished without such equivalence (e.g., Foxx, 1993; Kazdin, 1993). Definitions of random assignment are reminiscent of definitions of random sampling primarily because the same fundamental process is being used. Basically, random assignment involves a procedure by which subjects are assigned to groups in such a fashion that each subject in the study has an equal change of being placed in any of the treatment or comparison groups (Moberg, Piper, Wu, & Serlin, 1993). Within this general procedure there are several techniques for actual implementation.

Captive Assignment.   In some cases researchers will have the total sample identified and available at the outset of the investigation (as opposed to situations in which all the subjects are not present at one time). The subjects in this situation are said to be *captive*. This makes it possible to actually know, from the outset, which subjects, by name, will be in which experimental group. Consequently, somewhat different operational techniques are used to randomly assign subjects than are used in other situations.

When the researcher has the total sample captive, procedures for random assignment to the experimental conditions are simple. Individuals in the sample are listed by name, forming a frame. Once this is completed, the experimenter executes what is essentially a miniature random sample for each of the treatment groups. This might be done using the fishbowl arrangement as mentioned before. Subjects are assigned consecutive numbers from 1 to N. These numbers are then written on individual slips of paper, placed in a fishbowl, and thoroughly mixed. This can also be done by placing the subject's name on the slip rather than a corresponding number. Once either names or numbers are in the receptacle, the subject groups may be randomly drawn. If, for example, the study involved two conditions, the first half of the total sample that is drawn from the fishbowl might form the first group n and the remaining sample constitutes the second group. Thus, if the sample N equaled 50 individuals, the first 25 slips of paper drawn would constitute the group for treatment A and the remaining 25 would be assigned to treatment B. The researcher may choose another procedure to achieve the same end. For example, the decision may be to use the first subject for group A, the second for B, the third for A, the fourth for B, and so on, in an alternating fashion until both groups are complete. In either case, there is little reason to suspect that bias has been systematically introduced that would make the groups different.

Random number tables may also be used efficiently to assign subjects to groups. As before, it is necessary to formulate a list of the subjects in some sort of order. This process may be conveniently accomplished with an alphabetical listing. Once this is completed, the random number table is used to assign treatment to the subjects in consecutive order beginning with the first name and proceeding through the list. Using the previous example in which there were two experimental conditions, the researcher would be interested only in the digits 1 and 2 as they appeared in the table (each digit representing one of the groups). The researcher can then begin at any point in the random unit table and proceed systematically in any direction (horizontally or vertically). If the first digit encountered is 2, the subject in the first list position is assigned to group 2. If the second and third digits are 1, those individuals occupying the second and third list positions are assigned to group 1. This procedure is continued until group ns are completed. The researcher ignores irrelevant digits (those other than 1 or 2 in this example) and similarly ignores either 1 or 2 after that respective group n is completed. Therefore, after the 25th subject is assigned to group 2, the remaining encounters with 2 in the table are ignored. Using the random number table is generally more convenient than drawing from a fishbowl, particularly when large numbers of subjects are involved (unless, of course, you really enjoy cutting up all those little slips of paper).

*Turn to page 283 and complete
Simulation 9.3*

Sequential Assignment.   Often researchers do not have the entire sample captive (the actual names are not all present before beginning the study) and a different assignment procedure is necessary. The term *sequential assignment* is often used for the method involved in assignment for these circumstances. In a situation in which researchers do not have the exact sample drawn, they may be operating from a subject pool (drawn in a representative fashion). Consequently, the researchers do not know exactly which individuals from that pool will ultimately serve as subjects. Additionally, the experiment may be conducted over a period of time rather than at a single sitting. Under these conditions, the researchers may gather data on three or four subjects one day, another three or four the second, and so on. Individuals from the subject pool are then presented for the study on a sequential basis. When they do present themselves, the subjects must be assigned to one of the treatment conditions in such a fashion that will guard against the formulation of biased or unequal groups. Such a setting is not at all uncommon in studies in which subjects are individually tested or individually interviewed (Braucht & Reichardt, 1993). If there are many subjects in the study, it is usually impossible to test all subjects in a day.

A slight modification of the fishbowl procedure may be used for this situation. Suppose a working study was being conducted with an N of 50 and two experimental conditions (cell n of 25 each). The researcher may simply place 50 slips of paper in the fishbowl, 25 with condition A written on them and 25 with condition B. As the first slip is drawn, its specified condition (A or B) is listed, and so on, until all slips have been drawn and their respective conditions listed in order. Once this step is completed, the experimenter is ready for the first subject to appear. That subject is assigned to the group indicated by the first slip drawn, the second subject is assigned to the second slip drawn, and so on. Using these procedures, it is not likely that the subject groups will be systematically different.

A similar procedure may be implemented using shuffled cards or data sheets premarked by condition. Twenty-five cards would be marked with condition A and 25 with condition B. These cards are then shuffled thoroughly (recall the importance of a thorough shuffling—casual shuffling is often not random). Once completed, the first subject to appear is assigned to the condition appearing on the first card. As before, the sequential testing of subjects corresponds to the sequence of shuffled conditions.

Alternative procedures for sequential random assignment are also available through the use of random number tables. This may be done by assigning digits to represent each of the conditions for which groups are to be formed. If, for example, six experimental conditions were being studied, then the digits 1 through 6 would be used in the random number table. Suppose it has been determined that cell *n*s for this same experiment will be 20; this would result in a sample *N* of 120 subjects. If the first number encountered is 5, then the first subject to appear will be assigned to condition 5. Likewise the second may be assigned to 3, and so on, until the total of 120 subjects with 20 per group has been obtained. If group 5 is completed with 20 subjects, then subsequent encounters with digit 5 in the table are ignored. Usually, a complete list is made of the group sequence (e.g., 5, 3, 1, ...) before the experiment begins, including the full complement of subjects to be assigned. This way the sequence of assignment is predetermined randomly before each subject appears for testing. Computer programs are also available that are specifically designed for sequential assignment situations (Braucht & Reichardt, 1993).

Occasionally, a researcher will wish to exert a bit more control than is possible with the randomized procedures described above. As an illustration, take the six-condition experiment just described. Table 9.1 presents an example of the sequence of subject assignment to conditions. For discussion purposes, however, only a portion of the assignment sequence is provided (recall that the entire subject list will include an *N* of 120). Despite the fact that this is only a partial list, a bias problem is evident in this portion. Note that there is no individual assigned to condition 4 until the 22nd subject appears. Although the groups will most probably even out by the time the 120th subject is reached, the cell *n* for condition 4 must be obtained in greater proportion from the later subjects than other groups. The problem would be more pronounced if a smaller total *N* were involved in the study. It is not unreasonable to suspect that certain subject variables may be operative in the promptness with which subjects appear for experimentation (e.g., motivation, interest, or compulsiveness). These variables, which are essentially unknown but highly probable, may well be influential in the way in which a subject performs the experimental task. If such influences are operative in, for example, the first 30 or so subjects to appear, condition 4 is likely to be systematically different from the other groups (by the time the 30th subject appears, the group count is as follows: group 1, five subjects; group 2, five subjects; group 3, seven subjects; group 4, two subjects; group 5, five subjects; group 6, six subjects).

One method of circumventing the above problem is through *block randomization*. This procedure considers a block to be a sequence in which each condition appears once. The researcher draws subjects at random within a block, ignoring all digit repetitions until each condition has appeared once (the completion of a block). As soon as each condition has appeared, a new block is begun, and this procedure is

TABLE 9.1   Example of Assignment-Sequence List for Six-Group Study

Subject Number	Group Assigned	Subject Number	Group Assigned
1	5	36	2
2	1	37	3
3	6	38	1
4	3	39	4
5	2	40	5
6	3	41	6
7	6	42	2
8	2	43	6
9	1	44	4
10	5	45	5
11	5	46	3
12	6	47	1
13	3	48	3
14	1	49	4
15	2	50	5
16	2	51	1
17	1	52	2
18	6	53	6
19	5	54	6
20	3	55	1
21	3	56	4
22	4	57	3
23	6	58	5
24	4	59	2
25	3	60	5
26	1	61	4
27	6	62	2
28	5	63	6
29	2	64	1
30	3	65	3
31	1	66	5
32	2	67	4
33	4	68	1
34	5	69	3
35	6		

repeated until the sample N is totally assigned to conditions. Table 9.2 presents an example of the previously assigned subject pool that has been sequenced using block randomization. Each block in the table is set off by a horizontal line under the condition digit that completes the respective block. The subject assignment to conditions is considerably different from what was exemplified in Table 9.1. Because of the control imposed by block randomization, the group proportions existing

TABLE 9.1 Example of Assignment-Sequence List for Six-Group Study

Subject Number	Group Assigned	Subject Number	Group Assigned
1	5	36	5
2	1	37	4
3	6	38	1
4	3	39	2
5	2	40	6
6	4	41	3
7	5	42	5
8	3	43	3
9	2	44	1
10	4	45	6
11	1	46	5
12	6	47	4
13	2	48	2
14	6	49	3
15	1	50	5
16	4	51	2
17	5	52	1
18	3	53	4
19	5	54	6
20	2	55	5
21	1	56	2
22	4	57	3
23	3	58	1
24	6	59	4
25	5	60	6
26	2	61	6
27	4	62	5
28	1	63	2
29	3	64	1
30	6	65	4
31	6	66	3
32	1	67	1
33	4	68	5
34	3	69	6
35	2		

by the time the 30th subject appears are substantially changed. Beyond this control, however, the assignment within blocks is random, presenting little reason to expect systematic bias between group characteristics.

*Turn to page 284 and complete
Simulation 9.4*

Comments. It should be evident from the preceding discussion that all random-assignment procedures do not absolutely ensure the absence of bias between groups. Free random-assignment procedures (those without nonchance controls such as were imposed in block randomization) are occasionally vulnerable to the generation of nonequivalent groups. Although such bias occurs infrequently, the statistical theory on which random procedures are based indicates that atypical groups will appear by chance a certain percentage of the time.

There are precautions that may be taken by the researcher to circumvent such occurrences. Captive assignments may permit the researcher certain checkpoints that are not possible with sequential assignment. By virtue of the actual identification of all subjects before beginning the study, the researcher may be able to determine equivalency of groups on a preexperimental basis. To accomplish this, relevant measures must either be available or be administered before the initiation of experimental procedures. Because the exact composition of groups is known, groups may be compared on these preexperimental measures before administering the treatments. If the groups are statistically different, they may be thrown back into the sample pool and reassigned until they are equivalent. Such procedures are not possible with sequential assignment because the exact individuals serving as subjects in each group are not identified prior to beginning the experiment. Although this is a useful safeguard, its helpfulness depends on the relevance of the preexperimental measure. If the measure is not related to the experimental task (e.g., if the task involved discrimination learning and the preexperimental measure is shoe size), it may be of little use in estimating group equivalency with respect to related subject variables. The preexperimental group comparison also presumes that other unmeasured, experimentally related variables are not different. It is important to remember that precise equivalency may not be determined in a "money-back-guaranteed" fashion. However, the use of certain controls in combination with random procedures greatly enhances confidence that the groups are probably not different in a significant manner.

Sequential assignment does not permit the same preexperimental checkpoints that captive assignment does. However, certain precautions may be taken. Despite the fact that researchers do not have actual subject names available, they do have the information necessary to scrutinize the sequence of assignment. It is always prudent to carefully examine the assignment sequence list to identify possible idiosyncrasies that may result in biased assignment of subjects to conditions. Such an atypical sequence was evident in Table 9.1. If a potential problem is noted, the investigator may then exercise some control options. One possibility may be to specify some a priori rules and reassign in a free random fashion. These rules may be that no more than three (or some specified number) consecutive subjects may be assigned to any one treatment condition. Likewise, the block-randomization procedure may be a desirable option to control for extremes in assignment sequence occurring by chance. Sequential assignment (sometimes termed *trickle-process* since the subjects trickle in) requires some additional vigilance regarding the formulation of equivalent groups (Braucht & Reichardt, 1993).

There is also a procedure that can be used which does not actually advance group equivalency but does guard against flagrant misinterpretation of results. Recall the previous discussion of preexperimental measures on subjects that are related to the experimental task. Because complete groups are not identified, such data are not useful before instituting the treatment. These measures may, however, serve for a group comparison on a post hoc basis or after the study has been completed. Such comparisons would provide the researcher with information concerning the pretreatment status of the groups. If groups are not different, the researcher can interpret the data as if group equivalency were in effect (at least assumed) before the treatment. If, on the other hand, the groups appear different on a pretreatment basis, considerable care must be exercised in the interpretation of results (if the data are amenable to meaningful interpretation at all). An alternative to this last possibility may be found through the use of specific statistical procedures. Analysis of covariance is a method whereby statistical equivalency may be imposed to facilitate interpretation of results if pretreatment differences exit. This procedure, however, in no way offsets the desirability of group equivalency that exists as a part of actual group composition (Howell, 1995; Wampold & Drew, 1990).

The importance of subject assignment procedures cannot be overemphasized in studies in which group comparisons are being made. In group studies, this is a central concern in the technical soundness of an investigation. It demands the researcher's careful attention both in terms of planning and in terms of implementation.

Assignment by Controlled Methods

Earlier we discussed certain subject assignment procedures in which the researcher exerted certain controls rather than using free random assignment. Such subject assignment procedures primarily rely on *chance*, with the controls or restrictions being imposed as added modifications. This section explores methods that primarily rely on *control* and, in some cases, use chance procedures as secondary modifications.

The first method that comes to mind under controlled assignment is *experimental matching.* There are several procedures that generally fall under matching approaches. In general, experimental matching differs from random methods in that the researcher attempts to force group equivalency on a given dimension using data that are available on a preexperimental basis. For example, suppose it had been determined that measured mental age was an important variable related to subject performance on a given task. Under such circumstances, the researcher may wish to have groups that are equivalent on mental age. Using experimental matching, the researcher would see to it that the groups involved were not different on mental age.

There are some alternatives in the way an experimental match may be implemented. A researcher may decide to perform a group match, in which case the only concern is that group means and variances be equal. Because the primary concern with a group match involves the composite representation of the control variable (i.e., means and variance), this is the focus of monitoring during group formulation. Usually, the entire sample is listed in rank order on the control measure (mental age in the earlier example). With this completed, the highest subject is usually arbitrarily assigned to one of the conditions (e.g., treatment 1). The second highest subject is then assigned to treatment 2, the third to treatment 3, and so on, until one subject has been assigned to each condition. Once that has been accomplished, the usual procedure is then to reverse the order (begin with treatment 3, then 2, then 1, for purposes of assigning the second subject in each group). This procedure is continued until a complete cell n has been constituted for each treatment and the total N assigned. Although this procedure will usually generate little difference in group means, it is frequently the case that the researcher will carefully monitor group means to ensure similarity. If statistically different means do occur in following such procedures, it is not unusual to find group mean adjustments being made. Because the group mean is the concern, adjustments may be made by subject substitution. The use of such procedures to control means occasionally makes it difficult to achieve equal variances between groups at the same time (Christensen, 1994). Although this difficulty has been noted by experimental methodologists, procedures for avoiding the difficulty have not received serious attention. It is not uncommon for group matches to focus primarily on means.

A second approach to conducting an experimental match involves the assignment of *matched pairs*. Assignment of matched pairs, as the label suggests, is a procedure whereby a subject-to-subject match is accomplished, again, for purposes of formulating presumed equivalent groups. To perform such a subject assignment, the researcher has a preexperimental measure that is related to performance on the experimental task. The researcher then scrutinizes all the scores in the sample, searching for subjects with equal or nearly equal scores. If three groups are to be formed, three subjects must be drawn with "matched" scores. Such subjects are then assigned to each of the three conditions. This procedure is continued until cell ns are completed.

A basic requirement for either group matches or subject-by-subject matches is the preexperimental measure on which the control dimension is based. The match measures are usually obtained in one of two fashions: (1) by using a task that is separate but highly related to that which is involved in the treatment, or (2) by using the initial performance level on the treatment task. The first source of match data seems self-explanatory, but there are specific concerns that must be addressed. Probably the most pressing area involves the strength of the relationship between scores on the control measure and performance on the experimental task. It is prudent for the researcher to have statistical evidence of such relationships either from previous research or from pilot correlations computed in preparation for the experiment. If the researcher merely assumes a relationship, the design is seriously weakened in terms of control.

The second source of match data involves initial subject performance on the experimental task. This is frequently a convenient method of obtaining control dimension data. Inherent in this procedure, however, are certain requirements concerning the logistic characteristics of the experimental task. First, it is obvious that the task must be constructed in a fashion that requires multiple trials or responses from the subjects. Some learning tasks are designed this way and permit a series of trials until the subject's performance reaches a given criterion level. Then, to implement the match, the researcher provides each subject a few trials on the experimental task. After this has been accomplished, performances on these trials are scrutinized and the match is performed. Finally, the remainder of the experiment is conducted with the difference in treatments being implemented.

The use of the initial performance for match data has an additional concern that must not be ignored. This involves the strength of the relationship between performance on the initial trials (match data) and total performance. It seems likely that performance on a given task ought to be highly related to subsequent performance on that same task. This may not be the case in all circumstances. In fact, on some experimental tasks the initial phases of performance are quite different from the later performance scores. It is not wise, therefore, to assume a relationship in the absence of some evidence, even on the same task.

Experimental matching enjoyed considerable popularity in the earlier years of behavioral science. However, there are several difficulties that were encountered with this procedure that have led researchers to move more in favor of random techniques as a means of equating groups. The move toward random techniques was precipitated by Fisher's classic work published in 1925 entitled *Statistical Methods for Research Workers.* Although the move has been gradual, it has been of sufficient magnitude to generate statements such as that of Campbell & Stanley (1963) who suggested that "matching as a substitute for randomization is taboo even for quasi-experimental designs" (p. 185). The nature of difficulties with experimental matching has been discussed widely (e.g., Christensen, 1994; Wampold & Drew, 1990), and these difficulties are of sufficient importance that the beginning researcher needs to be at least introduced to them. Because there are situations in which it is not possible to effectively use random assignment, knowledge concerning the pitfalls of experimental matching becomes doubly important when it must be used.

From the outset, certain logistical restrictions are evident with experimental matching. Using either group procedures or matched-pairs procedures, it is necessary to have preexperimental data available on subjects before assignment to groups. To have these data available, it is necessary that the sample be captive (in the sense of actually having individuals identified). If the exact individuals were not identified (such as was described under sequential assignment), the researcher could not obtain match data and perform a preexperimental match.

One of the most perplexing problems with experimental matching involves the control variable itself. Because any given variable is chosen as the one on which groups are matched, it is assumed to be an important factor for control. It has been repeatedly stated that such a variable should not be used based only on assumptive evidence of importance, although it is not unusual to find this to be the primary basis for choice. In both group and matched-pairs procedures, it is important that sound evidence of the relationship between the match variable and the performance on the experimental task be available. Beyond the relationship question, there are some additional implicit assumptions that concern the match variable.

Although it is not uncommon to encounter match design studies with more than one control variable, for the moment examine the case in which subjects are matched on one dimension. By selecting that variable for matching or control, the researcher is explicitly indicating its perceived importance. At the same time, one must ask certain questions concerning the other variables on which subjects were not matched. (Remember, the focus is momentarily on the case of matching on a single dimension.) Because there is no match on the multitude of other possible dimensions, the assumption may be made that they are not important for control. The reasoning here is highly tenuous. The point is that the logic used in selecting the match variable (that it is important) is not easily reversed (that those not selected are not important). Yet by ignoring other variables, the design itself may suggest such reasoning.

It is evident that the unattended variables may indeed create problems. In the process of matching subjects, the researcher is, in fact, placing subjects in groups in a fashion that is systematic. A serious unknown is the degree to which this process introduces systematic bias between the conditions on the unmatched (perhaps unknown) variables. In fact, there is reason to suspect that this may have occurred. Random assignment, on the other hand, gives little reason to expect systematic differences between groups. The very process involved is aimed at creating groups that are unbiased on both known and unknown variables. This is a strength that is built into random assignment that is absent in matching procedures.

The researcher using matching procedures for subject assignment frequently selects more than one variable for control. It is not uncommon to read matching studies in which several dimensions were controlled ("subjects were matched on sex, IQ, socioeconomic status.."). Two concerns need to be addressed under such circumstances. Despite the addition of more control variables, the issues previously discussed remain as design concerns. First, human subjects are extremely complex. It is almost inconceivable that all the possible dimensions that may influence subject performance can be considered and controlled. The unknown or unattended influences are still highly suspect as potential contaminators. The second concern is one of logistics: as the number of match variables increases, the difficulty of implementing a match is also greatly increased. It is enough of a task to find matched subjects on a single dimension. The magnitude of the problem is increased severalfold just by adding one additional control. Finding an adequate match with more than two controls creates several additional problems. Because of the difficulty in performing such a match, the precision with which it is accomplished is frequently sacrificed. Such sacrifices usually begin with rather small deviations (e.g., subjects were matched on measured IQ within plus or minus 5 points) but are necessarily increased as the subject pool nears exhaustion.

The difficulties discussed above are generally more prevalent in pair-match procedures than group-match procedures. The fact remains, however, that these are pitfalls that are encountered in using any experimental match designs. Random subject assignment provides a more powerful procedure when it can be used. Additionally, the use of random assignment with analysis of covariance is also preferable to experimental matching on a number of dimensions.

Comments

Although we have discussed several different procedures for subject selection and assignment, one question remains unanswered: Which procedure is the best? This question cannot be answered in a general way that speaks to all conditions. Under varying circumstances, different procedures are more appropriate. Likewise, the convenience often required in a field setting may alter the exact procedures required. Despite our preference for random-assignment procedures, there are times when matching may be more practical. The one factor that should be kept in mind, however, is that convenience or pragmatic considerations cannot intercede to the degree that rigor is sacrificed. Although the pressure of different situations often makes this tempting, if such sacrifice is permitted the study probably is reduced in terms of usefulness.

The replacement of lost subjects frequently presents a difficult problem. Many researchers operate with a subject pool drawn from the larger population. This is an appropriate manner in which to replace lost subjects, assuming that the subject pool is constructed in a careful manner that will permit reasonable generalizability. However, certain precautions must be taken. First of all, subject mortality may represent a serious problem in group studies (previously discussed in detail in chapter 8). If subjects are lost differentially from groups, the replacement of subjects may create an internal-validity problem. It is not unusual to be faced with considerable lack of information about lost subjects. In particular, there is a question regarding why they were lost. Also, if subjects were replaced randomly from a pool, are the replacements similar to those who were lost? For example, if the lack of subject vitality is a prime reason for mortality (e.g., the weaker rats die), randomly sampled replacements will most likely be different. Random sampling will probably include strong as well as weak subjects. Because the lower subject vitality is (hypothetically) the reason for mortality, the group composition has a good probability of being changed by the replacements (if all subjects lost are weak and replacements are equally divided, weak and strong, the group as a whole becomes stronger). Besides resulting in internal-validity bias, replacements may alter the generalizability of results.

Simulations

Simulation 9.1

Topic: Population definition

Stimulus Information: This simulation represents one part of a hypothetical population frame construction for sampling purposes. The population is defined as "all third-year male students enrolled in West Rebew State." Computer printout material was generated for all students and coded with the digit 1 for first-year students, 2 for second-year students, and so on. Below is a reproduction of one page of that printout.

Tasks to Be Performed: Construct a portion of the population frame from the list presented. Do so by placing an X by each name that will become part of that population frame.

For feedback see page 285.

Bacco, F. Donald	1
Bach, Jay T.	3
Bachman, Thomas	4
Back, Donald R.	2
Back, Laura J.	6
Backer, Jane Z.	3
Backman, Fred	1
Bacon, R. Myrtle	3
Bacon, Robert F.	3
Badger, Mike	3
Bagley, David	6
Bagley, Penny	2
Bailey, Bob Jo	3
Baird, James V.	6
Baird, Sally Jo	1
Banks, Vernon L.	4
Bannon, Diane	2
Barber, Anne L.	2
Barger, George	3
Barber, Jeanne	1
Barclay, Larry	3
Barclay, Robert B.	1
Bardin, Robyne Anne	3
Barker, James R.	3
Barker, Sara	4
Barnes, Linda F.	2
Barnes, Mike L.	3
Barnes, Scott	2
Barnhart, Cyrus F.	1
Barnumm, Daniel	4
Bennett, Ellen	6
Berg, William J.	3
Bernard, Clifford	4
Berrett, Colleen	3
Best, Sandy	4
Bigelow, Randy L.	3
Bigelow, Robert W.	3
Bragg, Raymond J.	3
Brassiere, Newland	1
Burns, Sallie	2
Burton, Archibald	4
Butkus, Lowell Tom	1

Random Number Table

For the next few simulations you will need a random number table. A short table is provided Random number tables are simple to use. Specific instructions will be included with each simulation concerning how to use the table in the particular task presented.

	Column					
Line	1	2	3	4	5	6
1	10480	15011	01536	02011	81647	91646
2	22368	46573	25595	85393	30995	89198
3	24130	48360	22527	97265	76393	64809
4	42167	93093	06243	61680	07856	16376
5	37570	39975	81837	16656	06121	91782
6	77921	06907	11008	42751	27756	53948
7	99562	72905	56420	69994	98872	31016
8	96301	91977	05463	07972	18876	20922
9	88579	14342	63661	10281	17453	18103
10	85475	36857	53342	53988	53060	59533
11	28918	69578	88231	33276	70997	79936
12	63553	40961	48235	03427	49626	69445
13	09429	93969	52636	92737	88974	33488
14	10365	97336	87529	85689	48237	52267
15	07119	61129	71048	08178	77233	13916
16	51085	12765	51821	51259	77452	16308
17	02368	21382	52404	60268	89368	19885
18	01011	54092	33362	94904	31273	04146
19	52162	53916	46369	58586	23216	06691
20	07056	96728	33787	09998	42698	06691
21	48663	91245	85828	14346	09172	30168
22	54164	58492	22421	74103	47070	25306
23	32639	32363	05597	24200	13363	38005
24	29334	27001	87637	87308	58731	00256
25	02488	33062	28834	07351	19731	92420

Simulation 9.2

Topic: Random sampling

Stimulus Information: You have been assigned the task of evaluating a piece of instructional material. The group for which the material is designed is defined as those children who range in age from five to seven years. Your subject pool (presumably representative of all children in that age range) has been listed, and corresponding numbers have been assigned to each child's name. The numbers run from 1 to 85.

Tasks to Be Performed:

1. Using the random number table provided on page 282, draw a sample from the subject pool to be used in the study. The size of the sample is 30.

2. Construct the subject list using the code numbers that appear in the table.

Use of the Random Number Table: For purposes of this simulation, begin in the upper left corner of the table (column 1, line 1). Place your ruler vertically on column 1 in such a way that it covers all but the first two digits in each line. When you have done this, you should see the following digits for lines 1 to 5: 10, 22, 24, 42, and 37. You are using the first two digits in each number because your population frame has 85 individuals in it, and 85 is a two-digit number. If your population frame had 120 individuals, you would cover all but the first three digits.

Now, proceed down the column and list all the relevant numbers for your sample. Recall from the text that relevant numbers include those in the frame and ignore a given number the second time it appears. When you reach line 25, begin in the same fashion in column 2 until you have your 30 subjects.

For feedback see page 286.

Simulation 9.3

Topic: Random assignment—captive

Stimulus Information: You are conducting a study that involves two comparison groups. Your total sample is 50 subjects, and they are to be assigned to the two groups. The individuals are already identified by name, so you can implement a captive random assignment.

Tasks to Be Performed: Using the random number table on page 282, assign the subjects on the following page to groups A and B using captive random assignment.

Use of the Random Number Table: The technique for this simulation is similar to that in simulation 9.2. First, begin in the upper left corner of the table (column 1, line 1). Then, place your ruler vertically on column 1 in such a way that it covers all but the first digit in each line. When you have done this, you should see the following digits for lines 1 to 5: 1, 2, 2, 4, and 3. You are using only the first digit in each number because you only have two groups, for these purposes, identified as 1 and 2. Both are single-digit designations, and you therefore need only single-digit options for assignment.

Now proceed down the column and assign the subjects to the respective groups (1 or 2) in the order that they appear. Ignore irrelevant digits. Begin again in column 2, 3, and so on, until you have completed your assignment. Review the text pages if further direction is necessary.

By the way, you will run out of columns on this one (that is, you will not have 25 subjects in either group when you finish column 6).

1. Robert		26. Kay
2. Myrna		27. Carole
3. Ralph		28. Phil
4. John		29. Don
5. Sally		30. Walt
6. Sherry		31. Bonnie
7. Lois		32. Doug
8. Andy		33. Steve
9. Joel		34. George
10. Thomas		35. Mary Ann
11. Eugene		36. Sandra
12. Dennis		37. Larry
13. Anna		38. Rick
14. David		39. Joy
15. Earl		40. Virginia
16. Lorraine		41. Sonia
17. Maurice		42. Anita
18. Terry		43. Bruce
19. Carl		44. Suzanne
20. Ken		45. Alice
21. Wilmer		46. Barbara
22. Anne		47. Clyde
23. Alan		48. Karle
24. Kevin		49. Kent
25. James		50. Travis

When you get to this point, change ruler positions so that only the last digit shows in each column and begin again in column 1. You could begin again anywhere, but for feedback purposes, use the last digit (which will result in 0, 8, 0, 7, and 0 for lines 1 to 5).

For feedback see page 286.

Simulation 9.4

Topic: Random assignment—sequential

Stimulus Information: You are conducting a study that involves two comparison groups. Your total sample is 50 subjects, and they are to be assigned to the two groups. The identity of the individuals, however, is not specifically known to you. They will appear in the lab in an undetermined order, which will require that you use sequential assignment to form your groups.

Tasks to Be Performed: Using the random number table provided on page 282, assign the following subject positions to groups 1 and 2 so that when the actual subjects appear, they may be sequentially assigned to a group.

1.	18.	35.
2.	19.	36.
3.	20.	37.
4.	21.	38.
5.	22	39.
6.	23.	40.
7.	24.	41.
8.	25.	42.
9.	26.	43.
10.	27.	44.
11.	28.	45.
12.	29.	46.
13.	30.	47.
14.	31.	48.
15.	32.	49.
16.	33.	50.
17.	34.	

Use of the Random Number Table: For purposes of this simulation, use the random number table in exactly the same fashion as you did in Simulation 9.3. The only difference in this case is that you will be assigning the subject positions (represented by the numbers just presented) to groups because you do not know what the names are yet.

For feedback see page 287.

Simulation Feedbacks

Simulation 9.1

As indicated in your text, the population frame is constructed by designating all the potential subjects, by name, who have the characteristics indicated in the population definition. Recall that the population was defined as "all third-year male students enrolled in West Rebew State." From the partial list that you have, certain students should have an X by their name, thereby becoming part of your population frame. The students listed below should have an X by their name. These are male students with a code of *3* for year of enrollment.

Bach, Jay T.	3
Bacon, Robert F.	3
Badger, Mike	3
Bailey, Bob Jo	3
Barber, George	3
Barclay, Larry	3
Barker, James R.	3

Barnes, Mike L.	3
Berg, William J.	3
Bigelow, Randy L.	3
Bigelow, Robert W.	3
Bragg, Raymond J.	3

Other students in the original list did not combine the characteristics of both male and code 3. Occasionally, you may encounter some difficulty determining characteristics from the information provided. For example, names have definite regional differences in terms of whether they are given to males or females (Bob Jo Bailey). If confusion exists, you must confirm sex by seeking additional information in some way. By the way, Bob Jo is from the southern United States.

Simulation 9.2

The exact subjects who will become a part of your study will vary depending on which part of the random number table you use. Since you are instructed to begin in the upper left corner, here is a list of subject codes that would appear from this approach.

10	7	46
22	51	39
24	2	6
42	1	72
37	52	14
77	48	36
85	54	69
28	32	40
63	29	61
9	15	12

The children whose names appear beside these code numbers are your subjects. Other digits were ignored (e.g., the number 99 in column 1, line 7) because they were not part of your population frame (which only went to 85) and were therefore not relevant.

Simulation 9.3

The exact assignment would, of course, differ depending on the random number table used (or the point of beginning in this table).

Because you were instructed where to begin and how to proceed, here is a list of the names and numbers of the subjects, once again, with their group codes in parentheses. This would mean that since Robert has a (1) beside his name, he will be in group 1, and so on.

1. Robert (1)	26. Kay (1)
2. Myrna (2)	27. Carole (1)
3. Ralph (2)	28. Phil (2)
4. John (2)	29. Don (1)
5. Sally (1)	30. Walt (1)
6. Sherry (2)	31. Bonnie (1)
7. Lois (1)	32. Doug (1)
8. Andy (1)	33. Steve (1)
9. Joel (1)	34. George (2)
10. Thomas (2)	35. Mary Ann (1)
11. Eugene (2)	36. Sandra (2)
12. Dennis (2)	37. Larry (1)
13. Anna (2)	38. Rick (1)
14. David (1)	39. Joy (2)
15. Earl (2)	40. Virginia (1)
16. Lorraine (3)	41. Sonia (2)
17. Maurice (1)	42. Anita (1)
18. Terry (1)	43. Bruce (2)
19. Carl (1)	44. Suzanne (2)
20. Ken (2)	45. Alice (2)
21. Wilmer (2)	46. Barbara (1)
22. Anne (1)	47. Clyde (2)
23. Alan (1)	48. Karle (2)
24. Kevin (2)	49. Kent (2)
25. James (1)	50. Travis (2)

Note that Clyde, Karle, Kent, and Travis (at the end of the list) all received group 2 assignments. The reason for this (regardless of which numbers came up in the table) is that when Barbara was assigned to group 1, that made a total of 25 subjects in group 1. The remaining individuals were then placed in group 2 to make that group complete.

Simulation 9.4

As before, the exact assignment would differ depending on which table you used and where you began in the table. If you did follow the procedure outlined, then, you would obtain the following subject-position assignment:

1. (1)	8. (1)	15. (2)	22. (1)
2. (2)	9. (1)	16. (2)	23. (1)
3. (2)	10. (2)	17. (1)	24. (2)
4. (2)	11. (2)	18. (1)	25, (1)
5. (1)	12. (2)	19. (1)	26. (1)
6. (2)	13. (2)	20. (2)	27. (1)
7. (1)	14. (1)	21. (2)	28. (2)

The complete listing of position assignments is not presented here because it is exactly the same as that obtained in Simulation 9.3 and presented in the Simulation 9.3 feedback. Check back to see if you need further feedback. They are the same because you had the same number of subjects, they were assigned to the same number of groups, and the table was used in exactly the same way. If the situation were different in terms of any of these factors, the subject position sequence would also be different.

Measures, Instruments, and Tasks

Many details must receive attention in a research investigation beyond the basic design or plan. The successful completion of a research project involves a series of interrelated parts. This chapter addresses those parts of an investigation that are commonly referred to as measures, instruments, and tasks.

Selection of Criterion Measures

It is important for a researcher to select a criterion measure during the planning of an investigation. The *criterion measure* is synonymous with the term *dependent variable* and refers to that which is being measured in the study. It is important to reemphasize the distinction between dependent variables and the *independent variable* (sometimes referred to as the *experimental variable*) used in experimental studies.

The independent variable is the factor being studied. If a researcher is comparing the effectiveness of two instructional techniques (e.g., method A versus method B), the independent variable is the method of instruction. In the above example (method A versus method B) the researcher is not measuring the method of instruction; the method of instruction is being studied as an independent variable. What is being measured is the effectiveness of the method of instruction. If the instruction methods were designed for teaching reading, the immediate task would be to determine how effectiveness might be assessed. One approach is to measure reading comprehension by the number of correct responses made by subjects on a test. In such an example, the number of correct responses would be the criterion measure.

Thus, criterion measure refers to that which is measured or counted. It is the metric (measure) used to assess the impact or outcome of the independent variable or treatment (Fraenkel & Wallen, 1993). If a researcher were conducting a descriptive study of the height of a particular group of individuals, the criterion measure might be specified in terms of inches. Many students are somewhat confused by the term *criterion* used as a modifier for measure. The term is primarily a result of traditional usage. In the example of reading comprehension, the criterion or acceptable method for assessing this construct was the number of correct responses. The term *criterion* is not used in the same sense as a performance goal to be achieved (such as the idea that students must reach a certain performance level or criterion before they are certified as having passed a course). Instead, it is a means of measuring the actual level of performance that a subject accomplished.

One area that must receive attention is the level of *specificity* regarding the criterion measure selected. It is important to distinguish between those factors that can and cannot be measured. In making such distinctions there are some constructs that cannot be measured directly. Their existence (of the degree to which they exist) must be inferred from the measurement of certain *attributes* that are observable and are believed to indicate something about the more abstract construct. An example of such a construct is learning. It has long been acknowledged in experimental psychology that one cannot measure learning directly. One can, however, infer that learning exists or has occurred through observation of certain performance dimensions. In this example, learning is considered the broader construct, whereas the performance (e.g., number of correct responses) is an attribute of learning.

Because abstract constructs are not directly measurable, they cannot be considered for use as criterion measures. The attributes of the construct, because they are observable, countable, or in some fashion amenable to having a metric applied, achieve the level of specificity that must be present in a criterion measure. The construct usually represents a more global or abstract construct (e.g., self-concept, intelligence, or anxiety), whereas the attribute is a more specific, definable, observable type of factor that reflects something about the nature of the construct.

Obviously, the relationship between a criterion measure and the construct under investigation is critical. One must be assured that the criterion measure selected is indeed an attribute of the construct being studied. This is frequently a troublesome area for beginning researchers. There are not prescribed rules for determining that the presumed relationship between criterion measures and constructs being studied is sound (Christensen, 1994). Frequently, previous research has resulted in the establishment of accepted criterion measures. A researcher can then rely on this research as a guidepost that will facilitate the process. When such guidance is absent, however, the researcher must rely on experience, judgment, and intuition to assess the logical relationship between a given criterion measure and the factor being studied. For example, in a descriptive study of a selected group's height, the suggested criterion measure may be inches. This is a logical criterion measure because the inch is the primary unit for determining length in the United States. It would be foolish, however, to attempt to describe a particular group's height using a criterion measure of ohms. Even beyond the matter of accepted measurement units, a criterion measure of ohms does not hold an intuitive or logical relationship to the purpose of a study that involves a description of height. Likewise, if the purpose of an investigation was to test a particular dimension of a psychological theory, the criterion measure selected should have a logical or established relationship to that psychological construct. Usually, one would not want to use performance on mathematical computation problems as a measure of self-concept. The behavior that is observed or counted as a criterion measure must have a stronger intuitive relationship to the construct being studied than is evidenced between computation of mathematics problems and the elusive construct of self-concept (Fraenkel & Wallen, 1993).

Many other concerns must also be addressed in selecting criterion measures. Assuming that a researcher has attained a measurable level of specificity and that the relationship of the measure to the topic is acceptable, there may still be other decisions to be made. It is not unusual to be faced with two or three possible criterion measures that are acceptable with respect to specificity and the relationship to the construct under investigation. Under such circumstances, the choice may be based on several considerations.

One characteristic that may suggest the selection of a given measure over other alternatives is the communication efficiency of the measure. Which measure is the most efficient means for investigating and communicating about a given problem? In the example concerning the descriptive study of height, it was suggested that the criterion measure of inches might be appropriate. Of course, the inch is not the only measure for height. People who are horse enthusiasts are well acquainted with a measure of height known as hands. For a descriptive study of human height however, hands would seem to be a less efficient measure than inches. Because nearly everyone in the United States who reads a report concerning the height of humans is accustomed to using inches, hands would probably have to be translated into the more orthodox measure. Such a translation is cumbersome and unnecessary because of the availability of inches as an alternative, so there is good reason to prefer the use of inches in the first place. This choice is predicated on the assumption that the hands measure does not have other properties that make it more desirable.

Another consideration in the selection of a criterion measure is the *sensitivity* of the measure (Christensen, 1994). It is possible that one measure might be more sensitive to subject performance differences than the alternative being considered. It is always preferable to use the most sensitive measure available, assuming that other considerations do not make its use undesirable (such as subject reaction or other logistic difficulties). For example, in cognitive psychology, a great deal of research has been conducted on the learning of verbal material. Because of the extensive work in verbal learning, a sophisticated technological base has been developed with specific subareas of investigation. A substantial amount of research has been conducted that focuses on the rate at which subjects acquire knowledge. Two possible criterion measures for rate of acquisition serve well to exemplify the sensitivity issue.

For the purpose of illustration, let's say that the subjects are required to learn a list of eight paired words (e.g., dog-fist, lion-water, baby-sky, etc.). One attempt at each of the eight pairs is defined as a *trial*. As a criterion measure, a researcher records the number of trials it takes a subject to make three correct responses on each pair. An alternative criterion measure might involve counting the number of errors a subject makes in reaching the three-correct-response level of proficiency. In this example, the number of errors is the more sensitive measure, whereas the number of trials represents a more gross measure. This is the case because a subject may make a variable number of errors (reflecting variation in acquired knowledge) within a list trial. Consequently, the number of trials may be the same for two subjects, but substantial differences may exist in the number of errors committed. Because errors seem more reflective of the knowledge being acquired, it is the more sensitive measure and is preferred as a criterion measure. Although this example comes from experimental research, the same issue is equally important in other investigations.

In summary, there must be a logical relationship between the measure and the topic being studied (it must be an attribute of the construct). The measure must be specific and observable (one must be able to determine its existence either by counting or in some fashion certifying its existence or absence). Finally, it should be efficient and sensitive to performance differences.

*Turn to page 309 and complete
Simulations 10.1 and 10.2*

Instruments and Tasks

Instruments or tasks presented to subjects must generate behavior that may be recorded in the form of the criterion measure. Consequently, there must be a logical relationship between the instrument the researcher selects and the constructs being studied. The instrument or task must be so designed as to generate behavior that is presumed to be an attribute of the object-topic under investigation. For example, suppose a researcher was conducting a survey on the political affiliation of a particular group of people. To determine a subject's political affiliation, the researcher must generate some response from the subject that will identify the individual's political party. An efficient way of obtaining this type of data involves a mailed questionnaire, or it can be done by personally interviewing the subjects. In the first case, the questionnaire is the instrument that generates the subject's response, and in the latter the subject's response is given directly to the interviewer. Either of these approaches could serve the purpose of providing an acceptable criterion measure for the study. The selection of which approach to use depends on many considerations.

Instruments and tasks vary greatly from one investigation to the next. Some experimentation may actually include a task that the subjects perform and their performance results in the criterion measure. Others may involve the administration of a test instrument of some type. Nonexperimental and qualitative research may be undertaken by means of surveys (questionnaires or interviews) and observation studies. In both surveys and observation studies, there is often some instrument used to generate data. The researcher must give careful attention to the instrument's characteristics, advantages, and potential problem areas.

The process of generating the actual data in an investigation may be conceived of as an interaction between certain subject characteristics and the properties of the task or instrument. This implies that once a subject perceives the stimulus of the task, responsivity is altered in some fashion. For example, it is likely that a subject's responsivity is altered somewhat if a part of the treatment or task involves receiving an electric shock. It is reasonable to expect that such an experience may result in anxiety, a heightened sensitivity, or any number of changes in subject properties.

A researcher must be doubly concerned about altered subject properties in situations in which the same subjects are administered more than one treatment or measure. In the strictest sense, subjects cannot be assumed to be the same after the first measure has been taken. This was exemplified in several sections in Chapter 8. There are times, however, when it is not feasible to do anything but administer multiple measures. When multiple measures are administered, the researcher seems to have two basic options: (1) systematically administer one measure before the other or (2) rotate the order of administration in some fashion.

If one measure is obviously less vulnerable or sensitive to subject changes, then that measure should be administered after the other. An example of this is a situation in which teachers were supposed to evaluate certain instructional materials and the researcher also wanted to know how much information the subjects had about the material. The measure evaluating instructional materials should be administered first. The evaluation measure is probably more vulnerable to subjects' emotions or attitudes than an information test. If the subjects did not do well on the information test, the evaluation might be systematically lowered. It is doubtful, however, that subjects will do less than their optimum on an information test because of the evaluation rating. Therefore, it seems reasonable that the evaluation measure should precede the information test.

If there is little apparent difference in measure sensitivity, sequence of administration is not relevant. Under these circumstances, the researcher usually desires some assurance that neither measure systematically comes before the other, thus creating an influence that cannot be accounted for. To accomplish this, measures are generally counterbalanced (i.e., measure A then B; B then A) or randomly ordered. All that these latter procedures do is equally mask or mix the influence of each respective measure on the other.

The types of instruments and tasks that can be used in research are nearly endless. They are limited only by the researcher's imagination and the specific nature of the study. Differences are clearly evident between tasks even when several investigations are part of a program of research on the same topic. Researchers are constantly attempting to refine their instruments or study a slightly different dimension of the same construct. Because these types of variations are a routine part of science, it makes little sense to present a list of specific tasks or instruments as being representative or desirable. Researchers must become well acquainted with the literature in their particular area of investigation to identify those instruments that may be useful or could be modified to function effectively. There are, however, certain potential difficulties that are somewhat generalizable to various types of tasks and various types of instruments. These problem areas should be carefully considered as one selects a task or adapts one that already exists.

Task Performance Range

One of the most frequent problems encountered in task selection, particularly with regard to experimentation, involves the range of performance that the task will permit. The performance range of a task refers to the variation in responses possible within the limits imposed by uppermost and lowest possible performance scores on the task. Take the example of a hypothetical achievement test that is being used as a task. Suppose the number of correct responses is being scored as the criterion measure. If the total number of questions on the test is 25, the performance range would have a ceiling of 25 and a floor of zero (no correct responses). The desirable situation, of course, is to have the task designed so that the subjects can perform without being limited by the task itself. Unless this is the case, the level of performance probably reflects the task limits rather than the experimental treatment (e.g., the method of instruction). In many cases it is difficult to select or contrive a task that will permit subjects to perform fully to their ability without being hampered in some fashion by task performance range.

Ceiling Effect. If subjects in an investigation (or a subgroup of subjects) perform the task so well that they "top out," this is a ceiling effect. A ceiling effect occurs when the performance range is so restricted or limited on the upper end that many subjects cannot perform to their greatest ability (Kazdin, 1992). Such results would be called an *experimental artifact* because they represent an artificially determined performance level generated by constraints of the experiment rather than constraints of ability. The term *ceiling effect* accurately describes what happens to the subjects. This may be aptly illustrated by an analogy. Suppose a researcher were to conduct a descriptive study concerning the jumping ability of a professional basketball team, using as the criterion measure the upper height reached (in feet and inches) on a wall by each subject's right hand while jumping as high as possible. The results would look rather strange if the study were conducted in a room with an 8-foot ceiling. Not only would the ballplayers' performance be restricted by the ceiling, the researcher might end up with some brain-injured subjects (certainly the 7-footers).

More in the realm of behavioral science, Figure 10.1A provides a visual example of results in which a ceiling effect was operative. In this hypothetical experiment, subjects with mental retardation were compared with subjects of average intelligence to assess the effectiveness of two teaching methods. The number of correct responses on a test served as the criterion measure with a task performance range of 0-25. If the researcher is not alert to the apparent ceiling effect, an incorrect interpretation of these results may be made. One interpretation might suggest that there is a differential effectiveness between teaching methods for some subjects, but not all. Method A seems superior to method B for subjects with mental retardation, but that difference is not evident with average subjects. This would be a logical interpretation if the average subjects had not performed at or near the upper limit of the performance range. Because their group means are so close to the task ceiling, one might suspect that their performance represents task limitations rather than the effectiveness of teaching methods. This possibility becomes even more likely when one considers the fact that the results are presented as group means. Because the means for the average group are so near 25, there was undoubtedly a large proportion of those subjects who made correct responses on all test items. One has no way of knowing how many correct responses they might have made if the task ceiling has been raised.

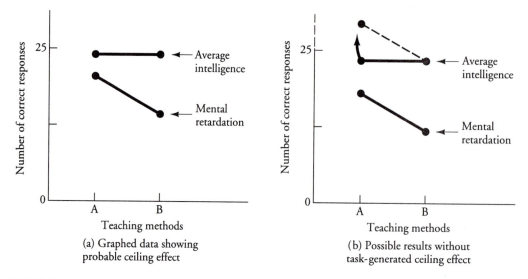

(a) Graphed data showing
probable ceiling effect

(b) Possible results without
task-generated ceiling effect

FIGURE 10.1

Figure 10.1B portrays hypothetical results that might have been obtained if the task performance range had been expanded in terms of
upper limits. Interpretation of these data is much different from what
was previously suggested under the conditions of the ceiling effect.
The data presented in Figure 10.1B suggest that teaching method A is
more effective than method B for both average subjects and those with
mental retardation. This represents important information that was not
evident in Figure 10.1A. It is also information that is not obtainable because the imaginary study in Figure 10.1A would not permit its observation. Thus, with a ceiling effect operative, one does not know whether
the lack of difference existed between method A and method B with
average subjects was because (1) the methods were not differentially
effective or (2) the range of task performance was so restricted that
these subjects could not perform to the best of their ability. The situation represented in Figure 10.1A is often referred to as a result in which
possible differences are *masked.*

Floor Effect. Task restrictions may occur at the lower end of the
performance range as well as the upper end. In situations where variation in subject performance is restricted by the lower limit of the task,
results are influenced by what is called a floor effect (Kazdin, 1992). In
the previous example, zero correct responses was the lower limit of
possible subject performance. Because zero responses is the floor with

any task, the difficulty of the material itself becomes a primary determiner of lower limit.

Figure 10.2A presents results of a hypothetical investigation in which a floor effect appears. Using the same research variables as before, the number of correct responses serves as the criterion measure for a comparison of teaching methods with subjects having mental retardation and subjects with average intelligence. Because the mean correct responses for the subjects with mental retardation are so near zero, one suspects the task floor is limiting possible performance variation. Again, unless the researcher is alert to this apparent artifact in the data, the interpretation may well be in error. If the floor effect were ignored, the data in Figure 10.2A might result in an interpretation that method A was more effective than method B for average subjects only. One does not know whether the absence of differences between methods A and B in subjects with mental retardation is caused by the fact that methods are not differentially effective or that the task itself was so difficult that possible influence of the methods is masked.

Figure 10.2B portrays hypothetical results from this same study that might have been obtained if the task performance range had been expanded with regard to lower limits. In this case, such a change might have been accomplished by using less difficult material for the test. Easier items might have permitted the subjects with mental retardation to exhibit some performance variation. Although the floor is still zero correct responses, one has reason to believe that variation of the subjects with mental retardation on less difficult material is more representative of their ability to perform than was the case when the lower limit

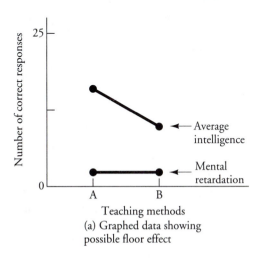

Teaching methods
(a) Graphed data showing
possible floor effect

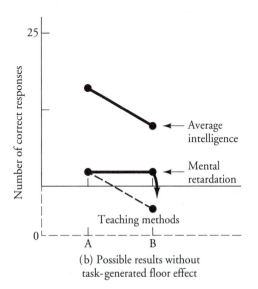

(b) Possible results without
task-generated floor effect

FIGURE 10.2

was masking performance. Interpretation of these data, as before, would probably be different from the interpretation for data in Figure 10.2A. It would now seem that method A was more effective than method B for both groups of subjects.

Alteration of Task Performance Range

It is desirable to find a task performance range that does not limit the response variation of subjects. Because the objective is to study subjects (their behavior, physiological sensitivity, ability, etc.), logically the subject must be permitted to perform. As a researcher progresses in a program of research, it is not uncommon to find that alteration of the task range is necessary. Usually, determination of the need to expand the performance range is based on results that involve an apparent floor or ceiling effect.

As suggested earlier, expanding the performance range of the task may be accomplished in a number of different ways. What actually occurs in an experimental setting is that the subject interacts with the task. The task presents a certain set of properties, and the subject uses a certain set of abilities (e.g., visual perception, auditory perception, or physiological maturity). These two components of subject and task combine in some fashion to generate the results observed. To obtain nonartifactual data with respect to performance range, researchers may alter either of these two components. Thus far, it is the task that has been altered. Depending on the circumstances, a researcher may elect to use different subjects (e.g., younger or brighter) to avoid performance range problems. Younger subjects, for example, may circumvent a ceiling effect if performance level is related to age. Experimenters must, however, be somewhat cautious in using a subject change to alter performance range problems. If there is a substantial change in the subject description, it is probable that a different organism is being studied (i.e., developmental differences). This is a particularly delicate matter if the primary focus of the research is the subject (e.g., response properties of the subject). It is not always the case, however, that the subject is the central focus. There may be investigations in which the primary interest is the task (e.g., stimulus properties of a given instructional material). Under such circumstances the researcher may be more willing to change subject characteristics than task properties.

Subject characteristics are more commonly the focus of investigation than task properties. Therefore, alteration of task properties represents the most common approach to circumventing a floor or ceiling effect. The fashion in which this may be accomplished was clearly exemplified in a series of studies that investigated the effects of organizing material on the subjects' recall performance (Drew & Altman, 1970; Freston & Drew, 1974; Simpson, King, & Drew, 1970). The Simpson, King, and Drew study compared the recall of subjects with and without mental retardation on two lists of words. The first was organized by conceptual category (e.g., fruits and trees) and the second was randomly organized (conceptually unorganized). Table 10.1 summarizes the results in terms of mean correct responses by group and experimental condition. The total number of words (and possible correct responses) was 25. Inspection of the group means in Table 10.1 suggests that the performance of normal subjects was limited by the task ceiling. These results represent, essentially, the same type of data contamination evident in Figure 10.1A. Thus, the researchers were not able to determine from this study whether organization of material has an influence on the recall of individuals of normal intelligence. This lack of information then became the central question for a subsequent study.

For the Drew and Altman study, a change in task was necessary to circumvent the ceiling effect. Only subjects of normal intelligence were used in this study. The age was lowered slightly but not sufficiently to be concerned about the problem of studying a different developmental level. To expand the performance range, two levels of material difficulty were used. Additionally, the list of words that each subject received was lengthened to 30 words. The easier list had a difficulty level that approximated that used in the Simpson et al. study. A second set of words was then constituted with a difficulty level substantially above the first. Table 10.2 summarizes the results in terms of mean correct responses by list difficulty and organization. Analysis of the data indicated that a significant difference did occur between performance on organized and unorganized material. At least from this, it is evident that a ceiling effect had been sufficiently circumvented to permit differences to appear. Inspection of the means, however, suggests that performance on low-difficulty material was approaching the ceiling although not nearly as much as in the previous work. This was expected because the low-difficulty was essentially the same level as that used by Simpson et al., with the exception of being slightly longer.

TABLE 10.1 Retarded and Nonretarded Mean Correct Responses by List Organization

| | List Organization | |
Subject Classification	Unorganized	Organized
Nonretarded	23.73	24.00
Retarded	12.67	17.29

Note. Adapted from "Free recall by retarded and nonretarded subjects as a function of input organization" by R. L. Simpson, J. D. King, & C. J. Drew, 1970, *Psychonomic Science, 19*, p. 334. Copyright © 1970, Psychonomic Society.

TABLE 10.2 Mean Correct Responses as a Function of List Difficulty and Organization

	List Organization	
List Difficulty	Unorganized	Organized
Low	23.73	24.27
High	15.80	17.27

Reprinted with permission of publisher from: Drew, C. J., & Altman, R. (1970). Effects of input organization and material difficulty on free recall. *Psychological Reports, 27,* 335-337.

The Drew and Altman study exemplifies the variety of minor adjustments that may be made to influence the interaction between subjects and the task. The age level of subjects was slightly different from that in the Simpson et al. study (range of 19-24 years, whereas the first study had an age range of 21-27 years). This probably had little or no influence, considering the age of the subjects. It is a technique that can be used, although a dramatic change in subject age may result in a developmentally different subject. This would be more of a problem with subjects who were younger than those used in these studies. A second minor adjustment was made by increasing the list length from 25 to 30 words. Lengthening the task must also be done somewhat cautiously because extremely dramatic changes may also alter the nature of the study. Care must be taken to avoid letting the lengthened task become a test of endurance instead of accomplishing the actual purpose of the investigation. Usually, this problem is avoided by running a quick pilot test of the task.

Thus, adjusting the performance range may be accomplished in a number of fashions. Decisions are usually made on the basis of clinical experience and inspection of previous task-subject interactions. For example, further adjustments were made in a third study that Freston and Drew conducted following those just described. A different population was under investigation that had some unique properties causing concern. Notably, this third group was diagnosed as having learning disabilities and was expected to have greater variation than had been expected in either of the previous studies. Great variability in performance seems characteristic of this population. Additionally, this variation was expected at both ends of the performance range. Consequently, three levels of material difficulty were used to ensure that subject performance would fall within the task limits. These were designed as follows: (1) a low-difficulty list that was easier than even the low-difficulty material in Drew and Altman, (2) an intermediate difficulty list that fell, approximately, between the high and low list in Drew and Altman, and

(3) a high-difficulty list that had a difficulty level above that in previous studies. As the results were analyzed, it was apparent that the judgment had been correct. All means were nicely plotted and well within the performance limits imposed by the task (Freston & Drew).

Performance Range: Quasi-Experimental Designs

Task performance range difficulties present a particularly challenging problem in certain quasi-experimental designs. Recall from Chapter 8 that a quasi-experimental design is one in which an experimenter is comparing groups that are different on the basis of some preexisting condition. Examples of quasi-experimental studies are found throughout the research literature in sociology, psychology, education, medicine, and many other disciplines. The previously cited studies in which subjects with mental retardation were compared with subjects of normal intelligence represent classic quasi-experimental designs. Likewise, investigations comparing different cultural groups or physiologically different groups are examples that would be considered quasi-experimental.

The problem arises in attempting to design a task with sufficient performance range to cover the broad range of response variation present in all groups. For example, studies in child development may necessitate a minimum of three levels of chronological age to obtain even a rough picture of developmental trends in performance. In many cases, it is somewhat difficult to ascertain much developmental information from only two levels. Three or more levels permit a more complete developmental picture. Even with three age levels, the performance range may be extremely problematic. Imagine the difficulty in designing a task that will permit performance of groups with mean ages of four, six, and eight years. Likewise, the problem is equally challenging for groups that are deviant on other dimensions. Such preidentified subject classifications as high, average, and low achievement bring with them vast differences in background information and, likely, wide performance ranges. When planning an investigation, a researcher must be cautious in selecting the task if a quasi-experimental design is involved. A pilot test of the task with each type of subject group will probably be necessary to determine the degree to which the task will appropriately serve. This is more advisable than investing resources in a full-blown investigation that obtains results contaminated by performance-range restrictions.

*Turn to page 309 and complete
Simulations 10.3 and 10.4*

Questionnaires

To a beginning researcher, questionnaire studies may seem to be the easiest type of investigation to undertake. All one does is put the questions to be asked on paper, mail them out, then sit back and wait for the data to roll in. This simplicity, however, is deceptive. There are many intricacies to questionnaire studies that are not apparent on the surface, and some of them relate directly to the instrument. This section will provide a brief examination of some issues pertaining to the construction of the questionnaire instrument.

The questionnaire represents the link between a researcher and the data. It must, in large part, stand on its own because a researcher is not usually present to prompt a response or clarify areas in which the subject may be confused. This leads to a point of departure for designing the instrument. Because a researcher cannot personally work with each respondent, it is important to solve as many problems as possible as the questionnaire is being constructed. One critical factor is to anticipate the difficulties that may arise. This type of process was previously encountered in the planning of experiments. The researcher's task is to keep Murphy's Law from ruining the study. This can be partially accomplished by asking a series of questions.

In general, a researcher wants to know what factors might make a subject fail to respond and/or what might lead a subject to give inaccurate responses. First and foremost, the respondent must be convinced that the study is legitimate and worth the effort of response. Part of this task may be managed through appropriate sponsorship and a well-written cover letter (Bailey, 1994). However, the questionnaire must also contribute to this goal. The amount of effort required on the part of the respondent is important—the less effort, the better. The questionnaire should not be so lengthy that it requires a great deal of time and effort to complete. This directly pertains to the type of questions asked. If there are many open ended questions, the respondent may not be willing to take the time to write out the answers—whereas the same information might be obtained by questions for which the subject can merely check alternative responses. These brief examples illustrate the importance of the manner in which the questionnaire is designed and lead directly to some of the more specific issues involved in instrument construction for this type of study.

The questions being asked in a questionnaire are central to the data collection process. They must be clearly worded so that there is minimal chance for the respondent to be confused. As noted before, the best protection against problems such as this is a limited pilot test of the instrument prior to beginning the study. This is a crucial step and should always be conducted to avoid serious inaccuracies and inconsistencies in the data. However, in addition to the pilot test, there are several points that need attention as the questions are being written.

One problem that must be avoided involves items that actually have *two questions included in one*. An example of this might be a question like "Does your company have an explicit recruitment policy for ethnic minorities and women?" This type of question is very typical of oral conversation but causes serious difficulties on a questionnaire. The problem is the use of the word *and*, which may cause confusion for the respondent. What response should be given if the department has a policy for minorities but not for women? If the question is read literally, a *yes* answer can be given only if policies exist for both. A negative response might result if there is not a policy for women, minorities, or both. The question might be worded more clearly by substituting *or* for *and*, or it might be separated into two questions. Items should always be reviewed carefully to ensure that only one question is involved in each (Bailey, 1994).

All possible precautions should be taken to avoid *ambiguous questions*. Certainly, the example presented above was vague in terms of what response was really desired. There are, however, other types of ambiguity that a researcher should avoid, such as terminology. Certain words may not be well known to the respondents and may therefore be ambiguous. (Researchers should not expect respondents to use a dictionary unless they are willing to settle for a very low response rate.) On the other end of the continuum, there may be some terms everyone thinks they know but that have been used so much and so loosely that the meaning has become very fluid (as in the case of slang terms or phrases). Such terms or phrases may generate very inconsistent responses because they have different meanings to different people. Thus, a researcher must be cautious regarding the use of uncommon terms as well as those that are commonly used. The best safeguard against ambiguity in a questionnaire is a pilot test of the instrument or at least a critical review by an independent but alert group of colleagues.

The points mentioned above alluded to potential problems related to the wording used in questionnaires. However, *wording level* warrants re-emphasis. A delicate balance must be maintained between precise and colloquial language. After a researcher avoids the obvious problems of "four-bit" words and slang, attention should be turned to the general level of wording of the questionnaire. For this consideration, the primary concern must be the sample of subjects being studied in the survey. If the respondents are considered "well educated," the language level may be somewhat higher than if they are less educated. At times, there may be an inclination to use slang phrases to establish rapport with the respondents (e.g., studying adolescents' opinions of music). Here again, caution must be exercised because of the problems with slang terminology. The same slang phrases may have widely varying definitions for adolescents in California and in Ontario, and may change weekly.

Particular care must be taken when a survey involves *sensitive topics* (e.g., sex, drinking habits, use of drugs). Such topics raise the probability that respondents may not return the questionnaire or may respond inaccurately. Although this is a persistent problem, there are some precautions that can be taken in questionnaire construction that may help. One of the difficulties just mentioned was the possibility of inaccurate responses; subjects may be inclined to answer in a manner that they think is socially appropriate rather than being completely honest. Questions may be worded in a fashion to partially offset such tendencies. For example, the same item could be phrased two different ways:

1. Do you smoke marijuana?
    Yes_____ No _____

    If yes, how often?
    Once a week _____
    Once a month _____
    Every day

2. How often do you smoke marijuana?
    Once a week _____
    Once a month _____
    Every day _____
    Never _____

Subjects may give socially appropriate (or "legally appropriate") answers in either case, but there is less chance of this happening in question 2. The wording in number 1 makes it very easy to say *no*, whereas the second wording makes it somewhat more difficult. Other approaches to sensitive topics include wording the question in a manner suggesting that the practice is widespread or that there is no consensus regarding what is socially appropriate. Some might suggest that sensitive topics such as those noted above should simply be avoided because of the response problems involved. Certainly, less sensitive topics do not present as many difficulties, but researchers cannot avoid an area of investigation just because it may be troublesome to study. Often, it is just such topics that really need to be investigated.

The *order* in which questions appear may also have an influence on subjects' responses. For example, it is usually best to place the easily answered questions first. In this way, respondents may become more committed to completing the questionnaire as they proceed because they have already spent time on the task. Similarly, if there are sensitive questions or open-ended items requiring more effort, these are best placed at the end of the questionnaire. Even if the subject refuses to answer these more specific items, the responses to the other questions have already been provided and there is greater likelihood that the instrument will be mailed back.

There are many considerations involved in the construction of a questionnaire. Only a few have been examined here. Beginning researchers who anticipate undertaking such an investigation should consult reference volumes specifically focusing on these types of studies and instruments (e.g., Bailey, 1994; Berdie, Anderson, & Niebuhr, 1986). Many of the issues discussed in this section are also relevant to constructing structured interview protocols. Such interview studies are similar to questionnaire surveys except that an interviewer personally reads the questions to the subjects and records the responses.

Turn to page 311 and complete Simulation 10.5

Observation

Studies employing observation for data collection were discussed in Chapters 6 and 7. These earlier discussions emphasized that the observer is the central factor in such data collection. This is somewhat different from other types of research in which an instrument or task is of central importance (e.g., as the questionnaire is in questionnaire surveys). There are, however, certain instrument considerations that must receive attention in observation research. Observers must have some means of recording the data. This section will provide a brief examination of data-recording instruments that can be used for observation studies. There are certain types of observation that impose relatively little structure on the data recorded, whereas others involve a great deal of structure. Observations in qualitative studies often favor the former circumstances. Quantitative observation, with more structure, is the primary focus of this discussion because the data-recording instrument is a major source of structure.

Observation recording instruments may be very simple, or they may be quite complex, depending on the nature of the study. The data sheet will probably be quite simple if an investigation is aimed at recording information on only a few behaviors. More complex instruments are obviously necessary for studies involving many behaviors or many subjects who are being observed simultaneously. One important guideline in developing an observation instrument pertains directly to this complexity factor. The instrument should never be more complex than is necessary to serve the purposes of the study. Complex instruments require more effort from the observer than those that have simple formats. As more effort is required, there is a greater likelihood that errors will be committed during data collection. This obviously generates more inaccurate data and may contribute to reduced interobserver reliability. A delicate balance must be struck between a format that is sufficiently precise to meet the needs of the study and one that is as simple as possible and convenient to use.

Formats for observation instruments will vary, depending on the data-recording method being used. For example, the format might be very simple if the researcher is merely counting occurrences—the *tally* method. Figure 10.3 illustrates a data-recording format using the tally method for the aggressive behavior study discussed in chapter 6. Note that the categories of behavior are provided on the form for the observer.

The data instrument might look quite different if the observer were using a *duration* recording method. Duration data involve the amount of time that the subject is engaged in the target behavior. In this case, the observer will note the time that the behavior begins (i.e., by starting a stopwatch) and when it terminates (i.e., by stopping a stopwatch). This process of starting and stopping the stopwatch may continue (without resetting the watch to zero) for a specified period such as a 1-hour reading lesson. The data then would be the total amount of time that the subject was engaged in the target behavior (e.g., self-stimulation) during that 1-hour observation session. Figure 10.4 illustrates a data form for the duration recording method.

	Subject: David	
Aggressive behavior	Session 1	Session 2
Physical		
Peer	𝈦	//
Adult	/	
Verbal		
Peer	𝈦 //	𝈦 ///
Adult	//	/
Nonagressive behavior		
Physical		
Peer	/	
Adult	/	///
Verbal		
Peer	//	/
Adult	/	////

FIGURE 10.3   Observation Data Sheet Using the Tally Recording Method

Subject: _____   Target behavior: _____

Observer: _____   Date: _____

Location: _____   Activity: _____

Session number: _____

Time ended: _____   Total behavior
                                       (duration read
Time started: _____   from watch)

Total session length: _____   _____ hr. _____ min.

FIGURE 10.4   Data Form for Duration Recording Method

Observation studies may also use the *interval* method of recording data. Such procedures focus on whether or not a particular behavior occurred during a given interval. The observer would simply place a check mark or a code symbol on the recording form if the behavior occurred during the specified interval. Figure 10.5 illustrates an interval recording form. The codes in this example are simple: *P* represents physical aggressive behavior, *V* represents verbal aggressive behavior, and a blank interval box means that neither of those target behaviors occurred during that interval.

Observation instruments can obviously take many forms as indicated by the examples presented above. As with most research, the specific format must often be tailored to fit the investigation being planned. A beginning researcher may find it helpful to review current literature in the area being studied or consult volumes that focus in greater depth on observational recording systems. Developments in electronic technology have also contributed to observation as a data-collection technique. Figure 10.6 illustrates a hand-held bar-code reader that is used to collect coded data and automatically enter it into a computer memory for later analysis. Bar-code symbols, much like those we encounter in retail stores, are used and assigned to certain behaviors as one would the codes noted above. When an observer sees that behavior occur, the wand is passed over the code and the occurrence is recorded. This type of equipment relieves the stress on observers and increases reliability of the data collected.

Subject: _____David_____   Observer: _____Mary_____

Date: _____5/16_____   Activity: _____Playground recess_____

Session number: _____12_____   Time started: ___9:15 a.m.___

Target behaviors and codes: _____Physical agression = P,_____

___verbal agression = V_____

Interval length: _____15 seconds_____

1	VP	2	P	3	V	4	PV	5	V	6	
7		8	V	9	P	10	P	11	P	12	VP
13	V	14		15		16	V	17	V	18	P
19	VP	20	V	21		22		23		24	
25		26		27	P	28	P	29	V	30	VP

FIGURE 10.5 Data Form for Interval Recording Method

FIGURE 10.6 Barcode Data Recording

Simulations

Simulations 10.1 and 10.2

Topic: Criterion measures

Background Statement: The data that are collected in a study represent the researcher's evidence of how the subject interacted with the task. Specification of the measure to be recorded is, therefore, a crucial part of planning any investigation. It is also a frequent area of difficulty for the beginning researcher.

Tasks to Be Performed:

1. Read the following stimulus material, which is a summary statement about a hypothetical study.
2. Suggest a criterion measure that might be appropriate for the investigation.

Stimulus Material for Simulation 10.1: A teacher in your school wishes to compare the effectiveness of two reading programs. The study has been designed in a traditional experimental framework with two groups of subjects, one receiving one program and the second receiving the other program. Suggest the criterion measure(s) that may be appropriate.

For feedback see page 312.

Stimulus Material for Simulation 10.2: A study is to be initiated with a young girl who has been in preschool for six months. The teacher is extremely concerned because the child is withdrawn and does not interact with the other children. This has become a problem because much of the daily activity involves spontaneous or free play in small groups. It has been determined that this behavior will be the target for modification through reinforcement contingencies in a time-series design. Suggest the criterion measure(s) that may be appropriate.

For feedback see page 312.

Simulations 10.3 and 10.4

Topic: Performance range

Background Statement: The performance range in an experimental task is a crucial issue if the data obtained are to truly represent the subjects' ability to perform. Certain studies are particularly vulnerable and require considerable ingenuity on the part of the experimenter to design an appropriate task.

Stimulus Information: The simulation you are presently performing involves an investigation that is developmental in nature and focuses primarily on a subject question concerning the development of classification concepts in children. One study has been conducted before yours, and you are using it as a point of departure for designing your own. The study is focusing on the cognitive development of classification concepts and does not involve instruction per se as an experimental variable. Your study is to be a follow-up on previous work. The data presented in the stimulus material are to be used as a point of departure.

Tasks to Be Performed for Simulation 10.3:

1. Inspect the following data table from the earlier study.
2. Graph the data to facilitate inspection.
3. Do you see anything in particular that should receive your attention in planning your own study?
4. If there are problems, what changes seem in order to circumvent those problems?

Stimulus Material for Simulation 10.3:

Mean Correct Responses on Classification Task Performance*

	Material Difficulty	
Subject Age Group (years)	*Low*	*High*
3 to $4^{1}/_{2}$	22.0	12.7
5 to $6^{1}/_{2}$	28.6	16.3
7 to $8^{1}/_{2}$	29.2	22.8

* Thirty items on the classification task.

For feedback see page 313.

Tasks to Be Performed for Simulation 10.4:

1. Inspect the accompanying data table from the earlier study. Note the criterion measure (different from that in Simulation 10.3).
2. Graph the data to facilitate inspection.

3. Do you see anything in particular that should receive your attention in planning your own study?
4. If there are problems, what changes seem in order to circumvent those problems?

Stimulus Material for Simulation 10.4:

Mean Trials to Criterion on Classification Task Performance*

Subject Age Group (years)	Material Difficulty	
	Low	*High*
3 to $4^1/_2$	6.1	29.2
5 to $6^1/_2$	3.0	16.7
7 to $8^1/_2$	1.5	6.3

* The task will permit one trial performance to reach criterion. Therefore, the best possible performance is one trial to criterion.

For feedback see page 314.

Simulation 10.5

Topic: Questionnaire construction

Background Statement: One very important factor in questionnaire construction involves the manner in which questions are worded. This has been a continuing problem for survey researchers and must receive careful attention in the planning process. The simulation you will perform here focuses on questionnaire wording.

Tasks to Be Performed:

1. Inspect the wording of the questions presented below.
2. Identify any wording that may cause response problems.
3. Rewrite the questions to circumvent the difficulties.

Stimulus Material for Simulation 10.5:

1. Do you mow and trim your lawn regularly?   Yes ___ No ___
2. Do you have a florulent yard?   Yes ___ No ___

For feedback see page 315.

Simulation Feedbacks

Simulation 10.1

As with any problem in which one is given a general task to perform, a variety of specific responses may be expected. The crucial issue here is whether you were sufficiently specific and operational that what you specified can be measured and is a logical criterion measure for the topic. Hopefully, the following will serve to exemplify such specificity for at least one possible measure.

You have already had some practice that applies to this simulation. Remember Simulation 4.5? It dealt with a reading study. Pursue this same approach again.

First of all, the criterion measure must be a way of determining the effectiveness of the reading programs. One way of assessing the effectiveness of reading instruction is to measure a student's reading comprehension. However, as noted previously, the term *reading comprehension* is not specific enough to tell you what you are going to count. Frequently, reading comprehension is determined by counting the number of correct responses on a test dealing with a passage the students have read. Correct responses will serve adequately if reading comprehension is what you wish to assess. Do you have something else you want to measure? Is it specified in a measurable form?

Simulation 10.2

As before, there may be a number of different responses that are appropriate for this simulation. You should check with your instructor to determine if what you listed is on target. A few guidelines are presented below for general feedback.

First, specificity and operational definitions are crucial. Not only are you faced with the issues of defining some behavior that is measurable and countable, you are also going to have to have that behavior sufficiently well described so that an observer will know the behavior (whatever it is) when it occurs. In this case, you will want to select one or two countable behaviors involving the child's interaction with other children. Perhaps these could be verbal interaction or appropriate physical interaction such as cooperative play or the sharing of toys. Additionally, it will be necessary to specify a time frame. This might involve a statement such as "frequency of verbal interactions per 2-minute observation." How did you do? Can you measure it?

Simulation 10.3

The problem with the data may be obvious to you immediately. The instruction to graph the data was included because we have found visual inspection of graphs to be helpful. Your graph might involve some specific characteristics that are different, but generally the data may be visually presented as shown.

From the graphed data, it becomes obvious that the previous study was plagued with a serious ceiling effect. This probably prevented at least the groups of subjects who were 7 to 8 and 5 to 6 years old from performing as well as they might have. If there are only 30 possible items, certainly means of 29.2 and 28.6 included scores of 30 from several subjects.

What does this mean for your study? You will obviously want to avoid the ceiling effect. Because the major focus of the research involves child development, your options would favor altering material in the task rather than the subjects' ages. One approach might entail changing the present high-difficulty material to the low-difficulty condition. This would certainly be a possibility because difficulty is only relative and the means in the right-hand column of the table do not appear to be restricted by a ceiling.

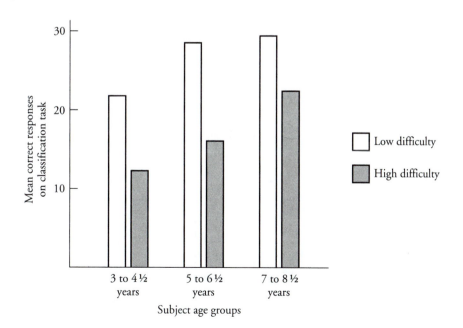

Simulation 10.4

The graph for the data in this Simulation (see p. 311) would look something like that shown here.

What problem did you note with these data? If you said that a ceiling effect was operating, you were exactly right! If you said it was a floor effect, you fell into a trap. The trap was not set up intentionally to frustrate you; this is an area where even experienced researchers often have to take a second look. Here is what happened.

Essentially this set of data could be from the same study presented in Simulation 10.3, but the criterion measure that was recorded has been changed. Before, mean correct responses was used, which meant that the higher number indicated better performance. This time, the measure is the number of trials that a subject takes to reach a proficiency criterion. Using this measure, the lower the number, the better the performance. If a subject takes only two trials to reach proficiency, the performance is better than that of a subject who takes five trials to reach proficiency. Consequently, a ceiling effect is operating with the older group that received low-difficulty material. Why? It is possible to reach proficiency in one trial (see the footnote to the table). If the older group has a mean of 1.5 trials, there are a good number of them who are reaching proficiency in one trial. Consequently, their ability to perform is being restricted by the task.

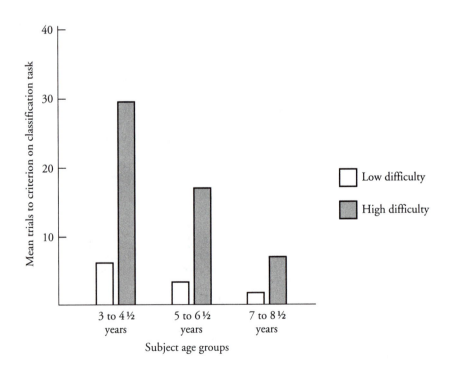

What changes are in order for your study? Again, the focus is child development, so the favored option probably involves a change in the material. The high-difficulty material looks all right because the means are nicely distributed without an apparent restriction in performance range. Probably the same adjustment that was suggested in the feedback for Simulation 10.3 should *not* be made because if a still more difficult list were developed, a floor effect might result with the younger children (there is already a mean trials to criterion of 29.2 with them). Perhaps the best option would be to develop a new set of easy material that has a difficulty level somewhere in between the two that are presented in the table. This could be hoped to avoid the ceiling yet not present other problems. A pilot test will be in order before launching the experiment to see if the material appears appropriate.

Simulation 10.5

These questions present some obvious problems. Question one represents a classic example of two questions in one item. The tip-off here is the use of the term *and*. The respondent may mow regularly but not trim; therefore, what response is appropriate? This problem could be solved by replacing *and* with *or*. A second approach might involve writing two separate questions, one addressing lawn mowing and the second focusing on trimming. The first question also includes a vague term pertaining to how often the activity is undertaken. *Regularly* might mean one thing to one respondent and another to a second. It probably would be better to specify how often in the question (e.g., weekly, every two weeks, monthly).

The second question is one of those that uses a "four-bit" word that is unnecessary and likely unknown to most respondents. *Florulent* is not a term that is in many individuals' vocabulary. The question could simply have said, "Does your yard have flowers?" or "Do you have a flowery yard?" and been much more appropriate.

How did you do on this simulation? Can you think of other similar examples?

Research Design Related to Statistics

We have emphasized throughout this text that the research process should be thought of as a series of vitally interrelated parts. It becomes necessary to highlight this fact once again by noting that there is a crucial relationship between the design of a study and the statistical tools used. Frequently this relationship is not clearly conceptualized by the beginning student of research. Consequently it is not uncommon to find an investigation that is designed to ask a particular type of question and statistical techniques used to analyze the data that are more appropriate for a different type of design. The purpose of this chapter is to examine the relationship between research design and the statistical techniques used. Additionally, several topics involve considerations preliminary to the selection of the appropriate statistical tool.

The use of statistical analyses is limited to investigations that have collected quantitative data or have in some fashion converted part of the data into numerical format. It is not unusual for studies that use qualitative methodology to also supplement the qualitative descriptive information with some quantitative data which may be summarized using statistical analyses. Mixed method research (i.e., studies employing both quantitative and qualitative procedures) are becoming more popular as researchers recognize their utility and become increasingly comfortable crossing the methodology boundaries (e.g., Crawford & Christensen, 1995; Hart, 1994). Qualitative analyses will be examined in Chapter 15. This chapter will discuss matters that are important for consideration as you prepare to select the appropriate statistical analysis for quantitative data.

Throughout the portion of this book that deals with data analyses it will be necessary to keep in mind the scope of the text. It is not the intent to provide a detailed discussion of how to use statistical tools. This has been accomplished in a variety of textbooks that focus either solely or largely on statistical methods (e.g., Bruning & Kintz, 1987; Howell, 1995; Wampold & Drew, 1990). Neither is it the intent, nor would it be possible, to examine all the specific techniques that are available for data analysis. Rather it is the purpose of this portion of the text to provide an introduction to the area of statistical analysis, to indicate how these techniques fit in the overall scheme of the research enterprise, and to suggest generally some of the analyses that may be applied in certain situations.

Statistics: What and Why

Many students, and even a fair number of faculty, view statistics with a mixture of fear, hatred, reverence, skepticism, and aversion, all derived from the many myths and illusions that surround the topic as a required set of courses for graduate degrees. Such views, both openly and subtly expressed, are commonly encountered by most researchers. During the days when Ph.D's required foreign languages, it was alleged that three were required for the degree, German, French, and Statistics. Why do such attitudes prevail concerning the statistical aspects of research?

We have noted a reaction additional to those mentioned that may shed some light on this question. A high proportion of beginning students are fearful of the area of statistics. (Recognize it? The sweaty palms, tight stomach, and frequent outbursts of nervous laughter?) This fear is often accompanied by an absence of knowledge concerning what statistics are. It may be that the emotional attitudes are related to this lack of knowledge and understanding about what statistics are and why they are useful. An example of such a lack of knowledge came to our attention several years ago when a student asked if a statistical test was an instrument to be administered to the subjects in a study in addition to the reading test. Admittedly, this student was just beginning to learn about research, but the question still was a red flag concerning the entering knowledge of some individuals who have little background. Statistical methods are procedures for *analyzing the data* (scores), which have already been obtained from administration of the research task or instrument to the subjects. This section will discuss briefly the whats and whys of statistical methods.

Once the data are collected it is the researcher's task to scrutinize the scores, draw certain conclusions concerning the subjects' performance, and interpret the data in terms of the original research question. To interpret the data it is necessary that the researcher have a way of looking at the scores that will provide a clear picture of what happened in the experiment. Seldom* can this be reliably accomplished by merely inspecting the numbers or performance scores. Visual inspection usually permits attention to only loose questions, and answers to such questions are frequently vague. It may be possible to determine that George scored about as well as most subjects or that Sally obtained the highest score in all groups, but little can be said about group performance. Groups are often the basis for a research question (such as "How well can this group be expected to perform on task X?" or "Which is more effective, treatment method A that group 1 received or treatment method B that group 2 received?") The researcher has to be able to speak in terms of group performance if the group represents the basis for answering the research question. Statistics represent summary and analysis procedures that permit the researcher to determine group performance characteristics in a manner that is far more precise and convenient than visual inspection of the raw data.

There are statistical tools available for nearly every conceivable research purpose or question. Two broad categories of purpose are generally involved in behavioral research—descriptive and inferential.

As the term indicates, *descriptive* studies have the primary purpose of describing a sample or group of individuals. The description may involve annual income, average height, educational achievement, or any of a number of different dimensions. Descriptive studies usually do not intend to go beyond the process of providing a picture of the group that is being investigated.

Inferential research, on the other hand, has a substantially different purpose. An inferential investigation, although it may describe a group, also has the purpose of drawing implications from the data with regard to a theory, model, or body of knowledge. It may be that the researchers are testing the soundness of some psychological theory, making some predictions with regard to student success, or determining which of several treatment approaches is more effective. In accomplishing this purpose, they are inferring beyond the behavioral facts of the data to some abstract concept or to some generalized situation. This inference goes beyond a reporting of "what is" and is the characteristic of inferential research that distinguishes it from descriptive research. In reality the distinction between inferential and descriptive studies may be somewhat blurred. It is not difficult at all to find examples of investigations that involve both purposes to some degree. The distinction is being made here for instructional convenience in examining different statistical methods.

Different statistical procedures are designed to facilitate the func-

---

* It is particularly difficult to obtain a clear picture of the results by merely inspecting the scores when groups are used. Graphed raw data from time-series studies using only one subject are more amenable to interpretation by visual inspection.

tions of descriptive and inferential studies. These general categories of statistical techniques are generically identified as descriptive statistics and inferential statistics. The former provide a summary of the data from which a description can be made (e.g., average height or range of intelligence). Descriptive statistics make it possible to conveniently scrutinize characteristics or performance (see Chapter 13). Inferential statistics have a different purpose (see Chapter 14).

Statistics are used to perform research functions that cannot be accomplished without them. In descriptive research, statistics provide a convenient and precise summary of the data that permits the researcher to describe "what is" or "what happened" in situations for which mere visual inspection of the data would be insufficient. Far from being an academic exercise or hurdle (designed to generate hives, poor complexion, and general ill health in students), statistics serve practical purposes in research.

Which Statistic? Foundations of Tool Selection

Statistics play an important role in the overall process of quantitative research. This statement is not meant to contradict earlier discussions, which attempted to deemphasize them. Previously, statistics were characterized as "*just* tools." This earlier characterization intended to emphasize to the beginning researcher that the research process involves a *series* of important segments, with statistics representing only one. This is the perspective that has been maintained throughout the text and is an accurate view of research and its components.

Many statistical tools are available to the researcher for different purposes. To select the appropriate technique, certain considerations must receive attention. The remainder of this chapter will examine one of the basic factors that a researcher must consider in selecting the statistic to be used—the different types of data that may be collected.

The Nature of the Data

The importance of selecting an appropriate criterion measure was previously discussed. This decision is crucial. The researcher must now consider several factors that relate both to the research question and to the type of statistical tools that may be applied.

Criterion measures represent a means of describing real world events or occurrences (such as a child's behavior). It is essential that the criterion measure or data accurately represent or parallel the events, otherwise the research question intended for investigation may not be what is actually being studied. For example, numbers have the property known as *identity*. A number is unique and is not exactly the same as any other number. If a number is used as the criterion measure representing an event, the event should also have the property of identity. That is, there should be reason to believe that the event so designated is unique from other events. Numbers also have the property of *order*. One number is less than or greater than another on some continuum. Occurrences to which such a type of measure is applied should also have order. If one event is represented by a given number (e.g., six) and a second event is represented by a higher number (e.g., seven), there should be a sound basis for believing the second event to be larger or greater on some continuum than the first. This may be exemplified by ranking the relative heights of basketball players. By lining the team up in order from the shortest to the tallest, it is possible to rank each individual in terms of height relative to the others on the team. Numbers are also characterized by the property of *additivity*. By adding together two numbers, one can obtain another number, which is different or unique. This last property is important for most of the arithmetic operations performed in analyzing data. Without additivity, arithmetic operations cannot be performed on the data and accurately reflect the circumstances or events in the actual observation setting. Although there is some disagreement regarding the importance of data properties, there is little question that interpretation of results requires attention to the issue (Howell, 1994).

Not all of the events that are studied in behavioral science have all the properties of identity, order, and additivity. Different events have certain properties but not others. This does not mean that they are not legitimate topics for investigation or that data cannot be recorded on them. It does, however, emphasize the necessity of specifying a criterion measure that parallels the observed phenomenon. Different types of data are amenable to different types of analysis. It is crucial that the beginning researcher become acquainted with measurement scales to make appropriate decisions in selecting the statistical tool needed.

Nominal Data.   The first type of data to be discussed is called nominal data, occasionally referred to as categorical or classification data. Nominal data represent the most primitive type of measurement. They are useful when all that can be accomplished is the assignment of events to categories. For example, an item on a questionnaire may require a *yes* or *no* response from the subject. Under such circumstances all that can be determined from the data is whether a subject's response falls into one or the other of two categories. Other examples are found in biological classification systems, psychiatric diagnostic categories, and many other areas both in and beyond the boundaries of science.

The essential element to be noted with regard to nominal data is that the information, whether in the responses, attributes, people, or characteristics, is in the form of categories that are distinct and mutually exclusive, *without an apparent underlying continuum*. If numbers are used to designate categories (e.g., response type 1 or response type 2), they serve only as identification labels (Howell, 1994). Such numbers would not represent any magnitude or order continuum and could be replaced with any symbol that would conveniently and effectively discriminate one category from another (e.g., group A or group B). Nominal data have the property of identity, since presumably each category is completely different from the other categories.

Ordinal Data.   The second type of data to be discussed is known as ordinal or *rank-order data.* Ordinal data move measurement from the qualitative discrimination between events, which is characteristic of nominal data, to a more quantitative basis of assessment. Ordinal measurement is characterized by the ability to rank order events on the basis of an underlying continuum. Thus the ranks denote *greater than* or *less than* on the dimension being assessed.

A variety of situations exemplify ordinal data. The earlier ranking of basketball players with regard to relative height would result in ordinal data. Likewise, ordinal data may be generated by the frequently used Likert or 1 to 5 scale. Recall the yes-no questionnaire response example mentioned under nominal data. It is possible that this dichotomous response option might be transformed to a Likert scale with an underlying continuum representing relative degree of agreement. This could be accomplished by following the stimulus statement with a response format such as:

Highly disagree	*Disagree*	*Neutral*	*Agree*	*Highly agree*
1	2	3	4	5

The respondents could provide considerably more information regarding how they viewed the stimulus statement with this type of format than by merely selecting a dichotomous response of yes-no or agree-disagree. With this type of data the researcher is able to discriminate between those subjects who are only mildly in disagreement with the statement and those who are firmer in their position. The relative firmness of the viewpoints is all that may be determined, however. The actual amount of difference between any two response possibilities is not known. One cannot say that the difference between any two responses represents an equal interval (for example, the amount of difference in agreement between 1 and 2 is not known to be the same as that between 3 and 4). Thus the serial order of responses may be determined so that a response of 4 is relatively more in agreement with the statement than a response of 3, but one does not know what the actual interval is. Ordinal data have both the properties of identity and order, but since the interval is unknown, additivity is not present.

Interval Data.   The third type of data to be examined is called interval data. Interval data have all the properties of nominal and ordinal data plus added information concerning the interval units. When interval measurement is possible, the researcher is working with known and equal distances between score units. With interval data it is not only possible to determine greater than or less than but also the magnitude of a difference in the underlying continuum of what is being measured. If, for example, the differences between scores are equal (for example, the differences in score units generated by subtracting 10 from 25 and 20 from 35 are both 15), then there is a corresponding equivalence in property magnitude differences. Interval data are characterized by all three number properties: identity, order, and additivity.

Common examples of interval data include calendar time and temperature as measured on centigrade and Fahrenheit scales. Differences in the score units on these measures represent known and constant magnitude differences in the factor being measured. The example measures also involve a property that is characteristic of interval data, *an arbitrary zero point.* Temperature perhaps exemplifies this characteristic most vividly. Temperature measured as 0º on the centigrade scale reads 32º on the Fahrenheit scale, whereas 0º F is the same as -17.8º C. Thus the zero point is arbitrary, attained at different points depending on which scale is used, and in neither case does 0º indicate the complete absence of temperature. (Absolute 0º in temperature is on the Kelvin scale.) Likewise the calendar time or numbering of years was rather arbitrarily begun on the Christian calendar with the birth of Christ.

Measurement in behavioral science does not achieve interval status as frequently as it does in the physical sciences. For example, data generated in cognitive psychology and education are often recorded in the form of the number of correct responses or the number of errors committed (as measures of, say, learning or forgetting). The researcher seldom knows whether the units represented by such measures are equal, making it difficult to say with certainty that interval data are being obtained. Usually the behavioral researcher will assume that the units approximate equality unless the data are obviously ordinal or nominal. This assumption, if reasonably in harmony with the properties of what is being measured, provides more latitude in terms of statistical methods that can be used.

Ratio Data.   The fourth and final type of data to be discussed is known as ratio data. Ratio data have all the properties of interval data but are distinguished in that the zero point is not arbitrary. A zero score on a ratio scale *does* signify total absence of the property being measured.

Examples of ratio data are primarily found in physical measurement and seldom in behavioral science. As noted in the previous section, temperature measured on the Kelvin scale (also known as the absolute zero scale) conforms to the characteristics of ratio measurement. Likewise height, weight, and time (to perform) are examples of ratio scale data. Occasionally behavioral scientists will be interested in time (such as response latency) or some other measure that appears to be a ratio scale. This type of measure, however, is not frequent. Work is primarily conducted in the nominal, ordinal, and interval scales. Fortunately, there are few statistical procedures that require ratio data characteristics, and consequently the primary focus in this text will be the first three types of data.

Turn to page 323 and complete Simulations 11.1, 11.2, 11.3, and 11.4.

Simulations

Simulations 11.1, 11.2, and 11.3

Topic: Nature of the data

Background Statement: In many cases you will be presented with data that have already been collected. Frequently it is up to you to determine what type of data is involved in the study. This will require knowledge and experience with different data types so that you can make subsequent decisions concerning data analysis.

Tasks to Be Performed:

1. Review the following stimulus material, paying particular attention to the nature of the data collected.
2. Answer the following questions concerning the data that are being recorded:
   a. What type of data is involved in the study?
   b. What properties do the data have and why?

Stimulus Material for Simulation 11.1: The feedback for simulation 4.4 suggested one approach to having teachers evaluate instructional material. This suggestion included an example of a 1 to 5 scale such as:

Excellent		Average		Poor
1	2	3	4	5

In view of what was discussed in Chapter 11, respond to the two questions under part two of the task to be performed above.

For feedback see p. 325.

Stimulus Material for Simulation 11.2:   Suppose you are faced with the situation in which teachers are predicting job success for their high school students. In accomplishing this task they are asked to categorize their pupils into groups of "successful" and "unsuccessful." In view of what was discussed in Chapter 11, respond to the two questions under step two of the task to be performed.

For feedback see p. 325.

Stimulus Material for Simulation 11.3:   In this simulation suppose that you have been asked to serve as a consultant for a medical research program investigating the use of certain drugs with infants. One of the topics of interest is possible side effects of the medication. The project director suspects that the child's temperature may be seriously elevated when the drug under study is administered. The criterion measure here, then, is temperature. In view of what was discussed in Chapter 11, respond to the two questions under step two of the task to be performed.

For feedback see p. 325.

Simulation 11.4

Topic: Nature of the data

Background Statement: As noted, both in this chapter and previous simulations, the nature of the data is something that a researcher must be able to determine to complete later tasks in the investigation. Occasionally different types of data may be generated even though the same phenomenon is being assessed.

Tasks to Be Performed:

1. Review the following stimulus material, which involves the assessment of age.
2. Identify the type of data involved in each of the examples (A, B, and C).

Stimulus Material:

A. Ten subjects are classified and placed in one of three categories:

Classification 1	Classification 2	Classification 3
Young	Middle-aged	Old

B. Ten subjects are ranked from youngest to oldest.
C. The ages of ten subjects are recorded.

For feedback see p. 325.

Simulation Feedbacks

Simulation 11.1

As noted in Chapter 11, the data generated by a rating scale such as this are ordinal in nature. This is the case because the different numbers on the scale denote *greater than* or *less than* in terms of the teacher's perception of the quality of the material. A rating of 1 indicates a more positive assessment than a rating of 3. This is, however, a relative statement, and you do not know what the difference between those two ratings means in terms of a quantity or amount.

The properties of ordinal data are identity and order. These are two of three possible properties that numbers may have, the third being additivity. Since ordinal data do not have the property of additivity, certain arithmetic operations cannot be performed (such as adding or subtracting). This is not necessarily "bad" because a rating does provide a relative indicator of the teacher's perception of the material. It does, however, have considerable importance for later decisions about what analysis should be applied.

Simulation 11.2

As noted in Chapter 11, the data generated by a categorical sorting are nominal in nature. What was accomplished was the assignment of events, in this case pupils, to a classification of either successful or unsuccessful.

Nominal data have the property of identity. Each category is unique from the other and any symbol (e.g., numbers or letters) could be used. The identification of such data as nominal is important for later decisions on analysis.

Simulation 11.3

The data generated by temperature as a criterion measure (at least as assessed by a thermometer) can be considered interval data. When you are working with such data, you have known and equal distances between score units and an arbitrary zero point. These are characteristics that are applicable to the criterion measure in this simulation.

Interval data have all three number properties—identity, order, and additivity. This provides considerable latitude in what can be done in terms of analysis.

Simulation 11.4

Despite the fact that the same dimension—age—is being assessed in all three examples, the types of data differ because of the ways in which the measure is recorded. Example A is nominal data, since categories are used. Even though an underlying continuum exists, the subjects are only grossly classified into one of three categories. Example B involves ordinal data, since the subjects are ranked from youngest to oldest. Since only ranks are recorded, you have no information about the magnitude of age difference between ranks 6 and 7, or whether it is the same as the difference between ranks 3 and 4. Example C is at least interval data and perhaps ratio (depending on whether one can determine an actual zero age). If in doubt, it is frequently wise to be conservative in deciding the level of measurement (interval in this case). It makes little difference in this example, since most of what can be done with ratio data can be performed on interval data.

Chapter 12

Data Tabulation

One of the first tasks to be accomplished after the data are collected is to summarize what has been recorded. This is a process that requires careful planning before beginning. The current chapter examines data tabulation and some preliminary facets of presenting the data. Much of what is discussed relates to formats which are appropriate for data aggregation and presentation for publication purposes. However, we have found that many of the formats are also very useful for writing the research report.

Aggregating Data

As noted in Chapter 11, it is difficult to determine how well subjects performed by simply visually inspecting the raw data. It is necessary to summarize the data in some form to facilitate analysis, interpretation, and presentation to the research consumer. We will examine a number of procedures that are useful for data tabulation and presentation.

Ranks

One helpful first step in examining the data is to place subjects in rank order according to their performance scores. For example, suppose one had 24 subjects with scores such as those found in Table 12.1. It is difficult to interpret what subjects' performance represents when the raw data are presented in this manner. However, subjects' performance scores can be more easily interpreted when they are ranked such as in Table 12.2.

TABLE 12.1 Subject Performance Scores (Unranked)

Subject	Score	Subject	Score
Robert	91	Terry	60
Myrna	84	Carl	103
Ralph	84	Kay	105
John	97	George	102
Sally	108	Carole	107
Sherry	59	Phil	105
Eugene	110	Don	100
Andy	106	Walt	196
David	67	Bonnie	101
Earl	85	Kent	110
Laurie	82	Anita	99
Maurice	95	Alice	109

Reviewing Table 12.2 we see that Eugene and Kent performed the best of all subjects and Sherry had the poorest performance. This table also illustrates that there may be tie scores for subjects. Both Eugene and Kent scored 110 on the task and their ranks are 1.5 (split between 1 and 2). The next subject (Alice) receives the rank of 3 since 1 and 2 have already been used. Researchers seldom use raw subject performance scores for presentation in a report or publication. In fact, to include the subjects' names in such a report would violate privacy. Most human subjects committees require that investigators destroy subjects' names after the data collection is complete. However, aggregating data in the form of tables such as 12.2 is very useful in preparation for data analysis, either descriptive or inferential (see Chapters 13 and 14).

Grouping

If the list of scores is long (e.g., 120 subjects) the researcher can shorten it by grouping scores. Table 12.3 illustrates how data from such a set of scores may be grouped. (Note that these are an entirely different set of scores from those in Tables 12.1 and 12.2.)

Using this approach, the data are grouped into intervals. In Table 12.3 X is the *midpoint* of the respective interval. The f in Table 12.3 refers to the *frequency* with which scores fall into a given interval (e.g., a score of 63 would be given a value of 62 and there were two scores assigned that value). The midpoint and frequency are used for certain statistics as we will see in Chapter 13. It would have been quite laborious to list each score individually for the data in Table 12.3. Of course each score was listed originally as the researcher aggregated the data. However, for purposes of inspecting the data, the format in Table 12.3 is more informative and convenient.

TABLE 12.2 Ranked Subject Performance Scores

Subject	Score	Rank
Eugene	110	1.5
Kent	110	1.5
Alice	109	3
Sally	108	4
Carole	107	5
Andy	106	6.5
Walt	106	6.5
Phil	105	8.5
Kay	105	8.5
George	102	10
Bonnie	101	11
Don	100	13
Anita	99	14
John	97	15
Maurice	95	16
Robert	91	17
Earl	85	18
Myrna	84	19.5
Ralph	84	19.5
Laurie	82	21
David	67	22
Terry	60	23
Sherry	59	24

TABLE 12.3 Hypothetical Example of Grouped Data

Score Interval	X	f
60-64	62	2
55-59	57	1
50-54	52	6
45-49	47	10
40-44	42	20
35-39	37	18
30-34	32	19
25-29	27	16
20-24	22	13
15-19	17	9
10-14	12	2
5-9	7	3
0-4	2	2
		$N = 120$

One factor to be considered in grouping raw data is determining the *size* of score intervals. This is typically dictated by two rules of thumb which have evolved over the years. The first is that the number of intervals should generally not exceed 20 or be fewer than 10 (commonly the number is between 10 and 15). With a smaller number of intervals there will obviously be fewer to contend with in any inspection or analysis. However, the smaller number of intervals necessitates a larger interval size; thus, using midpoints introduces more error since any given score may be more units away from its interval's midpoint score than if the interval were smaller. Use of a larger number of intervals results in smaller interval size, reducing the error by making all scores closer to their intervals' midpoints. A large number of intervals, however, may be somewhat more cumbersome. Most sets of data can be grouped appropriately with 10 to 15 intervals.

A second rule of thumb for determining the size of intervals is that certain score ranges are preferred for intervals. There is some difference of opinion regarding exactly what these ranges are. For the most part, however, intervals of 2, 3, 5, 10, and 20 units are seen as being the most preferred. While these intervals will cover most sets of data, there are some that are more convenient than others. If a researcher is using an interval of 2, he or she has not grouped the data a great deal *unless* there is a very small range in the scores and a rather high frequency at each interval. Thus an interval of 2 is likely to be useful only in rare instances. Additionally, intervals with an odd number of score units are more convenient to use than those with an even number of score units. It is much easier to understand and establish the midpoint of an interval of say 3 or 5 than one of 4 or 6 since it is a whole number. Refer again to Table 12.3 where we see, for example, an interval of 60 to 64. This is a 5-unit interval including scores of 60, 61, 62, 63, and 64, which makes the midpoint very easy to establish. The *exact* limits of the interval are 59.5 to 64.5, and consequently any scores falling between these exact limits are considered to be in the interval. With minor modifications on the earlier interval examples, one can cover most data sets and employ intervals that all are constituted with odd-numbered score units (e.g., 3, 5, 9, 19).

Turn to page 338 and complete Simulation 12.1

Another factor to be considered in grouping data is where to begin and end the intervals. There is no reason to begin far below the lowest subject's score or continue far beyond the highest subject's score. Thus, if our subjects' scores ranged from 23 to 79 on some hypothetical task, it makes little sense to begin with an interval of 0 to 4 and end with an interval of 85 to 89. Several of the intervals on either end of the range would have an f of 0 and therefore be useless (even if the scores *possible* on the task ranged from 0 to 100). Additionally, in beginning the intervals it is most natural to begin with a score unit that is a multiple of the interval. This would suggest that if the interval is 5 the interval might begin with 15, 20, or some other multiple of 5. For our hypothetical task we have a range of 23 to 79 or 56 score units. If we used an interval of 3 we would have too many intervals (56 divided by 3 equals 18.67). An interval of 5 will result in an appropriate number of intervals (56 divided by 5 equals 11.2 or 12 intervals). Therefore, we will use an interval of 5, beginning with 20 to 24 and ending with 75 to 79.

Turn to page 340 and complete
Simulation 12.2

Tables

Tables are used in research reports to summarize data or other information that cannot conveniently or effectively be presented in the narrative of the text. Tables are more expensive to prepare and publish than text and therefore should be used judiciously (American Psychological Association, 1994). An appropriately constructed table supplements rather than duplicates textual material and can save space in circumstances in which a lengthy or complex narrative would be required to present the same information. However, tables must be carefully planned and constructed or they may detract from a reader's understanding of the data.

The general rule in constructing tables is that they be as simple and clear as possible while still presenting all the information necessary to complement the text. In general tables should proceed so that they read from top to bottom and left to right. They are numbered consecutively using arabic numerals as they appear in the text (e.g., Table 1, 2, etc.). This numbering system is modified somewhat for most textbooks, where tables are numbered consecutively for each chapter (Table 12.1, 12.2, and so on for Chapter 12). The researcher preparing a report should indicate where a table is to appear in the text with instructions to the editor and printer as soon as is practical after reference to the table is made in the text. For example, if we were to refer to Table 3 in this sentence, then we would break the text with instructions like those below. We would then continue the text in a routine narrative fashion. Such a break may occur in the middle or at the end of a paragraph. The actual table is prepared on a separate manuscript page and placed at the end of the manuscript for submission to the editor of a journal or textbook.

Insert [hypothetical] Table 3 about here

A table must be able to stand alone and therefore should be clearly labeled. The title should be sufficiently complete and descriptive that a reader can understand what is contained therein by simply inspecting the table. Abbreviations should not be used in a table unless they are commonly understood or parenthetically explained. Some explanations may be placed below the table although they should be kept to a minimum. These explanations, usually termed *notes,* come in three types. A *general* note provides explanations or qualifying statements regarding the whole table. General notes appear at the foot of the table and may refer to the source of a table if it was reprinted from another publication or in some other fashion provide the reader with information pertaining to the table in general. They appear as: Note. Adapted from…. *Specific* notes are used to explain or elaborate information about a particular part of the table contents. These are designated by using a lowercase letter superscript such as [a], [b], beside the specific part of the table being explained and the same superscript preceeding the explanation at the foot of the table. The third type of table note typically used in behavioral science involves *probability levels.* These are employed when the table presents statistical analysis results and use asterisks in the body of the table with corresponding explanations at the foot of the table (e.g., $*p < .05$, $**p < .01$). (Probability statements such as these will be explored more completely in Chapter 14.) If more than one type of note is used for the same table, they should appear at the foot in the order from general to specific to probability (American Psychological Association, 1994).

The title of a table is placed at the top and the body begins with a single horizontal line (called a rule) across the width of the table immediately beneath it. Beneath the first rule there is a space in which the columns of the table are labeled so the reader knows what data or information are presented in each column. Directly below these labels is another horizontal rule followed by the body of the table. At the end of the table body a final horizontal rule appears (below which are the notes if there are any). Rules within the table body should be restricted to only those that are essential for clarity. Vertical rules are seldom used. All rules should be made with a pencil since it is occasionally necessary to change them when a printer sets type.

For the most part tables should be constructed so they can be fit on the width of a journal page. Only in rare cases should a table be constructed that requires it to be placed sideways on a page. One should consult the publishing requirements and characteristics of the journal or publishing organization for specific space limitations.

For the beginning researcher it is important to keep in mind that tables should augment, clarify, or save space in the text. They should not be used unless they are necessary and/or facilitate understanding by the reader. If information can be conveniently and effectively incorporated into the narrative, a table is probably not necessary or appropriate. As usual, a researcher preparing tables for a report should consult the intended publishing outlet for unique or specific details regarding format (e.g., *Publication Manual of the American Psychological Association,* 1994). Each publisher is somewhat different with respect to requirements. We have presented information that pertains only to the general preparation of tables.

Turn to page 341 and complete
Simulations 12.3 and 12.4

Graphing Data

It is widely accepted that visual representation of data is an extremely useful tool in research. Graphs often provide a dramatic statement of the results for which narrative and/or tabled numbers are difficult to comprehend. Graphs attract a reader's attention, clarify points or results, and in some cases save space in a publication (which is very expensive). There is no single type of graph that serves every purpose in research. This section will examine a variety of factors pertaining to the utilization of graphs.

When to Graph

Graphs serve several purposes in the overall research process. Many investigators find graphs to be extremely valuable as they are examining the data in preparation for writing the research report. Working graphs are constructed in order to provide a pictorial representation of how subjects performed. It is from these working graphs that writing proceeds. Such graphs may or may not appear in the final publication of the report, depending on how clearly and succinctly the authors were able to express the results in narrative form. Experience has shown that using working graphs (often in rather crude form) in this fashion is particularly helpful for beginning researchers.

The decision to use a graph in a report (particularly for publication) must be made with great care. Simply adding graphs capriciously to a report is inappropriate. With respect to publication, it should be remembered that figures (all illustrations other than a table are called *figures*) are typically quite expensive to prepare and reproduce. The most important point to consider is whether the graph is really necessary. The *Publication Manual of the American Psychological Association* (APA) states of a figure that "If it duplicates text, it is not necessary. If it complements text or eliminates lengthy discussion, it may be the most efficient way to present the information" (1994, p.142). Thus one should employ graphs in reports only when they are needed to clarify and/or augment the text or when they will save space by eliminating the need for lengthy narrative. Determining the need for a figure primarily rests with the author although journal editors will not hesitate to require inclusion or deletion as the manuscript is reviewed. It is always good practice to have a colleague read your report in manuscript form to receive feedback regarding the clarity of the narrative as well as potential need for figures. Often the investigator is so close to the study that important points are inadvertently omitted or expressed poorly.

Types of Graphs

There are many different types of graphs used in behavioral science. Figure 12.1 illustrates a variety of different approaches to graphing the same data. This experiment investigated the types of errors committed by subjects with mental retardation by learning stage on an associative learning task. (Subjects of average intelligence were also studied but those data are not presented here to conserve space.) Errors were classified into four types: 1) extra list intrusions (responses that were not on the list of material to be learned), 2) omissions (failure to respond), 3) stimulus intrusions (subjects giving a stimulus word instead of a response word as an answer), and 4) misplaced responses (subjects answering with a response that was supposed to be paired with another stimulus). Learning stage was divided into three blocks, each containing several trials.

Each type of graph presents the data in a somewhat different manner, and the choice of which approach to use would depend on the nature of the narrative. The author(s) might select one over another based on the theoretical basis for the study which may largely direct the line of reasoning and writing. Bar graphs are simple and very flexible in terms of how they may be used. Line graphs are also very flexible but are typically used to depict change over time such as in time-series studies or those involving repeated measures on the same subjects. Pie graphs are often used when percentages are employed as the criterion measure (percentages may also be portrayed with other graph formats). Graphs such as the paired bar example are useful when multiple criterion measures need to be visually compared. The example formats presented in Figure 12.1 are illustrative rather than exhaustive.

Preparation of Graphs

There is considerable variation in the manner in which graphs are prepared in behavioral science. Much depends on the particular journal or publishing house involved in producing the printed document. However, there are certain general guidelines that are customarily followed. The APA provides a list of standards for figures as follows:

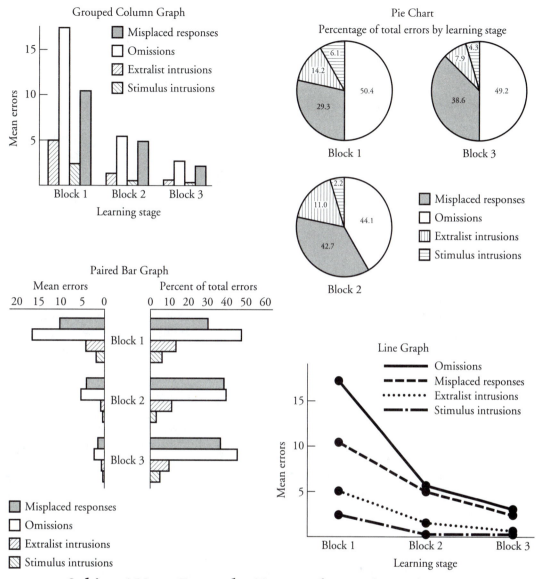

Grouped Column Graph

Misplaced responses
Omissions
Extralist intrusions
Stimulus intrusions

Mean errors

Block 1 Block 2 Block 3
Learning stage

Pie Chart
Percentage of total errors by learning stage

Block 1: 6.1, 14.2, 29.3, 50.4

Block 3: 4.3, 7.9, 38.6, 49.2

Block 2: 2.2, 11.0, 42.7, 44.1

Misplaced responses
Omissions
Extralist intrusions
Stimulus intrusions

Paired Bar Graph

Mean errors
20 15 10 5 0

Percent of total errors
0 10 20 30 40 50 60

Block 1

Block 2

Block 3

Misplaced responses
Omissions
Extralist intrusions
Stimulus intrusions

Line Graph

Omissions
Misplaced responses
Extralist intrusions
Stimulus intrusions

Mean errors

Block 1 Block 2 Block 3
Learning stage

Subjects' Mean Errors by Type and Learning Stage

Error Type	Block 1	Block 2	Block 3
Extralist Intrusions	4.875	1.250	.458
Omissions	17.250	5.041	2.875
Stimulus Intrusions	2.083	.250	.250
Misplaced Responses	10.041	4.875	2.250

FIGURE 12.1   Data Graphed Four Different Ways

Adapted from C. J. Drew and W. R. Berard, 1970, "Errors of retarded and nonretarded subjects by learning stage." *Psychonomic Science, 20*,65-66. Copyright © 1970, Psychonomic Society.

The standards for good figures are simplicity, clarity, and continuity. A good figure

- augments rather than duplicates the text;
- conveys only essential facts;
- omits visually distracting detail;
- is easy to read—its elements (type, lines, labels, symbols, etc.) are large enough to be read with ease in the printed form;
- is easy to understand—its purpose is readily apparent;
- is consistent with and is prepared in the same style as similar figures in the same article; that is, the lettering is of the same size and typeface, lines are of the same weight, and so forth;
- is carefully planned and prepared.

(APA, 1994, p. 142)

As noted, these standards are quite general and there are a number of other preparation factors that are common practice. In general a graph should read from left to right and bottom to top. The experimental variable is plotted on the horizontal axis, and in cases where it represents a comparison between differing magnitudes of the variable (e.g., years—1982, 1983, 1984; age—10, 12, 14; dosage—5cc, 10cc, 15cc; etc.) the format should proceed in an increasing manner from left to right. The criterion measure is plotted on the vertical axis and should read from bottom to top. Where feasible, the vertical scale should be arranged so that zero shows at the bottom of the vertical axis. If it is not practical to include the full scale on the vertical axis including the zero, the axis should be broken with a double slash as shown in Figure 12.2. A double slash may also be used to break the horizontal axis if the graph is likely to be misinterpreted by the absence of a zero on the experimental variable. This is also illustrated in Figure 12.2.

Graphs may be prepared in nearly any size as long as they are easily read. Most editors will either reduce or enlarge the figure to fit their publishing format. However, greater clarity is achieved by reduction of the graph provided rather than enlarging it to fit the format. From the standpoint of proportion, the vertical axis should be about two thirds the length of the horizontal axis. It is always prudent to consult the specific guidelines of the particular publisher for details concerning size and proportion requirements before the graph is prepared for the final manuscript (e.g., APA, 1994).

It is essential to clearly label all aspects of a figure. A graph should be able to stand alone, which makes this labeling so important. The title of the figure should be complete so that a reader knows what information is being presented. Both vertical and horizontal axes should be clearly labeled (e.g., learning stage, age, treatment sessions, mean errors, IQ, mean correct responses, etc.) and the calibration provided on both

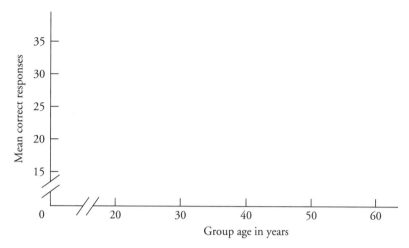

FIGURE 12.2   Example of Breaking Axes to Show Zero for Experimental Variable and Criterion Measure

axes (e.g., block 1, block 2, block 3; 0, 5, 10, 15; etc.). Without complete and clear labels a figure is often unintelligible. The title of a figure is typically placed below the graph and most commonly capitalizes all important words. With respect to placement of figures (and tables for that matter) the researcher writing the report will have to indicate where they should appear in the manuscript. This is usually accomplished by breaking the manuscript as soon as possible after reference to the figure is made in the narrative with instructions to the editor and printer. Such instructions are very simple. For example if we were to refer to Figure 2 in this sentence then we would insert the following in the text.

Insert [hypothetical] Figure 2 about here

Obviously there is a great deal of latitude with respect to the preparation of graphs. Once again, specific details are usually available from the organization or publisher that produces the publication. Additionally, it is often helpful to review some manuscripts that have been published by your colleagues to see how graphs were prepared.

Graphing Faux Pas

Many of the errors committed in graphing data have received attention in the guidelines presented above. However, there are some additional points that need to be mentioned. The cardinal rule for graphing data is that it should be *clear and not misleading.* This requires that a graph be as simple as possible. An overly complex graph is no easier to understand than a lengthy narrative or a complex set of numbers. Simplicity and complete labeling will usually solve problems of clarity.

Graphs may also be misleading if they are not carefully conceived and prepared. It was noted in the preceeding section that the vertical axis should be about two thirds the length of the horizontal axis in most cases and that calibration of the vertical axis should go to zero if practical. This rule of thumb creates a commonly accepted proportion between the two axes. When these guidelines are not followed the result may be a graph that is visually very misleading. One must also be very cautious about misleading readers by using charts or graphs that present geometric figures of different sizes to represent magnitude of the criterion measure. For example, suppose we were to use the diameter of three different size circles to chart average annual income level for three levels of education. We may be quite accurate in drawing the circles' size according to diameter but they might be very misleading because what strikes the reader visually is the *area* of the circle, not the diameter. It is generally prudent to avoid graphing approaches that can be interpreted in terms of area rather than linear relationships. The exception to this area rule is the pie graph of percentage where it is commonly accepted that the complete pie is 100 percent (even where the percent is labeled as in Figure 12.1).

We all commit graphing errors from time to time. Researchers are usually so completely immersed in their projects that they may understand figures that are quite confusing or unintelligible to a reader approaching the topic cold. One of the most useful precautions against making such an error is to have the graph and report manuscript reviewed by a colleague.

*Turn to page 342 and complete
Simulations 12.5 and 12.6*

Simulations

Simulation 12.1

Topic: Grouping Data

Background Statement: Grouping raw data often facilitates inspection and further analysis. There are a number of guidelines that should be followed in grouping data to maximize effective tabulation in this form.

Tasks to Be Performed:

1. Review the following grouped data set.
2. Identify any problem(s) that you see with respect to the manner in which these data are grouped.
3. Suggest how the data might be more effectively grouped and explain your rationale.

Stimulus Material: Lowest score = 1, highest score = 71.

Hypothetical Grouped Data Set

Score Interval	X	f
69-71	70	1
66-68	67	1
63-65	64	2
60-62	61	0
57-59	58	2
54-56	55	1
51-53	52	4
48-50	49	5
45-47	46	7
42-44	43	8
39-41	40	13
36-38	37	10
33-35	34	18
30-32	31	23
27-29	28	19
24-26	25	0
21-23	22	20
18-20	19	15
15-17	16	10
12-14	13	6
9-11	10	2
6-8	7	0
3-5	4	2
0-2	1	1

For feedback see page 344.

Simulation 12.2

Topic: Grouping Data

Background Statement: Raw data collected on a large group of subjects is frequently difficult to use without further tabulation. Grouping raw data often facilitates inspection and further analysis. This frequently involves taking the data in the form it was collected and transferring it to a sheet that summarizes it in a manner that is usable. In performing this operation there are certain matters that require attention (e.g., number of intervals, interval size).

Tasks to Be Performed:

1. Review the following material.
2. Select intervals that are appropriate for grouping the data set presented in the stimulus material. Indicate why you selected the intervals you did.
3. Present the data in tabular form similar to that illustrated in Table 12.3 including the midpoint and *f* columns.

Stimulus Material: You have been employed for the summer as a research assistant in the psychology learning lab. Some of the work in the beginning involves data that were collected in a learning experiment conducted earlier. As the junior research assistant in the lab, you have been given the tedious job of tabulating the data in preparation for descriptive analysis. The criterion measure was number of errors committed by subjects in learning the task.

Data Set

Donald B.	13	Robert B.	13	Fred R.	34
Jay T.	34	Robyne A.	33	Sara F.	23
Thomas B.	42	James R.	6	Lowell B.	10
Donald R.	26	Jane Z.	31	Tom L.	14
Laura B.	63	Linda P.	23	Dan B.	46
Fred A.	3	Scott E.	21	Sandy S.	43
Myrtle R.	37	David B.	62	Joe S.	14
Bob D.	51	Vern L.	48	Sallie P.	29
George J.	38	Archy T.	36	Ray J.	31
Ellen C.	63	Barbara B.	43	Bonnie S.	20
Ann T.	8	Grant W.	39	John A.	17
Connie M.	9	Lloyd S.	46	Robert W.	33
Randy L.	41	James D.	5	Cyrus R.	14
Larry B.	27	Jeanne G.	13	George L.	23
Anne L.	22	Dianne B.	42	James V.	61

Mike B.	36	Ben E.	16	Anne. R.	30
Bruce W.	18	Ed P.	25	Claude G.	26
Marla D.	28	Jane F.	30	Mike R.	33
Hans P.	34	Billy W.	35	Danny K.	36
Hal H.	38	Michelle K.	41	Randall C.	43
Mark E.	47	Dan P.	56	Susan P.	58
Toby L.	18	Dean M.	25	Harry B.	28
Mike H.	30	Winston M.	34	Kathy R.	35
Mary A.	36	Margie S.	41	Nancy S.	43
Carl A.	47	Carl T.	56	Charles P.	25
Earl T.	28	Lee I.	34	Clara P.	41
John M.	43	Bill M.	47	Bob W.	28
Bob C.	47				

For feedback see page 344.

Simulation 12.3

Topic: Data Tables

Background Statement: Tabular presentation of data can be an effective and efficient means of presenting information in a research report. Decisions of how and when to include tables require careful consideration and planning on the part of the investigator.

Tasks to Be Performed:

1. Review the tabled data presented here.
2. Comment on the table noting any problem(s) you see.
3. Suggest how you might resolve any problem(s) you noted.

Stimulus Material:

TABLE 4 Mean Errors by Psychotic and Nonpsychotic Subjects on Meaningful and Nonmeaningful Material

Subject Classification	Meaningful Material	Nonmeaningful Material
Psychotic	22	21
Nonpsychotic	10	20

For feedback see p. 345.

Simulation 12.4

Topic: Data Tables

Background Statement: Tables can be an effective and efficient means of presenting data in a research report. Construction of a table requires careful planning and attention to a number of rules of thumb.

Tasks to Be Performed:

1. Review the following data set.
2. Construct a table of the data according to the guidelines provided in the text.

Stimulus Material: The criterion measure represented by these data is mean correct responses. Subjects are those with mental retardation and those with average intelligence; the material is of two types: high associative strength and low associative strength. Measures were taken at three recall periods: immediate, after 24 hours, and after 15 days. The data are as follows:

- average intelligence, high associative strength, immediate = 13.45
- average intelligence, high associative strength, 24-hour = 13.88
- average intelligence, high associative strength, 15-day = 13.75
- average intelligence, low associative strength, immediate = 12.74
- average intelligence, low associative strength, 24-hour = 12.75
- average intelligence, low associative strength, 15-day = 11.20
- mental retardation, high associative strength, immediate = 13.12
- mental retardation, high associative strength, 24-hour = 11.79
- mental retardation, high associative strength, 15-day = 9.33
- mental retardation, low associative strength, immediate = 12.16
- mental retardation, low associative strength, 24-hour = 9.62
- mental retardation, low associative strength, 15-day = 6.62

For feedback see page 346.

Simulation 12.5

Topic: Graphing Data

Background Statement: Graphs and other figures provide an effective and efficient means of presenting information to augment the narrative of a research report. There are a number of guidelines that should be followed in graphing data which require careful planning on the part of the investigator. A poorly constructed graph can easily detract rather than add to the understanding of research results.

Tasks to Be Performed:

1. Review the graph presented in the stimulus material.
2. Note any problem(s) that you see in the graph and indicate why it/ they represent errors if they do.
3. Suggest how you might resolve any errors you identify.

Stimulus Material:

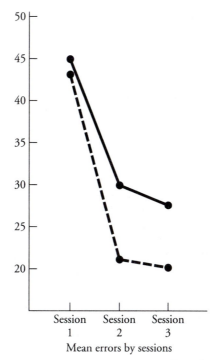

Mean errors by sessions

For feedback see page 346.

Simulation 12.6

Topic: Graphing Data

Background Statement: Graphing data requires an investigator to consider several factors. These include basic decisions regarding when to use a graph as well as attention to a number of guidelines regarding its preparation.

Tasks to Be Performed:

1. Review the data tabled in Simulation 12.3.
2. Prepare a graph of the data in Simulation 12.3.
3. Aside from following the instructions provided here because you were told to, how would you treat the data in Simulation 12.3 and why?

For feedback see page 347.

Simulation Feedbacks

Simulation 12.1

The most evident problem with the manner in which these data are grouped relates to the interval selected. The score range in this data set is 70 score units. With an interval size of three score units the investigators created a situation in which it was necessary to have 24 intervals in order to include the full range of subject performance. As indicated in the text, 10 to 15 intervals will cover most score ranges and 20 is generally considered the upper limit. The investigators in this hypothetical study exceeded 20 and did not need to do so. Inspection of the data indicates that there are a rather large number of intervals with low frequencies, particularly at both ends of the distribution.

More effective grouping of the data presented could have been achieved by using a larger interval. Assuming that we want to employ an odd-numbered interval for convenience, we could have tried either five or seven as an interval size. Using an interval size of five would have generated 15 intervals. This is determined by dividing our score range (70) by five, which equals 14, plus we have to add one more interval since the highest subject performance was 71 and 14 intervals would only get us to 70. Fifteen intervals is within the preferred range. If we used an interval size of seven, we would have 11 intervals since dividing 70 by seven equals 10 plus adding one to include the subject that achieved a score of 71. Of the two options we might prefer an interval size of five to reduce a bit the error of using the midpoint for further calculations.

Simulation 12.2

Our first task in selecting intervals for this data set involves determining the number and size of intervals to be used. The data indicate that we have a score range of 60 score units, with the lowest number of errors being 3 and the highest 63. For convenience recall that we probably would like to use an interval with an odd number of units. You will also recall that we would not like to exceed 20 and would prefer to have somewhere between 10 and 15 intervals. Dividing our score range by a potential interval size of three it appears that we will need 20 intervals. Actually an interval size of three will get us only to a score of 59, so we would have to add two more intervals to include the highest error score of 63. This would result in 22 intervals which is more than is desirable. A potential interval size of five score units will result in 12 intervals plus one in order to include the high error score of 63. Thus if we use an interval of five we would have 13 intervals, which appears to be appropriate. A seven-unit interval size would result in 10 intervals which is at the lower limit in terms of the number commonly used in behavioral science. For our purposes an interval size of five seems to be the most serviceable option. The table of grouped data may appear as follows:

Hypothetical Grouped Data Table

Score Interval	X	f
60-64	62	4
55-59	57	3
50-54	52	1
45-49	47	7
40-44	42	11
35-39	37	10
30-34	32	14
25-29	27	11
20-24	22	5
15-19	17	4
10-14	12	7
5-9	7	4
0-4	2	1

Simulation 12.3

The most evident problem with the table in this simulation is that it probably is unnecessary. The study is a simple two-factor design with two levels on each experimental variable (2 x 2). Information presented in the table is limited to mean errors for each condition. It is difficult to imagine how this could not be presented just as effectively in the narrative, thereby eliminating the distraction to a reader of having to refer to the table as well as the added expense of preparing and printing a table. With no more information than we have here, the data could probably be effectively incorporated into the text. (As we will see later, providing only the means is probably too limited with respect to data presentation.)

Another area in which there is a problem involves the construction of the table. Although this is a minor point, recall that one seldom, if ever, uses rules inside the body of a table. The only time they might be employed is if they are essential to understanding a complex set of data. These data certainly are not sufficiently complex to warrant the internal horizontal rule, and vertical rules are not used at all in most behavioral science reports.

Simulation 12.4

There are, of course, a number of formats that might be employed for the data provided. One approach might appear like Table 1 below.

TABLE 1   Mean Correct Responses as a Function of Recall Period, Subject Classification, and Material Associative Strength

Subject Classification/ Material Associative Strength	Immediate	24-hour	15-day
Average/HAS[a]	13.45	13.88	13.75
Average/LAS[b]	12.74	12.75	11.20
Retardation/HAS	13.12	11.79	9.33
Retardation/LAS	12.16	9.62	6.62

[a] HAS = High Associative Strength
[b] LAS = Low Associative Strength

Simulation 12.5

The problems with the graph presented in this simulation are many. First of all it is very poorly labeled. The title does not adequately describe what information is graphed. It is not clear what "sessions" means and the "mean errors" is vague. Neither of the axes is labeled and the horizontal axis does not even have the points quantified (e.g., session 1, 2, 3?). One might assume that the vertical quantification represents mean errors, but without a label we are left with this being only an assumption. A further labeling problem relates to the internal part of the graph. We are presented with two data lines that appear to represent different populations or different materials or something else. One line is solid whereas the other is broken, which would make the viewer definitely infer that they represent two data sources, but since there is no legend we do not know what these sources are.

Other problems with the graph emerge when we examine the axes. First the axes are not drawn in proper proportion. The vertical axis is over twice as long as the horizontal axis. Our guidelines indicate that the vertical axis should be only about two-thirds as long as the horizontal axis. Additionally, the vertical axis should be broken and show zero at its foot. Without the break, the vertical axis is misleading and the distance between where the zero point should be and the 20 is out of proportion with the scale. The distance between an imaginary zero and 20 is about one-fourth the distance of the next 20 score units (i.e., between 20 and 40). This graph should be redrawn with attention given to the difficulties noted above (e.g., labeling, axis proportion, axis break, etc.).

Simulation 12.6

There are a number of formats that might be employed to graph the data which were tabled in Simulation 12.3. One way that the graph might look follows.

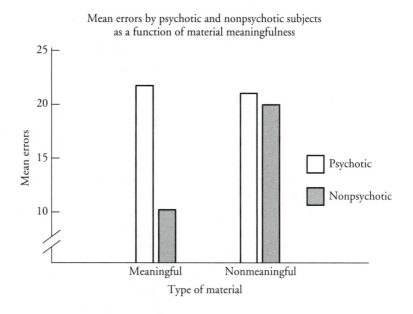

Mean errors by psychotic and nonpsychotic subjects as a function of material meaningfulness

In response to task 3, probably the major consideration is whether or not one even needs a figure for these data. As you will recall from Simulation 12.3, we noted that the data were so simple that they probably could be presented in the text and a table was not needed. The same point is likely relevant here. It is probably not a sufficiently complex set of data to warrant the time and expense involved in preparing and printing a graph.

Chapter 13

Statistics for
Descriptive Purposes

Once the data have been collected and raw scores tabulated, a researcher usually has several operations to perform. In nearly all cases, the first process is data compilation in some form that describes the group performance. Compilation or data summary in descriptive form beyond those discussed in Chapter 12 involves the use of descriptive statistics. Two general categories of descriptive statistics are commonly used— measures of central tendency and measures of dispersion. *Measures of central tendency* provide an index of where the scores tend to bunch together or of the typical score in the group of scores. *Measures of dispersion,* on the other hand, describe the amount of variability among the scores in the group (Spence, Cotton, Underwood, & Duncan, 1992). As evident in Chapter 12, measures of central tendency and dispersion are frequently used in graphs and tables. Consequently these two chapters are interrelated in data description.

One preliminary note should be made regarding the researcher's objective in compiling a descriptive data summary. If the primary intent of an investigation is describing the group, the researcher may well terminate analysis with the computation of descriptive statistics. Such statistics will provide the information necessary for the goal of group description. It is possible, however, that the investigation has an inferential purpose beyond mere group description. If this is the case, descriptive statistics represent preliminary computation necessary to perform further data analysis. Thus descriptive measures are commonly computed regardless of whether the investigation is a descriptive or inferential study. In the first case, the descriptive statistics are probably terminal operations, whereas in the latter case, they are preliminary operations in preparation for further analysis.

More often than not the actual computation of statistical analysis is accomplished using a computer. A variety of software programs are available that will perform both descriptive and inferential analyses, and may even print out tables and graphs of the data in draft form. Such programs have become nearly standard tools for researchers in all areas and greatly reduce some of the more tedious aspects of data analysis. Desktop computers can typically perform the analyses necessary for the vast majority of research projects in education and the social sciences. It is vital, however, that researchers understand very well what statistical analyses are appropriate for which types of questions and designs. Computer technology cannot make those decisions and depending on statistical consultants is very risky. Such consultants frequently know a lot about statistics but little about research design. You should know what analysis or analyses you need for your study and ask the consultant (if you are using one) to compute *that* analysis. (Occasionally they have to be convinced, but it is your study.)

Central Tendency Measures

Data may be summarized and presented in a number of ways. Frequently it is desirable to be able to characterize group scores with a single index that will provide some idea of how well the group performed. This requires a number that is representative of the distribution of scores that were obtained. One type of index commonly used for such group description involves numbers that reflect the concentration of scores, known as central tendency measures. Three measures of central tendency are generally discussed, the *mean*, the *median*, and the *mode*. Each measure has slightly different properties and is useful for different circumstances.

The Mean

Probably the most familiar measure of central tendency is the mean. The mean or *arithmetic average* is obtained by simply adding the scores for all subjects together and dividing this total by the number of individuals in the group. In a spelling test, the mean might be 25 correctly spelled words. These data might appear like the example in Table 13.1.

The example just given involves a mean calculated on actual raw data scores. This procedure becomes somewhat laborious if many individuals are serving as subjects. An alternative is to compute a mean on data that are grouped into intervals. For this procedure, the data are grouped into intervals as discussed in Chapter 12 and in the example in Table 13.2. Because each score does not have to be summed individu-

TABLE 13.1 Hypothetical Raw Scores on Spelling Test

Subject	X
1	33
2	6
3	25
4	35
5	10
6	30
7	25
8	32
9	35
10	19
	Total = 250

ally, the computation is considerably easier. In Table 13.2 we find one additional column over what we saw in a similar table in Chapter 12— fX. The values in the fX column are generated by multiplying the midpoint value (X) by the frequency (f) (e.g., 6 times 52 is 312). The fX values are then totalled and the mean is obtained in the same manner as before, by dividing the total scores (fX total) by the number of individuals (N can be obtained as indicated in the table by adding the fs, since each f represents a subject). The mean for this example turns out to be 33.29.

TABLE 13.2 Hypothetical Example of Grouped Data Approach Used in Computing Means

Score Interval	X	f	fX
60-64	62	2	124
55-59	57	1	57
50-54	52	6	312
45-49	47	10	470
40-44	42	20	840
35-39	37	18	666
30-34	32	19	608
25-29	27	16	432
20-24	22	13	286
15-19	17	9	153
10-14	12	2	24
5-9	7	3	21
0-4	2	1	2
		$N = 120$	Total = 3,995

As you might expect, using the grouped data approach for calculating means introduces a certain amount of error into the computation. This error occurs when scores are assigned the interval midpoint value and, although not serious in most cases, must be kept in mind when data are being summarized. Because of this error, it is usually preferable to compute raw data means unless the number is so large that the process is simply too cumbersome. If grouped data means are used, the researcher must remember that some error may be present in the means. As noted in Chapter 12, greater error is likely with larger intervals than with smaller intervals, since the midpoint of the smaller interval is likely to be closer to a given exact score. Of course, if intervals are reduced considerably, the computation task becomes more laborious, somewhat like the use of raw data.

The mean has occasionally been likened to the fulcrum on a seesaw. This analogy places the mean at the center of gravity or "point of balance" in a distribution of scores (Spence, et al., 1992, p.23). Consider the first example of a mean as presented in Table 13.1. If this distribution of scores were placed on a seesaw, it might appear somewhat like Figure 13.1. The mean of 25 is positioned as the fulcrum, with the individual scores represented as weights placed at the appropriate distances from the center. The score deviations away from the mean are then noted as plus and minus values on their respective sides of the fulcrum. These deviations are then summed for each side, and the total minus deviations are equal to the total plus deviations (+40 and –40). This is characteristic of means as a measure of central tendency and is essentially the formal definition of a mean: *the total signed deviations around a mean equal zero* (+40 added to –40 equals zero).

The Median

A second measure of central tendency is the median. The median is a *point in the distribution that has exactly the same number of scores above it as below it when all scores are arranged in order.* The specific point at which the median exists in a given distribution is slightly different depending on whether the number of individuals in the group is odd or even. If N is even, then the median is a hypothetical score value midway between the two scores that occupy the midpoint in the distribution. Suppose one wished to determine the median in the series of

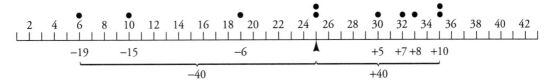

FIGURE 13.1   Center of Gravity Effect of Deviations around Mean

scores that follows: 3, 5, 6, 9, 10, 12, 14. Because there is an odd number of individuals ($N = 7$), the score that occupies the midpoint in the distribution becomes the median; in this example it is 9. In another series of scores, determining the median is slightly different. Consider the following: 3, 5, 6, 9, 10, 12, 14, 16. There is now an even number of scores ($N = 8$), which places the median midway between the two middle scores. In this case, the interval between 9 and 10 is one unit on the scale. Midway between the two would involve half of that interval or 0.5. The median is therefore 9.5.

The examples and discussion of medians thus far have involved raw data scores. Medians may also be obtained with data that are grouped by interval. The process is essentially the same. For example purposes, turn to Table 13.3. Since N is 32, the median will be at a point where 16 scores fall above and 16 below. Counting individuals up from the bottom in the f column yields $2 + 2 + 9 + 10 = 23$, which is beyond the median point. To obtain exactly 16, some but not all of those cases that fall into the score interval of 15 to 19 must be taken. Looking at the next lower interval, $2 + 2 + 9 = 13$, which is only 3 short of the 16 needed for the median. Therefore, take 3 of the 10 cases in the score interval of 15 to 19. For computation purposes, those ten scores must be assumed to be spread evenly throughout the interval even though they probably are not in reality. With this assumption, the median point can be determined by proceeding $3/10$ of the distance into the interval. Since the interval distance is 5 units, $3/10$ of that equals 1.5 units. This 1.5 units must now be added to the lower limit of the score interval of 15 to 19 to obtain the median.

At this point we need to be reminded about interval limits which were discussed very briefly in Chapter 12. The *exact* limits of any interval are actually midway between the intervals that are usually specified. In Table 13.3 the exact limits for the specified median interval (15 to 19) would be 14.5 to 19.5 (29.5 and 34.5 for interval 30 to 34, 24.5 and 29.5

TABLE 13.3 Illustration of Grouped-Data for Median Determination

Score Interval	f
30-34	2
25-29	1
20-24	6
15-19	10
10-14	9
5-9	2
0-4	2
	$N = 32$

for interval 25 to 29, and so on). Thus if 1.5 units are added to the exact lower limit of the median interval (14.5), a score of 16 is obtained, which is the median for this example. (Note that in this example the median *score* was 16 and that it was also necessary to find the *point* at which 16 scores were above and 16 below—the definition of a median. The two 16s are a coincidence, and obviously other examples might result in differences between the median score and the number of cases needed to obtain that median.)

The grouped-data procedure for determining the median is particularly useful when a large *N* is involved in the study. This approach is considerably easier than ordering the actual scores for many individuals.

The Mode

The third measure of central tendency to be discussed is the mode. The mode is simply an indicator of *the most frequent score or interval.* For raw data or actual score distributions, the mode would be defined as that score that occurred most frequently (i.e., more subjects obtained that score than any other score). For data grouped into intervals, the midpoint of the most frequently occurring interval is considered to be the mode. For example, in the distribution of scores illustrated in Table 13.3 more scores fell into the interval of 15 to 19 than any other interval. Since the midpoint of that interval is 17, this would be considered to be the mode.

Occasionally more than one score or interval will appear with modal frequencies. If two scores (or intervals) occur more frequently (and with equal frequency) than other scores, the distribution is said to be *bimodal.* This term is used somewhat loosely on occasion when the two modes are not precisely equal, although the score that occurs most frequently (between the two) is distinguished as the *major mode,* whereas the less frequent score is called the *minor mode.* A distribution with only one most frequently occurring score is termed *unimodal.*

Comments on Selection

As might be expected from the foregoing discussion, the mean, median, and mode have a variety of different properties and are useful in different situations. From the outset the type of data collected has considerable influence on which measure is preferred. If nominal data have been gathered, the mode is the only central tendency description that may be used. Ordinal data, on the other hand, will permit the use of the median as well as the mode. Interval and ratio data, since they both include additivity, permit the computation of a mean in addition to the other central tendency measures.

Some difference of opinion exists regarding such firm statements as those just presented; but in all cases a researcher must be concerned about the meaningfulness of the central tendency measure selected. It makes little sense, for instance, to present a median or mean when categorical (nominal) data are being scrutinized. Even if numbers are used to designate the categories, they are merely serving as labels and could easily be replaced by letters (e.g., A, B, C) or by any other convenient designation that would permit discrimination. The numerals thus do not say anything about the properties being observed except that they have identity and are discriminable (there is no underlying continuum of quantity). Certainly one could perform arithmetic operations on the label numbers, but such manipulation would have no meaningfulness with regard to the property. For example, suppose there are two categories, male and female, designated with numbers 1 and 2. It makes little sense to obtain an arithmetic mean. (What does 1.5 mean in terms of these categories?)

Ordinal data do not present such a clear situation as nominal data. Mean ranks found in research literature may or may not be appropriate depending on the situation. Ordinal data vary considerably in terms of how nearly the ranks represent magnitude as well as order. In some cases the data fit into a lower-level ordinal scale and represent only gross directionality. In such situations a median is usually the preferred measure of central tendency. On other occasions the ranks may suggest considerably more concerning magnitude even though exact interval equivalence is not a certainty. Under such circumstances the use of a mean is meaningful in terms of the property being measured to the degree that magnitude statements may be approximated. Again, researchers must remain cognizant of their purpose, that of being able to say something meaningful about the topic. Mere manipulation of numerals does not fulfill this purpose.

The mean is by far the most frequently used measure of central tendency in behavioral research. There are several reasons why this occurs. One important reason involves purposes of research other than description. If researchers are conducting an inferential study, it is likely that they will wish to compute additional analyses on the data. The mean is amenable to further arithmetic manipulation and is thus more useful for many of the additional operations necessary in inferential statistics.* The median and mode, on the other hand, are more frequently terminal descriptive statistics. It should be noted again that because of the arithmetic operations involved in computing a mean, interval or ratio data are usually preferred for this measure of central tendency since they have the property of additivity.

Depending on the shape of the distribution, the three central tendency measures may have the same score values or different values in

---

*The mean, however, is not the only measure used in inferential studies. This will become evident in chapter 14 when nonparametric and parametric inferential statistical techniques are discussed.

a given set of scores. If the distribution is shaped like the example in Figure 13.2, the mean, median, and mode will have the same score value. This unimodal, symmetrical distribution results in all three central tendency measures being at the same point in the curve.

Distributions that are not unimodal *and* symmetrical result in a somewhat different picture of the central tendency measures' placement. For example, distribution A in Figure 13.3 is symmetrical but *not* unimodal. In fact, this distribution appears to have the double-hump appearance of a bimodal distribution. Distribution A therefore is characterized by two modes, which makes it impossible for the three central tendency measures to have the same score value. However, the median and mean in distribution A still have the same score value. This is to be expected when symmetry exists in the way that the scores are distributed.

Distributions B and C in Figure 13.3 represent a central tendency picture different from either of the other examples. Both of these distributions are characterized by being asymmetrical in shape. When distributions are asymmetrically shaped, they are known as *skewed* distributions. Distribution B illustrates what is called a *positively skewed* distribution, whereas distribution C is an example of a *negatively skewed* set of scores. The direction of the skewness is referenced toward the tail or point of the curve. Since measurement scales commonly read from left to right in an ascending fashion, the term *positive* is used when the tail is toward the upper end of the scale and *negative* when the tail is toward the lower end. Note the positioning of the central tendency measures in skewed distributions B and C. Such skewness in distributions tends to generate different score values for each of the measures. The mode, as usual, is positioned at the hump or most frequent score. The median is positioned at the middle of the distribution, whereas the mean tends to be nearer the tail than the other measures.

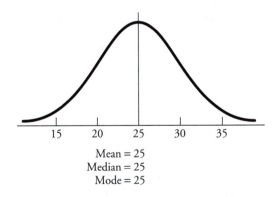

Mean = 25
Median = 25
Mode = 25

FIGURE 13.2   Example of a Unimodal Symmetrical Distribution of Scores

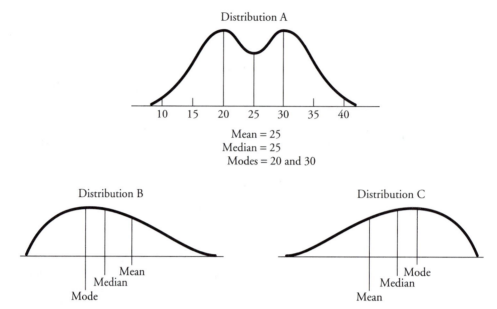

FIGURE 13.3   Central Tendency Measure Placement in Various Distribution Shapes

It is evident from the previous discussion that all three measures of central tendency may vary from sample to sample with regard to the exact score value that each represents. This will occur as a result of the way in which the scores are distributed as well as individual differences in the scores regardless of distribution shape. The mean tends to be somewhat less likely to substantially change position than the median and mode. This greater stability increases the desirability of the mean as a measure of central tendency in most samples. There are, however, occasions when this is not the case. If a particular sample includes a few atypical or extreme scores, the mean may give a distorted picture of the distribution. For example, suppose a sample of individuals is being described in terms of annual income. Say the sample includes primarily those individuals in the middle income bracket, with the exception of one person who has a multi-million-dollar yearly income. In this case the mean is likely to suggest a much higher average income than is actually typical. If such extreme scores are involved in a distribution, the median may well provide a more adequate description of central tendency than the mean. It is frequently advisable to provide more than one measure of central tendency if accurate description is essential. This is particularly important if distributions are skewed as in illustrations B and C in Figure 13.3.

The choice of which measure of central tendency to use depends entirely on what the researchers want to do and in what fashion they wish to describe their sample. If the investigators want to guess a given subject's score and to be *exactly correct* most often, the mode is the best score to pick. This is simply because more subjects obtained that score than any other score in the distribution, which raises the likelihood that the researchers would guess exactly right. For purposes of purely descriptive research, the median is a very functional measure (Hays, 1988). Despite the fact that it is somewhat less stable than the mean, the median is not so affected by extreme scores and thus is often more descriptive of the typical score. Additionally, it is easily communicated. Beyond the realm of descriptive research, for inferential purposes the mean is usually the preferred measure over the median or mode. It uses the data more fully and is amenable to a number of further analyses that are often employed in inferential research. As with other areas of the research process, selection of a central tendency measure must be accomplished on the basis of research purpose (Spatz, 1993; Spence, et al., 1992). Rigid adherence to a particular measure at all times is inappropriate.

***Turn to page 363 and complete
Simulations 13.1 and 13.2***

Dispersion Measures

Describing a set of scores in terms of central tendency furnishes only one descriptive dimension of the distribution, where the performance levels tend to be concentrated. In performing this function, the central tendency measure, whether it is the mean, median, or mode, attempts to characterize the most typical score with a single index.

A second important way of describing scores involves measures of dispersion. Dispersion measures provide an index of *how much variation there is in the scores*, that is, to what degree individual scores depart from the central tendency. By determining where the scores concentrate and to what degree individual performances vary from that concentration, a rather complete description of the distribution is available. In fact, in the absence of a dispersion description to accompany the central tendency measure, knowledge about a given set of scores is rather limited. An example will serve to illustrate this point. Assume that two members of a bowling team are practicing seriously for a tournament. During the last month of practice before the tournament, they maintain an ongoing record of their scores to determine averages with their newly acquired skill level. Figure 13.4 illustrates the distribution of scores for both bowlers. Note that both individuals have the same average (mean) score of 193, yet their bowling performances are considerably different. Tom is an extremely consistent bowler. He can be relied on to fill most of the frames and hit for a reasonable number of strikes. He seldom shoots below 180 but likewise seldom has bowled above 206. Richard's score, on the other hand, is all over the place. Although he has the same average score of 193, his ball placement is erratic. When he is hitting well, his score runs well up into the 200s, but during an off night he is fortunate to break 100. During the last month when scores were recorded (for purposes of this book, of course) he bowled a 282 the first game on one night and followed with a second game of 104.

Information provided by the central tendency measure in the above example is limited. Much more is known about the two bowlers' performance by also viewing the distributions of scores with respect to variability in performance. One may wish to make some decisions concerning next year's bowling team based on such information. In discussing variability indices, three measures of dispersion will be examined, the *range*, the *semi-interquartile range*, and the *standard deviation*. Each provides somewhat different information.

The Range

The range is the simplest and most easily determined measure of dispersion. As suggested by the term, the range refers to the *difference between the highest and lowest scores in a distribution*. If Richard's highest score during his month of bowling practice was 282 and his

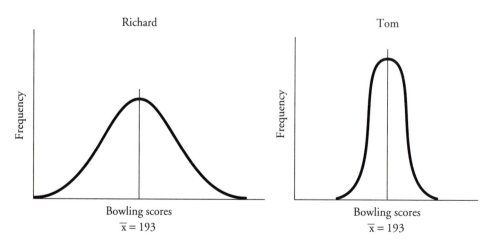

FIGURE 13.4 Hypothetical Distribution of Bowling Scores for Two Bowlers

lowest score was 96, the range for the month's performance would be 282 minus 96, or 186 pins.

The above example illustrates the ease with which the range in a set of scores may be determined. This provides a quick index of variability, which gives additional information beyond the central tendency measure. Unfortunately, the usefulness of the range is somewhat limited because it uses little of the data available in a set of scores. It is determined entirely by the two extreme scores. Since the extreme scores may be capricious, the range may fluctuate a great deal. Its usefulness is primarily limited to preliminary data inspection. After all, an extreme score may be generated by a number of factors that are not particularly representative of the subject's usual performance (e.g., physical or emotional trauma or irregularities in materials or instrumentation).

The Semi-Interquartile Range

The second measure of dispersion to be examined is the semi-interquartile range which circumvents some of the difficulties noted regarding the range (Spence, et al., 1992). Before exploring this measure, however, certain related items require attention. Initially, it is necessary to distinguish between *quartiles* and *quarters.* The hypothetical distribution illustrated in Figure 13.5 is divided into four sections or quarters. The points used for accomplishing this division, designated Q_1, Q_2, and Q_3, are known as quartiles. Thus the quartiles are *points on the measurement scale that serve to divide a distribution of scores into four equal parts.* A subject's score may fall *in* a given quarter or *at* a given

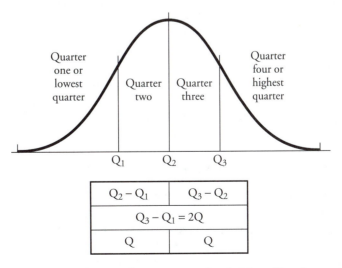

FIGURE 13.5 Hypothetical Symmetrical Distribution of Scores Divided into Quarters Using Quartiles

quartile, but not in a quartile, since the quartile represents a point on the scale.

Strictly defined, the semi-interquartile range is *half the range in scores represented by the middle 50 percent of the scores.* Turn again to Figure 13.5 to examine this definition more closely. The middle 50 percent of the scores in this distribution represents those scores between Q_1 and Q_3. To establish the first and third quartiles, a simple counting procedure is involved. Q_1 may be determined by counting up from the bottom of the distribution until a fourth of the scores have been encountered. If there were 48 subjects in the total group, then 12 would be a fourth of 48. The twelfth score up from the lowest would be at the first quartile. Similarly, the twelfth score down from the highest would be at the third quartile Q_3. Midway between these two points is the second quartile or Q_2. Note that since Q_2 is the midmost score in the distribution, it coincides with the median. The semi-interquartile range is represented by the difference between Q_1 and Q_3 divided by two, or

$$\frac{Q_3 - Q_1}{2} = \text{Semi-interquartile range}$$

For example, if Q_1 was at 36 in the hypothetical distribution of scores and Q_3 was at 92, then the semi-interquartile range would be calculated: $92 - 36 = 56 \div 2 = 28$ score units. The semi-interquartile range is generally represented by Q, thus in the example $Q = 28$.

If the distribution is symmetrical as in the one in Figure 13.5, the semi-interquartile range is the same as either $Q_2 - Q_1$ or $Q_3 - Q_2$. This changes, however, if an asymmetrical or skewed distribution exists as exemplified by Figure 13.6.

The semi-interquartile range is a measure of dispersion that, like the total range, is easily determined and does not involve complicated computational operations. It is, however, superior to the range as a dispersion index. It is a more stable measure, primarily because it uses much more of the available data than the range. As such it provides a much more complete picture as to how the scores are distributed along the scale of measurement.

The Standard Deviation

The third measure of dispersion to be discussed is the standard deviation (SD). By far the most commonly used index of variability, the SD involves somewhat more complicated computational procedures.

The SD may be thought of as *a measure of variability in the scores around the mean.* The mean is therefore the reference point, and the SD provides a description of the distribution of individual scores around that point. In fact, the actual deviation of each score from the mean

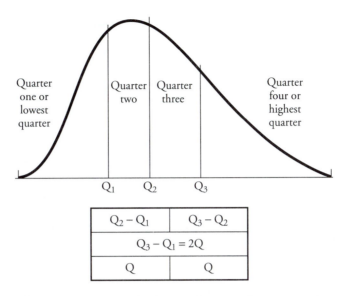

$Q_2 - Q_1$	$Q_3 - Q_2$
$Q_3 - Q_1 = 2Q$	
Q	Q

FIGURE 13.6   Hypothetical Skewed Distribution of Scores Divided into Quarters Using Quartiles

(Mean - X) is used in calculating SD. The SD, in one sense, might be thought of as an average of all the deviations from the mean. Let us turn to Figure 13.7 for an illustration to facilitate this discussion.

The SD is expressed in score units and represents a width index along the measurement scale. The width of this index becomes greater when the scores of a distribution are more variable and narrower as the scores are more concentrated around the mean. Referring back to our example concerning bowlers, the SD of Richard's scores will be considerably larger (wider) than that of Tom's scores. Richard's distribution looks much like the hypothetical illustration in Figure 13.7, whereas Tom's scores are much more concentrated. Although this example involves a distribution of scores in a single individual (intraindividual variability), it is obvious that a single measure taken on a group of individuals would also result in a distribution of scores and can be conceived in the same fashion. This is called interindividual variability.

Figure 13.7 represents a hypothetical set of scores that are normally distributed. The term *normal* in this context should not be viewed literally with other distribution shapes being thought of as abnormal. It is actually defined in terms of certain mathematical properties that determine its shape and was not developed as a description of actual events in the real world. A more descriptive term might be *bell-shaped* distribution. Note the percentages indicated for each standard deviation in Figure 13.7. These percentages remain constant for any set of normally

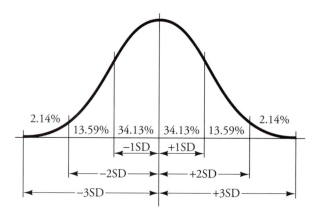

FIGURE 13.7 Normal Distribution with Standard Deviation Divisions

distributed scores. Thus for a normal distribution one can expect that about 68 percent of the scores will fall between +1 and -1 SDs. (This also translates into 68 percent of the area under the curve.)

Comments on Selection

Several issues are involved in the selection of which measure of dispersion is preferable. Certainly if a quick and easily computed index is needed, the order of preference is range, semi-interquartile range, and SD. Using convenience as the sole criterion for selection is questionable, however. The most stable and reliable index of dispersion is the SD, followed by the semi-interquartile range, with the range being the least stable measure. Likewise, if additional statistical computation beyond mere description is in order (e.g., inferential studies such as group comparisons) and the type of data permit, the SD should be the choice.

Somewhat like the mean, the SD is affected by a few atypical, extreme performances (highly skewed distribution). When such a situation exists, the SD does not provide as accurate a description of score dispersion as the semi-interquartile range. Thus if an extremely skewed distribution is obtained, Q is preferable over the SD. Q is frequently viewed as a natural dispersion companion when the median is used for central tendency.

Consideration must also be given to the type of data collected when selecting the measure of dispersion. If the SD is to be used, data must certainly have the property of additivity. This would limit the use of the SD to interval and ratio data. The range and Q may also be used with interval and ratio data, but the SD requires at least interval data. If ordinal data are collected, range and Q may be used. Nominal data, however, present a rather different situation, since the only property present is identity. Measures of dispersion, since they assess variability along some assumed continuum, are not usefully applied to data without such a continuum. Therefore, when working with categorical data, descriptive summaries are best accomplished using modal statements for determination of which category(ies) received the concentration of responses. Beyond this, description can probably best be facilitated by frequency graphs for each category.

Although guidelines have been presented concerning which dispersion measure may be used under what conditions, it is evident that considerable judgment is required on the part of the researcher. As in other areas of the research process, rigid rules are not applicable in all situations. If the Q will provide a more *accurate description* than the SD (despite the availability of interval data), then it should be used. The basic purpose of accurate description must be kept in mind when determining which tool to select.

*Turn to page 364 and complete
Simulations 13.3 and 13.4*

Simulations

Simulations 13.1 and 13.2

Topic: Central tendency measures

Background Statement: Descriptive statistics are frequently useful for summarizing group performance. Central tendency measures provide a single index that is representative of the concentration of scores or where the scores tend to be bunched. One of the determining factors in the choice of which central tendency measure should be used is the type of data collected.

Tasks to Be Performed for Simulation 13.1:

1. Review the following stimulus material.
2. Answer the following questions:
   a. What type of data are involved in the example?
   b. What central tendency measure should be used and why?
   c. What score represents the central tendency measure?

Stimulus Material for Simulation 13.1: You are a coach for a university golf team. The department of health, physical education, and recreation has developed an instrument that is supposed to assess your team members in terms of their probability of tournament success. This instrument involves a pencil and paper test that has a score possibility of 1 to 7. The best possible score is 1, and 7 is the worst. These scores are based on ratings of performance by a highly qualified judge who has several years of experience as a golf coach. Your varsity team takes the test and scores are transmitted to you in the following form.

Name	Score
Peggy	2
Joseph	5
Roberta	7
John	4
Judy	1

Respond to the three questions in the previous section on task to be performed.

For feedback see page 366.

Tasks to Be Performed for Simulation 13.2:

1. Review the following stimulus material.
2. Answer the following questions:
   a. What type of data are involved in the example?
   b. What central tendency measure should be used and why?

Stimulus Material for Simulation 13.2:   You are working on a research program for a large drug firm. The laboratory has developed a new formula for use with tiny infants that will presumably reduce the vulnerability to pulmonary problems. A serious elevation in temperature is suspected as a potential side-effect difficulty. The criterion measure here, then, is temperature. Respond to the questions under part two of the tasks to be performed.

For feedback see page 366.

Simulation 13.3

Topic: Dispersion measures

Background Statement: Dispersion measures provide an index of how much variation exists in a set of scores. Such information is an important addition to the description provided by central tendency measures.

Tasks to Be Performed:

1. Review the following stimulus material and all of Simulation 13.1, including the feedback.
2. What dispersion measure is appropriate for this situation and why?

Stimulus Material: You have been asked to consult with a group of students who are conducting their first research project. The data involved ratings on 52 golf students in terms of their probability of tournament success. The same instrument is being used as in Simulation 13.1.

For feedback see page 366.

Simulation 13.4

Topic: Dispersion measures

Background Statement: Dispersion measures provide an index of how much variation exists in a set of scores. Such information is an important addition to the description provided by central tendency measures. Selection of a given dispersion measure may be influenced by a number of factors.

Tasks to Be Performed:

1. Review the following stimulus material.
2. What dispersion measure is appropriate for each of the situations presented?

Stimulus Material: You have been serving as a scout for a professional basketball team. You have just returned to your office late one evening after watching two potential recruits. You were able to observe both players during seven different games each, so you have considerable data on them. Suddenly the head coach calls and wants a quick summary of the players' scoring. Both individuals had the same mean points scored during the seven games (22.3). What measure of dispersion might you give the coach on such an immediate basis (you don't even have your pocket calculator with you)? What measure of dispersion might you give on your written scouting report, which you can submit after a bit more time?

For feedback see page 366.

Simulation Feedbacks

Simulation 13.1

The data presented are ordinal data since they are generated from a rating scale that does provide evidence of greater than and less than but does not provide information concerning the interval between any two scores. This is the type of example that was used in discussing ordinal data in Chapter 11 as well as in previous simulations.

The central tendency measure of choice for these data is the median. This choice is based on the fact that the median does not require arithmetic operations such as adding, subtracting, or dividing. These operations generally should not be performed on ordinal data since the property of additivity is not present. The median is preferable over the mode for ordinal data although both may be used.

The score representing the median in this example is 4.

Simulation 13.2

First of all, assume that the instrument to be used in data collection is a thermometer, since this is the usual instrument. The data that will be collected can be considered to be interval data. In such cases one is working with known and equal distances between score units and an arbitrary zero point. These are the characteristics of interval data.

The central tendency measure of choice for these data is the mean. Since interval data include the property of additivity, the arithmetic operations necessary to obtain a mean can be appropriately performed. When this is possible, the mean is usually preferred because it makes use of as much information as possible (which the median and mode would not in this case). The only circumstances in which the mean would not be preferred would be if there is a highly skewed distribution.

Simulation 13.3

The dispersion measure of choice is most likely the semi-interquartile range because it is frequently viewed as a natural companion when the median is used. More important, however, is the fact that ordinal data will not generally permit the use of a standard deviation, since additivity is not present. The semi-interquartile range will provide more information than the range, since more of the available data are used.

Simulation 13.4

Since you are so pressed on the phone, you are really likely to need a measure of dispersion that is quickly obtainable without much computation. For the purpose noted in the stimulus material, the range will probably serve adequately, and you can get the coach off the phone. For your written report you may wish to use a measure that will use more of the information available. Your data are at least interval in nature and therefore have the property of additivity. With this in mind, the standard deviation would probably be the dispersion measure used in your report.

$$Chapter\ \ 14$$

Statistics for Inferential Purposes

The Inferential Purpose

General Background

We mentioned earlier that certain quantitative investigations have a purpose beyond mere description. Commonly called *inferential* studies, they have the purpose of drawing implications from the data to some setting, subjects, or materials other than those that were directly involved in the completed study. In some cases such studies are testing the applicability of a theory, model, or body of knowledge in a new setting or with subjects that have not previously been explored. In other cases studies may be investigating the effectiveness of one or more treatments or instructional techniques. Such studies are usually considered inferential by virtue of the suggestions that are generated (inferred) from the results. Certain preliminary issues similar to those examined with descriptive statistics also warrant discussion in terms of inferential statistics. One of the first involves what they are and what they do. Inferential statistics, like those used for descriptive research, are tools for analyzing data in a fashion that will address the question being asked.

It was noted very early in this volume that three general types of questions are typically explored in behavioral research—descriptive, difference, and relationship. Chapter 13 explored statistical procedures often used for descriptive studies. This chapter will focus on the two remaining types of questions—difference and relationship. These general categories of research questions are often involved in inferential research. As is evident from the material in earlier chapters, a broad spectrum of specific research questions may be examined within these two types.

The statistical techniques used for inferential research essentially tell a researcher whether the results obtained are different from chance; that is, what is the probability that chance could have generated the results? This is an important piece of information since the investigator would like to *infer* that the *treatment* generated the observed performance. For example, suppose a researcher is comparing the effectiveness of three instructional methods, *A, B,* and *C.* Students in the group receiving method *C* performed better on the test than did those receiving either *A* or *B.* It is important to know whether the difference was probably caused by the treatment or whether it represents normal variation in performance due to chance. If the differences are sufficiently dramatic that the probability of this result's being caused by chance is low (5 percent or less), then the differences are called *statistically significant.* Since the probability of chance is low, the researcher is inclined to infer that any differences are the result of the effectiveness of the instructional methods. To determine what the probability of chance is, the investigator applies a statistical test to the data. Thus for inferential research, statistics are the means by which researchers scrutinize their data to ascertain whether chance or the treatment probably generated the results. This cannot be determined by merely inspecting the raw data visually.

We noted that a chance probability of 5 percent or less is usually considered to be statistically significant. A brief expansion on this statement is appropriate at this point, particularly related to significance notation. You may have encountered such notation as $p < .05$ and $p < .01$ in reading research reports. The p refers to probability, and the statement as a whole means that the probability is less than 5 percent (or 1 percent, depending on which is used) that the obtained results were caused by chance. Strictly speaking, *only 5 times out of 100 would results such as these be expected due to chance influences.* Thus *95 times out of 100, when results such as these are obtained, they will be due to the treatment.*

Use of 5 percent as the cutoff point for statistical significance is actually arbitrary. This level was used early in the development of statistical procedures in behavioral science and has continued more out of tradition than because of any specific logic. Some researchers have maintained that a more logical basis should exist for determining what is and is not considered statistically significant. Despite these arguments, however, the 5 percent probability level of chance persists as the generally accepted upper limit for results to be considered statistically significant in most behavioral sciences.

Several statistical techniques are used in inferential studies. At times it seems that the multitude of different statistical tests is never-ending, particularly to the beginning researcher. Although there *are* many different statistical tests, they do not exist merely to cause hives in graduate students. Since there are many different research questions that may be studied, many different tools are necessary to apply to these problems. Just as the mechanic cannot make a screwdriver turn a nut, the researcher cannot make an inappropriate statistical test fit a question. Additionally, the mechanic cannot *only* remove screws and expect to disassemble an automobile. Likewise, researchers cannot *only* ask research questions for which they have statistics and expect to fully investigate the problem. In both cases a full range of tools must either be in hand or within reach (whether it be the toolbox or the reference textbook).

For the most part, various statistical tests merely represent variations on a few basic themes. This chapter will focus on the basic themes of statistical tests and indicate what types of variations are appropriate under what conditions. Only the more commonly used analyses will be discussed. The interested student may consult any one of many statistical texts for specifics regarding a particular technique that is not fully detailed in this volume.

Parametric and Nonparametric Issues

Many beginning researchers feel somewhat intimidated by the whole idea of dealing with statistics in general, let alone a breakdown of statistics into categories. However, the topic just discussed leads into such a categorization. A given research question and situation, like a $9/16$-inch bolt, requires a specific tool—in this case, a statistical tool.

Two general types of statistics have been developed and used in inferential research over the years, *parametric* and *nonparametric* tests. Both types of analyses serve the purpose of determining whether the results obtained are likely to be due to chance or to the variable(s) under study. Essentially the same types of research questions may be served by both parametric and nonparametric statistics. Either parametric or nonparametric analyses may be used in studies that investigate relationship questions or ones that investigate difference questions. This provides the researcher with a broad range of statistical tools that may be used. Selection of the appropriate statistical analysis depends on a number of factors including the nature of the data being collected, the size of the sample, and certain assumptions about the population. This section will explore those factors in preparation for subsequent sections, which will present a variety of specific tests.

Assumptions. When a researcher collects data on subjects, the data involve recording one or more scores on each individual. These scores represent a sample of all such possible scores in the universe. For example, recording the heights of 30 different subjects would result in 30 different scores. These 30 scores represent a sample of all possible different heights in the population. The population scores have certain characteristics or values such as a mean and a standard deviation (SD), and they are distributed in a particular manner.

Parametric statistics require a number of assumptions about the nature of the population from which the sample scores were drawn (Howell, 1995). For example, a given parametric statistic may require that the scores be normally distributed in the population. For that particular statistic to be appropriate, this assumption must be valid or the results of computation may not be accurate. The population values (e.g., mean, distribution, and SD) are known as *parameters,* and since this category of statistics requires assumptions about these values, they are called *parametric statistics.*

Because all the scores in the population are not recorded, the researcher has no way of verifying what the parameters are precisely. Consequently parameters or population values usually exist only in theory. Unless there is other information available (such as some massive study that previously recorded scores on the entire population), these values are truly assumptions. They are assumed to exist in a particular form that is in harmony with the requirements of the statistic that the researcher wishes to use. If, however, there is reason to believe (either by logic or previous information) that the population values do not conform to the requirements of a given statistic, the researcher would be in error to use that analysis.

The above statements should not be taken to mean that a researcher may capriciously choose a statistical analysis and decide that the assumptions are met by the data. These assumptions must be not only reasonable but supportable. If the soundness of any assumption is questionable, then a given statistical analysis should not be used. It is this reason that has generated the development and use of nonparametric statistics. Nonparametric statistics require fewer assumptions regarding the nature of the population from which the scores are drawn. This category of statistics has sometimes been referred to as *distribution-free.* This term may be misleading. It is *not* the case that no assumptions at all are involved; rather, that the nature of the population from which the scores were sampled is less frequently important. Requirements for nonparametric statistics more often involve the type of data and make fewer references to the population than parametric analyses.

Thus one of the differences between parametric and nonparametric statistics involves the assumptions that must be met. For parametric statistics to be appropriate, a researcher must be able to reasonably assume that certain characteristics are true about the population from which the scores were drawn (Howell, 1995). (Specific assumptions that are necessary for given analyses will be noted later in the chapter as selected tests are presented.) Nonparametric statistics do not, in general, require as many nor as rigorous assumptions.

Nature of the Data.   An additional difference between parametric and nonparametric statistical analyses involves the nature of the collected data. Four types of data were discussed in Chapter 11: nominal, ordinal, interval, and ratio. Each of these types of data were described as having different measurement properties. Nominal data have the property of identity, ordinal data have identity and order, and interval and ratio scales have identity, order, and additivity. These properties are important in terms of what statistical analyses can be appropriately performed (Spence, et al., 1992). Table 14.1 presents the four data types with their respective measurement properties and indicates the appropriate application of parametric and nonparametric analyses.

As indicated in Table 14.1, the application of parametric statistics is limited to data that are either interval or ratio in nature. This limitation is dictated by the mathematical operations involved in the computation of parametric statistics. These analyses require arithmetic manipulations on the actual score values such as addition and subtraction, as well as others that necessitate the property of additivity. Without this property such manipulations are meaningless, since they are not an accurate representation of real world events (e.g., if the digits 1 and 2 designate apple and orange categories, they cannot be added and result in a meaningful representation). Nonparametric statistics can be used with ordinal and nominal data since they do not require such mathematical manipulation on the actual score values. They may also be used with interval or ratio scales, since these data types *more* than satisfy the computational requirements of these analyses. *If,* however, other neces-

TABLE 14.1 Summary of Four Types of Data, Their Respective Measurement Properties, and Statistical Application

Data Type	Measurement Properties	Statistical Application
Nominal	Identity	Nonparametric
Ordinal	Identity Order	
Interval	Identity Order Additivity	Parametric as well as nonparametric
Ratio	Identity Order Additivity	

sary characteristics are present in interval or ratio data samples (e.g., distribution assumptions, adequate sample size), parametric statistics are generally preferred since they are more powerful and make more efficient use of data.

Thus the type of data recorded help to determine selection of the statistical analysis to be used. If a researcher collects data that are of the nominal or ordinal scale (e.g., yes-no or male-female categories; ranking or 1 to 5 rating scales, respectively), nonparametric analyses should probably be used (Howell, 1995; Spence, et al., 1992). If interval or ratio data are available, either parametric or nonparametric statistics may be employed. The decision in the latter case is made on other factors such as distribution assumptions (previously examined in a general fashion) and sample size.

Sample Size. As suggested by previous comments, the sample size must also be considered when selecting a statistical analysis. If few subjects are used for experimentation (e.g., $N = 6$ to 8), there is little alternative. Nonparametric analyses are more appropriate. Such a small number of subjects does not represent much of a sample of behavior. With such a limited sample, the mathematical operations required by parametric statistics (e.g., computation of means) become highly questionable as to accuracy. Unless replicated several times with only six subjects, there is the distinct possibility that an atypical sample has been drawn and that the performance is not at all representative. Although this is always a problem, the use of parametric statistics may suggest a false sense of security regarding the accuracy of the portrayal.

This raises an immediate and practical question. What is an adequate sample size for using parametric statistics? If a definitive answer were available, this section could have been much shorter, perhaps one or two lines. Judging from the massive amount of literature available in the statistical area, such an answer is not possible. It has been our general rule of thumb that groups (*ns*) of less than 12 or 14 are questionable in terms of using parametric statistics. This means that if two groups are being compared (treatments A and B), then each group should contain at minimum 12 to 14 subjects before parametric tests may be used confidently. Certainly 15 and even 20 per group increases the comfort with which the parametric mathematics may be performed, but the concern here is minimums. "Rules of thumb" are, of course, not hard and fast rules. Researchers must use their best judgment and consultation resources. The fact remains that with *ns* much less than those noted above, the confidence in parametric analyses is substantially reduced, and nonparametric statistics are preferred.

Parametric and nonparametric statistical analyses have primarily been discussed in terms of group studies that use traditional experimental designs. This type of research has historically made greater use of statistical analysis than have investigations using single-subject experimental designs or many nonexperimental studies. There is, however, a continuing interest in the application of statistical procedures that are not traditional experimental in nature (e.g., Edgington, 1980a, 1980b, 1980c; Onghena, 1992; Wampold & Worsham, 1986). The interested student may wish to consult these references for more detailed information regarding the use of statistical analyses in single-subject investigations.

Comments on Parametric and Nonparametric Statistics. As noted above, three general areas are involved in selecting parametric versus nonparametric analyses: assumptions about the nature of the population distribution, the type of data that are collected, and the sample size. In all of these areas, parametric statistics have been the standard and more rigorous in terms of requirements. Parametrics require *more stringent assumptions* about the population distribution of scores, necessitate *more sophisticated data,* and require *larger sample sizes.* This does not, however, imply that nonparametric analyses are a panacea for researchers who do not wish to attend to these factors. Nonparametric statistics do not represent tools that may be applied in a capricious manner, with an expectation of the same outcome. The advantage of nonparametric statistics involves the characteristics already described. They may be used in situations in which knowledge is lacking concerning the population distribution or in which the necessary assumptions for parametrics cannot be met. They may be used in studies in which small samples are drawn and with more primitive types of data. *If,* however, *the necessary requirements for parametric statistics are met, they are preferred over nonparametric analyses* for a variety of reasons. Parametric statistics are more powerful than nonparametric analyses when they can be used (Keppel, 1991). Additionally, they make more efficient use of data. If the data are of an interval or ratio scale, nonparametrics are wasteful in terms of the information used with respect to that which is available in such measurement (Howell, 1995; Keppel, 1991). One further advantage offered by parametric statistics involves greater flexibility with regard to the types of research questions to which they may be applied. This is particularly evident with more complex studies in which more than one variable is under investigation. Thus when it is possible to satisfy the requirements for parametric analyses, they should be favored over nonparametric statistics. When this is not possible, the use of nonparametrics provides the researcher with an alternative that is much more powerful than mere visual inspection of the data.

*Turn to page 399 and complete
Simulations 14.1, 14.2, and 14.3*

Difference Questions: Which Statistic and When

From the beginning of this text a distinction has been made between difference and relationship questions. By way of review, difference questions are involved in studies that *compare.* Such comparisons may be between the performances or answers of two or more groups (e.g., in which the groups receive different treatments or in which the groups are compared on a survey regarding something like annual net income), within a group but between different conditions (e.g., pretest-posttest experiments or answers to questions before and after an election), or within a single subject but between different treatment conditions (e.g., baseline-treatment-reversal comparisons). Relationship questions, on the other hand, explore the degree to which two or more phenomena relate or vary. This type of investigation might ask: As intelligence varies, what *tends* to happen to reading ability? As intelligence increases in a group, does reading ability tend to also increase, or does it tend to decrease? (Another example mentioned in Chapter 1 involved length of marriage, perhaps measured in years, and annual net income measured in dollars.) Relationship studies involve recording data on a sample of subjects (e.g., both intelligence and reading scores). With two measures on each individual, the researcher then computes a correlation coefficient to determine how the two variables relate in the group, rather than comparing them.

Difference questions and relationship questions require two distinctly different types of statistical approaches. The purpose of the present section is to discuss difference questions and briefly examine the type of statistical techniques that may be employed for data analysis. Relationship statistics will be presented in a subsequent section of this chapter.

Many variations and combinations of difference questions may be asked. For nearly any type of difference question that may be invented, there are statistical techniques that may be appropriately applied. In the course of this discussion, both parametric and nonparametric analyses will be noted.

Comparing Two Data Points

The first type of difference question to be examined involves comparing two data points. In this context, the term *data point* refers to a performance record, score, or summarization of scores such as a group mean. The two data points could be summarized performance records on two groups (e.g., mean correct responses by groups A and B, median ranking by groups A and B), two performances by the same group (e.g., in a pre-post investigation), or two performances by a single subject (e.g., baseline performance compared to postintervention performance in a behavior modification experiment). There could be several variations on these types of arrangements. It has been our experience that, with the basic design and statistical frameworks in mind, a researcher can apply appropriate variations on these themes for a given research problem.

Independent Comparisons

Throughout this text examples of two group comparisons with one experimental variable have been used. (Group A receives one treatment method, group B receives a second treatment method, and the experimental variable is method of treatment.) This is one of the simplest types of experiments to conceptualize with essentially a single focus: Is there a difference in effectiveness between treatment method A and B? Other things being equal, this question becomes: Does group A perform differently than group B? The term *independent* indicates that the scores under condition A are not affected by or do not affect those in condition B. For practical purposes this means that the two groups are constituted by different subjects (which is not the case with, say, a pre-post investigation). Consequently there is no reason to believe that the performances are not independent.

Two groups may be compared under circumstances in which the researcher is faced with a weaker data scale (nominal or ordinal measurement) or few subjects per group or both. As was noted earlier, either of these conditions would require the use of nonparametric statistics. Under other conditions in which interval data are approximated, the required distribution assumptions are reasonable, and a more adequate sample is tested, parametric analyses are appropriate.

Parametric Analysis.   For comparisons in which interval or ratio data are recorded, it is common to compare the mean of the scores obtained by group A with the mean of group B. This process is testing for differences between two independent means. Since means are being specified, it is assumed that the appropriate data have been recorded that will permit the necessary mathematical manipulations.

Two parametric statistics are available for this situation, the *z* test and the *t test for differences between independent means*. The *z* test is useful for samples with more than 30 individuals in a group. The *t* test is similar to the *z* test except that it is also applicable for groups equal to or less than 30. Since the *t* test is more flexible in terms of the number of subjects (e.g., $n = 12$ to 30 or above), it is almost universally used in comparisons of two means.

As suggested by its inclusion as a parametric statistic, the *t* test requires interval or ratio data and group samples (*ns*) of about 12 or more. In addition to these requirements, the *t* test assumes that the criterion measure is normally distributed in the populations from which the means are drawn and that both also have equal variation in terms of the criterion measure. If these assumptions are reasonable (or if there is little reason to believe that they are drastically violated), the *t* test for differences is a powerful and convenient analysis for comparing two independent means. It is simple to compute, and formulas may be found in nearly any introductory statistics text (e.g., Grimm, 1993; Vernoy & Vernoy, 1992). For step-by-step procedures, the reader is directed to the volume by Bruning and Kintz (1987). Remember that the test to be used is the *t* test for differences between *independent* means. The reason for this emphasis becomes evident later as a variation of the *t* test is examined.

Nonparametric Analysis. Nonparametric statistical analyses may be used under certain conditions in which parametric statistics cannot be applied. For situations in which two independent data points are to be compared, there are analyses that can be used with both nominal and ordinal data.

Two nonparametric analyses will be mentioned for investigations in which nominal data have been recorded. The reader will recall that nominal data are characterized by categorical representation of events. For example, yes-no responses on a questionnaire and performances that are scored as pass-fail or successful-unsuccessful would be considered nominal data.

If a small number of subjects are used (total *N* less than 20), a useful statistic for comparing two groups is the *Fisher exact probability test.* This test might be used in comparing, say, groups A and B if the data collected involved categories (scores) such as pass versus fail. Table 14.2 illustrates diagrammatically how such a comparison might be made. Fisher's test is simple to compute, and procedures may be found in Hays (1988). If the sample is large, however, the computation becomes laborious if calculated by hand. In situations in which *N* is greater than 20, it is much easier to use the *chi-square (χ^2) test for comparing independent samples.*

The chi-square test for two independent samples, like Fisher's exact probability test, may be used with nominal data. The previous example (groups A and B that had performance categorized as either pass or fail) will also serve satisfactorily for the chi-square test. The question is essentially: Does group A differ from group B in terms of how many

TABLE 14.2 Example of How Comparisons Might Be Made Using the Fisher Exact Probability Test

	Performance Categories	
Groups	Pass	Fail
A	*n*	*n*
B	*n*	*n*

subjects passed as opposed to how many failed? The chi-square test is preferred when N is greater than 20. This test requires a cell size (n) of at least five. Thus in Table 14.2 none of the categories (e.g., group A, passed; group B, failed) should have less than five individuals so categorized, if the chi-square test is to be used. If this requirement is not met, such as group B having only three individuals who passed, Fisher's test should be applied instead. Computational procedures for the chi-square may be found in a number of statistics texts (e.g., Howell, 1995; Spence, et al., 1992).

Two nonparametric analyses will also be mentioned briefly for studies in which ordinal data have been collected. Again, by way of review, ordinal data are characterized by the ability to rank order events on the basis of an underlying continuum. The ranks denote greater than or less than on the dimension being assessed, a property that is not necessarily characteristic of categories. The example of a rating scale of 1 to 5 was used in Chapter 11. The reader may wish to refer to this chapter for additional review and examples.

When data are of at least an ordinal scale, two groups may be compared using the *median test.* Using the previous example, this analysis addresses the question of whether there is a difference between the medians of group A and group B. The median test may be used with a variety of sample sizes. Individuals interested in computational procedures should consult Spence, et al. (1992) or other texts that provide details on this technique.

A second nonparametric analysis that is useful for comparing two independent samples of ordinal data is the *Mann–Whitney U test.* This is a powerful nonparametric analysis for comparing two groups for which rank-order data have been collected. This test also may be used with a variety of sample sizes and with different sample sizes in each group (e.g., group A, $n = 1$, and group B, $n = 3$, up to group ns of 20). Beyond group ns of about 20 the Mann–Whitney U test becomes somewhat laborious if computed by hand. Readers who need to use this test in such situations can consult Howell (1995) for appropriate procedures.

Nonindependent Comparisons

Nonindependent comparisons of two data points represent a considerably different situation from that of independent comparisons just discussed, although they are variations on the same theme. The nonindependent comparison is almost defined by characteristics that are *not* the case for independent comparisons. In an independent situation, the scores in condition A are not affected by or do not affect those under condition B. In practice this has generally meant that the two groups (conditions A and B) are constituted from different subjects. In a nonindependent situation, on the other hand, there is some reason to believe that scores under condition A have some effect on those under condition B. This might be the case if repeated measures were taken on the same subjects. For example, Fred's performance is measured under condition A and then again under condition B. Since Fred's performance is recorded under both conditions, there is reason to believe that the two scores are not independent because his score in one condition may well have some influence on his score in the other. (There is *no* way that his reading ability in one performance test is not going to have some relationship to his performance on another test.) Similarly, if a subject learns a great deal from taking the pretest, that performance will likely have an influence on the posttest performance. In either of these situations a different set of statistical procedures is appropriate than was the case for independent comparisons. These procedures are the topic of this section.

Parametric Analysis.   Probably the most frequently used parametric statistic for this type of comparison is the *t test for differences between nonindependent means.* As the name suggests, this analysis is a computational variation on the *t* test previously discussed for independent comparisons. Since it is a parametric statistic, at least interval data and a sample size of 12 or more are required. Additionally, the assumption of a normally distributed criterion measure should be reasonable if the *t* test is to be appropriately applied. This test could be used in circumstances in which a pretest mean is to be compared with a posttest mean or where two experimental treatments are administered to the same group (in either case, the same group is being tested under both conditions). Remember that for comparing two nonindependent means, the *t* test to be used is different from that used for independent means. Computational procedures may be found in nearly any introductory statistics text (e.g., Grimm, 1993; Howell, 1995). Several name variations commonly appear with this analysis including *t* test for nonindependent means, correlated *t* test, and *t* test for related means. These terms are used interchangeably and all designate the same analysis.

Nonparametric Analysis.   Recall that nonparametric statistics are useful in situations in which parametric analyses are inappropriate. A variety of nonparametric analyses may be used to compare two nonindependent data points. When nominal data have been collected, the *McNemar test for significance of changes* is a useful analysis and is particularly appropriate for pre-post designs.

If ordinal data have been recorded, two nonparametric analyses are available—the *sign test* and the *Wilcoxon matched-pairs signed-ranks test.* Both of these tests, once again, are used for situations in which performance is assessed on the same subjects at two different times.

The sign test is so named because the signs + and - are used as integral parts of the computation. This test is easy to use and may be applied with rather small samples (e.g., *N* = 6). One assumption must be reasonable for appropriate application of the sign test: this analysis does require that the variable being assessed and scored in terms of ranks must have a continuous distribution. An example may serve to clarify what is meant by this assumption. Suppose all the students in a given group are being ranked in terms of height. The continuous distribution requirement simply assumes that there is a continuum of heights possible underlying the ranks of 1 to 15 (if there are 15 in the group). No other assumption is required.

The Wilcoxon matched-pairs signed-ranks test is the second nonparametric statistic to be mentioned for ordinal data. This analysis is more powerful than the sign test because it takes into account the magnitude of differences between scores rather than merely indicating in what direction change occurred. (Using the sign test, the direction of change is all that is considered. A change in one direction is denoted by a +, whereas a change in the other direction is designated as a -.) Because the Wilcoxon test makes greater use of the actual ranks, it does require that the experimenter be able to roughly judge the magnitude between ranks. When this can be reasonably done, the Wilcoxon test is preferred over the sign test. Computational procedures may be found in a number of sources (e.g., Howell, 1995).

It should be kept in mind that both of the above analyses ask the question: Is there a significant difference between two sets of related performances? This question may take the form: Is there a difference in this group's performance on the pretest as compared to the posttest? These analyses may also be employed in studies in which the same group might be given two experimental treatments (e.g., both A and B) and which is not the pretest–posttest format.

*Turn to p. 400 and complete
Simulations 14.4, 14.5, and 14.6*

Comparing More Than Two Data Points

One Experimental Variable

The discussion of statistical analyses thus far has focused on comparing two data points (e.g., comparing performances of two test situations such as two means or medians). This discussion has examined comparisons that were independent as well as those that were nonindependent. In all cases the comparisons were between two groups or performances with one experimental variable involved. Recall for a moment the many hypothetical examples of groups A and B in which two treatment techniques are compared. There is one experimental variable, method of treatment, with two types (conditions A and B) representing the specific conditions compared. Likewise if a time-series study is conducted, baseline performance is compared to performance under treatment. In this case the experimental variable may be designated as level of positive reinforcement. The two specific conditions within this experimental variable are the absence versus presence of the treatment (baseline versus treatment). In a similar fashion a pre-post experiment may be conceived of as a comparison of absence versus presence of the treatment with a single experimental variable.

Frequently a researcher wishes to conduct a study in which one experimental variable is involved, but more than two specific conditions exist within that variable. Expanding the previous example, a study may be conducted that investigates methods of treatment but compares three or more specific types (groups A, B, C, etc.). Experiments of this type are merely variations on the previous basic theme with *one experimental variable under study*. The only change represented is that more than two specific conditions are compared within that experimental variable. Instead of two drug dosages, the researcher may wish to compare performance under five levels of dosage (amount of drug treatment being the experimental variable). These variations do, however, require the use of statistical analyses different from those previously discussed.

Independent Comparisons. Independent comparisons of three or more data points, with one experimental variable, should be viewed in much the same fashion as independent comparisons in general. Independence, once again, means that the scores under condition C are not influenced by those under conditions B, A, and so on. As before, this usually takes the form of different groups of subjects for each condition. Figure 14.1 illustrates how five conditions might be designed to test the effects of variation in level of drug dosage. For the present purpose, 20 different subjects have been assigned to each of the five different experimental groups, making this an independent comparison design.

If the researchers have collected interval or ratio data, they are in a position to consider the use of parametric statistics. Perhaps the most

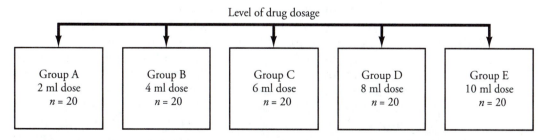

FIGURE 14.1   Independent Comparison Design with One Experimental Variable and Five Specific Conditions

commonly used statistic for this type of comparison is the *one-way analysis of variance for comparing independent means.* Shortened to one-way analysis of variance or ANOVA, this test is a powerful technique for comparing three or more means. It is important to emphasize that this discussion is about a *one-way ANOVA for independent comparisons.* Variations of the basic ANOVA will recur in later discussions with different types of designs. One of the reasons for the popularity of ANOVA is its great flexibility for different designs.

The ANOVA provides a convenient analysis for making a simultaneous test for differences among the five means of performance scores by the subjects in Figure 14.1. As noted earlier, ANOVA is a parametric statistic. Several assumptions must be reasonable before it can be appropriately applied. The type of data must be suitable for this type of analysis, interval or ratio. Additionally, four other assumptions are usually considered as being required: (1) the scores recorded are normally distributed in the population, (2) the variation in scores is approximately the same for all groups in the experiment (i.e., the score variation in group A is about the same as that in groups B, C, and so on. This is commonly referred to as the *assumption of equal variance or homogeneous variances.*), (3) the observations or scores are independent, and (4) the performance variation in the total sample is a result of additive influences. Although these assumptions may appear overwhelming to a beginning researcher, in practice it is obvious that they are not. ANOVA is simply used too frequently for them to present an unsurmountable obstacle. Over 20 years ago Edgington (1974) reported that "71% of the articles using statistical inference [in APA journals] used analysis of variance" (p. 25), and this high level of usage continues (Howell, 1995). In reality some latitude is possible with respect to how rigorous one must be about meeting these assumptions precisely. Considerably more detail regarding these assumptions, as well as computational procedures, may be found in most statistical texts that present inferential analyses (e.g., Grimm, 1993; Winer, Brown, & Michels, 1991).

As with other research situations, there are occasions when nominal or ordinal data are recorded with the intent to compare more than two data points (still within the realm of one experimental variable). Under these conditions, of course, one must turn to nonparametric statistics for analysis purposes. Using the same basic design arrangement that was presented in Figure 14.1, suppose for a moment that there are nominal data with which to work. This might be the case if there were some sort of dichotomous categories regarding the subjects' health status (e.g., "cured" versus "not cured"). The different groups can be statistically compared under this type of situation by using the *chi-square test for k independent samples.* The chi-square test for this comparison is a simple expansion of the analysis that was mentioned previously for comparing two groups. The term *k* is used to designate the number of groups being compared. For the example in Figure 14.1, *k* would be equal to 5, since there are five groups. However, as a part of the general title of the analysis, k is used to indicate "several, depending on the exact number of groups in the experiment." As before, the cell size (*n*) needs to be at least 5 or more. Thus this test would not be appropriate if there were only three or four in any cell. The discussion presented previously for chi-square remains appropriate for its application here and, as before, computational procedures may be found in a variety of statistical textbooks (e.g., Spence, et al., 1992).

Two statistical analyses are appropriate for comparing more than two independent data points if ordinal data have been collected—the *median test* and the *Kruskal-Wallis one-way analysis of variance by ranks*. The median test for this situation is an extension of the median test that was previously mentioned for comparing two data points (in fact it is frequently designated as the *extension* of the median test). Computational procedures may be found in many texts covering non-parametric statistics (e.g., Howell, 1995; Spence, et al., 1992).

The Kruskal-Wallis one-way analysis of variance by ranks represents a second statistical technique that is useful for comparisons of *k* independent data points when ordinal data have been collected. The requirements of this analysis are essentially the same as those for the extension of the median test presented above. The Kruskal-Wallis, however, is more efficient because it makes use of more of the available information than does the median test. Consequently, when the experimental situation permits use of either test, the Kruskal-Wallis is preferred.

Nonindependent Comparisons. Occasionally a researcher may wish to compare three or more data points that are not independent. Such a situation might arise if, for example, the same subjects were tested three times with some treatment or event occurring between the measurements. Figure 14.2 illustrates how such an investigation might be designed. The same subjects are given a pretreatment measure (measure 1), then the first 20 practice trials of the learning task are administered. This is then followed by a midexperiment assessment (measure 2), the next 20 practice trials and, finally, the third test (measure 3). This type of study can easily be viewed as an extension of the pre-post design mentioned previously with the addition of a third test. Expansions may, of course, involve more than three data collection points (e.g., four, five, … *k*). On occasion the treatment that intercedes between measurements may involve only the passage of time rather than application of an active treatment. In all cases in which multiple measurements are administered, a researcher must be cautious about the effects of the testing itself, as noted in Chapter 8.

If the researcher has collected nominal data and wishes to compare three or more nonindependent data points, a useful analysis is the *Cochran Q test*. Such a situation might occur if the design involved testing the same subjects under three different drug dosages. The data

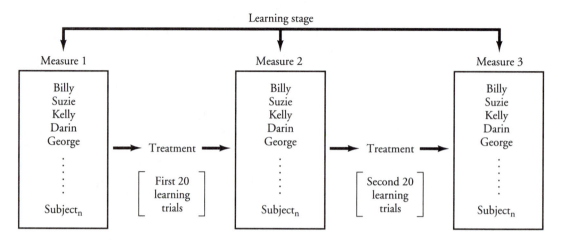

**FIGURE 14.2 Nonindependent Comparison with One Experimental
Variable and Three Data Points**

might be recorded as "cured" versus "not cured," thus falling into the
categorical type of measurement. This example is merely used for illustrative purposes, and it is necessary to remain aware of the design problems that would be presented by such an experiment. One obvious
difficulty would be the multiple treatment interference problem, which
was noted as affecting both internal and external validity in Chapter 7.
Certainly there would have to be some assurance that the effects of
drug dosage 1 were not still operating when the dosage 2 condition was
implemented. Computational procedures for Cochran's Q may be found
in Hays (1988).

If the recorded data are ordinal in nature, three or more nonindependent data points may be statistically compared using the
Friedman two-way analysis of variance by ranks. Although the title
includes the term *two-way* (usually suggestive of two experimental
variables), this analysis is appropriately discussed here because it actually makes a one-way comparison. To illustrate, suppose that the study
concerning drug dosage was arranged as in Table 14.3. The Friedman
analysis compares the ranks between the dosage conditions, which,
since there is one experimental variable (level of drug dosage), is a
one-way comparison despite what the analysis title suggests. Because
the same subjects are tested under all conditions, this situation falls into
the nonindependent data point comparison category. The Friedman technique may be used with small samples and is relatively simple to compute (Spence, et al., 1992).

If the researcher has collected interval or ratio data, parametric statistical techniques may be considered for analysis purposes. With this

TABLE 14.3 Example of Nonindependent Comparisons between Three Drug-Dosage Conditions

Subject	Dosage Conditions		
	2 ml	6 ml	10 ml
1			
2			
3			
4			
.			
.			
.			
n			

level of data and assuming that other factors are present such as an adequate sample size and a reasonable assurance that assumptions are approximated, the task at hand is essentially one of comparing three or more nonindependent means. Probably the most commonly used statistical test for such a comparison is the *analysis of variance for repeated measures* (with one experimental variable—thus a one-way ANOVA for *repeated* measures). The *repeated* distinction is important to highlight. Previously, a one-way ANOVA for comparing independent means (resulting from different groups' performance) was discussed. The present discussion refers to a one-way ANOVA for comparing three or more *nonindependent* means (resulting from repeated measures on the same subjects). The computational procedures are somewhat different and may be found in most statistical texts that focus on inferential statistics.

*Turn to page 403 and complete
Simulations 14.7 and 14.8*

Two Experimental Variables

The discussion of statistical procedures has thus far focused on situations in which one experimental variable is being investigated. (The term *experimental variable* is being used generically here as before; it essentially refers to comparisons that may be made whether the study is an experiment in the true sense or a comparison between data points in a nonexperimental study such as a survey.) Hypothetical studies in which two or more data points are compared (such as performance under three different instructional techniques) within the single experimental variable (method of instruction) have been examined. Frequently studies are conducted in which more than one experimental variable is of interest in the same investigation. This section will discuss statistical data analysis in situations with two experimental variables under study. You may wish to review the design sections on this type of investigation in Chapter 5.

You will note that there will be less emphasis on nonparametric analyses in this discussion than in previous sections, a reflection of a point made earlier in this chapter. Parametric statistics offer greater flexibility in terms of the types of questions asked, particularly with regard to more complex designs involving more than one experimental variable. Do not interpret this as freedom to apply parametric analyses under all conditions in which two or more experimental variables are studied. Restrictions concerning the type of data, sample size, and assumptions are still operative.

Independent Comparisons.   An investigation with two experimental variables that involves independent comparisons merely represents a conceptual combination of more simple designs. Figure 14.3 illustrates a hypothetical investigation with two experimental variables, material difficulty and amount of practice. Comparison A, which represents the material difficulty variable, has two specific levels, high-difficulty material and low-difficulty material. Comparison B, the amount of practice

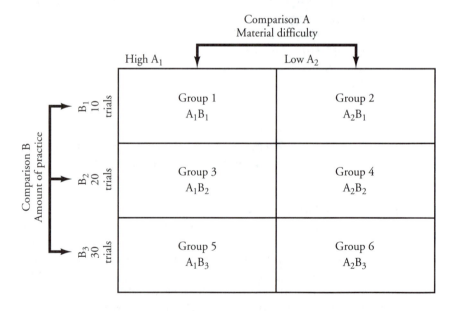

FIGURE 14.3 Hypothetical Independent Comparison with Two Experimental Variables

variable, has three levels of 10 trials, 20 trials, and 30 trials. Thus there are six different data points to be compared. This is an independent design since there is a separate group of subjects for each condition (randomly assigned).

An investigation such as that in Figure 14.3 is usually designed for situations in which parametric analyses can be applied, since non-parametrics are so cumbersome with complex studies. This, of course, means that interval data are collected, cells include 12 or more subjects, and the researcher is reasonably sure that the assumptions of normal distribution and equal variance are approximated. If these elements are present, the most popular statistical technique for this situation is the *two-way analysis of variance for comparing independent means*. This analysis is an extension of the independent ANOVA noted previously under independent comparisons with one experimental variable.

By now it should be evident that the ANOVA is an extremely flex-ible statistic that may be computationally modified to fit a variety of research designs. This is an important factor in its great popularity and contributes to its frequent appearance in the research literature. In addi-tion to its flexibility, however, the ANOVA is an extremely powerful analysis, often viewed as the standard against which other techniques are compared. Computational procedures for this analysis are really rather simple and certainly less formidable than many beginning re-searchers think. They are found in most statistical texts under titles such as two-way ANOVA, two-factor ANOVA, and ANOVA for double-classification experiments.

If the requirements are not met for parametric statistics, the researcher will have to resort to nonparametric analyses. In an experiment such as that exemplified above, data analysis becomes cumbersome. Common nonparametric techniques previously reviewed constitute the main choices from which selection may be made. In such a situation the experimenter has little choice but to analyze one comparison at a time while ignoring the second experimental variable. This would mean, in the example just given, that two independent data points would be compared (high versus low difficulty) by combining the performances of groups 1, 3, and 5 for high difficulty and groups 2, 4, and 6 for low difficulty (refer to Figure 14.3). The second variable would then have to be analyzed comparing the three amounts of practice, 10 trials (by com-bining the performance scores of groups 1 and 2) versus 20 trials (groups 3 and 4) versus 30 trials (groups 5 and 6). Such an approach is obviously more laborious and does not provide as much information. It may, how-ever, be the only option if parametric analysis is not appropriate.

Mixed Comparisons. Mixed designs have previously been introduced in Chapter 5. Review of this material will alert the reader to the fact that mixed designs involve studies with at least two experimental variables, in which *independent comparisons are made on one variable and* *repeated measures are used on the second.* For the purposes of this section, use the example in Figure 14.3. This independent design would be altered to a mixed design if it were set up with different groups for each level of variable B that received both high- and low-difficulty material. The different groups for each level result in three *different* groups of subjects, the independent comparison variable. Receiving both high- and low-difficulty material constitutes repeated measures on the difficulty variable. Such a design is illustrated in Figure 14.4.

As noted earlier, investigations that are designed in this fashion are usually planned with the intent of using parametric statistical analyses. If the requirements for such computation are met, the *two-way mixed analysis of variance* would be an appropriate analysis for this type of experiment. This is another variation on the basic ANOVA theme, which further illustrates its great flexibility. Computational procedures are somewhat different from those presented before and essentially combine the components of independent analysis with those for repeated measures. "Mixed" ANOVA is used in the same sense as the "mixed" design described earlier. Details for computing this analysis may be found in a variety of statistical texts that include discussions of inferential statistics.

Investigations that will not permit the use of parametric analyses (e.g., inappropriate data, small samples, or drastic assumption violation) would again require the application of nonparametric techniques.

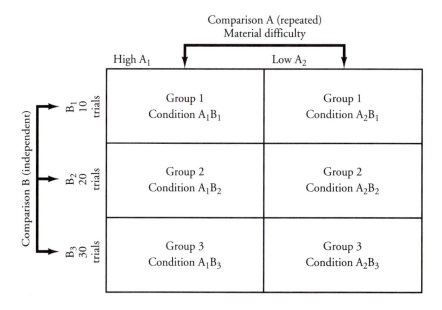

FIGURE 14.4 Hypothetical Mixed Comparison with Two Experimental Variables

Basically the same approach as that described in the previous section would be applied. Data from one variable at a time would be analyzed using the appropriate nonparametric statistic (e.g., either two or *k* data points, independent or nonindependent, depending on the situation). As with two-factor studies or more complex experiments, nonparametric analyses are considerably more cumbersome.

*Turn to page 404 and complete
Simulation 14.9*

Logical Extrapolations: More Complex Designs

The phrase *more complex designs* has been used in this chapter in a relative sense and generally as a means of referring to studies with more than two experimental variables. The term is not meant to connote complex in the sense of "difficult." It has been our experience that some of the most "difficult" experiments are really made difficult by virtue of ill-defined problems that have not been distilled to operational form. On the other hand, some of the "easier" pieces of research often involve several experimental variables (*complex* in the sense of the number of variables) but are made easy in the sense that they are clearly and operationally defined.

Using More Complex Designs.   For purposes of the present discussion, the phrase *more complex designs* is used generally to refer to studies asking difference questions with three or more experimental variables. Such designs have already been introduced in Chapter 5 and considered briefly. This type of study is conducted when the researcher wishes to examine three or more experimental variables simultaneously. Diagrammatic representations of such studies are somewhat more difficult than with two variables. Figure 14.5 illustrates an experiment with three variables. This diagram, although totally hypothetical, involves variable A (with two levels, A_1 and A_2), variable B (with three levels, B_1, B_2, and B_3), and variable C (with two levels, C_1 and C_2). This experiment might be labeled a 2 x 3 x 2 design in a research report, with the numerical designations referring to the specific levels in each variable.

If the experiment illustrated in Figure 14.5 involved different subjects for each cell group, it would be considered a totally independent design. This would mean that 12 separate groups of subjects would be used. As before, the term *independent* is used to indicate that the scores in any given cell do not have an influence on the scores in any other cell. This, of course, precludes repeated measures on any variable. Using

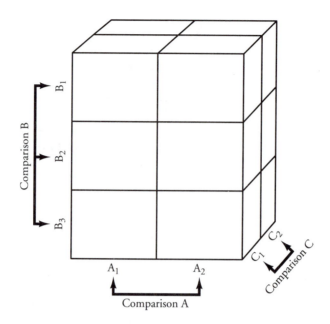

FIGURE 14.5   Diagrammatic Representation of a Hypothetical Study with Three Experimental Variables

this example, suppose for the moment that the basic requirements for parametric analyses are met. This would mean that interval or ratio data had been collected, that each cell had 12 or more subjects, and that the assumptions of normality and equal variance were reasonable. If these elements were present, data could be conveniently analyzed using a *three-way analysis of variance for independent comparisons*. This analysis will yield a great deal of information and, as before, merely involves computation extensions of the more simple ANOVA procedures discussed earlier. Computation procedures are not difficult but become increasingly tedious as the design becomes more complex, if you are calculating by hand.

Now examine this same design assuming that it is not possible to use parametric statistics. As noted during the discussion of studies with two experimental variables, such a situation makes data analysis cumbersome since nonparametric statistics are not nearly as flexible in terms of application to more complex designs. Probably the best approach under such conditions would involve analyzing the comparisons separately (e.g., comparison A, then B, and finally C). The basic nonparametric approaches to perform such analyses have been described earlier in this chapter. Hopefully an investigator would plan ahead sufficiently and either ensure the appropriateness of the study for parametrics *or* design a simpler investigation.

Reconsider the three-factor experiment that was illustrated in Figure 14.5. It may be that the researcher will want to obtain repeated measures on one or more of the experimental variables. If this is the case, the design becomes a three-factor mixed design, since it combines independent comparisons on some experimental variables (e.g., different groups for variables A and B) and repeated measures on others (e.g.,

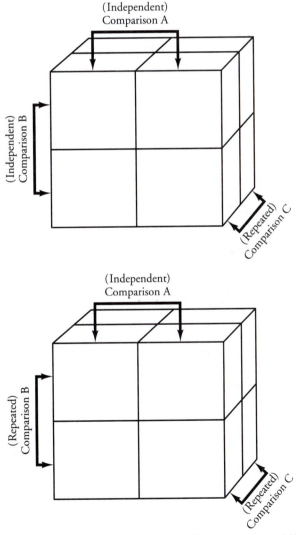

FIGURE 14.6 Option Examples for Three-Factor Mixed Design

variable C). This type of design was introduced previously in Chapter 5 and is illustrated in Figure 14.6. Note that two examples are shown in Figure 14.6. One indicates comparisons A and B as being independent, and comparison C is the variable on which subjects receive repeated measures. For this experiment four different groups of subjects would be necessary, and they would all be measured twice (under the two C conditions). The second example in Figure 14.6 indicates only variable A as independent, and repeated measures are obtained on both variables B and C. Only two groups of subjects would be used in this example, and both groups would be measured under all B and C conditions. Both of these examples are considered mixed designs.

If the studies in Figure 14.6 include the appropriate elements for parametric statistics, the data can be analyzed using the *three-way mixed analysis of variance.* This technique is an extension of the mixed ANOVA discussed earlier. Slight computational modifications are made depending on whether one or two variables are independent.

Problems with More Complex Designs.   The last section described more complex designs that may be used to investigate difference questions and statistical procedures that can be applied for data analysis purposes. Studies were discussed that included three experimental variables. The researcher may wish to conduct an investigation that includes even more experimental variables (e.g., four, five, or more). Such studies may be implemented and data analyzed using logical extrapolations of what has been discussed previously. There are analysis of variance procedures that can be computed for such designs, both totally independent as well as mixed (e.g., four-way ANOVA). In fact, as computer use has become increasingly sophisticated, there have been a number of sophisticated analysis procedures that make the computational capability nearly limitless. There are, however, some serious problems involved in using such complex designs.

As the complexity of an investigation increases, it becomes more difficult to create and maintain a mental image of the various components included in the study. It has been our experience that one of the most effective means of conceptualizing a study is to draw a picture of it much like the diagrams that have appeared throughout this text. Most people are accustomed to visualizing phenomena primarily in a two-dimensional fashion (particularly as they illustrate on paper). It is possible to draw three-dimensional designs such as those in Figures 14.5 and 14.6, but when presented with additional factors to illustrate, the task becomes difficult. This results in a conceptualization problem, particularly for the beginning researcher. Related to this difficulty is the task of interpreting results from a complex experiment once the data are analyzed. Remember, analysis of the data is *not* the end product of research. There is little reason to conduct an investigation unless the *results can be meaningfully interpreted.* Such interpretation frequently becomes overwhelming when the design is complex. Thus, although the design and analysis capability exists for highly complex experiments, the interpretation of simpler studies is far easier and more straightforward. More importantly, this may well result in a more meaningful outcome in terms of practice and theory.

A variety of statistical procedures have been discussed thus far in this chapter. The questions and conditions under which each might be most appropriately applied have been examined. Obviously these are general considerations; specifics may alter somewhat the analysis chosen. However, these general guidelines may be very helpful to the beginning researcher and are summarized in Table 14.4.

TABLE 14.4   Summarized Inferential Statistics for Difference Questions

Type of Analysis	Type of Comparison		
	Independent	*Nonindependent*	*Mixed*
Two data points			
Parametric	z test t test for independent means	t test for nonindependent means	
Nonparametric			
Nominal data	Fisher exact probability test Chi-square test	McNemar test for significance for changes	
Ordinal data	Median test Mann–Whitney U test	Sign test Wilcoxon matched-pairs signed-ranks test	
More than two data points			
One experimental variable			
Parametric	One-way ANOVA (indep.)	One-way ANOVA (repeated measures)	
Nonparametric			
Nominal data	Chi-square test for k ind. comparisons	Cochran's Q test	
Ordinal data	Median test Kruskal-Wallis test	Friedman test	
Two experimental variables	Two-way ANOVA (indep.)		Two-way ANOVA (mixed)

Relationship Questions: Which Statistic and When

Thus far our focus has been on statistical procedures that may be applied to a variety of difference questions. The purpose of this section is to briefly describe techniques that may be used for data analysis when the researcher is investigating a relationship question.

By way of review, relationship questions are involved in studies that explore the *degree to which two or more phenomena relate or vary together.* Such an investigation might examine the relationship between height and weight *(as height varies, what tends to happen to weight?).* For this type of study the researcher records both height and weight on a sample of subjects. With two measures on each subject, the data are then analyzed by computing what is known as a correlation coefficient. The correlation coefficient provides an estimate of the degree to which the variables measured relate. The coefficient itself is the outcome of the computation and may range from +1.00 to –1.00. (Most results fall between these extremes, such as +.70, –.50, etc.) Correlations that result in coefficients with a plus sign are known as *positive correlations.* Such results indicate a positive relationship, which means that the two variables tend to vary in the same direction (as height increases weight also tends to increase, or as height decreases weight also tends to decrease). Coefficients with a minus sign are known as *negative correlations.* Negative correlations indicate inverse relationships between the two variables. They tend to vary in opposite directions; as one increases the other tends to decrease. (For example, as the frequency of cardiac arrest increases in a population, longevity tends to decrease.)

A correlation that results in a +1.00 coefficient indicates a strong positive relationship between the two variables being measured. Sometimes known as a *perfect positive correlation,* a +1.00 coefficient indicates that each time one variable either increases or decreases, the second variable also exhibits an increment change in the same direction. (e.g., each time height increases, weight also increases.) Similarly, a –1.00 correlation is indicative of a strong relationship of an inverse nature. In such a situation, each time there is an increase in one variable there is a decrease in the second. Correlation coefficients that are closer to zero indicate a much weaker relationship between the two variables being measured. A zero correlation suggests that there is no systematic variation at all between the two variables, either positive or negative.

Statistical significance in relationship studies essentially means the same thing that it does in comparative investigations. Once the sample is selected and the measures recorded, the data are then analyzed using one of a variety of computational formulas. This results in a correlation coefficient such as has just been discussed. The researcher then checks this coefficient statistically to determine whether it is significant. If the correlation obtained is statistically significant ($p < .05$ or $p < .01$), it is doubtful that the relationship observed is a result of chance. The researcher is then likely to interpret the data as suggesting that a relationship does exist between the two factors measured.

A word of caution is in order concerning the interpretation of correlational studies. A high correlation coefficient, even if it is statistically significant, should *not* be taken to mean that the variation in one factor (e.g., height) *causes* variation in the second factor (e.g., weight). Causation should *not* be inferred from correlational data. A high correlation coefficient merely indicates that the two variables tend to vary systematically, either together for positive correlation or inversely in the case of negative correlation. Such a relation permits the prediction of one variable from knowledge about the second but does not permit statements about causation. Many factors that may vary systematically in this world do not actually act on one another. They may both, for instance, be acted upon by some additional factor or series of factors.

A second note is also appropriate at this point in terms of interpretation of correlation coefficients. It was noted above that 1.00 correlations (either + or -) rarely occur and that coefficients such as .70, .50, and so on are more frequent. Perhaps because of the way the correlation coefficient is presented, a .70 correlation is occasionally *misinterpreted* as representing the percent of variation in common between the two variables being measured. This is an inappropriate interpretation and, in most cases, inaccurate. A .70 correlation does *not* mean that 70 percent of the time when one factor varies, the second measure also changes. In fact, if one is interested in the percent of variation in common, the obtained correlation coefficient should be squared. Using the previous example, a correlation of .70 actually indicates less than 50 percent variation in common between the two measures (.70 x .70 = .49 or 49 percent). This presents a picture different from the previous misinterpretation of a .70 coefficient. There are certain formulas that include correction factors in computation (primarily reliability formulas used in test construction). In general, however, a correlation should not be taken as representative of percent.

The term *correlation* is a general label for the type of analysis used in relationship investigations. Actually several specific techniques are used in different situations, much as was encountered with statistics for difference questions. In selecting the appropriate correlational technique for analysis purposes, the researcher must pay close attention to the type of data that have been collected on both variables (i.e., nominal, ordinal, interval, or ratio). The reader may wish to review the discussion concerning different types of data found in Chapter 11.

Perhaps the most commonly known correlation technique is the *Pearson product-moment correlation.* This analysis may be used when *both of the measures recorded* (criterion measures 1 and 2, height and weight in the previous example) *are either interval or ratio data.* The symbol for the product-moment correlation is *r,* which is occasionally used to refer to correlation in general. This use of the symbol is actually incorrect since it specifically denotes the product-moment analysis. The product-moment *r* is a highly popular correlation technique, primarily because it provides a stable estimate of relationship. When the data permit its use, this is definitely the preferred analysis. Computational procedures may be found in most standard statistical texts (e.g., Bruning & Kintz, 1987; Howell, 1995).

Two correlational techniques may be used if the *data collected are ordinal* (i.e., the measures on *both* measure 1 and measure 2 *are in the form of ranks*). The more widely known analysis is the *Spearman rank-order correlation,* which is also known as *rho.* The second technique is *Kendall's tau,* which may also be used when both measures are in the form of ordinal data. Kendall's tau is preferred over the Spearman correlation when only a small sample is available (*N* less than 10). It is, however, somewhat more difficult to compute, and when the sample size permits, the Spearman rho should be employed. Computational procedures for Spearman's analysis may be found in most statistical texts (e.g., Bruning & Kintz, 1987; Howell, 1995). Computational procedures for Kendall's tau are somewhat less available but may be obtained from Hays (1988) as well as Bruning and Kintz (1987).

Data in the form of a dichotomy (e.g., successful–unsuccessful) may also be submitted to correlational analysis. Because a dichotomy represents categories, data of this type fall into the nominal level of measurement. Two correlational techniques may be used with this type of data.

If the data on *both variables* represent an *artificial dichotomy,* the analysis to be applied is the *tetrachoric correlation.* A note of explanation is in order regarding artificial dichotomy. An artificial dichotomy would exist if the experimenter arbitrarily divided performances into two categories. This might be the case with the "successful–unsuccessful" example above, in which someone has rather arbitrarily defined what is successful and unsuccessful performance. If such data are recorded on both measures, the experimenter can obtain a correlation using the tetrachoric procedure.

A second type of dichotomous data may also be correlated. When data on both variables represent *true dichotomies,* the analysis of choice is the *phi coefficient.* A true dichotomy exists when the categories are relatively clear-cut and are not determined arbitrarily. An example of this type of situation might be the absence versus presence of a student's response. Assuming that the determination of whether the student responded is clear-cut, such data would be considered a true dichotomy. When such data are recorded on both measures, an estimate of relationship can be obtained with the phi coefficient.

The discussion thus far has examined correlational techniques that may be used with nominal and ordinal data as well as interval and ratio data. In each case, however, the procedure was designed for the *same type of data on both of the measures being correlated.* That is, if the analysis under discussion was appropriate for rank data (Spearman's rho, Kendall's tau), this type of data was required on both measure 1 and measure 2. A limited number of techniques are available that permit correlation when data on one measure are of one type and data on the second measure are of a different type. The remainder of this section will present two such correlational procedures.

The concepts of artificial and true dichotomies have already been encountered. Consider for a moment a situation in which the researcher has data in the form of an *artificial dichotomy on one measure* and *interval or ratio data on the second measure.* Recall that the artificial dichotomy data will be the result of two arbitrarily defined categories. If a researcher wishes to correlate such data with interval or ratio data the *biserial correlation* may be used. This type of situation might be encountered if, for example, the investigator wanted to determine the relationship between success or failure in a physical fitness test and speed in a 100-yard dash. In this example the time to run the 100-yard dash may be considered interval or ratio data. The other measure, recorded as pass-fail on the physical fitness test, is artificial dichotomous data, since the score represents an arbitrarily determined category.

A precautionary note is in order in terms of use of the biserial correlation. It was previously noted that the extreme limits for any correlation are +1.00 and –1.00. In computation of the biserial correlation, it is mathematically possible to exceed these limits, particularly if the measures are not normally distributed. This is a characteristic of this particular formula of which the researcher should be aware. Otherwise a correlation of 1.15 might result in wasted searching for a computational error that really is not there. Such a result is generated by the relative lack of precision in the technique, emphasizing the preference of measures other than the artificial dichotomy when possible.

If the data involve a *true dichotomy on one measure* and *interval or ratio data on the second measure,* an estimate of relationship may be obtained by using the *point biserial correlation.* Recall that a true dichotomy is the result of clear-cut categories such as male-female. This is a different situation from that presented by the artificial dichotomy. The point biserial correlation is frequently used in investigations that relate sex categories to performance on tasks that generate at least interval data. Modifying the earlier example, the point biserial procedure might be used to correlate sex categories with performance in a 100-yard dash. This analysis is closely related to the powerful product-moment correlation and does not have the mathematical idiosyncrasy noted for the biserial technique (exceeding the 1.00 range). Computation procedures for the point biserial correlation may be found in Bruning and Kintz (1987).

Examination of statistical procedures for relationship questions has been limited to situations in which two variables are of interest, such as the well-worn examples of height and weight as measures 1 and 2.

More complex techniques are available to permit correlation of more than two variables. These analyses, however, generally require a knowledge of and degree of comfort with statistics that are frequently not present in the beginning researcher. Consequently, these procedures have been omitted to maintain the conceptual integrity of an introductory presentation.

A variety of statistical procedures have been discussed here for relationship questions. The conditions under which each might be most appropriately applied have also been examined. Clearly these are general considerations and the particular conditions of a given investigation might alter the analysis used. These general guidelines, however, may prove useful to beginning researchers and are summarized in Table 14.5.

TABLE 14.5   Summarized Inferential Statistics for Relationship Questions

Type of Analysis	Parametric Conditions	Nonparametric Conditions
Same data type on both measures		
Interval or ratio	Pearson product-moment correlation	
Ordinal		Spearman rank-order correlation ($N > 10$) Kendall's tau ($N < 10$)
Nominal		Phi coefficient (true dichotomy) Tetrachoric correlation (artificial dichotomy)
Different data types on the two measures		
Nominal (artificial dichotomy) and ratio or interval		Biserial correlation
Nominal (true dichotomy) and ratio or interval		Point biserial correlation

Turn to page 405 and complete Simulations 14.10 and 14.11

Comments

The discussion of inferential statistics presented in this chapter has by no means been exhaustive. Not all of the myriad of statistical tools have been discussed, nor has any single technique been explored in great depth. The purpose of this chapter has been simply to provide an introductory description of selected analyses that might be applied under a variety of research circumstances. The nature of the presentation has been intended to give the reader an overview of various types of statistical tools and to provide a guide as to when they might be used. Certainly more comprehensive knowledge will require consultation of a variety of texts that have the sole purpose of presenting statistical analyses. Likewise, information on computational procedures and formulas has intentionally been omitted from this chapter. This was done on the assumption that such inclusions might detract from the student's necessary grasp of the purposes and uses of various analyses. The result has been a frequent reference to other sources for computational information. Without fail an attempt has been made to consider these references carefully to select those that are elementary and clear yet accurate in their presentation. We hope the student now has a general knowledge (or can refer back to this chapter) of what statistic to use when. Armed with this background, it will be a much simpler task to make sense of and apply the basic statistical tools used in behavioral research.

Simulations

Simulations 14.1, 14.2, and 14.3

Topic: Parametric versus nonparametric statistics

Background Statement: Selection of the appropriate statistical tool is an essential first step before the data are analyzed. It will do no good to perform computations correctly if the incorrect analysis has been used. The choice between parametric and nonparametric statistics rests essentially on three factors as noted in the text: assumptions, nature of the data, and sample size. Since the assumptions exist primarily in theory (unless evidence exists that suggests a problem) your practical decision may have to be based primarily on the latter two.

Tasks to Be Performed:

1. Review the following stimulus materials.

2. Indicate whether you would be inclined to use parametric or nonparametric statistics and why.

Stimulus Material for Simulation 14.1:   You are conducting a study in which two reinforcement techniques are being compared to determine which is most effective. Two groups of children have been formed by random assignment with 20 subjects in each group. The data are collected on a scale that rates behavior on a scale of 1 to 7 with 1 representing nondisruptive and 7 representing highly disruptive behavior.

For feedback see page 406.

Stimulus Material for Simulation 14.2:   You are working as coaching assistant for the varsity basketball team at Southern Grant University. The coach is planning a defense strategy for the year. To accomplish this task, you have been asked to analyze the scoring patterns of players who are 6 feet 5 inches or less in height as compared to those 6 feet 6 inches or above. The league tends to be rather evenly distributed in height. When you break it out, the league has 60 players in the shorter group and 60 in the taller group. Your measure is the number of points scored per game played last year. What type of statistical test will you use, parametric or nonparametric? Why?

For feedback see page 406.

Stimulus Material for Simulation 14.3:   You are conducting a study for a research laboratory on a rare eye disease. This is a progressive ailment, and the project director is interested in any differences between individuals who are in the early stages versus those in the late stages of the disease. One of the symptoms is an atypical flutter of the upper lid. The question, then, is whether a difference exists in the frequency of upper lid flutters between early- and late-stage patients. The criterion measure is the frequency of upper-lid flutters per two-minute observation period. Since the disease is so rare, there are only three subjects in each group. What type of statistical test will you use, parametric or nonparametric? Why?

For feedback see page 406.

Simulations 14.4, 14.5, and 14.6

Topic: Comparing two data points

Background Statement: The actual determination of which statistical test should be used depends on several factors. As was noted earlier, the type of data and the sample size are important general considerations. The specific test selection will then be further narrowed by the question being addressed (e.g., comparing two independent groups or comparing pretest and posttest scores). Such a selection process frequently involves considering several alternatives. We have found it unnecessary to try to memorize all the possible alternatives. Consequently you are encouraged to refer to the relevant portion of the chapter in responding to this simulation. Such reference is realistic in terms of the actual research process since many researchers do not believe it is worth the effort to memorize the alternative statistical tests and the specific situations in which they are appropriate. The more frequently used tests become easily remembered after they are used a few times.

Tasks to Be Performed:

1. Review the following stimulus materials.
2. Indicate which statistical test you would select for data analysis and why.

Stimulus Material for Simulation 14.4: Suppose you are back at your previous job as coaching assistant for the varsity basketball team at Southern Grant University. Recall that in Simulation 14.2 you were asked to compare the scoring of those players 6 feet 5 inches or less with those 6 feet 6 inches or above. This is a study that compares two groups of 60 subjects each. Your criterion measure was the number of points scored per game played, which represented at least interval data.

Now walk through a few of the preliminary steps before you get to the actual test selection.

1. The first step is to determine what summary or descriptive statistic will be used. Do you want to compare group means (mean points scored for group 1 as compared with mean points for group 2), medians, or modes? Since you have interval data, group means are most likely appropriate. So, the first decision is made; you are comparing two means.

2. Are these independent means or are they nonindependent? Since two different groups are involved (as opposed to the same group measured twice as in a pre-post situation), you have little reason to believe that the performances are not independent. Therefore, in the absence of any compelling argument otherwise, these are probably independent groups.

3. Now, what statistical test would you suggest? Review the relevant chapter pages if you wish. Recall that the feedback for Simulation 14.2 suggested the general type of statistic (parametric) because of the sample size and the type of data.

For feedback see page 406.

Stimulus Material for Simulation 14.5:   You have been asked to work in a psychology laboratory. The topic of your first investigation involves comparing the effectiveness of two treatment techniques. Two groups of children have been formed by random assignment with 15 subjects in each group. Treatment is administered and measurements are then taken. The data are collected on a scale that rates behavior from 1 to 7, with 1 representing nondisruptive behavior and 7 representing highly disruptive behavior.

Review briefly what is involved in this study by asking a few specific questions.

1. Is this an independent or a nonindependent comparison?
2. What type of data are being collected, and what does this suggest relative to the selection of parametric versus nonparametric analyses?
3. What is the size of the sample and what does this suggest?

Now, what statistical test would you suggest? Review the relevant chapter pages if you wish.

For feedback see page 407.

Stimulus Material for Simulation 14.6:   You have been asked to serve as a statistical consultant for an environmental research team that is studying certain aspects of pollution control. A new facility that has been constructed in the valley has proved effective in reducing pollution in other parts of the country. One expected result is a reduction in the frequency of sinus infection symptoms as the pollution is reduced. A sample of 100 individuals has been randomly selected for the study. The subjects will be examined three times during the first 15 days of the month (pollution device not operative) and three times during the second 15 days of the month (pollution device operating). The data will involve recording the number of symptoms for each subject, computing an average for all subjects on the first 15 days, and comparing that with the mean for all subjects during the second 15 days.

Review briefly what is involved.

1. Is this an independent or a nonindependent comparison?
2. What type of data are being collected, and what does this suggest relative to the selection of parametric versus nonparametric analyses?
3. What is the size of the sample and what does this suggest?

Now, what statistical test would you suggest? Why? Review the relevant chapter pages if you wish.

For feedback see page 407.

Simulations 14.7 and 14.8

Topic: Comparing more than two data points

Background Statement: See background statement for Simulations 14.4, 14.5, and 14.6.

Tasks to Be Performed:

1. Review the following stimulus material.
2. State which statistical test you would select and why.

Stimulus Material for Simulation 14.7: You are working again as a research consultant for that well-known drug firm in the East. The laboratory has developed a new formula for use with tiny infants that will presumably reduce their vulnerability to pulmonary problems. One concern, however, is the possibility of undesirable side effects. A serious elevation of temperature is suspected as a potential problem. Consequently three different compounds have been developed in an attempt to circumvent this difficulty.

The laboratory wishes to conduct a study comparing the three compounds to determine whether any of them will be less influential on temperature elevation. Three groups of infants will be randomly constituted with 20 subjects each. The data will be recorded in degrees Fahrenheit.

Review briefly what is involved.

1. How many experimental variables are indicated in this study, and what is it (what are they)?
2. Is the study independent, nonindependent, or mixed?
3. What type of data are being collected, and what does this suggest relative to the selection of parametric versus nonparametric analyses?
4. What is the size of the sample, and what does this suggest?

Now, what statistical test would you suggest? Review the relevant chapter pages if you wish.

For feedback see page 408.

Stimulus Material for Simulation 14.8: You have been employed by a health spa to direct a new weight reduction program. Since this is a new program, the owner has asked that you conduct a careful study to monitor its effectiveness. As you ponder your assignment, you come to the conclusion that you will assess your enrollees over a period of time, taking a measurement before they actually begin, one midway through the program, and a final measure at the end of the four-month course. Since this program is conducted as a group endeavor, all of the first participants will begin at the same time and move through the four-month sequence simultaneously. You have 30 individuals in your group and your criterion measure is weight.

Review briefly what the problem involves.

1. Identify the experimental variable or variables.
2. Is the study independent, nonindependent, or mixed?
3. What type of data are being collected and what does this suggest relative to the selection of parametric versus nonparametric analyses?
4. What is the size of the sample and what does this suggest?

Now, what statistical test would you suggest and why? Review relevant chapter pages if you wish.

For feedback see page 408.

Simulation 14.9

Topic: Comparing more than two data points

Background Statement: See background statement for Simulations 14.4, 14.5, and 14.6.

Tasks to Be Performed:

1. Review the following stimulus material.
2. Indicate which statistical test you would select and why.

Stimulus Material: Once again you are serving as a consultant for that well-known drug firm in the East. The laboratory has refined a new medication that influences heart rate, but it still needs to test two forms of the drug (compound A and compound B). The laboratory director also needs information on dosage and wants to test the effects of a 5 ml. dose versus a 10 ml. dose. Four groups have been constituted by random assignment with 30 subjects in each. The criterion measure is heart rate per minute.

Review briefly what is involved.

1. How many experimental variables are indicated in this study and what is it or what are they?
2. Is the study independent, nonindependent, or mixed?
3. What type of data are being collected and what does this suggest relative to the selection of parametric versus nonparametric analyses?

4. What is the sample size and what does this suggest?

Now, what statistical test would you suggest and why? Review relevant chapter pages if you wish.

For feedback see page 409.

Simulations 14.10 and 14.11

Topic: Relationship between two measures

Background Statement: See background statement for Simulations 14.4, 14.5, and 14.6.

Tasks to Be Performed:

1. Review the following stimulus material.
2. Indicate which statistical analysis you would select and why.

Stimulus Material for Simulation 14.10: You have been asked to serve as a consultant for a major research firm in a large metropolitan area. One of the initial studies involves investigating the relationship between certain variables that are thought to be important. The project director has obtained height and weight measures on a random sample of 500 individuals residing in the area. You have been asked to suggest a correlational analysis that is appropriate for use in estimating the relationship between these measures. What analysis will you suggest and why? You may wish to review the relevant chapter pages.

For feedback see page 409.

Stimulus Material for Simulation 14.11: The Superintendent in your school district has been conducting some investigations on pupil achievement during the past year. She gathered preliminary data on a small sample of students last year ($N = 8$), particularly focusing on reading and mathematics. In this small study, she had the teacher rank each student in terms of performance in reading and math. She then correlated the ranks using the Spearman rank-order correlation. She wants to follow up this year with a much larger sample ($N = 50$), also using ranks, and has asked your advice. Initially she wants to know if she used the correct analysis last year, and secondly she wants to know whether the same analysis is appropriate with the larger sample that has been proposed. What is your advice and why? You may wish to review the relevant chapter pages.

For feedback see page 409.

Simulation Feedbacks

Simulation 14.1

The general category of nonparametric statistics would be appropriate for use in the study presented. The nonparametric choice is based on the type of data that are collected. The rating scale has been a recurring example of ordinal data throughout the text. Reference to Table 14.1 indicates that nonparametric analyses are the only possibility with such data. The sample size was certainly adequate for parametric statistics, but the previously mentioned type of data consideration will not permit parametric statistics use since the property of additivity is not present.

Simulation 14.2

The general category of parametric statistics can be appropriately selected for the study presented. This selection is appropriate because both the type of data and the sample size will permit such use. The data are at least interval (actually they are probably ratio), and the group size is more than ample.

Simulation 14.3

The general category of nonparametric statistics can be appropriately selected for this study. Nonparametrics are necessary because of the extremely small number of subjects. The data (frequency of upper-lid flutters) are at least interval and probably ratio, since there really could be zero occurrences. Therefore, although the data are strong enough for parametric analyses, the small sample requires nonparametrics.

Simulation 14.4

As noted on p. 376, two statistical tests are appropriate for situations such as that presented in the stimulus material, the *z test* and the *t test for differences between independent means*. The *z* test may be used since the samples are over 30, but the *t* test may also be used (in fact, the *t* test may be used for samples both above and below 30). Either test may be employed in the situation presented. The *t* test is more popular and is probably one of the most widely used statistical tests for such circumstances because it can be more flexible in terms of sample size.

Simulation 14.5

First run through the questions in the stimulus material.

1. You have information in the stimulus material that indicates two groups of 15 subjects each were formed. Consequently there is little reason to believe that the performances are not independent. It seems you have an independent comparison.

2. As you have noted throughout the text and previous simulations, a rating scale such as this is generally considered to be generating ordinal data. Reference to Table 14.1 indicates that nonparametric analyses should be used with ordinal data.

3. The sample size of 15 per group is not terribly relevant, since you must use nonparametrics with ordinal data. It may, however, influence your choice of a specific test within the nonparametric category.

As noted on p. 378, two statistical tests are appropriate for ordinal data comparing two independent data points, the *median test* and the *Mann-Whitney U test*. Either test will be appropriate, although the Mann-Whitney U test is perhaps the more popular with samples under 20.

Simulation 14.6

First run through the questions in the stimulus material.

1. The stimulus material indicates that one group of subjects will be evaluated before and after the pollution device is in operation. Essentially this is a pre-post study with data on the same subjects being gathered before and after the treatment is started. Thus this is a non-independent comparison.

2. The data involve counting sinus symptoms before and after treatment. As you will recall from Chapter 11, this type of data presents a somewhat uncertain situation but is usually treated as interval data if it is not clearly ordinal. For your purposes, assume interval data are present, which means parametric analyses may be used if the sample size is adequate.

3. The sample size noted is 100 subjects. This is more than adequate for using parametric statistics.

Reference to p. 379 indicates that the *t test for differences between nonindependent means* may be used in situations such as you have here. Reread this section to refresh your memory on this analysis. It is a popular test and appears frequently in the literature.

Simulation 14.7

Run through the questions in the stimulus material.

1. One experimental variable is involved in the study. As was noted in Chapter 4, exactly what it is labeled may vary in terms of wording, but it probably would be called something like "type of drug compound." So you have one experimental variable and three specific conditions under it (compounds A, B, and C).
2. The comparison is independent since three different groups of subjects were formed, one to receive each of the drug compounds.
3. The data can be considered to be interval data (in fact, temperature is one of the examples of interval measurement in the text). This suggests that parametric analyses may be considered if other requirements (e.g., sample size) are met.
4. The sample size noted is 20 subjects in each group which is generally considered adequate for parametric statistics.

Given the contingencies noted above, probably the most popular statistical test is the *one-way analysis of variance for comparing independent means.* Consequently the ANOVA will be used to determine whether there is a statistically significant difference in the mean temperature between the groups being treated with the different compounds.

Simulation 14.8

Run through the questions presented at the last of the stimulus material.

1. One experimental variable is involved. As before, the exact wording may vary, but it would probably be called something like "stage in weight loss program" (since you are dealing with assessment in three stages, pre-, mid-, and postprogram measures).
2. The comparison is a nonindependent design, since the same subjects are being assessed at three different times.
3. The data may be considered as ratio (weight is one of the examples of ratio data in Chapter 11). This suggests that parametric analyses may be considered if other requirements are met (e.g., sample size).
4. The sample size of 30 is generally considered adequate for parametric statistics.

Given the contingencies noted above, probably the most popular statistical test is the *analysis of variance for repeated measures.* The ANOVA will be used to determine whether there is a statistically significant difference in group mean weight between the preprogram, midprogram, and postprogram assessment points.

Simulation 14.9

Run through the questions in the stimulus material.

1. Two experimental variables are involved, type of drug (compound A compared with compound B) and dosage (5 ml. compared with 10 ml.).
2. The study is totally independent (both variables are independent comparisons) since four different groups of subjects were randomly constituted (one for compound A, 5 ml.dose; one for compound A, 10 ml.dose; one for compound B, 5 ml.dose; one for compound B, 10 ml.dose).
3. The data can at least be considered interval, perhaps ratio, in nature. This suggests that parametric analyses may be considered if other requirements are met.
4. The cell size of 30 per group is generally considered adequate for parametric statistics.

Given the contingencies noted above, probably the most popular statistical test is the *two-way analysis of variance for comparing independent means.* The two-way ANOVA is suggested because two experimental variables are involved in the study, and the data and sample are appropriate.

Simulation 14.10

Height and weight may both be considered to be at least interval data (in fact, they have been used as examples of ratio data). Reference to p. 395 indicates that when both measures to be correlated are either interval or ratio data, the *Pearson product-moment correlation* may be used. This is perhaps the most commonly known correlation technique and provides a stable estimate of relationship.

Simulation 14.11

Your first task is to somehow inform the Superintendent in a tactful manner that she probably used the incorrect analysis last year. Reference to p. 396 suggests that *Kendall's tau* is preferred for correlating ranks when a small sample is available (*N* less than 10). Once this delicate task is completed, you can compliment her on having foresight in anticipating this year's study. With samples greater than 10 the *Spearman rank-order correlation* is preferred for correlating ranks. If your advice is presented tactfully, you may even receive a merit increase in salary. Good luck!

Chapter **15**

Analyzing
Qualitative Data

We introduced qualitative principles of research design and methods of data collection in Chapter 7. The time-consuming nature of qualitative research should now be very apparent to you, along with its many advantages. Chapter 14 presented some commonly employed techniques for analyzing quantitative data. In this chapter, we turn to techniques the qualitative researcher uses to accomplish the same goals using data recorded as language rather than numbers. From the outset we should mention that computer software packages for analyzing qualitative data are becoming increasingly available and effective. As is the case with quantitative analyses, these software packages are designed for use primarily on desktop and laptop computers which now have ample power to perform the analyses. We do not make specific software recommendations here because titles are upgraded and change so frequently.

Qualitative data are collected over time in the form of systematic field notes, interview notes and transcripts, researcher journals and reflections, and archival records. These data can then be conceptually organized, beginning with preliminary pattern identification while still in the field (Carspecken & Apple, 1992; Patton, 1990). Qualitative data require careful analyses that employ much the same logic of pattern finding and pattern matching that dominates quantitative methods, in order to reveal patterns and principles that distinguish the social phenomenon under study. In Chapter 7, we emphasized that qualitative methods require rigorous inquiry on which consumers of the research can rely when drawing conclusions. The design and data collection principles we introduced provide the foundation for the inquiry, but, like the raw numbers recorded in a computer data file, they have no inherent knowledge value until they have been carefully analyzed. Many beginning researchers using qualitative methods underestimate the discipline and hard work necessary to turn interesting data into qualitative research through analysis. Collecting data in the field is often fascinating, even fun; analyzing the data systematically once the researcher has left the field is time-consuming and sometimes tedious, particularly if done manually. The rule of thumb that qualitative researchers often use to plan the time they need to complete a qualitative research project is "Time in the field equals time in analysis." In this chapter, we introduce the techniques that qualitative researchers use to complete this analysis.

First, we describe a few of the techniques that qualitative researchers use to organize data while still in the field. These techniques help qualitative researchers maximize the quality and appropriateness of subjects chosen for interviews, the observation sampling, and the search for archival data. Later and in greater detail, we discuss the variety of techniques employed to systematically analyze qualitative data once the researchers have left the field. These techniques distinguish the findings of well-designed and executed qualitative research from the insights provided by testimonials and stories. Each has its place and contributions to make. Unlike Nisbett and Ross (1980), we do not blanch with horror at the audacity of the novelist who takes up pen (or keyboard) to render insight into the human condition. Like them, we advise the committed qualitative researcher to seek patterns and themes in social life and not to commit the error of portraying unique circumstances as though they represent society and human behavior in general. But we remind the beginning researcher that qualitative researchers fall along the entire epistemological continuum from phenomenologist to positivist, and the scholarship they produce as a result of their inquiry methods may resemble the novelist's or the statistician's.

Preliminary Analysis

Preliminary field analyses can reveal possible patterns in the data that require additional data, broader sampling, or a search for new informants. Consequently, unlike the design, data collection, and data analysis steps carefully and sequentially followed in rigorous quantitative research, qualitative researchers engage in simultaneous and iterative processes of analysis *while still in the field* in order to point them toward important sources and types of data that they could not have predicted in the design phase of the study. A few techniques that assist in this process are: (1) team meetings of multiple researchers (or data sharing with other experienced researchers), (2) field note summaries, (3) data summary sheets, and (4) document directories.

Team Meetings

If a group of researchers is working on a project at the same time, meetings to discuss issues arising in the field and patterns the researchers are beginning to see provide a useful way to enhance the quality of the data gathering process. By comparing notes about their experiences and preliminary data, researchers can uncover new sources of data, learn about potential interview subjects, check the consistency of information being acquired by different interviewers or observers, assure the maximum consistency and breadth of archival data, and take advantage of the insights of other researchers.

If a qualitative researcher is working in the field alone, preliminary data should be shared with experienced qualitative researchers not in the field for reactions and suggestions. This step in the research process is not an odious burden on the outside scholar, and it assures the field researcher that the insights and questions of someone somewhat removed from the immediacy of the field will enhance the quality of the data-gathering process. The critic can point out places in an interview where a follow-up question was warranted, ask about relationships apparent in the data, and query the researcher about procedure decisions being made. An outsider's point of view on the data-gathering process is invaluable to the solo qualitative researcher.

Data Summaries

Ultimately, the form in which data are recorded and summarized in the field is a matter of personal preference and experience. It depends on the type of research, the focus of inquiry, and the preferences of the researcher. Many experienced qualitative researchers provide examples useful to the beginning researcher. Miles and Huberman (1994) illustrate numerous techniques for maximizing the benefits of preliminary analyses with multiple researchers while still in the field. Boxes 15.1, 15.2, and 15.3 are examples of data display options researchers can use as data begin to accumulate.

Yin (1989) also provides some examples that beginning qualitative researchers can adopt and adapt to their own particular research projects (see Boxes 15.4 and 15.5). You should practice using a variety of these summary format techniques so that you are skilled in managing your data *before* you move into the field for an extended qualitative research project. Individual researchers also can use these data display options to query their own data, seek new data sources, and point their data gathering in productive directions. Provisional counts of data points that reveal emerging themes can provide insight into issues around which interviews, instruments, or additional observation plans should be organized. New informants can be identified, new document sources found. And some inferences can begin to be developed on the basis of

BOX 15.1 Contact Summary Form: Illustration with Coded Themes (excerpt)

Contact Summary

Type of: Mtg. ___Principals___   ___Ken's office___   ___4/2/76___   Site ___Westgate___

contact: who, what group   place

        Phone _____   _____ _____   Coder ___MM___

              With whom, by whom   place

                                                             Date

        Inf. Int. _____   _____ _____   coded ___4/18/76___

              With whom, by whom   place

1. Pick out the most salient points in the contact. Number in order on this sheet and note page number on which point appears. Number point in text of write-up. Attach theme or aspect to each point in CAPITALS. Invent themes where no existing ones apply and asterisk those. Comment may also be included in double parentheses.

Page	*Salient Points*	THEMES/ASPECTS
1	1. Staff decisions have to be made by April 30.	STAFF
2	2. Teachers will have to go out of their present grade-level assignment when they transfer.	STAFF/RESOURCE MGMT.
2	3. Teachers vary in their willingness to integrate special ed kids into their classrooms—some teachers are "a pain in the elbow."	*RESISTANCE
2	4. Ken points out that tentative teacher assignment lists got leaked from the previous meeting (implicitly deplores this).	INTERNAL COMMUNIC.
2	5. Ken says, "Teachers act as if they had the right to decide who should be transferred." (would make outcry)	POWER DISTRIB.
2	6. Tacit/explicit decision: "It's our decision to make." (voiced by Ken, agreed by Ed)	POWER DISTRIB/ CONFLICT MGMT.
2	7. Principals and Ken, John, and Walter agree that Ms. Epstein is a "bitch."	*STEREOTYPING
2	8. Ken decides not to tell teachers ahead of time (now) about transfers ("because then we'd have a fait accompli").	PLAN FOR PLANNING/ TIME MGTM.

Source: Miles, M. B., & Huberman, A. M., *Qualitative Data Analysis* (2nd ed.), p. 54, Copyright © 1994 by Sage Publications, Thousand Oaks, CA. Reprinted by permission of Sage Publications, Inc.

BOX 15.2   Document Summary Form: Illustration

Document Form

Name or description of document: The Buffalo (weekly sheet)	Site: Carson
	Document: 2
Event or contact, if any, with which document is associated: Paul's explanation of the admin. team's functioning	Date received or picked up: Feb. 13
Significance or importance of document: Gives schedule for all events in the district for the week.	Date: Feb. 13

Enables coordination, knits two schools together.

Brief summary of contents:
Schedule of everything from freshman girls'
basketball to "Secret Pals Week" in the
elementary school.

Also includes "Did you know" items on the IPA
program (apparently integrating the IPA News).

And a description of how admin. team works
who is on team, what regular meetings deal with,
gives working philosophy (e.g., "we establish
personal goals and monitor progress" . . . "We
coordinate effort, K-12, and all programs" . . .
"We agree on staff selection"). Concluding
comment: "It is our system of personnel
management."

Also alludes to the 26 OPERATIONAL GUIDELINES
(Document 16)

((I'll guess that the admin. explanation does not appear
every week—need to check this.))

IF DOCUMENT IS CENTRAL OR CRUCIAL TO A PARTICULAR CONTACT
(e.g., a meeting agenda, newspaper clipping discussed in an interview),
make a copy and include with write-up. Otherwise, put in document file.

Source: Miles, M. B., & Huberman, A. M., *Qualitative Data Analysis* (2nd ed.), p. 55, copyright © 1994 by Sage Publications, Thousand Oaks, CA. Reprinted by permission of Sage Publications, Inc.

BOX 15.3   Illustration of a Start List of Codes

INNOVATION PROPERTIES		IP-OBJ	3.1
IP:	OBJECTIVES	IP-ORG/DD, LS	3.1.1
IP:	IMPLIED CHANGES—CLASSROOM	IP-CH/CL	3.1.4
IP:	IMPLIED CHANGES—ORGANIZATION	IP-CH/ORG	3.1.5
IP:	USERS SALIENCE	IP-SALIENCE	3.1.2
IP:	(INITIAL) USER ASSESSMENT	IP-SIZUP/PRE, DUR	3.1.3, 3.4, 3.5
IP:	PROGRAM DEVELOPMENT (IV-C)	IP-DEV	3.1.1, 3.3.3, 3.3.4

EXTERNAL CONTEXT		EC (PRE) (DUR)	3.2, 3.3, 3.4
EC:	DEMOGRAPHICS	EC-DEM	
	In county, school personnel	ECCO-DEM	3.2.3, 3.3, 3.4
	Out county, nonschool personnel	ECEXT-DEM	3.3.3, 3.3, 3.4
EC:	ENDORSEMENT	EC-END	3.2.3, 3.3, 3.4
	In county, school personnel	ECCO-END	3.2.3, 3.3, 3.4
	Out county, nonschool personnel	ECEXT-END	3.2.3, 3.3, 3.4
EC:	CLIMATE	EC-CLIM	3.2.3, 3.3, 3.4
	In county, school personnel	ECCO-CLIM	3.2.3, 3.3, 3.4
	Out county, nonschool personnel	ECEXT-CLIM	3.2.3, 3.3, 3.4

INTERNAL CONTEXT		IC (PRE) (DUR)	3.2, 3.3, 3.4
IC:	CHARACTERISTICS	IC-CHAR	3.2.2, 3.4, 3.5
IC:	NORMS AND AUTHORITY	IC-NORM	3.2.2, 3.4.3, 3.5
IC:	INNOVATION HISTORY	IC-HIST	3.2.1
IC:	ORGANIZATION PROCEDURES	IC-PROC	3.1.1, 3.2.4, 3.3, 3.4
IC:	INNOVATION-ORGANIZATION CONGRUENCE	IC-FIT	3.2.2

ADOPTION PROCESS		AP	3.2, 3.3
AP:	EVENT CHRONOLOGY—OFFICIAL VERSION	AP-CHRON/PUB	3.2.4, 3.3.1
AP:	EVENT CHRONOLOGY—SUBTERRANEAN	AP-CHRON/PRIV	3.2.4, 3.3.1
AP:	INSIDE/OUTSIDE	AP-IN/OUT	3.2.5
AP:	CENTRALITY	AP-CENT	3.2.2
AP:	MOTIVES	AP-MOT	3.2.6
AP:	USER FIT	AP-FIT	3.2.7
AP:	PLAN	AP-PLAN	3.3.3
AP:	READINESS	AP-REDI	3.3.4, 3.2.1
AP:	CRITICAL EVENTS	AP-CRIT	3.3.1

SITE DYNAMICS AND TRANSFORMATIONS		TR	3.4
TR:	EVENT CHRONOLOGY—OFFICIAL VERSION	TR-CHRON/PUB	3.4.1, 3.4.2, 3.4.3
TR:	EVENT CHRONOLOGY—SUBTERRANEAN	TR-CHRON/PRIV	3.4.1, 3.4.2, 3.4.3
TR:	INITIAL USER EXPERIENCE	TR-START	3.4.1, 3.4.2, 3.4.3
TR:	CHANGES IN INNOVATION	TR-INMOD	3.4.1
TR:	EFFECTS ON ORGANIZATIONAL PRACTICES	TR-ORG/PRAC	3.4.3
TR:	EFFECTS ON ORGANIZATIONAL CLIMATE	TR/ORG/CLIM	3.4.3
TR:	EFFECTS ON CLASSROOM PRACTICE	TR-CLASS	3.4.2
TR:	EFFECTS ON USER CONSTRUCTS	TR-HEAD	3.4.2, 3.4.3
TR:	IMPLEMENTATION PROBLEMS	TR-PROBS	3.4.1
TR:	CRITICAL EVENTS	TR-CRIT	3.4.1, 3.4.2, 3.4.3
TR:	EXTERNAL INTERVENTIONS	TR-EXT	3.4.3
TR:	EXPLANATIONS FOR TRANSFORMATIONS	TR-SIZUP	3.4.1, 3.4.2, 3.4.3
TR:	PROGRAM PROBLEM SOLVING	TR-PLAN	3.4.1, 4.4.2, 3.4.3

(continued)

BOX 15.3 *(continued)*

NEW CONFIGURATION AND ULTIMATE OUTCOMES	NCO	3.5
NCO: STABILIZATION OF INNOVATION—CLASSROOM	NCO-INNOSTAB/CLASS	3.5.1
NCO: STABILIZATION OF USER BEHAVIOR	NCO-STAB/USER	3.5.2
NCO: USER FIRST-LEVEL OUTCOMES	NCO-USER IOC	3.5.4
Positive and negative	NCO-USER IOC/+, -	
Anticipated and unanticipated	NCO-USER IOC/A, U	
Combinations (when appropriate)	NCO-USER IOC/A+, A-	
	U+, U-	
NCO: USER META OUTCOMES	NCO-USER META	
Positive and negative	NCO-USER META OC/+, -	
Anticipated and unanticipated	NCO-USER META OC/A, U	
Combinations (when appropriate)	NCO-USER META OC/A+, A-	
	U+, U-	
NCO: USER SPINOFFS AND SIDE EFFECTS	NCO-USER SIDE	3.5.5 (3.5.2)
Positive and negative	NCO-USER SIDE OC/+, -	
Anticipated and unanticipated	NCO-USER SIDE OC/A, U	
Combinations (when appropriate)	NCO-USER SIDE OC/A+, A-	
	U+, U-	
NCO: CLASSROOM INSTITUTIONALIZATION	NCO-INST/CLASS	3.5.5
NCO: STABILIZATION OF INNOVATION—ORGANIZATION	NCO-INNOSTAB/ORG	3.5.6
NCO: STABILIZATION OF ORGANIZATIONAL BEHAVIOR	NCO-STAB/ORG	3.5.7
NCO: ORGANIZATIONAL INSTITUTIONALIZATION	NCO-INST/ORG	3.5.8
NCO: ORGANIZATIONAL FIRST-LEVEL OUTCOMES	NCO-ORG IOC	3.5.9
Positive and negative	NCO-ORG IOC/+, -	
Anticipated and unanticipated	NCO-ORG IOC/A, U	
Combinations (when appropriate)	NCO-ORG IOC/A+, A-	
	U+, U-	
NCO: ORGANIZATIONAL META OUTCOMES	NCO-ORG META	3.5.9
Positive and negative	NCO-ORG SIDE OC/+, -	
Anticipated and unanticipated	NCO-ORG META OC/A, U	
Combinations (when appropriate)	NCO-ORG META OC/A+, A-	
	U+, U-	
NCO: ORGANIZATIONAL SPINOFFS AND SIDE EFFECTS	NCO-ORG SIDE	3.5.9 (3.5.7)
Positive and negative	NCO-ORG SIDE OC/+, -	
Anticipated and unanticipated	NCO-ORG SIDE OC/A+, A-	
Combinations (when appropriate)	U+, U-	
NCO: INSTITUTIONAL EXPANSION	NCO-INNOGRO/ORG	3.5.8
NCO: ORGANIZATIONAL REDUCTION	NCO-INNODWIN/org	3.5.8

EXTERNAL AND INTERNAL ASSISTANCE (SEPARATE CODES FOR EXTERNAL, PEER, ADMINISTRATIVE)

ASS:	LOCATION	AS-LOC	3.6.1
ASS:	RULES, NORMS	ASS-RULE	3.6.1
ASS:	ORIENTATION	ASS-ORI	3.6.2
ASS:	TYPE	ASS-TYPE	3.6.3
ASS:	EFFECTS	ASS-EFF	3.6.4
ASS:	ASSESSMENT BY RECIPIENTS	ASS-ASS	3.6.5
ASS:	LINKAGE	ASS-LINK	3.6.6

EMERGING CAUSAL LINKS		CL	
CL:	NETWORKS	CL-NET	N.A.
CL:	RULES	CL-RULE	N.A.
CL:	RECURRENT PATTERNS	CL-PATT	N.A.
	Within site	CL-PATT/LS	N.A.
	Intersite	CL-PATT/OS	N.A.
CL:	EXPLANATORY CLUSTER (researcher)	CL-EXPL	N.A.
	(respondent)	SITECL-EXPL	N.A.

QUERIES		QU	
QU:	SURPRISES	QU-!	N.A.
QU:	PUZZLES	QU-Q	N.A.

Source: Miles, M. B., & Huberman, A. M., *Qualitative Data Analysis* (2nd ed.), pp. 59–60, copyright © 1994 by Sage Publications, Thousand Oaks, CA. Reprinted by permission of Sage Publications, Inc.

preliminary patterns in the data. Qualitative researchers must become expert at maximizing serendipity.

Qualitative researchers also must be sensitive to normative expectations in the setting—what is expected of the members of the group by other members of the group. This is why the researcher-reflections section of systematic field notes is so important. It provides a record of the thinking and beliefs of the field researcher at each stage of the research. Subjective judgments made by the researcher can unfairly bias attitudes toward normative expectations and lead to premature and inaccurate preliminary conclusions. Eventually, patterns in the data may emerge as system-wide relationships that can be reconstructed through the data. However, prudent qualitative researchers treat all cautiously preliminary findings developed while still in the field and in relation to their own thinking at the time the data were recorded or obtained. Preliminary patterns provide insight into promising sources and types of data, but they should not be treated as *findings* until data are re-analyzed from the distance of time and place after the researcher leaves the setting. (See Chapter 7 for a discussion of the impact of time away from the setting on the reliability and validity of findings.)

BOX 15.4 Relevant Situations for Different Research Strategies

Strategy	Form of Research Question	Requires Control Over Behavioral Events?	Focuses on Contemporary Events?
Experiment	how, why	yes	yes
Survey	who, what,* where how many, how much	no	yes
Archival analysis (e.g., economic study)	who, what,* where how many, how much	no	yes/no
History	how, why	no	no
Case study	how, why	no	yes

* "What" questions, when asked as part of an exploratory study, pertain to all five strategies?

Source: Yin, R. K., *Case Study Research: Design and Methods* (rev. ed.), p. 17, copyright © 1989 by Sage Publications, Newbury Park, CA. Reprinted by permission of Sage Publications, Inc.

BOX 15.5

Protocol Question

B. How is the Title I program organized, who is employed by Title I, when are decisions made, and who makes them?

Sources of Data:

___ Title I director

___ Assistant Superintendent for Compensatory Education

___ Organization chart

___ Job descriptions

Sample Strategies:

___ Obtain or draw an organizational chart that shows the location of the Title I office.

___ List the type and number of instructional and noninstructional Title I personnel (including Title I specialists, coordinators, managers).

___ To whom does the Title I director report?

___ Who reports to the Title I director?

___ Whom does the Title I director supervise?

What kinds of decisions does the director have to formally sign off and with whom?

___ Create an organizational chart of the Title I program (if one doesn't exist) that shows the directors and any intermediaries (either in schools or in the Title I office) and their relations to principals, regular teachers, and Title I teachers.

___ Fill in the following table by ranking the order in which the following decisions and events occur.

BOX 15.5 *(continued)*

	Order	Month Completed in Calendar 1981	Month Completed in Calendar 1980	Title I People Involved in Decisions
Determining Title I budget				
Hiring or firing of Title I staff				
Assigning staff to schools				
Purchasing of materials and equipment				
Deciding subjects and grades				
Testing students				
Selecting students				
Selecting schools				
Evaluating school programs				
Preparation and submission of application				

Source: Yin, R. K., *Case Study Research: Designs and Methods* (rev. ed.), pp. 76-77, copyright © 1989 by Sage Publications, Newbury Park, CA. Reprinted by permission of Sage Publications, Inc.

Post Data-Gathering Analysis

When the data-gathering stage of qualitative research ends, a researcher must leave the setting in order to achieve an intellectual and emotional distance from the people, place, and events studied. This need to remove oneself from the field even applies to field biologists who study animal behavior and need to remove themselves from the attachment they come to feel for their subjects (see for example, *Elephant Dreams* or Diane Fossey's work). Having left the field, the qualitative researcher can concentrate on the analytical techniques that will help enable the progression from data gathering toward the scholarship that reports the findings to consumers of this research. We will discuss only a few of these techniques in detail and recommend that the beginning researcher take special pains to become acquainted with the many options available. Analytical techniques consistent with more positivistic views of qualitative research include coding and counting, data summary sheets, matrices, charts, graphs, and tables. Techniques more consistent with phenomenological approaches to qualitative research include such things as thick description and criticism. Later in the chapter, we turn to the scholarly writing traditions that flow from these various types of data analysis.

Coding and Counting

At the beginning of this chapter, we reminded you about the phenomenological/positivist continuum along which researchers view the nature of social reality. Unlike quantitative research, which is planted firmly within the positivist perspective, qualitative research can vary along the full continuum—adopting views of knowledge that are totally subjective and phenomenological or totally objective and positivist. One of the authors' fellow researchers, a firmly entrenched quantitative positivist, likes to call her research "soft-headed positivism," because it falls outside the phenomenological traditions of anthropology. Methodological biases aside, however, the data display and analysis techniques chosen by the researcher do reveal very different assumptions about the kind of conclusions that can be drawn from qualitative data, the demands of rigorous analysis, and the systematic ways in which researchers can explore, explain, describe, and illustrate qualitative data and findings. Data display techniques such as those illustrated in Boxes 15.1 to 15.5 provide systematic processes for distilling data during analysis and draw on more positivist assumptions about qualitative research. These include such things as data coding, analytical matrices, and formal pattern matching that allow for data audits by other researchers through which the logic of analysis can be retraced and understood. They provide a qualitative analog for the statistical techniques discussed in Chapter 14. They also allow the analysis to reveal frequencies, intervals, intensity, and kinds of behaviors and can themselves be counted, allowing quantitative approaches to qualitative data. Before data can be recorded in matrices, charts, and tables, however, they must be distilled from language and text into abstract categories. Techniques of presentation and data analysis such as thick description, discourse analysis (Gee, Michaels & O'Connor, 1992), criticism (Eisner, 1993), classical (Dobbert & Kurth-Schai, 1992), and critical ethnography (Quantz, 1992) rely on phenomenological assumptions about the nature of social reality.

One of the first tasks a qualitative researcher working in the more positivistic tradition of qualitative research faces is to distill words into increasingly abstract conceptual categories or themes (Yin, 1991). These themes begin to emerge during preliminary analysis in the field. Through repeated and careful iterations, abstract concepts emerge that can be coded in the text and then displayed in any number of configurations as the researcher gradually understands the social behavioral implications of the findings (see Box 15.1).

Increasingly, computer programs are being used to organize text by codes and themes. These methods provide parsimonious and flexible alternatives to the reams of paper with which qualitative researchers work. Text that illustrates or represents a concept can be blocked and coded in the text and then the codes can be used by the researcher to assemble the data for further analysis and for writing the research report. For example, the responses from 100 interviews either transcribed into a text file or recorded as systematic field notes in a text file can be grouped by date, role of the respondent (e.g., teacher, parent, special educator, principal), interviewer, or any other general category. The same interviews also can be quickly reorganized by setting (school), level (elementary, middle, high school), environment (urban, socioeconomic, suburban, rural) or any other category. Once text has been carefully read and coded, it can be reorganized by theme or code. For example, the researcher can prepare a text file of all blocks of text coded as an example of concepts such as competitiveness, frustration, persistence or any other conceptual category represented in the data along with identifying information about the source. These processes can also be done with hard copies of text and have traditionally been done this way.

Various tables, charts, figures, and matrices can then be made using these distilled data. Patterns and relationships emerge from this process in vivid and visual ways that provide additional insight in the analysis. Miles and Huberman (1994) provide many useful examples of ways in which qualitative data can be displayed to enhance the reliability of the analytical process that can be used by beginning researchers as models.

These coding processes, whether accomplished on paper or using technological aids, provide a very important audit trail of the logic employed by the researcher during analysis. You will recall in Chapter 7 that we talked about ways in which the reliability of qualitative research can be enhanced. A *data audit* by another researcher (either part of the team or a colleague not involved in the research) can then test the logic of the analysis. Comparable data displays and presentations can also be used to compare one research setting with another, prepare case studies, or complete any number of analytical tasks. A qualitative researcher must be able to show how conclusions are drawn from the data as part of the analytical process in order for the consumers of the research to have confidence in the findings (Miles & Huberman, 1994; Patton, 1990).

As analytical codes are developed that represent central concepts emerging from the data, qualitative researchers can count the frequency with which these themes or issues appear, to develop a sense of the intensity, relative frequency, or distribution of concepts. Depending on the relative "objective" or "subjective" paradigm from which the researcher approaches the task, these analytical techniques can become increasingly quantitative in nature (Miles & Huberman, 1994). When multiple researchers are involved (one way of protecting the reliability of the research), they can do parallel analyses of the same raw data, compare their coding judgments, and discuss the emerging conceptual themes until they agree.

Regardless of the relativist/objectivist paradigm applied to the analysis, the record of the analysis should be as systematic as the records kept of raw data. This analytical trail provides a conceptual chain of logic that a peer or colleague can use to conduct a coding and analytical audit of the research. While no two scholars will reach exactly the same conclusions from any single data set, colleagues with equal or greater expertise should be able to follow the data/analysis/conclusion logic backward to understand how the researcher reached her or his conclusions. This process is a critical component of qualitative research and mimics the replicability process in quantitative, statistical analyses in its contribution to research rigor.

Data Summary Sheets

As we pointed out earlier, researchers use a variety of techniques to help organize their data into manageable forms while still in the field. After leaving the field, the need to organize the data becomes even more critical. As with data analysis in the field, data summary sheets are commonly used to summarize such things as findings from observation days, types of events, data related to a particular individual, or emerging themes. These arrangements can be set up by time, setting, type of subject, or individual. Thematic summaries of research on schools might include conversations between key leaders of groups in a school, criticisms about a discipline program shared with the secretaries by the teachers across time and by teacher, information about students referred to the assistant principal by teachers for disciplinary action, or previous action taken. Matrices, graphs, and charts can also help the qualitative researcher make sense of data.

Matrices

Once coding and counting are completed and summary sheets constructed, comparisons among variables, factors, or emerging themes are facilitated by the use of other data displays and analysis. Matrices constructed to promote such comparisons provide one such technique.

A matrix lays out one factor in relation to another providing for data cells across two factors. For example, a researcher investigating the disruptive behavior of special needs children in school might collect data observation data on a dozen children throughout the school day over a period of several weeks. After summaries of disruptive behavior are collected, a matrix that lays out the twelve subjects on one axis across the school day on another axis, with numbers of disruptive behaviors in the cells, provides one look at the children's lives in school. Another might compare children by teacher (if they move to different teachers during the day) and reveal the number of disruptive behaviors occurring under each teacher's supervision. Yet another might show types of behaviors recorded compared with settings in which the children spend the day (classrooms, physical education or recess, lunch, between classes, before and after school). The focus of the research and types of data emerging from the study would drive the choice of factors along which matrices could be built.

Graphs and Charts

Data points or matrix cell totals developed also can be displayed as graphs and charts that visually represent the findings emerging from analysis. Qualitative researchers interested in developing a sense of time or movement or in comparing cases, settings, groups, or individuals often use graphs and charts to explore differences and similarities. The crying patterns of 10 infants with colic by intensity over time laid out on a graph, for example, quickly and vividly portray the similarities and idiosyncrasies of various infants. Parents or caregivers provide another source of information. You probably can think of many other possible combinations of data that would reveal important information.

Pattern Matching

All the analytical techniques illustrated above provide ways for the researcher to compare and match patterns among abstract concepts emerging from qualitative data. This step is an important one, because it lays a foundation for trustworthy statements about the phenomenon under study. For example, a nonresearcher observing a daycare center when dropping off or picking up a child might say that the children seem to cry a lot. A researcher would observe the daycare center for many days, deliberately sampling observations over all times of the day and making sure to observe the children interacting with all their caregivers and with their parents. Crying patterns would constitute the focus of only one of many factors observed, and the researcher would then approach the analysis by child, by time of day, by caregiver, by age of child, and so forth. A statement might then be made that Eric cries for five minutes whenever his father leaves him at the daycare center or that two- to three-year-olds cry for half the time that eight-month-olds cry when their parents leave them. You can probably think of many matrices, charts, and graphs that a researcher interested in daycare might produce to understand children's and their parents' behaviors. Comparisons with children whose primary care takes place in their homes would then be warranted, as well, before general statements about children could be made. (Remember the call for research in the natural setting by Jerome Kagan discussed in Chapter 7.)

Inductive and Deductive Analyses

Inductive

The analytical methods described in the preceding discussion allow for a completely inductive method of analysis. Concepts, patterns, and themes emerge from the iterative logic employed by the researcher. The more naturalistic the inquiry (Lincoln & Guba, 1985), the more the researcher seeks to guard against any preconceptions or beliefs on the part of the researcher or any existing social theory to prebias the research. As we pointed out in Chapter 7, this even prevents the interviewer from tightly constructing the interview guide, because questions tend to direct the respondents' attention and attitudes in directions suggested by the researcher. What well-grounded quantitative researchers call theoretically based research, naturalistic researchers might call "preconceptions." However, qualitative research also can be designed to test social theories in natural settings characterized by the features we discussed in Chapter 7 (natural settings, small sample size, phenomena that cannot be manipulated). This type of research relies on a more deductive approach in which naturalistic data are analyzed using factors or variables from a social theory.

Deductive

Deductive qualitative research takes several forms. First, systematically collected data using naturalistic methods and very open-ended techniques can be analyzed using codes and variables from existing theory. The coding and counting techniques, data display, and data reduction methods described above then can be employed to test hypotheses or theoretical fit. Findings may confirm or disconfirm theory, but the test is in the form of language and text rather than probability (see Chapter 14).

Another way in which more deductive methods come into play in qualitative research relates to the research design prior to data gathering. A social theory may drive the original impetus for research, and the theory may include a strong conceptual framework proposing relationships and predicting outcomes. When this is the case, the researcher may design a more focused interview protocol deliberately designed to elicit responses along a particular vein. Observation sampling and archival research also would be directly related to the theory.

Two dangers face the qualitative researcher employing deductive methods. First, a too-directive interview or too-narrow observation schedule may fail and focus the research to a degree as to guarantee the affirmation of the theory or framework. We warned in Chapter 7 about "leading the witness" during an interview. In a deductive study, the researcher must take care not to "lead the research," resulting in self-fulfilling prophecy. This is true whether the data set is collected specifically for the study or whether an existing data set is used employing a post hoc analysis.

Second, important, even vital, information more relevant to a particular research setting may be missed entirely or misinterpreted. This is why it is so important that qualitative researchers seek out informants known to oppose a prevalent view, check emerging findings with participants to see if they are capturing the emic point of view accurately, and share their analysis and the logic of their data reduction with outside researchers or through a data audit. In Chapter 14, we noted that sophisticated statistical techniques applied to bad data produce the old "garbage in, garbage out" outcome. The same holds true during qualitative data analysis, but the danger holds for both bad data and bad analysis.

Phenomenological Analytical Techniques

The analytical techniques discussed so far tap into systematic traditions within the social sciences rather than into more literary traditions. Qualitative scholarship such as discourse analysis, critical theory, and criticism tap philosophical and artistic traditions. While space does not allow for an extensive description of these more phenomenological traditions, they differ substantially enough from analyses described previously to warrant some explication. We strongly urge those interested in these traditions to give rigorous study to the variety of intellectual traditions that inspire high quality phenomenological inquiry. For our discussion here, we rely on two of the most common in education and social science research—thick description and criticism. (See LeCompte et al., 1992 for a good review of phenomenological approaches to qualitative inquiry.)

Thick Description

Vividness and saliency contribute to readers' enjoyment of well-written journalism. While these characteristics do not make journalism into research, they illustrate the power of so-called thick description in the conduct of qualitative inquiry. Thick description places the consumer of qualitative research personally and vividly in the setting the researcher observed, through the use of prose. Like a gifted novelist describing a scene, the qualitative researcher writes prose that creates vivid sensual images of the setting and behaviors being observed. The sights, smells, and feelings of the social setting come alive for the reader. At the same time, the qualitative researcher must be sparse and accurate, avoiding purple prose that exaggerates and elaborates in the search for richness.

Description that meets both of these criteria—accurate and vivid—often is called thick description. It takes a great deal of talent and practice to be able to create for the reader the sense of being there with the researcher while resisting the temptation to embellish. Beginning researchers seeking to hone their observation and description skills often spend long hours sitting quietly, observing, and writing, much as art students spend long hours copying masterworks of art. When several students of qualitative inquiry describe the same setting and then critique one another's work, they develop a strong sense of the advantages and drawbacks of qualitative research. The vividness and salience that make thick description and the scholarship based on it compelling reading also place tremendous responsibility on the researcher. Up front, the point of view shapes the outcome.

This interdependence between point of view and findings exists in quantitative research as well. In Chapter 14 and in previous chapters, we emphasized that researchers must clearly acknowledge the assumptions on which their inquiry is based. In Chapter 14 particularly, we discussed the impact of the assumptions on which statistical techniques rely on research design and the critical dependence of the outcomes of analysis on respect for and adherence to these assumptions on the part of the researcher. In quantitative and qualitative scholarship, the researcher is responsible for stating clearly and directly what his or her assumptions and points of view are. The consumer of the research then can make informed judgments about how best to interpret and use the research.

Criticism

Another commonly used method of data gathering and analysis in qualitative research is criticism. While criticism relies on the same kinds of writing skills as thick description, it openly adds preferences, likes, and dislikes to the process. Elliot Eisner (1985, 1991, 1993) is among those who have applied criticism to social and educational research by promoting the application of processes of artistic criticism to observational research. This perspective relies on the analog of researcher as artistic critic (in the best sense). The observer describes while conveying personal taste and preference, even judgment, to the reader. Eisner called this process "rendering the ineffable", a way of combining art and science in social inquiry. The accomplished educational critic thus is able to capture by these methods the art and craft of teaching along with the science.

Criticism is firmly established in other traditions of social inquiry as well. Critical theorists take an openly hostile perspective on the heuristics, assumptions, and outcomes of traditional social sciences, and this point of view becomes a part of their methods and findings. More specifically, twentieth century critical theorists apply the methods of Marx and an anticapitalist perspective to the collection, analysis, and presentation of social science inquiry, arguing that purely positivist traditions carry an equally slanted bias toward western thought and science. (See Chapter 1 for a discussion of the roots of the social sciences.) These same criticisms of traditional methodologies are leveled by feminist theorists and others such as Afro-centrist scholars who rely on discourse analysis to illustrate how our very language biases the outcomes of our research and the implications of our findings.

The critical traditions in qualitative research are varied and complex. Before turning to the ways in which this scholarship is written and presented to consumers, we must emphasize that each new researcher must seek a scholarly tradition that coincides with his or her epistemological view—what is the nature of knowledge, how is it best obtained, how is knowledge conveyed to others? Self-knowledge will help facilitate this search.

Reporting Qualitative Research

The final test of qualitative research must lie in its ability to convey meaning and expand understanding while contributing to theory development and knowledge. Ultimately, the reader must be convinced, when reading the researcher's accurate description of methods and procedures, the report of findings, and the analysis and discussion, that the research conveys reliable and valid information about the situation under study and expands the reader's understanding of social and cultural experiences.

All three major methods for gathering qualitative data—interview, observation, and archival research—are used by qualitative researchers, regardless of the perspective they take during analysis and writing. Once the qualitative researcher leaves the field and switches roles to analyst, scholar, and writer, different research methods dramatically shape the nature of the study that emerges. The writer taking a totally phenomenological approach may write an extensive ethnography. Another scholar may employ the coding and counting methods described earlier that rely on searches for patterns and accept a more rationalistic view of qualitative research. Many traditional and emerging approaches to analyzing and reporting qualitative research exist. We limit our illustrations to three formats that are common in qualitative studies in education and social science research—ethnography, case study, and criticism.

Ethnography

Ethnography is the in-depth study of the culture of a particular group of people that results in a research report in the form of an ethnographic narrative. "Ethnography... is field study plus something special in the nature of interpretive emphasis" (Wolcott, 1992, p. 21). The ethnographer seeks to describe this culture and convey the patterned way of life, beliefs and ideologies, formal and informal interrelationships, and way of life represented by technology, architecture, art, literature (or stories), and other traditions that make up the culture, in a way that makes the ethnographer's interpretations credible and assures the reader that the ethnographer approached the study "without a lot of preconceptions about what she could expect to find" (Lancy, 1993, p. 36). This requires "direct, prolonged, on-the-spot observation". While the role of the ethnographer varies from site to site, a "sense of what is appropriate and of what will probably work can be conveyed by training" and "well-developed sensitivities about social interaction, self-other relations, and obtrusiveness" (Spinder & Spindler, 1992, p. 63, p. 64).

Good ethnography requires extended, meticulous, and perceptive data gathering and careful analysis. Many inexperienced researchers unsure of their statistical skills sometimes choose ethnography or other forms of qualitative research unaware of the major time commitment a good ethnography requires and the intellectual challenge careful analysis of ethnographic data presents. Before choosing ethnography, care should be given to research design that preserves important criteria for good ethnographic research. Spindler and Spindler (1992, pp. 72-74) provide eleven such criteria that researchers can use to help them design high quality ethnographies.

1. The context of observations is presented, both within the immediate setting and in extended contexts when appropriate.
2. Hypotheses emerge from the setting. "Judgment on what may be significant to study in-depth is deferred until the orienting phase of the field study has been completed."
3. "Observation is prolonged and repetitive. Chains of events are observed more than once to establish the reliability of observations."
4. The "native view" is given full voice with minimal "cultural translations".
5. Knowledge about the sociocultural reality in the setting is required to understand behavior and communication, and this knowledge comes from participants/informants.
6. The tools of research ("instruments, codes, schedules, questionnaires, agenda for interviews") should be generated on the site as part of the inquiry.
7. Accepting that cultures demonstrate common and distinguishing features, the ethnography acknowledges culture as changing adaptations to human life.
8. Much of sociocultural knowledge is tacit, not known or only ambiguously known to participants, so a major task of the ethnography is to elicit this knowledge and make it explicit. This process often causes discomfort, *because* tacit, implicit knowledge often is implicit because it is uncomfortable.
9. Because any informant being interviewed holds the native or emic insider view, interviews must not predetermine responses or impose preconceptions on the data.
10. Any technical data gathering techniques that enable the researcher to collect live, immediate, natural behavior can be used if not too intrusive and with permission.
11. The ethnographer should describe her or his role and interaction in the context of the study.

A number of ethnographers take what they call a *critical* perspective on ethnography. This distinction is important, because the intellectual role the ethnographer plays in the study is as a critic of the established perspective on knowledge. Critical ethnographers rely on a body of theory from critical sociology and philosophy that argues that:

> (1) the work must employ an organizing problematic that defines one's data and analytical procedures in a way consistent with its project; (2) the work must be situated, in part, within a public sphere that allows it to become the starting point for the critique and transformation of the conditions of oppressive and ineluctable moral and social regulation; and (3) the work must address the limits of its own claims by a consideration of how, as a form of social practice, it too is constituted and regulated through historical relations of power and existing material conditions. (Simon & Dippo, 1986, p. 197)

A critical ethnographer thus approaches the qualitative research process from an accepted point of view that capitalistic culture constrains social action. Profit, growth, and control by the social sciences and related disciplines are viewed as major impediments to the search for social reality through research. The researcher has and acknowledges having conscious political intentions in doing the research. (Aficionados of ethnography divide themselves into many other smaller categories as well, but this discussion is meant only as an introduction to the research approach.)

Along the phenomenological/positivist continuum, ethnographies fall on the unique, phenomenological side. Consequently, ethnographies should not be undertaken with specific hypotheses worked out in advance, coded instruments, or too highly defined categories for observation. The danger of carrying preconceptions into the study is too great when these techniques are used for an ethnography. Questionnaires and interview guides may be used, but they will be developed after the investigator has had time in the site collecting observations.

Case Study

The case study approach to qualitative research describes the *end product* of field study using observation, interview, and archival methods as much as it does a method. Case studies represent narrative descriptions of particular cases (students, teachers, schools). The case can be either the product or a data-reduction step that allows for comparison to other, similar cases in the search for parallel and contrasting patterns. Wolcott (1992) contends that every strategy for data gathering can be reported in case study format and thus challenges conceptualizations of the case study as a method for qualitative research only.

Despite differences of opinion about the method versus end-product views of case studies, some general characteristics of case studies will give a new researcher guidance about elements to include. Lancy (1993) summarized some of these attributes.

1. A case study includes a variety of data about a single subject at the level of study (individual, group, organizational). While case studies are more likely to include qualitative methods, many researchers advocate including qualitative and quantitative techniques (Smith, 1986).
2. Case studies rely less on phenomenological paradigms by delimiting in advance what will be studied and usually take a realist perspective.
3. Case studies address primary audiences such as the academic community or authoritative bodies such as school boards or administrators.
4. Case studies may be reported without publishing results. Publications for scholarly communities may use carefully written case studies as data for further analysis.
5. Case studies should be accessible, well-written, and address methodological issues.

6. The writer often assumes an evaluative stance, comparing case studies to each other or to some general standard.

7. The researcher draws conclusions and explicitly or implicitly makes recommendations for research, policy, or practice.

Many field researchers find comparative case studies to be compelling ways to convey the general patterns of human behavior observed through qualitative data. They also can be structured to make use of qualitative and quantitative data for maximum depth of understanding and to elucidate different aspects of the cases under examination (Yin, 1989).

Criticism/Connoisseurship

As we mentioned earlier, educational criticism or connoisseurship is most frequently associated with one of its most talented advocates and developers, Elliott Eisner. Modeled after the work of critics in literature, theater, film, music, and the visual arts, criticism relies on well-written, vivid descriptions of the setting to convey the ineffable reality of the situation to the reader. The result is a qualitative analysis that evokes some kind of experience in the reader, and the scholarship itself becomes a form of art.

From this perspective, the scholar becomes an educational critic with refined and well-developed "taste" who has the task of "rendering the essentially ineffable qualities constituting works of art into a language that will help others perceive the work more deeply" (Eisner, 1985, p. 191). Eisner maintains that criticism includes two essential features. First, it is an empirical experience in the Latin sense, "open to experience." The reader comes to understand the qualities and relationships in the situation being observed through criticism, not abstraction. Second, anything can be the subject of criticism: "the illumination of something's qualities" (p. 191).

The success of criticism depends on the ability of the scholar to perceive subtle, complex, and important features in a particular setting. It also depends on the ability to appreciate and describe those qualities. Unlike some scholars, Eisner differentiates between connoisseurship and criticism, arguing that "connoisseurship is the art of appreciation, criticism is the art of disclosure" (p. 193). Applying this concept to unstructured observation, one would look for what is significant in a classroom or school rather than counting events determined to be important in advance on an observation instrument.

What is significant in a social setting might have little to do with the incidence of a particular activity or statement but a lot to do with a single act or statement or with the organizational structure of the classroom or with the character of an assigned task or with the way in which a reward is given. Observation schedules are tools that can guide one's attention, but their mechanical use can blind one to what is significant. (Eisner, p. 194)

The report of an educational criticism is not meant to translate what happens but to vividly describe a situation in a way that will direct the reader to the significant aspects of the situation, event, or object. Criticism can be and usually is a very focused activity, can aim at a given emphasis such as a particular student's learning patterns, the character of classroom discourse, the visual environment, or the meanings embedded in the treatment of time.

Three aspects characterize educational criticism: descriptive, interpretive, and evaluative. The *descriptive* aspect identifies and characterizes, portrays, or renders in language the relevant qualities of the study. The *interpretive* aspect uses ideas from the social sciences to analyze and account for events and predict some of their consequences. The *evaluative* aspect requires that the scholar apply educational values and judge the value of a situation or circumstance.

Educational connoisseurship and the criticism that results convey a deeply evocative and personalized view of qualitative research approaches. While critics argue that it is the most subjective of methods, its supporters counter that the value and truthfulness of criticism can be tested by comparing its product with the social situation it describes and conveys. The proof is in the pudding, so to speak.

Summary and Conclusions

While many researchers who love statistical analyses find the time in analysis for quantitative research to be more fun than the data gathering stage, few qualitative researchers describe analysis as more fun than data gathering. This reality is unsurprising, because the deeply human and engaging process of data gathering often is the feature researchers find most attractive about qualitative research in the social sciences. As noted before, the advent of widely available computer analyses has freed quantitative researchers from many of the tedious aspects of analysis. Qualitative data analysis, even with the use of computer programs to facilitate data management, remains a labor-intensive, time-consuming process.

Nevertheless, for the researcher committed to "rendering the ineffable" and exploring the vividly salient depth and breadth of social life, qualitative research remains the methodology of choice. The rich traditions of qualitative research provide an immediacy of experience and an empathy in the reader unavailable for most consumers of quantitative research.

Increasingly, however, researchers in the social and behavioral sciences turn to mixed-methods designs, combining qualitative and quantitative methods. Mixed-methods designs reveal the immediate and individual experience in concert with the generalizable patterns of social life. They also pose interesting challenges to researchers. Important design questions arise about quality, the nature of knowledge, and the most productive heuristics available to researchers. Assumptions safeguarding the trustworthiness of analytical techniques require vigilant safeguarding. For those interested in crossing the boundaries, however, qualitative/quantitative mixed-methods designs offer an intriguing alternative to traditional research that adhered to traditionally sacred boundaries between research methods.

Turn to page 433 and complete
Simulations 15.1 to 15.6

Simulations

Simulation 15.1

Topic: Preliminary data analysis

Background Statement: Despite efforts to plan every step of the research process during the design phase, qualitative researchers often find that they did not predict all the people, settings, and documents that should be included in the research sample during data gathering. Consequently, decisions made in the field about additional subjects, observational sampling, and archival searches critically affect the quality of the research.

Tasks to Be Performed:

1. Read the following material.
2. Note leads in the data that should be pursued by the researchers. Recommend actions that should be taken before researchers leave the field.

Stimulus Material: A team of five field researchers is investigating the integration of handicapped students with mild to moderate degrees of special needs into three neighborhood middle schools in one district. One member of the team is assigned to observe each of the three schools. The other two travel to each of the sites conducting interviews with students, teachers, administrators, and parents. The team has been granted access to all student records (with identifying information removed) and all public space (e.g., classrooms, halls, lunchrooms) by the school district, schools, and educators. Parents were notified about the research project. They were asked to request that their children be omitted from the data-gathering process if they objected to their participation.

After three weeks of interviews and observations, team members are dissatisfied with the authenticity of their data. They finally meet to discuss their concerns. What issues do the team members need to address? What questions should they ask themselves? How should they proceed to plan for the rest of the data-gathering process?

For Feedback see page 438.

Simulation 15.2

Topic: Thick description

Background Statement: Description of a setting, events, and participants in a vivid, accurate, and parsimonious way poses a major challenge for qualitative researchers. Many researchers practice description for years and systematically review and critique each other's writing to improve their descriptive ability. Dry prose lacking in detail and purple prose that exaggerates limit and restrict the aspiring ethnographer.

Tasks to Be Performed: Choose a public setting in your college or university or an event, meeting, or setting in your workplace where you can observe unobtrusively. If possible, perform this task with one or more other students from your research design course. Station yourselves at various locations around the setting.

Stimulus Material: Describe your physical surroundings. As you write, imagine that your readers can visualize what you see. Describe the people, animals, buildings, plants, or other important features of the setting. What is happening; what can you hear, smell, and feel?

For Feedback see page 438.

Simulation 15.3

Topic: Inductive data analysis

Background Statement: Inductive analysis offers a particularly powerful way of using qualitative research methods to contribute new perspectives on existing theory and to provide new conceptual and theoretical constructs for further examination. The researcher using inductive analysis deliberately approaches the data with a perspective that is a tabula rasa—the blank slate. No preexisting knowledge, beliefs, or theories must interfere. Issues, themes, and concepts must arise directly from the data. The researcher must take special care to put aside past experiences and research. The time to return to the groundwork laid by other scholars is after not before analysis.

Tasks to Be Performed:

1. Print your systematic field notes from your observation completed as part of Simulation 15.2.
2. Collect your field notes and those of other students in your research design class for analysis as research data.
3. Read the collected field notes. List themes or issues you see imbedded in and emerging from these data. Give examples from the data to support you assertions of concepts emerging from observations.

For Feedback see page 438.

Simulation 15.4

Topic: Deductive data analysis

Background Statement: When qualitative researchers seek to examine the relationships between their field research and existing theory in the social scientists, they follow different analytical precepts than during inductive analysis. Hart (1994) undertook a deductive post hoc analysis of case study data of teacher work redesign.

Tasks to Be Performed: Read and critique the following analysis report. What precepts of deductive analysis were followed? What shortcomings in the analysis can you identify? What advice would you give to Hart to improve the quality of the study and the usefulness of its findings to consumers of the research?

Stimulus Material: Hart, A. W. (1994), "Creating Teacher Leadership Roles: The Impacts of Core Group Support," *Educational Administration Quarterly, 30*(4), 472–497. Copyright 1994 by The University Council for Educational Administration. Reprinted by permission of Corwin Press, Inc.

Data analysis for this paper followed established procedures for case study and naturalistic research when applying an existing theoretical framework to qualitative case data.... Transcripts of interviews and meetings, teaching observation notes taken by participants, journals, and field notes that earlier inductive analyses grouped under the general category of student performance effects were coded using basic concepts of role theory. Data summary sheets were prepared by collecting quotations and field note notations directly from the data. These summary sheets were, therefore, long collections of specific examples illustrating the manifestation of a concept in the raw data. Summary sheets also contained notations of the specific role (teacher, teacher leader, principal, etc.) associated with each entry, the school, and the date of occurrence. Comparison matrices then were developed to facilitate the analysis of interaction patterns. These matrices compared occurrences of data points illustrating each concept (and frequency counts) across time, by school, and by position, seeking insight into role-specific clues to strong feelings centered around perceptions of performance effects.

This analysis draws primarily on unpublished data originally grouped as participants' explanations for the new jobs' effects or lack of effects on student performance. These data were inadequately explained by work structure and redesign theories. While the teacher-to-student relationship clearly was important, previous analyses left it poorly elucidated. The present analysis is by no means exhaustive. The job characteristics model of work redesign, for example, suggests that the task, autonomy, and feedback features of the teacher leader and teacher specialist jobs might have affected their motivating potential (Hart, 1988). Pre-existing features of each school's social unit shaped events in the two schools (Hart, 1991). Yet, these initial differences were only part of the story. They framed the roles people played, but individual roles and the political jockeying among core groups also shaped this educational reform.

For Feedback see page 439.

Simulation 15.5

Topic: Ethnography

Background Statement: An ethnographer seeks to portray cultural life in a spirit of acceptance and with as little interpretation and translation from an outsider's point of view as possible. While the etic and emic points of view are critical, the etic perspective should enlighten and explain, not translate or judge. Critical ethnography takes an explicit political or analytical perpective based on assumptions about the epistemology and thought of western research traditions and approaches the portrayal of the culture from a specifically critical point of view.

Tasks to Be Performed:

1. Read two reports of ethnographic research. You may read Lightfoot, S. L. (1983), *The Good High School: Portraits of Character and Culture,* New York: Basic Books; Giroux, H. H. (1994), *Disturbing Pleasures: Learning Popular Cultures,* New York: Routledge; segments from Bateson's *Composing a Life, Black Elk Speaks;* or a research report of your own choosing.

2. Using the criteria laid out in the Ethnography section of this chapter, assess the ethnographic perspective taken by the author(s) in each report of research and classify it accordingly as ethnography, critical ethnography, discourse analysis, or connoisseurship. Defend your decision with evidence from the reports.

Stimulus Material: You have chosen an ethnography to read. The perspective of the author(s) drives the comments you should make in response to this simulation. Remember that ethnographies can be undertaken from many perspectives and can rely on research traditions that vary widely. Reflect this variety in your response.

For Feedback see page 439.

Simulation 15.6

Topic: Writing the research report

Background Statement: As with quantitative research, qualitative research reports must not only convey the findings and implications of the systematic inquiry but must provide sufficient detail for informed readers to determine for themselves the usefulness and trustworthiness of the findings.

Tasks to Be Performed:

1. Read the following material or use the analyzed material from your own and your classmates' thick description.
2. Summarize the analytical procedures followed by the author(s).
3. Describe the major qualities and shortcomings of the analyses in the stimulus material and defend your judgments.

Stimulus Material: You may have chosen to use your own and your classmates' thick description subject to analysis by you for this assignment. If so, proceed. If you would like to use other researchers' material you may turn to: Smylie, M.A., & Denny, J. W. (1990), "Teacher Leadership: Tensions and Ambiguities in Organizational Perspective," *Educational Administration Quarterly, 26*, 235-259; Bateson, M. C. (1990), *Composing a Life*, NY: Plume Books; or Baker, C. (1969), *Ernest Hemingway: A Life Story.* New York: Scribners. You may also choose ethnographic research reports you personally find compelling. Be sure to provide complete references to your instructor for ethnographies of your own choosing.

For Feedback see page 439.

Simulation Feedbacks

Simulation 15.1

The team members in this research project neglected several critical aspects of design and planning that need immediate rectification. First, they made no provisions for team meetings and discussions from the beginning of their field work. Second, they neglected fundamental differences between subgroups of the students in their sample—the nondisabled students and the students with special needs. Two immediate issues must be addressed: how can they secure more individualized data about students that will help them draw trustworthy conclusions, and what structures in their procedures need to be developed to establish and maintain team debriefing and preliminary data analysis sessions? Additional problems relate to the observation sampling established, archival data being collected (related to individual access), and the interviews.

The team must set regular meetings, agree on procedures for developing comparable data summaries and distillation processes, and immediately secure fully informed consent for expanding the depth of the inquiry appropriately. Your response should include some suggestions about how these steps can be taken and elaborated. See the discussion this chapter and discussions about informed consent and design in Chapter 7 for more information about preliminary data analysis.

Simulation 15.2

Thick description challenges qualitative researchers' observational and writing abilities. Most beginning researchers are more likely to over-embellish their descriptions in an attempt to be vivid than they are to omit descriptive prose. Yet accuracy is unrelated to floridity. Purple prose can omit critical details about the setting or observation, even as it seems over-blown. Read your description with accuracy, vividness, and completeness in mind. How well did you do? What would you do differently next time?

Now read and compare your thick description with the descriptions written by your classmates from different vantage points. What differences and similarities do you see? What do these differences and similarities tell you about the challenges of ethnographic field work?

Simulation 15.3

Inductive analysis stands or falls on the ability of qualified data auditors to trace the logic and reasoning used as the researcher moves toward conclusions during data analysis. For this simulation, you should be able to provide evidence of the way in which you used data from the research data set (your own or an existing set) to reach conceptual conclusions. Generalizations *must* flow from the data.

Simulation 15.4

This study is vulnerable to many of the dangers of deductive research in both qualitative and quantitative realms. The dangers are greater in qualitative data analysis, however, because of the truth of the adage "You find what you look for." The researcher took a number of steps to mitigate against this danger, including: (1) returning directly to the raw data, (2) developing analytical codes directly from the relevant theory, (3) preparing data summary sheets that use raw data to establish theory/data relationships, (4) examining data across precepts, subjects, and settings, and (5) exploring interaction relationships in the data. Additionally, the original interview data were not directed by questions based on the theoretical framework, nor were observation samples and archival searches. The danger inherent in asking questions that elicit responses that then appear as affirmations of theory was avoided in this design.

The researcher could have increased the reliability of the research in several ways. First, a data analysis audit by an independent researcher would have provided additional corroboration of data-coding decisions. Second, a follow-up study at the original research sites, organized around the theoretical framework conducted simultaneously with the post hoc analysis, could have provided a more longitudinal view of the schools as organizations and a more robust test of the theory. Although a follow-up study would have entailed additional expense, it would have provided a more powerful deductive test. Finally, a cross-tabulation analysis of the original case studies, inductive findings, and deductive analysis might have revealed relationships not discernible through a purely deductive process.

Simulation 15.5

As you by now are sure to have noticed, ethnography is not ethnography is not ethnography. Your analysis of the perspective taken by the author(s) should include a description of the features of ethnography from the perspective you adopt and evidence from the data to support your assertion that these features are present. You should be able to explicitly tie perspective (critical, connoisseurship ethnography) to data.

Simulation 15.6

Writing the research report poses a daunting challenge to researchers. While many scholars were reared with the injunction "if you can't write it, you don't know it," writing is the final hurdle many scholars face in their quest to communicate with other scholars. The research report also is the means through which the researcher seeks to communicate with others who could use their findings to improve their social lives.

Your analysis should have specifically enumerated the features of a research report drawing on a particular perspective. See relevant parts of the text for more information about the features of the report you should be able to describe and illustrate.

Chapter *16*

Completing the Research Process: Results Related to Behavior

It is not uncommon for beginning researchers to labor through the development of a research question, through the design and execution of a study, and even through data analysis, only to find themselves confronted with serious difficulty in terms of interpreting results. The frequency with which computer printouts of quantitative analyses are discarded in frustration is appalling, but not at all surprising. The intuitive leaps from quantitative data to behavior are difficult at best, but in fact these leaps are representative of a broader problem related to acquisition of a Gestalt-like concept of the research process. It should not be surprising that difficulties are encountered, since the process of interpretation, in fact the total process of research, is rarely taught formally. More often than not college or university instructors have mastered and are usually involved only in the instruction of segments of the research process. Indeed the segments most often taught lend themselves well to rote memorization but are not placed in the context of research as a thinking activity. Consequently, students may be well equipped with library research information, statistical computation skills, or 3 x 5 card details, but are unable to even approach the implementation of a study. The absence of an overall concept of the total research process not only impedes implementing research but often reduces the effective acquisition of even the segment skills.

This chapter will discuss the relationship between various segments of the research act with the intent of providing a Gestalt of the process, with the intention of putting these segments in functional perspective. Additionally, attention will be given to interpretation of results, which is a factor of vital importance to progress in behavioral science.

Research as an Integrated Process

There are a number of roadblocks that appear to deter research from being viewed as an integrated process. Perhaps the primary impediment is the previously mentioned fragmentation of the overall research act. This segmenting is generated in a variety of fashions, the most powerful of which may be the approach to teaching. Courses on statistics are often taught with little or no attention to how statistics relate to either the research question or the meaning of results. Similarly, writing is taught primarily from a term-paper framework with little attention focused on how to build a logical, reasoned case or how to articulate intuitive leaps from datum A to datum B to resulting conclusions. Since little effort is exerted to synthesize these disjointed parts, beginning researchers are often handicapped by the conceptual gaps existing between various segments of the research process. This may result in a limited perspective of research that is inharmonious with the total implementation of an investigation.

As noted previously, research actually represents a continuous process beginning with a theoretical construct or body of knowledge that generates a research question. The nature of the research question, in turn, dictates to a considerable degree the method to be employed. And all that has preceded relates to the interpretive discussion of results. (Certain qualitative researchers would contend that this series or sequence of events is inappropriate as indicated in Chapter 2. We acknowledge this viewpoint and are using the current framework only in a general fashion to facilitate discussion.) The gaps in conceptual continuity will be addressed in the following sections in an attempt to highlight the relationships among various segments of the research act. Conceptual gaps in the research process represent points at which the student has a high probability of encountering difficulties. Often these problems are extremely frustrating. Because the difficulty is one of a conceptual nature, it is not easily remedied. Were it, instead, one of a mechanical nature (e.g., computation decision or error), a remedy might easily be found in the form of advice from a colleague or consultant.

One of the first high-risk points encountered in the research process involves the intuitive (and actual) relationship between a theoretical construct and the research question. A second high-risk problem arises during translation of the research question into the method (which includes study design, data collection, and analyses). Finally, certainly of no little importance, are the conceptual relationships between re-sults and inferences or interpretations back to behavioral terms. These problematic areas represent vital and logical relationships that must be well understood if a researcher is to have the functional capacity to work in a variety of settings.

Theory Related to the Research Question

As noted, one of the first conceptual problem areas is represented by the relationship between the research question and a theoretical model or body of knowledge. Many people experience difficulty determining what an abstract theory or model means in behavioral terms. Essen-tially this is a deductive reasoning process that moves from the general statement of a theory to the specific behavioral performance.

A theory or model is an abstract framework that generally provides an overview of the inferred processes (e.g., learning) and how they operate. Since theory functions at an abstract level, it usually does not include specific statements regarding how a subject will behave under specific conditions. In the absence of exemplars, beginning students (and often the experienced researcher) may encounter difficulty in visualizing how the theoretical statements (sometimes called *postulates*) relate to a specific behavioral instance. Yet this process is vital to the development of a related research question.

One source of the translation difficulty is that students tend to view a theory as a total entity that must be related to behavior. Yet a model or theory often encompasses a rather broad area of behaviors that, when viewed as a whole, does not intend to predict behavioral specif-ics. A model is generally a composite concept such as learning and as such, it should be translated in terms of the various parts or dimensions of behavior that are included. Each behavioral dimension should be treated somewhat apart from the total model. By considering only one part of a theory or one statement within a total theory at a time, the specific contingencies of a situation may be more easily described and behavior under these more limited circumstances may be predicted. After the results are obtained, the findings are usually related back to the larger theoretical construct to test the behavioral dimension under study. Attempting to consider the total theory from the outset, however, seriously impedes the statement of a researchable question. This pro-cess may be compared to eating a pastrami sandwich. A person who tried to swallow the sandwich whole, would invariably choke and cer-tainly not derive pleasure from it nor be efficient in eating. On the other hand, one bite at a time from the sandwich is an approach that is easily translatable into operational terms and represents a manageable procedure.

Several steps may be useful in translating this analogy into the con-text of research. Students initially must hold the totality of a theory in storage while concentrating on one facet or dimension. Then with this segment of the model under focus the question becomes "What does this postulate mean in terms of behavior?" The answer to such a question needs to be situation specific if it is to predict behavior. For example, part of a theory under study may suggest, "Under variable reinforcement conditions a child who is socially immature should perform in a particular way." Since theory represents an abstraction, the empirical test of such a prediction becomes the task of research.

Continuing the process of asking progressively more specific questions, the researcher moves closer to a manageable research question. "If, under *these* (hypothetical) *conditions, this particular type of child* is expected to perform in a certain way, *then* how could I observe the behavior to either confirm or deny the prediction?" This question leads rather directly to the initial stages of study design and the specifics involved in the method to be used. It really represents several questions and resulting decisions that need attention. For example, how may the conditions specified by the statement be set up in the real world (or at least in a laboratory approximation of the real world)? How is the researcher going to know whether these conditions have exerted an influence? What is going to be observed or measured to represent the behavioral performance? (In quantitative studies, what is the researcher going to count, the number of correct responses?)

As suggested by the preceding discussion, the leap from a theory to a research question represents a dramatic increase in specificity. Intense application of the deductive process is involved as a researcher moves from a total theory or model to the particular facet under study and, in turn, to the research question. This funnel-like process may be hidden between the two visible end points, the generalized model and the specific, often molecular, research question.

For clarity it may be useful to proceed through a sequence of events from the beginning to the culmination of a piece of research. At the first stage, a possible researchable question could be "What are the effects of a variable reinforcement schedule as compared with continuous reinforcement on the recall performance of socially immature children?"

The Question Related to Method and Analysis

The next gap to be bridged is between the research question and the experimental method. Because of the specificity of the example research question above, translation to a tight, crisply articulated problem should not present great difficulty. The method basically must permit measurement aimed at answering the question posed. More specifically the method can be approached in terms of describing subjects, materials, and procedures. In terms of the example question, the subjects must in some fashion be determined to be "socially immature children." This gives us at least two dimensions to consider. First of all, who are "children?" This term suggests a chronological age range of people who are young enough to be considered children but not old enough to be thought of as adolescents. For these purposes it is sufficient to say that chronological age needs to be specified. The second dimension suggested by the above phrase is the necessity of determining that the subjects are "socially immature." How is this to be accomplished? It may involve some standardized evaluation instrument or it may mean that children are so classified by observations. At any rate, on some logical (and/or empirical) basis, if subjects are to be obtained who are relevant to the research question, they must be sampled from a group who will fall within the framework of "socially immature" children.

The next area of focus that relates investigation method to the research question is represented by the materials to be used. Materials or apparatus for the example question may include one or two factors depending on how the study will be implemented. Certainly it will be necessary to specify the materials to be used that relate to the phrase "recall performance." What is it that the children are going to recall? Even more specific on this point, how are these materials going to generate the criterion measure? If, for example, geography questions that require written responses are to be used, then is the researcher willing to contend that the number of correct responses represents recall? The point to be made here is simply that the materials chosen must also relate to the research question. In this example, the materials or research task must relate to what is considered to be recall.

The second dimension of materials discussion relates to reinforcement. If the subjects are going to be reinforced with tangible rewards (e.g., candy, tokens), reinforcement probably is best discussed under "materials." On the other hand, if verbal praise is to be used, the reinforcement part of the question receives attention under "procedures." Also, if tangible rewards are to be dispensed by machine or other apparatus, this should be described. These types of details need to be specified and their choice must relate to the research question being explored.

The third area of focus that relates study method to the research question is represented by the procedures that are actually put into operation. As with subjects and materials, the procedures must be relevant to the research question. This means that how the experimental conditions are to be implemented must be conceptualized in terms of the research question.

The next intuitive relationship requiring discussion is that which links the research question to the analysis of data. It is not uncommon among beginning students to pose a relationship question and yet to choose a design and analysis appropriate for a difference problem (or vice versa). The example research question suggests that the effects of variable versus continuous reinforcement are being compared. This is a difference question, which should be reflected by the design and the analysis technique employed. More specific information on the analysis segment has been presented in earlier chapters. The difficulty that often represents a conceptual gap involves the logical relationship between the research question and the selection of *which* analysis technique to use. It simply is not appropriate to approach a difference question with a correlation or a relationship question with a *t* test.

This section has emphasized the fact that the research process involves a series of highly interrelated segments. The relationships between these various areas are crucial and require specific focus because they are often overlooked in instruction and frequently not included in the conception of research held by beginning investigators. In review, this section has been a miniature replay of much of what has been discussed in greater detail in earlier portions of this text. We hope the overall view of research is no longer like a prism that distorts the relevant perspective of any activity area.

One important area of the research process remains to be discussed—interpretation of results. This area is strongly related to other activities in research and should not be viewed apart from the total research enterprise. It is highly dependent on all that has gone on before.

Interpretation of Results

Perhaps the most difficult conceptual gap to bridge is the relationship between the numbers obtained as results and the inference to behavior. This may result in part because many people without research experience extract little meaning from numbers and, in particular, statistical statements such as $p < .05$. Interpretation concerned with the meaning of results in terms of behavior requires that an individual must at least know what such statements mean. Assuming this level of knowledge is present (or amenable to acquisition), the relationship of results to inferences about behavior may begin with a series of questions. If, for example, the study involved a comparison of groups (a difference problem), the first question is usually "Did the groups perform differently?" This question may be answered by reviewing the results of the statistical test. Was there a significant difference? If they were different, which group had the higher performance? This latter question can be answered by simply inspecting the group means if mean scores are being used.

The next step really initiates the process of inference. What do the performance differences mean in terms of behavior? The researcher cannot get by with merely answering this question by saying that group 1 made more correct responses than group 2. That is evident in the results and adds no interpretive information. Inference requires attention to the psychology of behavior. The researcher must make some intuitive leaps regarding *why* group 1 made more correct responses than group 2. Would these differences have been predicted by the model that was discussed in the introduction? If so, in what fashion is the model supported? Would these data suggest that some particular psychological construct is operative in the process of learning? These questions exemplify the process of inference from results to behavior. Research that has a maximal impact on both theory and practice will attempt to push back the frontiers of understanding by using inference in this fashion.

An even greater challenge is represented by results that would not have been predicted by the model or theory being tested. Here again it is not enough to merely say, "These data would not support the theory of ...." The question must be posed as to *why* the data do not support the theory. Do the data, instead, suggest that an alternative model may be operating in the learning process? If so, this is an important and exciting finding. Perhaps the data suggest a modification of the model. This type of finding exemplifies the process of empiricism as it serves to shape models and theories. Fully interpreted results should include other possible explanations for the data if they do not support the theory under study.

Last but not least important, a researcher may choose to interpret what the results might mean for practice or clinical application. This process is particularly important in applied research endeavors. Do the data suggest that teachers might more effectively instruct if they were to use a particular reinforcement technique? Do the data suggest that instructional materials might be more effective for certain children if they were designed in a particular way? Results may suggest that a given counseling technique might be effective with a particular group of students. The point to be emphasized is that research results that are interpreted for application require the same intuitive inference processes relating data to the real world that were involved in inference from data to theory.

Interpretation for practice has not always been a respected activity for researchers. There has, however, been a substantial shift in philosophy regarding interpretation for practice in recent years. Not only is it given less of a peripheral status than was previously the case but it is being expected by journal editors under certain conditions. Whether interpretation for practice is attempted depends primarily on the audience for which the report is intended.

Drawing implications for practice and inference in terms of alternative models are two activities that represent a process that may be difficult for experienced researchers as well as the beginning student. Teaching these skills is an area about which little is known as well. One serious roadblock to such interpretation might be called *conceptual rigidity*, which can be illustrated by an example.

As noted, research often is launched from the framework of a theory, model, or some other explanatory conceptual framework. The relevant dimensions of this model have been discussed in the opening chapters, which gives the researcher a mental set to proceed with the study. This set may also work against the researcher when it comes to interpretation of results. If the researcher does not conceptually explore beyond the boundaries of the model, the mental set may become too rigid to permit alternative inference. The confinement of oneself strictly to the boundaries of the model is what we refer to as conceptual rigidity. The framework of the model is indeed useful and necessary to launch an investigation. The limits of such a framework, however, may become somewhat like conceptual fences. If researchers never go beyond those conceptual fences once the study is designed, they will find themselves less effective in terms of data interpretation. There are several resulting difficulties.

Initially, difficulty is encountered when the data do not fit between the conceptual fences. A quick examination of nearly any professional journal will indicate that this often occurs as evidenced by the frequency with which "results do not support..." whatever model is being tested. When data do not fit within the conceptual fences of a model, a statement that "these data do not support..." will not alone suffice. It is at this point that the researcher must go beyond the explanations provided by the model and either suggest an alternative theory that the data *will* support or suggest modifications of the model being tested.

Because the theory being tested seldom involves practice, implications in this area also involve conceptual fences. Often implications for practice are made more difficult because researchers are not generally in the field-practitioner role on a continuing basis. Thus in a real sense, the current set of experiences that are temporally and conceptually close to the researcher often do not involve clinical application or practice. Implications for practice therefore may require an even more dramatic assault on conceptual rigidity than model alternatives.

Researchers who are either unable or unwilling to inferentially explore beyond the boundaries of a model will reduce their impact even if the data were predicted by the model. At face value their discussions of results will appear somewhat sterile and unexciting to read. It should be emphasized that one must stay within the legitimate boundaries of the *data*. The researcher should, however, be willing to watch the subjects beyond the pure criterion measure level. Such observation often is revealing in a clinical sense and is not infrequently discussed during the interpretation. These observations should always carry a qualifying statement such as "Subjective experimenter observation suggested...." Science moves back the frontiers of the unknown at an incredibly slow pace. Without the help of such observations and their interpretation related to the data (which often generate further research), the movement would be even slower.

This chapter has emphasized some of the lesser known processes of research, primarily the judicious use of intuition and logic. We do not intend to give the impression that all researchers must do is gather data and then say whatever their imagination suggests. At all times a researcher must stay in close touch with what the data indicate in terms of logical leaps and inferences. The use of logic and conceptual relationships is, however, one of the most important processes in research. This chapter also highlights research as a dynamic, even creative act. Research does not always carry such a connotation for the uninitiated. Beginning researchers must, if they are to achieve the impact possible and desirable, learn to incorporate creative thinking into their repertoire of behavior.

How does one acquire the skills discussed in this chapter? As mentioned previously, the pat formula for such instruction is not presently known, at least to most professionals involved in research training. What is known is that with some prerequisite level of information acquired, most students progress most rapidly from practice. Once one begins to break down conceptual fences, the divergent thinking necessary seems best nurtured by experience at asking the additional questions. What are other psychological or theoretical explanations for the same results? What are modifications of the theory being tested that would predict the data obtained? To what practical setting might these results be relevant: curriculum planning, student diagnosis, counseling, placement, or treatment development?

It is not necessary for students to wait for their first study to practice the process of inference and data interpretation (although working on your own data is much more fun). In fact it is desirable to gain some experience before beginning the first study. We have used a simulation technique with our students that has shown considerable success. Simulations have been presented with most of the previous chapters in this text. Simulations for interpretation, however, require material of such length that presentation in this volume is not possible. If you are interested in such practice, you are encouraged to try the following procedures:

1. Select a journal article that is in an area familiar to you; if possible, let it be one in which you have done considerable reading, have considerable experience, or both.

2. The initial study should have a fairly simple design. As you become more experienced, more complex studies can be used (e.g., select a simple study that compares two groups for the first try).

3. Tape a piece of paper over the author's discussion section.

4. Read the article carefully up to the discussion section.

5. Now, write your own discussion of the results. Interpret the results in terms of the theory or literature reviewed in the introduction and in terms of what the results might mean for practice and future research. Be thoughtful during this process and review the current chapter if needed.

6. Remove the paper from the article and compare your discussion with that of the author. Did you hit the main points? Do not be concerned about the polish of your writing or differences in style. After all, the author may have been working and writing in the area considerably longer than you.

7. Practice, practice, practice.

Comments

It is evident that research is more than statistics. It is, in fact, a series of parts that have specific relationships and that strongly involve the use of mental exploration and intuition as well as logic. We hope you will begin to see research not as sterile and mechanistic but as the dynamic process that it is.

References

Abramovitch, R., Freedman, J. L., Thoden, K., & Nikolich, C. (1991). Children's capacity to consent to participation in psychological research: Empirical findings. *Child Development, 62,* 1100-1109.

Adler, P. (1990). *Requirements for inductive analysis.* National Institute on Drug Abuse Research Monograph Series, Monograph 98, 44-58.

Altenbaugh, R. J. (1991). *The teacher's voice: A qualitative analysis of teaching in twentieth-century America.* New York: Falmer Press.

Ambrose, A. (1978). Human social development: An evolutionary-biological perspective. In H. McGurk (Ed.), *Issues in childhood social development* (pp. 1-54). London: Methuen.

American Psychological Association (1989). *Ethical principles in the conduct of research with human participants.* Washington, D.C.: Author.

American Psychological Association. (1994). *Publication manual of the American Psychological Association* (4th ed.). Washington, DC: Author.

Anspach, R. R. (1991). Everyday methods for assessing organizational effectiveness. *Social Problems, 38,* 1-19.

Arrington, R. E. (1943). Time sampling in studies of social behavior: A critical review of techniques and results with research suggestions. *Psychological Bulletin, 40,* 81-124.

Asimov, I. (1960). *The intelligent man's guide to science* (Vol. One). New York: Basic Books Inc.

Ausubel, D. P. (1969). The nature of educational research. In W. J. Gephart & R. B. Ingle (Eds.), *Educational research: Selected readings* (pp. 5-13). Columbus, OH, Charles E. Merrill.

Bailey, J. S. (1992). Gentle teaching: Trying to win friends and influence people with euphemism, metaphor, smoke, and mirrors. *Journal of Applied Behavior Analysis, 25,* 879-883.

Bailey, K. D. (1994). *Methods of social research* (4th ed.). New York: The Free Press.

Baker, C. (1969). *Ernest Hemingway: A life story.* New York: Scribners.

Bateson, M. C. (1990). *Composing a life.* New York: Plume Books.

Baumrind, D. (1985). Research using intentional deception. *American Psychologist, 40*(2), 165-174.

Benjafield, J. G. (1994). *Thinking critically about research methods.* Boston: Allyn and Bacon.

Berdie, D. R., Anderson, J. F., & Niebuhr, M. A. (1986). *Questionnaires: Design and use* (2nd ed.). Metuchen, NJ: Scarecrow Press.

Best, J. W., & Kahn, J. V. (1989). *Research in education* (6th ed.). Englewood Cliffs, NJ: Prentice-Hall.

Beyer, J. (1995). *Standard Mathematical Tables* (30th ed.). Boca Ratan, FL: CRC Press.

Black Elk. (1961). *Black Elk speaks: Being the life history of a holy man of the Oglala Sioux.* Lincoln, NE: University of Nebraska Press.

Bogdan, R. C., & Biklin, S. K. (1992). *Qualitative research for education: An introduction to theory and methods* (2nd ed.). Boston, MA: Allyn and Bacon.

Borg, W. R., Gall, J. P., & Gall, M. D. (1993). *Applying educational research: A practical guide* (3rd ed.). New York: Longman

Bossert, S. T. (1979). *Tasks and social relationships in classrooms: A study of instructional organization and its consequences.* Cambridge: Cambridge University Press.

Braucht, G. N., & Reichardt, C. S. (1993). A computerized approach to trickle-process, random assignment. *Evaluation Review, 17,* 79-90.

Brown, P. (1992). Popular epidemiology and toxic waste contamination: Lay and professional ways of knowing. *Journal of Health and Social Behavior, 33,* 267-281.

Bruning, J. L., & Kintz, B. L. (1987). *Computational handbook of statistics* (3rd ed.). Glenview, IL: Scott, Foresman and Co.

Burdine, J. N., & McLeroy, K. R. (1992). Practitioners' use of theory: Examples from a workgroup. *Health Education Quarterly, 19,* 331-340.

Burrell, G., & Morgan, G. (1979). *Sociological paradigms and organizational analysis.* London: Heinemann Educational Books.

Campbell, D. J. (1987). Ethical issues in the research

publication process. In S. L. Payne, & B. H. Charnov (Eds.), *Ethical dilemmas for academic professionals* (pp. 69-84). Springfield, IL: Charles C. Thomas.

Campbell, D. T., & Stanley, J. C. (1963). Experimental and quasi-experimental designs for research on teaching. In N. L. Gage (Ed.), *Handbook of research on teaching* (pp. 171-246). Chicago: Rand McNally & Co.

Carspecken, P. F., & Apple, M. (1992). Critical qualitative research: Theory, methodology, and practice. In M. Lecompte, W. Millroy, & J. Preissle (Eds.), *The handbook of qualitative research in education* (pp. 507-554). New York: Academic Press.

Christensen, L. B. (1994). *Experimental methodology* (6th ed.). Boston: Allyn and Bacon.

Clark, C. M., & Ryan, L. (1993). Implications of statistical tests of variance and means. *Journal of Clinical and Experimental Neuropsychology, 15,* 619-622.

Cook, T. D., & Campbell, D. T. (1979). *Quasi-experimentation: Design and analysis issues for field settings.* Chicago: Rand McNally College Publishing Co.

Cook, T. D. & Campbell, D. T. (1990). Quasi experimentation. In M. D. Dunnette & L. M. Hough (Eds.) *Handbook of industrial and organizational psychology* (Vol. 1, 2nd ed.), (pp. 491-576). Palo Alto, CA: Consulting Psychologists Press.

Crawford, H. J., & Christensen, L. B. (1995). *Developing research skills: A laboratory manual.* Boston: Allyn and Bacon.

Cronbach, L. J., & Meehl, P. E. (1955). Construct validity on psychological tests. *Psychological Bulletin, 52,* 281-302.

Cusick, P. A. (1973). *Inside high school: The student's world.* New York: Holt, Rinehart and Winston.

Davis, H. T. (1941). *The analysis of economic time-series.* Bloomington, IN: Bloomington Press.

Deyhle, D. L., Hess, G. A., Jr., & LeCompte, M. D. D. (1992). Approaching ethical issues for qualitative researchers in education. In M. D. LeCompte, W. L. Millroy, & J. Preissle (Eds.), *The handbook of qualitative research in education* (pp. 595-642). San Diego: Academic Press.

Diener, E., & Crandall, R. (1978). *Ethics in social and behavioral research.* Chicago: The University of Chicago Press.

Dignan, M. (1993). Power analysis: A useful tool for designing health education and health promotion research. *Health Values: The Journal of Health Behavior, Education and Promotion, 17,* 54-57.

Dobbert, M. L., & Kurth-Schai, R. (1992). Collaborative Research: Methods of inquiry for social change. In M. D. LeCompte, W. L. Millroy, & J. Preissle, *The handbook of qualitative research in education* (pp. 93-160). San Diego: Academic Press.

Drew, C. J., & Altman, R. Effects of input organization and material difficulty on free recall. *Psychological Reports, 27,* 335-337.

Drew, C. J., & Berard, W. R. (1970). Errors of retarded and nonretarded subjects by learning stage. *Psychonomic Science, 20,* (2), 65-66.

Drew, C. J., Hardman, M. L., & Logan, D. R. (1995). *Mental retardation: A life cycle approach* (6th ed.). Columbus, OH: Charles E. Merrill.

Drew, C. J., Preator, K., & Buchanan, M. L. (1982). Research and researchers in special education: Status, training, and uniqueness among related disciplines. *Exceptional Education Quarterly, 2* (4), 47-56.

Edgington, E. S. (1974). A new tabulation of statistical procedures used in APA journals. *American Psychologist, 29,* 25-26.

Edgington, E. S. (1980a). Random assignment and statistical tests for one-subject experiments. *Behavioral Assessment, 2,* 19-28.

Edgington, E. S. (1980b). *Randomization tests.* New York: Marcel Dekker.

Edgington, E. S. (1980c). Validity of randomization tests for one-subject experiments. *Journal of Educational Statistics, 5,* 235-251.

Eisner, E. (1985). *The educational imagination: On the design and evaluation of school programs* (2nd ed.). New York: Macmillan.

Eisner, E. W. (1991). *The enlightened eye: Qualitative inquiry and the enhancement of educational practice.* New York: Macmillan.

Eisner, E. W. (1993). Forms of understanding and the future of educational research. *Educational Researcher, 22*(7), 5-11.

Ellis, H. C. (1992). Graduate education in psychology: Past, present, and future. *American Psychologist, 47,* 570-576.

Erickson, F. (1992). Ethnographic microanalysis of interaction. In M. D. LeCompte, W. L. Millroy, & J. Preissle (Eds.), *The handbook of qualitative research in education* (pp. 210-226). San Diego: Academic Press.

Evans, R. L., Dingus, C. M., & Haselkorn, J. K. (1993). Living with a disability: A synthesis and critique of the literature on quality of life. *Psychological Reports, 72*(3), 771-777.

Eysenck, H. J. (1992). Four ways five factors are not basic. *Personality and Individual Differences, 13,* 667-673.

Fisher, R. A. (1925). *Statistical methods for research workers* (1st ed.). London: Oliver & Boyd.

Fisher, R. A. (1926). The arrangement of field experiments. *Journal of the Ministry of Agriculture, 33,* 503-513.

Fisher, R. A. (1935). *The design of experiments* (1st ed.). London: Oliver & Boyd.

Fox, M. F. (1990). Fraud, ethics, and the disciplinary contexts of science and scholarship. *The American Sociologist,* (spring), 67-71.

Foxx, R. M. (1993). Sapid effects awaiting independent replication. *American Journal on Mental Retardation, 97,* 375-376.

Fraenkel, J. R., & Wallen, N. E. (1993). *How to design and evaluate research in education* (2nd ed.). New York: McGraw-Hill, Inc.

Freedland, K. E. , & Carney, R. M. (1992). Data management and accountability in behavioral and biomedical research. *American Psychologist,* May, 640-645.

Freeman, D. (1983). *Margaret Mead and Samoa: The making and unmaking of an anthropological myth.* Cambridge, MA: Harvard University Press.

Freeman, D. (1989). Fa'apua'a Fa'amu and Margaret Mead. *American Anthropologist, 91,* 1017-1022.

Freston, C. W., & Drew, C. J. (1974). Verbal performance of learning-disabled children as a function of input organization. *Journal of Learning Disabilities, 7,* 424-428.

Frontline (1994, Tuesday October 18). *School Colors.* Public Broadcasting System.

Gee, J. P., Michaels, S. & O'Connor, M. C. (1992). Discourse analysis. In M. D. LeCompte, W. L. Millroy & J. Preissle (Eds.), *The handbook of qualitative research in education* (pp. 227-292). San Diego: Academic Press.

Gelfand, D. M., & Hartmann, D. P. (1984). *Child behavior analysis and therapy* (2nd ed.). New York: Pergamon Press.

Gelfand, D. M., Jenson, W. R., & Drew, C. J. (1988). *Understanding child behavior disorders* (2nd ed.). New York: Holt, Rinehart and Winston.

Giroux, H. H. (1994). *Disturbing pleasures: Learning popular cultures.* New York: Routledge.

Glass, G. V., & Stanley, J. C. (1970). *Statistical methods in education and psychology.* Englewood Cliffs, NJ: Prentice-Hall, Inc.

Gregory, K. L. (1983). Native-view paradigms: Multiple cultures and culture conflicts in organizations. *Administrative Science Quarterly, 28,* 359-376.

Grimm, L. G. (1993). *Statistical applications for the behavioral sciences.* New York: John Wiley & Sons.

Guba, E. G. (1981). Investigative journalism. In N. L. Smith (Ed.), *New methods for evaluation: Techniques* (pp. 167-262). Beverly Hills, CA: Sage.

Guba, E. (1990). *The paradigm dialogue.* Newbury Park, CA: Sage.

Guba E. G., & Lincoln, Y. S. (1989). *Fourth generation evaluation.* Newbury Park, CA: Sage.

Guidelines for preparation of applications for review by General Institutional Review Board (1991). Salt Lake City: University of Utah.

Gurtman, M. B. (1992). Construct validity of interpersonal personality measures: The interpersonal circumplex as a nomological net. *Journal of Personality and Social Psychology, 63,* 105-118.

Hart, A. W. (1991). Leader succession and socialization. *Review of Educational Research, 61,* 451-474.

Hart, A. W. (1994). Work feature values of today's and tomorrow's teachers: Work redesign as an incentive and school improvement policy. *Educational Evaluation and Policy Analysis, 16*(4), 458-473.

Hart, A. W., & Bredeson, P. V. (1995). *The principalship: Professional visualization in action.* New York: McGraw-Hill.

Hays, W. L. (1988). *Statistics* (4th ed.) New York: Holt, Rinehart and Winston.

Henwood, K. L., & Pidgeon, N. F. (1992). Qualitative research and psychological theorizing. *British Journal of Psychology, 83*(1), 97-111.

Howe, K. R. (1985). Two dogmas of educational research. *Educational Researcher, 44*(8), 10-18.

Howe, K. R., & Dougherty, K. C. (1993). Ethics, institutional review boards, and the changing face of educational research. *Educational Researcher, 22*(9), 16-21.

Howe, K., & Eisenhart, M. (1990). Standards for qualitative (and quantitative) research: A prolegomenon. *Educational Researcher, 19*(4), 2-9.

Howell, D. C. (1995). *Fundamental statistics for the behavioral sciences* (3rd ed.). Belmont, CA: Duxbury Press .

Hser, Y. (1993). Data sources: Problems and issues. *Journal of Drug Issues, 23,* 217-228.

Janis, I. L. (1982). *Groupthink: Psychological studies of policy decisions and fiascoes.* Boston: Houghton Mifflin.

Kagan, J. (1978) *The growth of the child: Reflections on human development.* New York: Norton.

Kazdin, A. E. (1992). *Research design in clinical psychology* (2nd ed.). Boston: Allyn and Bacon.

Kazdin, A. E. (1993). Replication and extension of behavioral treatment of autistic disorder. *American Journal on Mental Retardation, 97*, 377-379.

Keith-Spiegel, P. (1976). Children's rights as participants in research. In G. P. Koocher (Ed.), *Children's rights and the mental health profession* (pp. 53-81). New York: John Wiley & Sons.

Keppel, G. (1991). *Design and analysis: A researcher's handbook* (3rd ed.). Englewood Cliffs, NJ: Prentice-Hall.

Kerlinger, F. N. (1973). *Foundations of behavioral research* (2nd ed.). New York: Holt, Rinehart and Winston.

Kosciulek, J. F., & Szymanski, E. M. (1993). Statistical power analysis of rehabilitation counseling research. *Rehabilitation Counseling Bulletin, 36*, 212-219.

Krathwohl, D. R. (1988). *How to prepare a research proposal* (3rd ed.). Syracuse, NY: Syracuse University Press.

Kratochwill, T. R., & Levin, J. R. (Eds.), (1992). *Single-case research design and analysis: New directions for psychology and education.* Hillsdale, NJ: Lawrence Erlbaum Associates.

LaFromboise, T. D., & Foster, S. L. (1992). Cross-cultural training: Scientist-practitioner model and methods. *Counseling Psychologist, 20,* 472-489.

Lancy, D. F. (1993). *Qualitative research in education: An introduction to the major traditions.* New York: Longman Publishing Group.

LeCompte, M. D., & Goetz, J. P. (1982). Problems of reliability and validity in ethnographic research. *Review of Educational Research, 52,* 31-60.

LeCompte, M. D., & Preissle, J., with Tesch, R. (1993). *Ethnography and qualitative design in educational research* (2nd ed.). New York: Academic Press.

Lee, C. C., & Workman, D. J. (1992). School counselors and research: Current status and future direction. *School Counselor, 40,* 15-19.

Lightfoot, S. L. (1983). *The good high school: Portraits of character and culture.* New York: Basic Books.

Likert, R. (1967). *The human organization: Its management and value.* New York: McGraw-Hill.

Lincoln, Y. S., & Guba, E. G. (1985). *Naturalistic inquiry.* Beverly Hills, CA: Sage.

Lincoln, Y. S., & Guba, E. G. (1990). Judging the quality of case study reports. *Qualitative Studies in Education, 3*(1), 53-59.

Lindsey, R. T. (1984). Informed consent and deception in psychotherapy research: An ethical analysis. *The Counseling Psychologist, 12*(3), 79-86.

Lortie, D. C. (1975). *Schoolteacher: A sociological study.* Chicago: University of Chicago Press.

Loughead, T. A., Black, R. J., & Menefee, L. A. (1991). Systematic approach to research training: Benefits for counseling practice. *Journal of Mental Health Counseling, 13,* 270-278.

Maestas, B., & Goldfield, P. (1989). *Sampling Basics.* Newbury Park, CA: Alexander Publishing.

Markus, H., & Zajonc, R. B. (1985). The cognitive perspective in social psychology. In G. Lindzey and E. Aronson (Eds.), *Handbook of social psychology, Vol. 1: Theory and method* (pp. 137-230). New York: Random House.

Mauch, J. E., & Birch, J. W. (1983). *Guide to the successful thesis and dissertation.* New York: Marcel Dekker.

McCall, W. A. (1923). *How to experiment in education.* New York: The Macmillan Co.

McDonnell, J., Hardman, M., McDonnell, A., & Kiefer-O'Donnell, R. (1994). *Introduction to people with severe disabilities.* Boston: Allyn and Bacon.

Mead, M. (1928). *Coming of age in Samoa.* New York: Morrow.

Miles, M. B., & Huberman, A. M. (1994). *Qualitative data analysis: An expanded sourcebook* (2nd ed.). Thousand Oaks, CA: Sage.

Miller, M. D., & Oshima, T. C. (1992). Effect of sample size, number of biased items, and magnitude of bias on a two-stage item bias estimation method. *Applied Psychological Measurement, 16,* 381-388.

Moberg, D. P., Piper, D. L., Wu, J., & Serlin, R. C. (1993). When total randomization is impossible: Nested randomized assignment. *Evaluation Review, 17,* 271-291.

Morgan, G. & Smircich, L. (1980). The case for qualitative research. *Academy of Management Review, 5,* 491-500

Morris, C. D., Niederbuhl, J. M., & Mahr, J. M. (1993). Determining the capability of individuals with mental retardation to give informed consent. *American Journal on Mental Retardation, 98,* 263-272.

Murata, P. J., Lynch, W. D., Puffer, J. C., & Green, L. A. (1992). Attitudes toward and experience in research among family medicine chairs. *Journal of Family Practice, 35,* 417-421.

Niles, S. G., & Sowa, C. J. (1992). Mapping the nomological network of career self-efficacy.

Special section: Career self-efficacy. *Career Development Quarterly, 41*, 13-21.

Nisbett, R. E., & Ross, L. (1980). *Human inference: Strategies and shortcomings of social judgment.* Englewood Cliffs, NJ: Prentice-Hall.

Onghena, P. (1992). Randomization tests for extensions and variations of ABAB single-case experimental designs. *Behavioral Assessment, 14*, 153-171.

Patton, M. Q. (1990). *Qualitative evaluation and research methods* (2nd ed.). Newbury Park, CA: Sage.

Paulhus, D. L., & Martin, C. L. (1987). The structure of personality capabilities. *Journal of Personality and Social Psychology, 52*, 354-365.

Peshkin, A. (1991). *The color of strangers, the color of friends: The place of ethnicity in school and community.* Chicago: University of Chicago Press.

Peshkin, A. (1993). The goodness of qualitative research. *Educational Researcher, 22*(2), 23-29.

Pincus, H. A. (1991). Research and clinical training in psychiatry: Inputs and outputs. *Psychiatric Quarterly, 62*, 121-133.

Provus, M. (1969). Evaluation of ongoing programs in the public school system. In R. W. Tyler (Ed.), *Educational evaluation: New roles, new means* (pp. 242-283). Chicago: NSSE.

Quantz, R. A. (1992). On critical ethnography (with some postmodern considerations). In M. D. LeCompte, W. L. Millroy & J. Preissle (Eds.), *The handbook of qualitative research in education*, pp. 447-507. San Diego: Academic Press.

Sahlin, N. E. (1991). Baconian inductivism in research on human decision-making. Special issue: Cognitivism and its discontents. *Theory and Psychology, 1*, 431-450.

Schatzman, L., & Strauss, A. L. (1973). *Field research.* Englewood Cliffs, NJ: Prentice-Hall.

Schon, D. (1983). *The reflective practitioner: How professionals think in action.* San Francisco: Jossey-Bass.

Searight, H. R. (1990). The neglect of qualitative evaluation in psychology training: Issues and alternatives. *Journal of Training and Practice in Professional Psychology, 4*(2), 33-43.

Sheridan, S. M. (1992). What do we mean when we say 'collaboration?' *Journal of Educational and Psychological Consultation, 3*, 89-92.

Sidman, M. (1960). *Tactics of scientific research: Evaluating experimental data in psychology.* New York: Basic Books.

Simon, R., & Dippo, D. (1986). On critical ethno-graphic work. *Anthropology and Education Quarterly, 17*, 195-202.

Simpson, R. L., King, J. D., & Drew, C. J. (1970). Free recall by retarded and nonretarded subjects as a function of input organization. *Psychonomic Science, 19*, 334.

Smith, M. L. (1986). The whole is greater: Combining qualitative and quantitative approaches in evaluation studies. In D. D. Williams (Ed.). *Naturalistic evaluation* (pp. 37-54). San Francisco: Jossey-Bass.

Smith, M. L., & Glass, G. V. (1987). *Research and evaluation in education and the social sciences.* Englewood Cliffs, NJ: Prentice-Hall.

Smith, S. S., & Richardson, D. (1983). Amelioration of deception and harm in psychological research. The important role of debriefing. *Journal of Personality and Social Psychology, 44*, 1075-1082.

Spatz, C. (1993). *Basic statistics: Tales of distributions* (5th ed.). Pacific Grove, CA: Brooks/Cole.

Spence, J. T., Cotton, J. W., Underwood, B. J., & Duncan, C. P. (1992). *Elementary statistics* (rev. 5th ed.). Englewood Cliffs, NJ: Prentice-Hall.

Spindler, G., & Spindler, L. (1992). Cultural process and ethnography: An anthropological perspective. In M. D. LeCompte, W. L. Millroy, & J. Preissle (Eds.), *The handbook of qualitative research in education* (pp. 53-92). San Diego: Academic Press.

Spradley, J. P. (1970). *You owe yourself a drunk: An ethnography of urban nomads.* Boston: Little, Brown and Co.

Spradley, J. P. (1979). *The ethnographic interview.* New York: Holt, Rinehart and Winston.

Staats, A. W. (1993). Redefinitions of the science-practice relationship without a framework for unity will fail. *American Psychologist, 48*, 58-59.

Stevenson, J. (1993). Problems in designing and carrying out longitudinal research. *Nordic Journal of Psychiatry, 47*, 27-39.

Sudman, S. (1976). *Applied sampling.* New York: Academic Press.

Svyantek, D. J., O'Connell, M. S., Baumgardner, T. L. (1992). Applications of Bayesian methods to OD evaluation and decision making. *Human Relations, 45*, 621-636.

Thomas, D. S., Loomis, A. M., & Arrington, R. E. (1933). *Observational studies of social behavior. Vol 1: Social behavior.* New Haven, CT: Yale University Institute of Human Relations.

Thompson, S. K. (1992). *Sampling.* New York: John Wiley & Sons.

Tsoi-Hoshmand, L. L. (1991). Clinical inquiry as scientific training. *Counseling Psychologist, 19*, 431–453.

Turnbull, H. R. III (Ed.), (1977). *Consent handbook.* Washington, D C: American Association on Mental Deficiency.

Van-Lill, J. B. (1989). The epistemological embarrassment of traditional research psychology. *South African Journal of Psychology, 19*, 153–161.

Vernoy, M. W., & Vernoy, J. (1992). *Behavioral statistics in action.* San Marcos, CA: Wadsworth.

Vidich, A. J., & Bensman, J. (1960). *Small town in mass society.* New York: Doubleday & Co.

Walker, E. F., & Lewine, R. R. (1993). Sampling biases in studies of gender and schizophrenia. *Schizophrenia Bulletin, 19*, 1–7.

Wampold, B. E., & Drew, C. J. (1990). *Theory and application of statistics: An intermediate text.* New York: McGraw-Hill.

Wampold, B. E., & Worsham, N. L. (1986). Randomization tests for multiple-baseline designs. *Behavioral Assessment, 8*, 135–143.

Warwick, D. P. (1973). Survey research and participant observation: A benefit-cost analysis. In D. P. Warwick & S. Osherson (Eds.), *Comparative research methods* (pp. 189–203). London: Hodder & Stoughton.

Watson, L. & Watson-Franke, M. (1985) *Interpreting life histories: An anthropological inquiry.* New Brunswick, NJ: Rutgers University Press.

Welch, M., & Sheridan, S. M. (1995). *Educational partnerships: An ecological approach to serving students at risk.* San Francisco, CA: Harcourt Brace Jovanovich.

Wheeler, D.L. (1994). Obtaining informed consent. *The chronicle of higher education, XL(21)*, A8–A9, A16.

Winer, B. J., Brown, D. R., & Michels, K. M. (1991). *Statistical principles in experimental design* (3rd ed.). New York: McGraw-Hill.

Wolcott, H. F. (1973). *The man in the principal's office: An ethnography.* New York: Holt, Rinehart and Winston.

Wolcott, H. F. (1992). Posturing in qualitative research. In M. D. LeCompte, W. L. Millroy, & J. Preissle (Eds.), *The handbook of qualitative research in education* (pp. 3–52). San Diego: Academic Press.

Wolcott, H. F. (1994). *Transforming qualitative data: Description, analysis, and interpretation.* Thousand Oaks, CA: Sage.

Yelibi, S., Valenti, P., Volpe, C., & Caprara, A. (1993). Sociocultural aspects of AIDS in an urban peripheral area of Abidjan (Côte d'Ivoire). *AIDS Care, 5*, 187–197.

Yin, R. K. (1989). *Case study research: Design and methods* (rev. ed.). Newbury Park, CA: Sage.

Yin, R. K. (1991). *Applications of case study research.* Washington, DC: Cosmos Corp.

Glossary

A-B design   A time-series design that involves two phases: A, in which the baseline data are collected before treatment is implemented; and B, in which data are recorded while treatment is under way. This design is not widely used because more sophisticated designs have been developed that provide stronger evidence.

A-B-A-B design   A time-series design that involves four phases. The first A represents baseline before treatment is implemented. The first B represents initial application of treatment. The second A designates removal of treatment and return to baseline conditions, whereas the second B represents a return to treatment conditions. This design is also known as a *reversal design.*

Analysis of variance (ANOVA)   A parametric statistical analysis used for simultaneously comparing three or more means. This is a popular procedure in behavioral research in which group designs are used. The ANOVA is highly flexible, and variations may be used for comparisons of independent groups, repeated measures comparisons, experiments with one experimental variable (one-way ANOVA), two experimental variables (two-way ANOVA), and more complex experiments.

Attributes   Refers to the observable, countable, or measurable dimensions of an object. For example, one cannot measure learning directly, but it is possible to infer that a certain amount of it has occurred by observing performance on a task. The performance is the attribute by which one infers that learning has occurred (such as number of correct responses on a test).

Baseline   The phase of phases or a time-series experiment in which data are recorded on the subject in an untreated state. Frequently, this is the first phase in which data are recorded before treatment is initiated. Performance under this condition is compared with performance of the subject during the treatment phase or phases.

Bias   Any influence that distorts the experimental results and thereby causes error in the findings. For example, the researcher may subconsciously favor one group of subjects over another and score them somewhat higher than a truly objective observer would. This would be experimenter bias and would threaten the soundness of results.

Bimodal distribution   A distribution that has two modes. If two scores occur more frequently than other scores (and with equal frequency), the distribution is said to bimodal.

Captive assignment   Assignment of subjects to experimental treatments when the total sample is identified and available at the outset of the investigation. This makes it possible to know which subjects, by name, will be in which experimental group at the beginning of an experiment.

Ceiling effect   An effect that occurs when the performance range of a task is so restricted or limited on the upper end that the subjects cannot perform to their maximum ability.

Cell   A particular experimental condition in a multi-group study. For example, in the ac diagram on the following page, there are four conditions (A_1, B_1, A_1B_2, and A_2B_2) and four corresponding cells.

Central tendency measures   Descriptive statistics that are used to summarize a group's performance in terms of where the scores tend to be concentrated. Three central tendency measures are commonly used (the mean, the median, or the mode), depending on the circumstances.

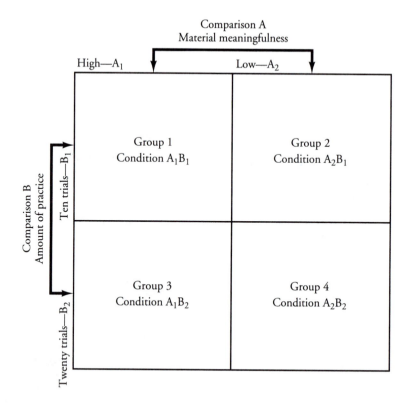

Cluster sampling   A type of subject selection that is useful when every individual in an entire population cannot be listed to form a frame but the population exists in groups or clusters (such as school districts, regions, or states). Instead of listing the individuals, the frame is formed by listing the clusters, and a representative sample of clusters is drawn. Subjects are then selected from the clusters.

Control, concept of   The process of holding all possible influences constant except the experimental variable, which is what is being studied. For example, if the researcher is comparing the effectiveness of reading programs A and B, the reading programs should be the only factor that is different between the groups. All other influences (such as intelligence or age) should be equivalent between the groups.

Correlation   A general term for the type of statistical analyses used in relationship studies. Correlational studies investigate the degree to which two variables (such as height and weight) vary together in a population. Such an investigation would be asking the question "As height varies (increases or decreases), what tends to happen to weight?"

Criterion measure   That which is being measured in a study. If, for example, a study were focusing on the height of a particular group, the criterion measure might be inches. Criterion measure is synonymous with the term *dependent variable.*

Criticism   A method of data gathering and analysis in qualitative research that includes preferences, likes and dislikes. The observer describes while also conveying personal taste, preference, and judgment to the reader.

Data   Generally, the information gathered during the course of a study to answer the question being investigated. The term *data* covers all information that may be recorded on subjects, such as age, intelligence, or performance scores (which are probably the criterion measure). Usually, the term is used with reference to criterion measure or performance scores.

Dependent variable *See* Criterion measure.

Determinism The assumption of science that there is a lawfulness in the events of nature rather than capricious and chaotic incidents. Events are assumed to have causes, and if all influences could be exactly duplicated, the event would recur in the same form.

Dispersion measures Descriptive statistics that are used to summarize a group's performance in terms of how much variation there is in the scores, that is, to what degree individual scores depart from the central tendency. Three dispersion measures are commonly used (the range, the semi-interquartile range, or the standard deviation), depending on the circumstances.

Double sampling A type of subject selection, sometimes called two-phase sampling, that is often useful for survey research. The term is descriptive of the process in that the investigators probe their subjects twice (e.g., as a more intensive follow-up on a cursory initial probe or as a follow-up for those subjects not responding to an initial questionnaire).

Empiricism An approach to inquiry emphasizing knowledge that comes through factual investigation, with the facts being obtained from sources external to the investigator. The primary means by which information is obtained involves direct experience or objective observation through the senses.

Ethnography A qualitative approach to research, the in-depth study of the culture of a particular group of people. The description of the culture conveys the way of life, beliefs, ideologies, formal and informal relationships, and many other dimensions of the culture's characteristics.

Experimental matching The assignment of subjects to experimental treatments in a manner that attempts to force group equivalency on a given factor (e.g., age IQ) by matching subjects on that factor.

Experimental mortality A threat to internal validity that occurs when loss of subjects changes the composition of the sample initially drawn. When this occurs, particularly if more subjects are lost from one group than from another group, the researcher may not have groups that are constituted in the same way that they were when the study was initiated.

Experimental variable That phenomenon that is under study; that factor that the researcher manipulates to see what the effect is. For example, if the researcher were interested in determining which of two teaching methods was more effective, the experimental variable would be the method of teaching. Experimental variable is synonymous with the term *independent variable.*

External validity The generalizability of results from a given study. External validity involves how well the results of a particular study apply to the world outside the research situation. If a study is externally valid or has considerable external validity, one can expect that the results are generalizable to a considerable degree.

Finite causation The assumption of science that natural events have a limited number of conditions that are responsible for their occurrence and that these conditions are discoverable. Finite causation essentially presumes that everything in nature is *not* influenced by everything else.

Floor effect An effect that occurs when the performance range of the task is so restricted or limited on the lower end that the subjects' performance is determined by the task rather than by their ability to perform. Under such conditions the task is so difficult that the researcher is unable to obtain any evidence about how the subjects can perform.

Generality, principle of A characteristic of a correctly stated experimental variable. If an experimental variable conforms to the principle of generality, it is stated in terms of the abstract variable being manipulated (e.g., the method of treatment rather than the particular conditions being studied—treatment method A compared with treatment method B.

Hawthorne effect A change in sensitivity or performance or both by subjects merely because they are in a study. This may occur when an experimental situation is sufficiently different from routine that subjects are somehow made to feel "special." The Hawthorne effect becomes a threat to internal validity when one group receives such a "special" treatment and another does not, thereby introducing a systematic difference between groups in addition to the experimental variable. This same effect is a threat to external validity but is called "artificial research arrangements" in the text.

History A threat to internal validity that occurs when specific events, in addition to the treatment, intervene between measurements. This threat is a particular problem in studies in which a pretest is administered, followed by treatment and then a posttest. The specific events may be occurrences such as an accident, playground fight, or similar specific intervening factors other than the treatment.

Hypothesis A statement used in research to help clarify the research question. It is presented as a declarative statement of prediction. Two basic formats are used, the *null hypothesis* and the *directional hypothesis*. The null hypothesis predicts no difference; for example, "Subjects will not differ in mean correct responses as a function of treatment method." The directional hypothesis predicts a difference and the direction of that difference; for example, "Subjects receiving treatment method A will make significantly more correct responses than those receiving treatment method B."

Independent group design Group research designs in which different subjects are used for each group. A group of subjects receives only one treatment, and therefore the scores in one condition are presumed independent of scores in another condition. This is distinguished from studies in which subjects may receive two or more assessments or treatments (repeated measures), and the scores in one condition cannot be considered independent of the scores in the other.

Independent variable See Experimental variable.

Instrumentation A threat to internal validity that occurs when changes in the calibration of a measuring instrument result in the alteration of the scores that are recorded. Instrumentation also refers to changes in calibration in human observers that may result as a function of systematic differences in the way they judge and record observations.

Internal validity The technical soundness of a study. A study is internally valid or has high internal validity when all the potential factors that might influence the data are controlled except the one under study. This would mean that the concept of control had been successfully implemented. If, for example, two instructional methods were being compared, internal validity would require that all differences between groups (e.g., intelligence, age) be removed except the differences in the instructional method, which is the experimental variable.

Interval data A type of data that has all three properties of numbers: identity, order, and additivity. Interval data have known and equal distances between score units and also have an arbitrary zero point. With interval data, it is possible to determine *greater than* or *less than* and the magnitude of a difference in the property being measured. Examples of interval data include calendar time and temperature as measured on centigrade and Fahrenheit scales.

Maturation a threat to internal validity that occurs when factors influence performance as a result of time passing. Such factors as growing older, hunger, and fatigue are considered maturational threats to internal validity when they are operating in a fashion that influences data in addition to the experimental variable.

Mean A central-tendency descriptive statistic obtained by adding all the scores for all the subjects and dividing the total by the number of subjects in the group; the *arithmetic average*. This measure of central tendency may be used with data that have the property of additivity, which includes interval and ratio data.

Median A central-tendency descriptive statistic that is a point in the distribution of scores with exactly the same number of scores above it as below it when all the scores are arranged in order. If there is an odd number of subjects (e.g., 9, 11, 15), the median is the midmost score. If there is an even number of subjects (e.g., 10, 12, 16), the median is the midpoint between the two scores that occupy the midpoint in the distribution. The median may be used with data that have the property of order (ordinal) as well as higher-level data such as interval and ratio types.

Mixed-group design   A group research design in which two or more experimental variables are involved, with independent comparisons (different groups) on one or more of the variables and repeated measures on the remaining variable or variables. The term *mixed* comes from the fact that in this type of design there is a mixing of components that are independent group comparisons with repeated-measures comparisons.

Mode   A central-tendency descriptive statistic that is the score in the distribution occurring most frequently. The mode may be used with nominal data. It may also be used with higher-level data such as ordinal, interval, or ratio; but it is the *only* central tendency measure that may be used in situations in which nominal data are collected.

Multiple-baseline design   A time-series research design in which data on more than one target behavior are simultaneously recorded. Phase changes from baseline to treatment are then staggered, with each behavior serving as the sequential control for the previously treated behavior, as in the accompanying diagram.

Multiple-treatment interference.   A threat to external validity that occurs when more than a single treatment is administered to the same subjects. Because the effects of prior treatments are frequently not dissipated by the time later treatments are administered, the generalizability of results from later treatments is reduced.

N   Generally, the total number of subjects in a sample. It is frequently used as a substitute for the term *number* (for example, "the total *N* for the study..." or "*N* equaled...").

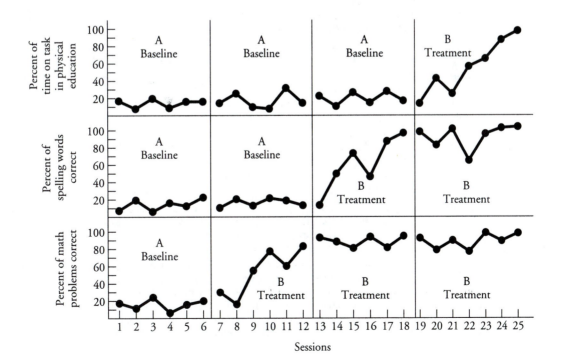

n   Generally, the number of subjects in a given treatment group or cell. For example, if a study has four groups, each with 20 subjects, then *n* would equal 20 (whereas *N* would equal 80).

Nominal data   A type of data that represents the most primitive type of measurement: the designation of occurrences into categories; also known as *categorical data*. This type of data has only the property of identity. All that can be accomplished is the assignment of events to categories (e.g., yes or no, male or female, pass or fail). There is no assumed underlying continuum between categories.

Nomothetic net   The structure of a theory in which data or results from studies are logically linked together to for the theory.

Nonparametric statistics   A general type of inferential statistics that does not require rigorous attention to assumptions regarding the nature of the population from which scores (data) are drawn. Nonparametric statistics often may be used in situations in which nominal and ordinal data are collected and in certain cases in which few subjects are used. These are useful tools in such situations because other statistics (parametric) are often not applicable.

Operational definition   A process whereby the researcher specifies all the steps (operations) and details of a research problem. By operationally defining the problem, each term (or procedural step) is taken in turn, and exactly what is meant by that term is specified.

Ordinal data   A type of data that is characterized by the ability to rank order events on the basis of an underlying continuum. The ranks then denote *greater than* or *less than* of the property being assessed. Ordinal data do not necessarily represent the known magnitude of the property being assessed.

Parametric statistics   A general type of inferential statistics that requires attention to several assumptions regarding the nature of the population from which scores (data) are drawn. Parametric statistics generally require at least interval data and usually necessitate a larger number of subjects than nonparametric analyses. When it is possible to apply parametric statistics, they are generally preferred because they are more powerful, efficient, and flexible in terms of application than nonparametrics.

Performance range (of a task)   The variation in responses possible within the limits imposed by the uppermost and the lowest possible performances on a task.

Phase change   A term used in time-series research designs to denote the point in time when experimental conditions are changed. There may be several phase changes, such as the point when the baseline condition is terminated and treatment is begun, when treatment is terminated and the baseline or untreated condition is reinstituted (in an A-B-A-B design), and so on.

Population   Any well-described set of people or events from which the researcher selects a sample of subjects.

Population frame   A complete list of all the individuals in the population. It is from this list that sampling actually takes place.

Proportional sampling   A type of subject selection procedure used to sample from subgroups in the same proportion that they exist in the larger population. For example, if individuals in the larger population were 80 percent brown-eyed and 20 percent blue-eyed, the sample would also be 80 percent brown-eyed and 20 percent blue-eyed.

Quasi-experimental design   A group study design in which the groups are formed from subject pools that are different before the experiment is begun, and this difference is the basis for the experimental variable. An example might be the comparing of groups from two levels of intelligence (group A with an IQ range of 75-90 and group B with an IQ range of 100-115). In this example, the level of intelligence is the experimental variable under study, and the two groups are preexperimentally different. Such a design is in contrast to a true experimental design in which both groups are formed from the same subject pool and become different after they are administered the respective treatments.

Random sampling   Also known as simple random sampling or unrestricted random sampling. This term refers to a selection procedure whereby each individual in the population frame has an equal chance of being chosen as a subject. Frequently, this procedure is implemented using a random number table or other technique that ensures each individual an equal chance of being selected.

Range   A descriptive statistic that is a measure of dispersion and refers to the difference between the highest and lowest scores in a distribution. This is the simplest and most easily determined measure of dispersion but is of somewhat limited usefulness.

Ratio data   A type of data that has all three properties of numbers: identity, order, and additivity. Ratio data have known and equal distances between score units and have a zero point that is not arbitrary. A zero score on ratio data signifies total absence of the property being measured. Examples of ratio data include temperature measured on the Kelvin scale and time (to perform).

Rationalism   An approach to inquiry that emphasizes an internal source of knowledge. Characteristic of inquiry in ancient Greek times, rationalism views the intellectual examination of ideas as the primary means by which knowledge progresses. Little if any emphasis is placed on the observable.

Relationship question   A type of research question that explores the degree to which two or more phenomena relate or vary together. For example, such a study might focus on the relationship between intelligence and reading comprehension. This type of study would essentially be asking, "As intelligence varies, what tends to happen to reading comprehension?" Relationship studies use correlation statistics for analysis of the data.

Repeated-measures design   A study design in which the researcher records data on the same subjects under two or more treatment conditions.

Research   A systematic way of asking questions that uses an orderly method of inquiry known as the scientific method.

Reversal design   *See* A-B-A-B design.

Sample   Those individuals or events that are selected from the population to serve as the subjects are known as the sample for a study. This term is also used as a verb (to sample), referring to the process of selecting individuals to serve as subjects.

Semi-interquartile range   A descriptive statistic that is a measure of dispersion and refers to half of the range in scores represented by the middle 50 percent of the scores. It is easily determined and may be used with ordinal data as well as interval or ratio data.

Sequential assignment   A procedure for assigning subjects to experimental treatments when the investigator does not have the entire sample captive (the actual names are not all present before beginning the experiment).

Skewed distribution   A term used as a general descriptor for distributions of scores that are not symmetrical.

Stable data   A term that has primary relevance to time-series experiments. It is crucial that the data be stable before a phase change is implemented in order to accurately assess the effect of changing conditions.

Standard deviation   A descriptive statistic that is the most commonly used index of variability. Computation of the standard deviation requires at least interval data and may be conceptualized as a measure of the variability of scores around the mean.

Statistical regression   A threat to internal validity that occurs when subjects have been assigned to a particular group on the basis of atypical scores. If this occurs, a subject's placement in, for example, group A may be in error because the score is atypical and the subject's more normal performance may be like that of the subjects in group B. If the misclassified subject (or subjects) then regresses (up or down) toward their average performance during the experiment, internal validity is threatened.

Stratified random sampling A type of subject selection procedure used in situations in which representative samples must be drawn from two or more population frames for a single study. Population frames are formed for each type of subject (e.g., different age levels), and random samples are then drawn from each frame.

Systematic sampling A type of subject sampling procedure in which every *k*th (e.g., every fifth) individual is selected from the list or population frame. Systematic sampling is convenient and useful if the list is arranged in such a way that the sequence is unbiased.

Test practice A threat to internal validity that occurs when the effects of taking a test substantially influence the scores of subjects on a second testing.

Thick description A term used in qualitative research that pertains to descriptions and analyses that are both accurate and vivid. Thick description is written in a manner that creates vivid sensual images of the setting and the behaviors being observed.

Triangulation Triangulation is used by qualitative investigators to build validity into their research database. Triangulation refers to the use of multiple sources of information to obtain data, including multiple informants, written documents or records, and any other information source that can be used to construct an accurate account.

t test A parametric statistical analysis used for comparing two means. Certain *t* tests are appropriate for comparing means of independent groups, whereas other computational formulas are used for comparing related means (as in a pre-post design).

Author Index

Subject Index